New Destination Dreaming

Immigration, Race, and Legal Status
in the Rural American South

Helen B. Marrow

Stanford University Press
Stanford, California

Stanford University Press
Stanford, California

Library of Congress Cataloging-in-Publication Data

Marrow, Helen B. author.
  New destination dreaming : immigration, race, and legal status in the rural American South / Helen B. Marrow.
    pages cm
  Includes bibliographical references and index.
  ISBN 978-0-8047-7307-2 (cloth : alk. paper) — ISBN 978-0-8047-7308-9 (pbk. : alk. paper)
    1. Hispanic Americans—Southern States—Social conditions. 2. Hispanic Americans—Legal status, laws, etc.—Southern States. 3. Latin Americans—Southern States—Social conditions. 4. Latin Americans—Legal status, laws, etc.—Southern States. 5. Immigrants—Southern States—Social conditions. 6. Southern States—Emigration and immigration. 7. Southern States—Rural conditions. 8. Southern States—Race relations. I. Title.
  F220.S7M37 2011
  305.868'075--dc22

                              2010047771

Typeset by Bruce Lundquist in 10/14 Minion

New Destination Dreaming

for all the "carolatinos"

and for J.R.P., one of those truly extraordinary people who come along only once in a while, and whose sheer presence make the world a better place

Contents

Illustrations

Acknowledgments

Writing my first book has been one of the most exciting, yet also one of the longest and most difficult, experiences of my life. I am deeply indebted to the many people who have helped me along the way. First and foremost are the four intellectual giants on whose shoulders I have tried my best to stand: Jennifer Hochschild, Katherine Newman, Mary Waters, and William Julius Wilson. Without their critical and constructive guidance, I would not be where I am today. For guiding me through the hardest and loneliest parts of the writing and revising process, Mary in particular deserves my utmost gratitude; she taught me how to survive and thrive in life and academia. To have someone as talented and yet also down-to-earth as she is, always cheering me on, inspires me to this day.

I also acknowledge the generous assistance of the National Science Foundation, the David Rockefeller Center for Latin American Studies and the Center for American Political Studies at Harvard University, the Rural Poverty Research Institute at Oregon State University, and Robert Wood Johnson Foundation, and the Faculty Research Awards Committee at Tufts University. Other invitations or financial support to present earlier drafts of this research were graciously provided by the American Sociological Association, the Association of Mexicans in North Carolina, Connecticut College, East Carolina University, the Eastern Sociological Society, Harvard University, the Latin American Studies Association, Pennsylvania State University, the Robert Wood Johnson Foundation, the Russell Sage Foundation, Tufts University, and the Universities of California at Berkeley, Davis, Irvine, and Los Angeles, the University of Illinois at Chicago, the University of Kansas at Lawrence, the University of Manchester, the University of Massachusetts at Boston, the University of Nebraska at Omaha, the University of North Carolina at Chapel Hill, the University of South Florida, the University of Southern California, the University of Texas at Austin, and the University of Virginia. Of course, all arguments and findings are my own and do not necessarily reflect the views of any of these supporting sources.

Moving on, I owe a tremendous debt to the many people who assisted me in the field. Although I cannot personally identify any of them here, I am especially grateful to my 129 interview respondents and the many other informants whom I encountered along the way. I hope that you all know who you are and that this book does you justice; I am truly grateful to you for opening up your lives so intimately to me!

Kate Wahl, my talented editor at Stanford University Press, and Robert C. Smith and David Griffith deserve enormous praise for slogging through the first draft of this book and for molding it into its current (and much improved) form. I thank them dearly for their time, attention, and patience. Many thanks also to assistant editor Joa Suorez and production editor Carolyn Brown at Stanford University Press, and to copyeditor Tom Finnegan, for their help and support.

A veritable host of other people helped me, in ways both big and small, to either brainstorm ideas or whittle them down into written form. They include Leisy Abrego, Richard Alba, Linda Allegro, Rene Almeling, Chris Bail, Katherine Bartley, Pete Benson, Irene Bloemraad, George Borjas, Susan Brown, Kara Cebulko, Aviva Chomsky, Rafaela Dancygier, Jennifer Darrah, Victoria DeFrancesco, Els de Graauw, Ben Deufel, Daniel Dohan, Katharine Donato, Elizabeth Durden, Katherine Fennelly, Nancy Foner, Kyna Fong, Michael Fortner, Cybelle Fox, Owen Furuseth, Elizabeth Fussell, Shana Kushner Gadarian, Herbert Gans, Hannah Gill, Shannon Gleeson, Tanya Golash-Boza, Roberto Gonzales, Marco Gonzalez-Navarro, Jennifer Gordon, Lourdes Gouveia, David Griffith, Jacqueline Hagan, Ken Haig, Luisa Heredia, Rubén Hernández-León, Nancy Hiemstra, Daniel Hopkins, Nadya Jaworsky, Tomás Jiménez, James H. Johnson, Jr., Karen Johnson-Webb, Jennifer Jones, Michael Jones-Correa, William Kandel, Philip Kasinitz, Neeraj Kaushal, Aarti Kohli, Elaine Lacy, Mark Leach, Taeku Lee, Peggy Levitt, Laura López-Sanders, Margarita Machado-Casas, Douglas Massey, Paula McClain, Eric McDaniel, Monica McDermott, Cecilia Menjívar, Pamela Metz, Cheri Minton, John Mollenkopf, Colin Moore, Sarah Morando, Hiroshi Motomura, Mary Newsom, Mai Nguyen, Emilio Parrado, Susan Paulukonis, Steven Pitts, Jeff Popke, Shannon Portillo, Julia Preston, Robert Putnam, Karthick Ramakrishnan, Maria Rendón, Nestor Rodríguez,

Wendy Roth, Rubén G. Rumbaut, Gabriel Ramon Sánchez, Alexis Silver, Audrey Singer, Barbara Ellen Smith, Angela Stuesse, Rachel Swarns, Rebecca Torres, Van Tran, Natasha Kumar Warikoo, Julie Weiss, Deborah Weissman, Kim Williams, Abby Williamson, Jamie Winders, and several anonymous reviewers at academic journals. If I have forgotten even more people, I apologize ahead of time and hope that it shows how far my gratitude truly extends.

Finally, all of my love also goes out to my wonderful family and friends. My parents, Molly and Jim Marrow, not only allowed and endured my presence in their home as I conducted my fieldwork in 2003–04 but helped make that experience infinitely more pleasant. I am extremely grateful for the opportunity to have spent so much time with them at this stage in my life and career, as well as for the resources and worldviews that they have somehow managed to pass down to me successfully. My brother, Owen Marrow, also joined in the effort to encourage greater institutional responsiveness to Hispanic newcomers in eastern North Carolina in the mid-2000s by teaching Spanish in local elementary schools and working with U.S. Census surveyors and local Hispanic associations to reduce official undercounts. One of my beloved grandmothers, Elizabeth Owen, has gained new interest in the immigrant communities in her home city of Lynchburg, Virginia, and even drives me around when I visit her to show them to me. My other grandmother, the late Jane Gregory Marrow Reed, was born in Shanghai at a much earlier and different stage of the American South's globalization; learning about how our life histories are continuing to weave together almost a century later has been truly fascinating. Not to be forgotten, countless friends have provided their support and entertainment over the past few years, lending me a shoulder to lean on, an ear to talk into, and a smile to brighten my days with; my life would be far less meaningful without each of you! And of course, last but never least, my husband, Mike Redd, has been the single best source of patience, love, and laughter a wife could ever hope for. He has encouraged me even in my darkest moments, and he constantly reminds me that building a good life involves both doing more than work and doing work I love.

When I started studying the sociology of immigration during my junior year in college at Princeton University, I never once imagined it would lead me "home." But in many ways, this book is the culmination of just that: a homecoming to the region, family, and people who raised me and then sent me out into the world to gather the tools to come back. Today, immigration has changed that home, visibly and audibly. It is my hope that this book will assist both long-term natives and newcomers alike to understand and share in the beauty—and also the collective challenge—that such change brings.

New Destination Dreaming

Introduction

Immigrant Incorporation in Rural New Destinations

I WAS BORN IN 1977 in a small town called Tarboro, North Carolina. Situated across a bend of the Tar River in the rural, eastern region of the Tarheel state, Tarboro is a typical small, lowland southern town.[1] On the one hand, natives take pride in it as a place where "everybody knows everybody." Youths grow up under strong community surveillance and in constant interaction with one another—they must, since there is only one each of most major social institutions in town. The level of social capital is also high, and old-timers still tell stories about the town's most beloved characters (including one rumored to have served as the inspiration for Ernest T. Bass on *The Andy Griffith Show*). As in many southern towns, Tarboro residents display a strong and deeply rooted sense of localism, which sociologist and southern regional scholar John Shelton Reed (1986) not only defines as people's "attachment to their place and people" but also documents as statistically stronger among southerners than among other Americans. The people of Tarboro frequently claim that strong community bonds, safety, affordability, and quality of life outweigh the negative facets of living in a small town—most notably boredom, lack of economic opportunity, and gossip-driven social control.

On the other hand, the surrounding county population is made up almost exclusively of non-Hispanic whites and blacks, the latter clearly poorer than and visibly segregated from the former. As in many southern towns, this "hard" segregation manifests in topographical divides marked off by river crossings and railroad tracks, further buttressed by other forms of "soft" segregation (Fischer and Tienda 2006). For instance, when I attended the local high school in the early 1990s, I never heard an explanation for why two homecoming queens were

crowned each year—one white and one black. (A decade later while research-
ing this book, I was told that the school instituted the policy to reduce racial
competition during the transitional years of the Civil Rights Movement.) Nor
did I ever hear an official explanation for why white students preferred going
to the prom while African Americans favored the homecoming dance instead,
even though both were officially open to all of us.

Such hard and soft divides were simply a fact of life for those of us coming
of age in this part of the United States at the end of the twentieth century. Indeed, although North Carolina as a whole has long been more progressive than
other southern states (Key 1984), its eastern region, known locally as "Down
East," is characteristic of the predominantly rural and impoverished "traditional" or "Deep South" now infamous throughout the world for a legacy of
poverty, slavery, and racial subjugation. Even today, natives describe this region
as a world away from, or the redheaded stepchild of, the central piedmont region of the state, home to the larger and better-heeled metropolitan areas such
as Raleigh, Charlotte, and Greensboro. It is also part of what scholars call the
rural southern "black belt," a large region stretching in an arc from eastern Virginia down to eastern Texas that was originally named for its dark soil and its
position as the center of plantation cotton agriculture, but that is now known
for a predominant African American population, persistent poverty, high unemployment, low education, poor health, and high infant mortality (Wimberley and Morris 2002).[2]

Given this seemingly dated description, one might wonder what a town like
Tarboro could possibly offer to the study of contemporary American immigration. After all, not only is it a starkly black-and-white kind of place, but most
of its natives can trace their ancestry back well over four generations before
identifying an ancestor (whether settler, immigrant, or slave) who was born
abroad. Natives of Tarboro, like other rural southerners, adhere less strongly to
the American immigration narrative, an incorporatist civic myth emphasizing
America as a country of voluntary immigrants, than do Americans elsewhere
(Schildkraut 2003; Winders 2009b). To illustrate, I once heard a Tarboro native
respond to the statement "This is America—we're all immigrants from somewhere else" by saying, "No, we're not. My great-great-granddaddy was born
right here in this county."

Indeed, scholars have shown that for close to two centuries natives living in
the traditional South have been the most isolated from immigration (Bankston
2007; Eckes 2005; Marrow 2011b; Odem and Lacy 2009; Reimers 2005).[3] In every
decade from 1850 to 1970, the South was home to a smaller percentage of im-

migrants than any other region of the country, a distinction it maintained even during mass immigration from Europe and Asia at the turn of the twentieth century and did not render until 1990, when the Midwest moved down to replace it as the least common region of immigrant settlement (Bankston 2007). Of course, the traditional South's social and cultural isolation is frequently overdramatized; a "legendary South of two isolated and homogeneous races" (Peacock, Watson, and Matthews 2005) was never entirely valid, and the region has always been embedded in complex transnational relationships, including with Spanish explorers and Spanish-speaking immigrants (Cobb and Stueck 2005; Mantero 2008). Nevertheless, scholars agree that the region was "relatively untouched" by immigration until very recently (Schmid 2003).[4]

I began to ponder what my hometown might offer to the study of American immigration in 2002, when I came across an early 2000 U.S. Census report documenting an emergent pattern of geographic dispersion among Hispanics/Latinos into areas of the country that have had little previous experience receiving post-1965 immigrants (Brewer and Suchan 2001).[5] The report showed that whereas the largest *absolute* concentrations of Hispanics/Latinos were still centered around the large, traditional urban immigrant gateways of the West and Northeast (see Map 1), such as New York, Los Angeles, and Miami, the greatest *relative* population growth over the 1990s had taken place in a variety of urban, suburban, and rural areas across the South and Midwest instead (see Map 2). Interestingly, North Carolina was the premier new destination state of the 1990s. At 394%, it posted the highest rate of Hispanic/Latino population growth among all U.S. states (with the Mexican-origin subpopulation of this population growing even faster, at 655%; McClain et al. 2003; Mohl 2003; Suro and Singer 2002). At 274%, it also posted the highest rate of foreign-born immigrant population growth among all U.S. states (again, with the Mexican-origin subpopulation of this population growing even faster, at 1,800%; Zúñiga and Hernández-León 2005a).

Over the next decade, I learned that geographic dispersion into such "new" or "nontraditional" destinations is one of the two major trends changing the face of contemporary American immigration. I learned that primarily Mexicans and secondarily Central and South Americans have been driving this process (Durand, Telles, and Flashman 2006; Massey and Capoferro 2008)—hence, why it was showing up more strongly among Hispanic/Latinos than among Asian Americans in the 2001 Census report I was reading. I also learned that geographic dispersion has been taking place at many levels, with immigrants moving across regions (into the South and Midwest), within regions (into new destinations in

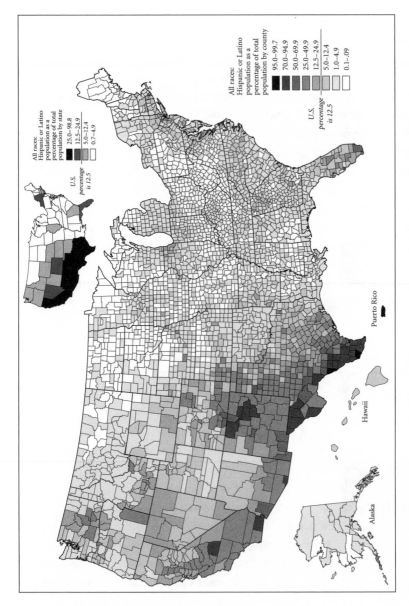

Map 1. Percentage of population, Hispanic or Latino (all races), 2000 U.S. Census. From Cynthia A. Brewer and Trudy A. Suchan (2001), "Mapping Census 2000: The Geography of U.S. Diversity," Census 2000 Special Reports (CENSR/01-1) (Washington, DC: U.S. Department of Commerce, Economics and Statistics Administration, U.S. Census Bureau [June]).

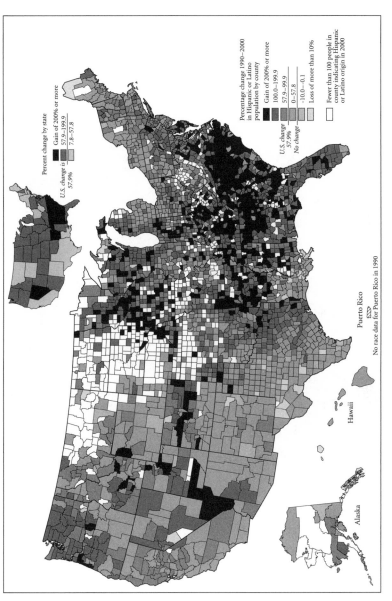

Map 2. Percentage growth in population, 1990–2000, Hispanic or Latino (all races), 2000 U.S. Census. From Cynthia A. Brewer and Trudy A. Suchan (2001), "Mapping Census 2000: The Geography of U.S. Diversity," Census 2000 Special Reports (CENSR/01-1) (Washington, DC: U.S. Department of Commerce, Economics and Statistics Administration, U.S. Census Bureau [June]).

Percent change by state

Gain of 200% or more

U.S. change is 57.9%

57.9–199.9

7.8–57.8

Percentage change 1990–2000 in Hispanic or Latino population by county

Gain of 200% or more

100.0–199.9

U.S. change 57.9%

0–57.8

No change

-10.0– -0.1

Loss of more than 10%

Fewer than 100 people in county indicating Hispanic or Latino origin in 2000

Puerto Rico

No race data for Puerto Rico in 1990

Hawaii

Alaska

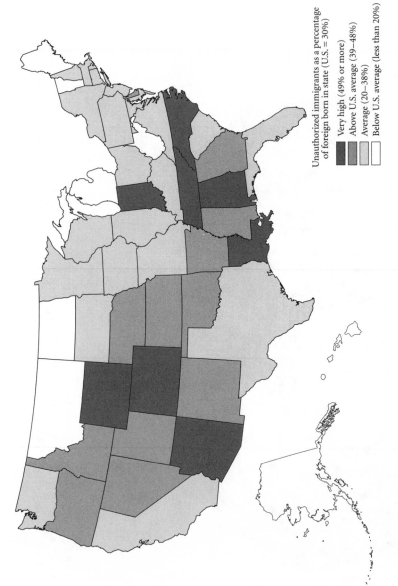

Map 3. Unauthorized immigrant population as share of foreign-born population, by U.S. state of residence, 2008. Reprinted with the permission of the Pew Hispanic Center from Jeffrey S. Passel and D'Vera Cohn (2009), "A Portrait of Undocumented Immigrants in the United States" (Washington, DC: Pew Hispanic Center [April 14]), http://pewhispanic.org/reports/report.php?ReportID=107.

Unauthorized immigrants as a percentage of foreign born in state (U.S. = 30%)

Very high (49% or more)

Above U.S. average (39–48%)

Average (20–38%)

Below U.S. average (less than 20%)

the Northeast and West), across metropolitan areas (into "emerging" and "pre-emerging" metropolitan gateways; Singer 2004, 2008), within metropolitan areas (into suburbs, where more than half of immigrants now reside), and even outside metropolitan areas entirely (into small towns and rural areas throughout the country).[6]

I further discovered that geographic dispersion has coalesced with the second major trend changing the face of contemporary American immigration: the extraordinary growth of what is called the "unauthorized" or "illegal" immigrant population.[7] Although the inflow of *new* unauthorized immigrants has fallen to almost zero since 2005, due primarily to a slackening American economy and secondarily to increased enforcement of border and interior immigration laws, by 2009 the unauthorized population had stabilized at roughly 11 million. Almost half of these people had entered the country since 2000, with more than 80% coming from Latin America. Together, they made up an unprecedented 30% of the total foreign-born population, 4.0% of the total American population, and 5.4% of the total American workforce.[8]

Simply put, because U.S. immigration policies enacted since the mid-1960s have actively shifted the primary routes of entry among Mexican and other Latin American immigrants away from legal and temporary avenues toward unauthorized ones,[9] and because foreign-born residents in the new destinations are on average more recent arrivals than those in traditional destinations, new destinations now post a higher proportion of unauthorized immigrants among their total foreign-born population than do traditional destinations (Passel 2005). To illustrate, whereas Map 3 shows that several southern, midwestern, and western new destination states ranked very high (more than 49%) or above average (39–48%) along this indicator in 2008, the six traditional immigrant destination states (California, Florida, Illinois, New Jersey, New York, and Texas) ranked only average (20–38%; Passel and Cohn 2009: 28).[10]

I realized that, taken together, geographic dispersion and the growth of the unauthorized population constitute a major shift in the demography and history of the United States at the turn of the twenty-first century. I immediately wanted to know more about why newcomers, particularly unauthorized ones, were settling in new destinations—particularly in small towns and rural areas across the South, which, like my hometown of Tarboro, have a long history of economic disadvantage and animosity toward nonwhites and outsiders (Saenz 2000). Fortunately, the burgeoning literature on new immigrant destinations was already beginning to address this question, and by now it has identified a complex array of economic and political factors that help explain immigrants' patterns of geographic dispersion.[11] Among them are economic and political push factors abroad, in American border enforcement policies, and in traditional immigrant gateways, including the profound economic dislocations associated with the process of economic development in Latin America; the Immigration Reform and Control Act of 1986; selective border militarization along the U.S.-Mexico border in the 1990s; California's anti-immigrant Proposition 187; and local "quality-of-life," minimum wage, and zoning ordinances enacted in large immigrant gateways, especially in Los Angeles (Light 2006). Also critical are economic and social pull factors in new destinations themselves, among them profound industrial restructuring processes across a variety of American industries; profound demographic shifts among America's native population (including aging, acquisition of education, economic mobility, out-migration, and so forth); direct and indirect immigrant labor recruitment;[12] and even a process migration scholars term "cumulative causation," whereby the existence and functioning of immigrants' own social networks, social capital, and institutions make migration streams into new destinations self-perpetuating even after other initial push and pull factors have dried up.

As a result, I decided to pursue a different range of questions, ones focused less on why immigrants have settled in new destinations and more on what has been happening to them since their arrival. Most generally, I wanted to know what life in new destinations has been like for these newcomers. And because contemporary immigration into the South has been concentrated disproportionately in metropolitan areas (Bankston 2007; Eckes 2005),[13] I especially wanted to know what life has been like for those newcomers living in small southern towns and rural areas, which, like my hometown of Tarboro, are still the most isolated from immigration. So I began asking various questions: How might the rural South influence newcomers' opportunities for economic mobility, in comparison not just to traditional immigrant gateways but also to nearby southern cities? How might the rural South similarly influence newcomers' quality of interaction with American natives? How might the rural South influence the lives and paths of unauthorized immigrants in particular, given their high proportion in new destinations? And how has the immigrant experience been playing out, similarly or differently, across various arenas of rural southern life—in workplaces typical of the old and new rural southern economy, in schools and other major social institutions, in the politics of community life, and, most importantly, in the rural South's strong and "binary" black-white racial structure? To be honest, I was pessimistic about what I might discover, since I expected immigration would be particularly unsettling to rural southerners, who often sense it as a threat to their "ideal of community produced by a traditional, deeply rooted society" (Bankston 2003: 127).

Essentially, I was asking the central questions that all scholars ask about how immigrants become incorporated into (as opposed to excluded from) American society (Bean, Brown, and Rumbaut 2006; Bean and Stevens 2003). However, I was doing so in a new place and with a few special twists. Past research on immigrant incorporation was centered disproportionately on the experiences of southern and eastern European immigrants in the major northeastern and midwestern cities, at the expense of other immigrant groups who settled in rural areas of the Midwest and Southwest (Alba and Denton 2004; Kasinitz 2004; Portes and Rumbaut 2006: 38–40; Telles and Ortiz 2008). Like its predecessor, the contemporary national research agenda has also centered on the experiences of immigrants in major immigrant gateway states and cities (Singer 2004, 2008). This includes the most influential studies of both the "1.5" and "second generation" children of immigrants and immigrant, Latino, and Asian political incorporation.[14] Consequently, examining processes of immigrant incorporation and exclusion in the rural South offered a unique opportunity to identify empirically how contextual features of life far away from traditional gateway cities shape the immigrant experience in the United States. Further examining such processes across a variety of institutional arenas could permit drawing together disparate strands of the literature on immigrant economic, social, and political incorporation, heretofore dominated by economists, sociologists, and political scientists, respectively.

Description of the Comparative Research

Early on, I realized that the questions I was asking lent themselves well to what is called, in the sociological literature on immigration, a "context of reception" approach. Developed most extensively by sociologist Alejandro Portes and his colleagues, context of reception emphasizes how the structural and cultural features of the specific contexts that immigrants enter influence their experiences and opportunities for mobility, *above and beyond* the role played by their own individual characteristics or motivations (Portes and Bach 1985; Portes and Borocz 1989; Portes and Rumbaut 2006: 91–102). In this model, the most relevant dimensions of context of reception that structure the mobility paths of immigrants and their descendants are the policies of the receiving government, the conditions of the receiving labor market, the characteristics of newcomers' own receiving ethnic communities, and the reactions of receiving non-ethnic communities. Looking at my questions this way, I saw that the sheer diversity of new immigrant destinations across the country, which range from rural agricultural markets to company towns such as Dalton, Georgia, to metropolitan areas such as Las Vegas (Zúñiga and Hernández-León, 2009), was a veritable goldmine. If I could use this diversity carefully to closely capture some of the distinct contexts of reception being offered to immigrant newcomers in the rural South, I could help move forward the domestic research agenda on immigrant incorporation (Ellis and Almgren 2009; Jones-Correa 2005a; Marrow 2005; Winders 2009b).

I eagerly set out to join the ranks of a set of pioneering scholars[15] who also recognized a need to employ direct comparative research on immigrant incorporation processes in new destinations to tease out if, how, and why they matter. Between June 2003 and June 2004, I returned to eastern North Carolina to answer my research questions by observing and interviewing Hispanic newcomers and non-Hispanic natives in two counties there. Because the South is a heterogeneous place—a fact frequently overlooked by natives from other regions—I wanted one of these counties to reflect the economic and demographic context of the new rural South, and the other that of the old rural South. Even though my research would often move me across county lines, I limited myself to focusing on counties because they continue to be important substate political units within the region that structure various aspects of residents' economic, social, and political lives (Bullock and Hood 2006). To ensure anonymity, I refer to these two counties by the pseudonyms "Bedford" and "Wilcox" throughout this book. For ease and consistency, pseudonyms beginning with letters close to *B* indicate places and entities within or near majority-*black* Bedford County; likewise, pseudonyms beginning with letters close to *W* indicate ones within or near majority-*white* Wilcox County. (The single exception is for business entities, which I refer to by pseudonyms that emphasize their area of expertise instead, such as "Poultry Processing Plant," "Textile Mill," "Tobacco Farm," and "Fabrico.") Unless otherwise indicated, I also use pseudonyms beginning with letters close to *B* and *W* to refer to all other counties in eastern North Carolina, as well as to all places and entities located within them (towns, trailer parks, nonprofit organizations, newspapers). However, I do not use pseudonyms for places in the central piedmont region of the state, or for state-level entities.

Bedford and Wilcox share some important features that make them characteristic of the racially binary rural South. First, racial and ethnic minority groups other than African Americans have little historical presence in either county, and separation of blacks from whites in each county runs deep. Second, at the same time both counties' populations are also small enough that everybody knows everybody and complete racial isolation is not possible. Consequently, although racial inequalities and tensions do exist, unlike the situation in many highly segregated gateway cities, what Erwin (2003) calls the "limits of space, resources, and opportunities for segregation" in rural areas also force members of all groups to interact in workplaces, neighborhoods, public spaces, and public schools (see also McConnell and Miraftab 2009; and Striffler 2009). As a result, almost everyone I interviewed reported having come into contact with someone outside their own group, usually in these spaces, and even if they did not know many people outside their own group personally, they at least knew something about one another.[16]

Yet Bedford and Wilcox also differ in several ways that are central to my analysis. Wilcox is characteristic of the new rural South. In the early 2000s, its population was majority white and had been growing for several decades, and its expanding low-wage agribusiness and food-processing industries and the rising number of immigrants since the mid-1980s had already attracted significant attention from academics, politicians, and the media. In fact, Hispanics made up fully 15% of Wilcox's official total county population in the 2000 U.S. Census, which was approximately half of the corresponding figure for African Americans (29%), without even considering the large potential undercount.

By contrast, similar to the county in which my hometown of Tarboro is located, Bedford is characteristic of the old rural South. In the early 2000s, its population was still majority black—Bedford is a historical center of North Carolina's section of the southern black belt—and had been declining for three decades. Because its economy still depended heavily on such smaller and declining low-wage southern industries as tobacco agriculture and routine manufacturing and textiles, Hispanics were settling in Bedford County in far fewer numbers than in Wilcox. In fact, they were only 3% of Bedford's official total county population in the 2000 U.S. Census, a figure far lower than the corresponding one for African Americans (58%). Interestingly, despite the decline in traditional industries, Bedford economic development and government officials had decided against construction of a large pork processing plant in the 1980s.

I chose to employ qualitative research methods because I was interested in the processes involved in immigrant incorporation in the rural South, especially as they are playing out for the Hispanic newcomers least likely to be captured in large-scale quantitative data, such as recent arrivals, unauthorized immigrants, and highly mobile seasonal farmworkers. In the end, the project drew on several forms of ethnographic research that I conducted in both counties, plus 129 formal interviews with foreign-born Latin American immigrants of varying nationalities, U.S.-born Hispanics (all but two of whom are "new-comers" to the traditional South), and key white and black native-born infor-mants, in both Spanish and English. As Table 1 shows, most of the foreign-born respondents in the sample hailed from Mexico (55.7%), had migrated directly to North Carolina from abroad rather than from another part of the United States (not shown), and lacked legal status (47.1%). This profile is consistent with the broader literature, which demonstrates that Mexicans predominate in

Table 1. Characteristics of respondents

	N	Percentage
Foreign-born Latin American immigrants	*70*	*54.0*
National origin		
Mexico	39	55.7
South America (Argentina, Chile, Colombia, Ecuador, Peru, Venezuela)	16	22.9
Central America (Guatemala, Costa Rica, El Salvador, Nicaragua)	14	20.0
Cuba	1	1.4
Legal status[a]		
Naturalized citizens	12	17.1
Legal permanent residents	12	17.1
"Nonimmigrant" workers (on work contracts or temporary visas)	7	10.0
Unauthorized immigrants	33	47.1
Unable to determine	6	8.6
U.S.-born Hispanics/Latinos	*18*	*14.0*
State of origin		
New York	6	33.3
Puerto Rico	4	22.2
Texas	2	11.1
Florida	2	11.1
Other states (MA, NC, OH, SC)	4	22.2
Legal status		
U.S. citizens	18	100.0
Key native informants	*41*	*32.0*
Race		
White	27	65.9
Black	14	34.1
Legal status		
U.S. citizens	41	100.0
Total	*129*	*100.0*

[a] See the Appendix on distinctions among legal permanent resident immigrants, unauthorized immigrants, and temporary "nonimmigrants."

North Carolina's foreign-born and Hispanic/Latino populations (at approximately two-fifths and two-thirds respectively); that the internal migration of Hispanics from other parts of the country to North Carolina has gradually given way over time to direct international labor migration (Leach 2004; Leach and Bean 2008; Marrow 2011b; H. A. Smith 2008; Torres, Popke, and Hapke 2006; Torres et al. 2003); and that as a new destination state, North Carolina has a high proportion of unauthorized immigrants (Johnson and Kasarda 2009; Kasarda and Johnson 2006; Passel 2005; Passel and Cohn 2009). I offer more detail on how I located my interview respondents, what kinds of ethnographic research I conducted, the measures I took to protect all research subjects' identities, and how I negotiated complex issues of entrée and identity in this project in the Appendix.

Contributions of the Rural Southern Context

The findings I present in this book are the culmination of research I carried out in Bedford and Wilcox Counties in 2003–04, and they help us begin to appreciate how the process of adapting to and becoming integrated into American life in rural southern new destinations not only differs from that taking place in traditional immigrant gateways but also varies among these new destinations themselves. Most important, the findings I present touch on the multiple comparisons I was able to pursue because of the similarities and differences in Bedford and Wilcox Counties' local economic and demographic contexts of reception. First, I was able to analyze Hispanic newcomers' experiences and opportunities for mobility in the context of expanding low-wage industries (such as food processing in Wilcox County) compared to stagnating or declining low-wage industries (such as tobacco agriculture and routine manufacturing/textiles in Bedford County). Second, I was able to analyze Hispanic newcomers' patterns of intergroup relations not only in similar binary rural southern racial contexts but also in majority-white versus majority-black ones. Third, I was able to analyze similarities in Hispanic newcomers' patterns of geographic and institutional incorporation across the two counties.

Based on these comparisons, the major argument of this book is that moving the focus of American immigrant incorporation research into the rural American South alters how we must think about three main things: assimilation, race relations, and political and institutional responsiveness to immigrants. In so doing, it reveals a more positive experience than we might have expected to find, given the rural South's reputation as the most economically depressed and racially intolerant region of the country.

Assimilation

Let's take assimilation first. Alba and Nee (2003) recently redefined *assimilation* as the state of achieving "parity in life chances" regardless of one's ethnic background. They further redefine the American "mainstream" as the place where people are located once their ethnic background ceases to matter in determining their opportunities and life chances (even while people can still maintain ethnic identity, and also while factors other than ethnicity, particularly social class, can still influence their life chances). Viewed this way, analyzing immigrants' experiences in the rural South forces us to rethink how much distance they and their descendants will have to travel, and in what direction, in order to achieve parity among mainstream American natives. This is because rural Americans have a lower educational level, work in agriculture at a higher rate, work in high-skilled professional and technical jobs at a lower rate, earn lower wages, and live in poverty at a higher rate than do their urban counterparts—especially in the rural southern black belt where much of this disadvantage is concentrated.

Although such indicators most certainly do not suggest that living in rural America is any better in material terms than living in urban America, what they do in an oversimplified way is reduce the economic and occupational distance that low-skilled immigrant newcomers and their descendants need to travel in order to gain entry and eventually "assimilate" into what is considered the local economic norm or mainstream. Stated differently, if we think of assimilation as a process whereby immigrants and their children converge toward the positions of the natives surrounding them, then it is plausible that, using a "subject-centered approach" (Zhou, Lee, Vallejo, Tafoya-Estrada, and Xiong 2008), newcomers might interpret and judge their incremental educational and economic progress as comparatively more successful in rural America than in urban America. Indeed, rural and small-town Americans often take great pride in their working- or lower-middle-class identity, whereas urban natives' ideas of what constitutes the local economic mainstream may both imply and require a higher level of educational or occupational attainment.[17]

Indeed, one key way that living in the rural South makes a difference to Hispanic newcomers' experiences and opportunities for incorporation and assimilation in America is by weakening the economic barriers separating them from local mainstream natives compared to what would be the case in many metropolitan gateways. I even find that food processing—the large, low-wage industry most characteristic of the new rural southern economy—was supplying important opportunities for some (although admittedly not all) of the Hispanic newcomers it employed to achieve limited economic stability and sometimes also "short-distance" upward mobility (Alba and Nee 2003). In Chapters 2 and 3, I identify key structural and institutional factors that were facilitating this lateral and short-distance upward mobility. I also show how it often compared favorably not only to that in low-wage, declining rural industries such as tobacco agriculture and routine manufacturing and textiles but also to that in metropolitan areas, where Hispanic newcomers noted they would most likely be working in low-wage service-sector jobs and confronting additional economic and noneconomic burdens that they associated with urban life.

I therefore argue that in the mid-2000s the new rural southern economy was not destining Hispanic newcomers to the ranks of an excluded and jobless "rainbow underclass" (Gans 1992; Portes and Rumbaut 2001; Portes and Zhou 1993; Zhou 1999). Rather, it was giving many of them limited yet much-needed economic stability that, combined with several other positive aspects of rural life (cited most strongly by lower-status newcomers of rural origins themselves; see Chapter 1), was helping them set the stage for their children's upward incorporation into a distinct sort of rural working class. In the mid-2000s, this boded cautious optimism, because some of the greatest Hispanic population growth in the rural South had occurred precisely in places where the food processing industry dominates the local landscape (Donato, Tolbert, Nucci, and Kawano 2007, 2008; Kandel and Cromartie 2004; Kochhar, Suro, and Tafoya 2005; Parrado and Kandel 2008), and because many Hispanic newcomers have been shown to undergo a process of "settling out" from agriculture into food processing, construction, or light manufacturing, and then into other industries and self-employment, as immigrant settlement matures (Dunn, Aragonés, and Shivers 2005; Griffith 1993, 2005, 2006, 2008).

Race Relations

Moving on to intergroup relations, I note that national public opinion studies consistently show that Americans view immigration in ambivalent terms, although small minorities on either end of the spectrum rally up in strong support and opposition to it (Burns and Gimpel 2000; Espenshade and Calhoun 1993; Espenshade and Hempstead 1996; Gimpel and Edwards 1999; Harwood 1986; Kohut, Keeter, Doherty, Suro, and Escobar 2006; Lee and Fiske 2006; Simon and Alexander 1993; Suro 2009). This picture of general ambivalence flanked by polarized support and opposition is now emerging in new immigrant destinations, too, where a range of scholars have found that ambivalence, confusion, variation, and even contradiction, as opposed to outright rejection and xenophobia, are the dominant responses to newcomers.[18]

Indeed, ambivalence and contradiction help explain why Hispanic newcomers in the rural South, especially lower-status ones, considered their lives in the rural South and their relationships with its mainstream natives to be positive, or at least neutral, rather than negative (see Chapter 1). Nevertheless, several features of the rural southern context also make a difference to Hispanic newcomers' experiences and opportunities for incorporation and assimilation in America by strengthening the cultural and racial barriers separating them from local mainstream natives compared to what would be the case in many metropolitan gateways. Together, the region's lack of immigrant history, its binary racial structure (Lee and Bean 2004; McClain et al. 2006, 2007), its large population of African Americans (Barreto and Sanchez 2009), its natives' more conservative political, moral, and religious values (Reed, 1986, 1993), and its natives' relative lack of pro-immigrant sentiment[19]—something Haubert and Fussell (2006) attribute to a lower educational level and stronger blue-collar occupational position among southerners than nonsoutherners—magnify the boundaries separating the region's two dominant groups (whites and blacks) from newcomers. These newcomers are easily marked and excluded as outsiders because of characteristics associated with being from somewhere else, notably foreign nativity, lack of English language ability, and even nonwhite or nonblack racial status (Bohon 2006).

In the mid-2000s, Hispanic newcomers in the rural South acutely felt this exclusion, and importantly they felt it more strongly from blacks than whites. In Chapters 4 and 5, I identify several key structural factors that were making black-Hispanic relations more contentious than white-Hispanic ones, in particular class structure, black population size, citizenship, and the institutional arenas in which groups were interacting. I also show how Hispanic newcomers' multiple interpretations of the meaning of discrimination (especially along the lines of citizenship) and their expectations about blacks interacted with conceptions of their work and worth. Consequently many began to distance themselves from African Americans in response to perceptions of civic and cultural ostracism as undeserving outsiders.

Combined with Hispanic newcomers' predominantly "nonblack" racial and ethnic identification, I therefore argue that in the mid-2000s the rural southern binary racial context was not fostering a "rainbow coalition of color" sense of identity among Hispanic newcomers and African Americans, wherein common experiences of racial discrimination can serve as a basis to unite, as nonwhites, despite other internal distinctions. This may well have been happening among small groups of political elites and black-brown coalition builders, but it was not generally the case among the masses. Rather, many Hispanic newcomers came to perceive that the boundaries separating themselves from whites, although existent, are somewhat more permeable than those separating themselves from blacks, or whites from blacks (see also Rose 2007). This suggests a classic pattern of racial assimilation, and it lends tentative support to predictions that a new black-nonblack color line (Gans 1999; Lee and Bean 2004, 2007, 2010; Sears and Savalei 2006; Yancey 2003) may be developing in the rural South—the very region where the African American population is still the largest, where the uniquely American racial binary has reigned most supreme, and where the pressures to divide whites from nonwhites have always been strongest.

Political and Institutional Responsiveness

Finally, although life in rural America certainly has its advantages (see Chapter 1), new destinations do exhibit a serious lack of institutional infrastructure to assist Hispanic newcomers and facilitate their civic and political integration (Gozdziak and Bump 2008; Massey 2008a; Price and Singer 2008; Shefner and Kirkpatrick 2009; Waters and Jiménez 2005). Rural new destinations suffer the most acute resource disadvantage in this regard. Not only are their newcomer communities often made up of recent arrivals with little human capital and political experience but these newcomers also often lack the critical mass, at least initially, to develop their own economies, services, networks, and organizations. Moreover, rural new destinations offer fewer services through which newcomers can make claims on government resources than do metropolitan areas, especially the traditional immigrant gateways; they also have fewer migrant-serving and community-based social and civic organizations through which newcomers can access assistance and advocacy (see Chapter 1).[20]

Consequently, a third key way in which living in the rural South makes a difference to Hispanic newcomers' experiences and opportunities for incorporation and assimilation in America is by depressing their chances for group-level descriptive political representation—that is, representation of their own interests as political actors. Many newcomers are actively prohibited (if they are unauthorized) from naturalizing, voting, and participating in electoral politics (Bullock and Hood 2006),[21] while others have fewer points of entry into electoral or nonelectoral politics than they would in larger urban areas. In such situations, newcomers' incorporation depends more strongly, at least in the early stages of settlement, on increased substantive political representation—that is, representation of their interests by other political actors.

However, in the mid-2000s I found little evidence of substantive responsiveness to Hispanic newcomers' needs among elected state and local politicians.

These politicians were not engaging in proactive efforts to reach out to Hispanic newcomers; they also questioned their accountability to Hispanic newcomers' interests, especially to those who are unauthorized immigrants and whom they did not necessarily see as deserving political constituents. Most surprisingly—defying dominant theories collected from the disciplines of political science, public administration, and sociology alike, which view bureaucracies as guided by politics and by the individuals who wield political power rather than vice versa—public bureaucrats working in a variety of local institutions were doing noticeably more than these elected politicians were to incorporate Hispanic newcomers and advocate on their behalf. In Chapters 6 and 7, I illustrate patterned differences in substantive responsiveness to Hispanic newcomers' interests and needs between elected politicians and public bureaucrats, as well as among public bureaucrats working in different types of institutions. I also show how attention to external government policies, which range from inclusive to exclusive across these institutional arenas, and bureaucrats' internal professional missions, which likewise range from service- to regulatory-oriented, help account for the patterns I uncovered.

I therefore argue that in the mid-2000s the rural southern political context was not necessarily fostering strong political incorporation among Hispanic newcomers. For this to happen, more proactive immigrant integration policies and greater attention from elected politicians are needed. Nonetheless, many Hispanic newcomers were still encountering some natives whom they perceived as kind and friendly, or who, by virtue of their strategic position in several service-oriented mediating institutions, support newcomers' quest for incorporation and upward mobility (Haubert and Fussell 2006; Jones-Correa 2008; Silver 2009). This suggests that an emergent pattern of bureaucratic rather than traditional political incorporation is under way in the rural South, whereby responsiveness to Hispanic newcomers' interests is being initiated not by elected politicians but rather by bureaucrats who are coming into frequent contact with newcomers and considering their professional role to be centered on dispensing resources to them in the name of promoting equity and the well-being of all community residents (Jones-Correa 2008; Lewis and Ramakrishnan 2007; Marrow 2009a; Van der Leun 2003, 2006).

. . .

Without discounting the significant challenges that Hispanic newcomers were experiencing, or the frustrations that some natives were also feeling, each of these things lent support to a cautiously optimistic view of newcomers' opportunities for incorporation and upward mobility in the rural South from the vantage point of the mid-2000s. They supported what Hirschman and Massey (2008) call an emerging "paradigm of immigrant inclusion" in the United States, in which intolerance toward newcomers is often tempered by growing norms of "intolerance for intolerance" and a positively valued "right to diversity" (Zúñiga and Hernández-León 2005a; see also Price and Singer 2008), as well as strong conceptions of natives and newcomers as functionally interdependent in various workplaces and institutions, particularly in depressed rural areas that are finding themselves battling long-term economic and demographic decline. From this vantage point, the rural southern context alters the American immigrant experience that we have come to understand from the existing literature in ways that are both sobering and promising. On the one hand, it widens the racial and cultural gulf between newcomers and natives and depresses their formal opportunities for political and civic integration. On the other hand, it offers newcomers—especially lower-status ones, who the existing literature shows face the most hostile contexts of reception in traditional immigrant gateways—strategic "holes" of opportunity in what they describe as safe, slow-paced, and friendly places where they can establish themselves and make a go at moving up.

Still, there are two major caveats to this cautiously optimistic picture. The first is that although the rural southern immigrant experience I uncovered is more positive than we might have expected it to be, it is arguably less so for African Americans than for whites or Hispanic newcomers. Still overrepresented at the bottom of the regional class structure, and with their Civil Rights Movement goals not yet fully realized, many rural African Americans perceived themselves to be bearing the brunt of low-skilled Latin American immigration's negative economic and social impact. Hispanic newcomers' perceptions of class-based competition with, and civic and cultural exclusion by, African Americans in the rural South poignantly reflect this. Therefore, black-brown tensions in a variety of arenas, both inside and outside the workplace, are an important feature of contemporary rural southern life that will need serious attention in the future—from whites, blacks, and newcomers alike—if tensions are to be defused and the development of a new color line dividing blacks from all other groups is to be avoided.

The second caveat runs like a thread through all of the chapters of the book: citizenship and legal status. As social scientist Barbara Ellen Smith (2006) eloquently points out, although the problems of the American South have historically centered around race and class (spawning social justice movements centered around collaborations of people of color and collaborations of workers, respectively), new questions related to immigration, citizenship, and legal status both complicate and frequently supersede these established frameworks. For many Hispanic newcomers living in the rural South in the mid-2000s, it was lack of citizenship or legal status, rather than race or class, that most seriously threatened their opportunities for incorporation and upward mobility in all of the institutional arenas I examined, and that most seriously depressed elected politicians' feelings of accountability to their interests and needs. Furthermore, as geographers Lise Nelson and Nancy Hiemstra (2008) astutely observe, the "discourse of illegality" that has become so prevalent in American politics and the media today provides rural southern natives with a publicly acceptable narrative for justifying immigrants' exclusion (Brettell and Nibbs 2010; Chavez 2008; Massey and Sánchez 2010) and also internalizes a harmful belief among immigrants that they can "never belong" (327).

As the most worrisome feature of the negative national-level context of reception toward Latin American immigrants at the turn of the twenty-first century, lack of legal status has placed many Hispanic newcomers in the rural South, like their counterparts elsewhere in the country, in a precarious position where they are made constantly subject to actual or potential policing and disenfranchisement as undeserving outsiders who do not belong (Bauer and Reynolds 2009; Cantu 1995; Chavez 2007; Massey and Sánchez 2010). Intentionally produced by American immigration law and border enforcement policies over the course of the twentieth century and exacerbated by recent increases in interior enforcement (Hincapié 2009; Massey and Sánchez 2010; Terrazas 2008),[22] this current system of excluding immigrants by legal status must be dismantled and reconfigured as soon as possible. This is imperative if downward mobility among Hispanic newcomers is to be avoided, intergroup relations and community trust improved, responsive American democratic politics rejuvenated, and the rise of a new system of legally sanctioned and socially institutionalized "Juan Crow" inequality (Lovato 2008) prevented. In the Conclusion, I discuss these policy implications and speculate on the negative impact of troubling changes that have occurred in the region since I conducted my fieldwork in 2003–04, particularly the growth in anti-immigrant sentiment and the passage of anti-immigrant policies and ordinances since 2005.

Geography

1 "I'm a Person Who Likes Tranquility a Lot"

Southern Region and Rural Space in the Hispanic Newcomer Experience

BY 2003, Vera had lived in the United States for 16 years. When she was a young child in the early 1970s, she spent four years living with her father in Dallas, and then in the border city of El Centro, California. After he was jailed for dealing drugs, Vera went back to their small village in Querétaro, Mexico, where she remained for the next 15 years. At 23 she returned on her own to the United States in 1991—this time to eastern North Carolina with a temporary H-2B visa in hand to work in crab processing, an industry that is spread over the state's coastal tidewater region (Griffith 1993, 1995b, 2006; Hall 1995). Over the next decade, Vera moved from one crowded crabhouse to another, to the orange groves in Florida, to a cucumber nursery and a dirt packing plant in two other southeastern states, and to the infamous Smithfield Foods pork processing plant in Tarheel, North Carolina (Associated Press 2007; Gartner 2007a, 2007b; LeDuff 2000) where she worked glazing cuts of ham. From Smithfield, Vera moved to the night shift in the worksite I call Textile Mill (a pseudonym) in Bedford County, to an aero-systems components manufacturing company in that same county, and finally to her current job as an ESL teacher in Bedford Elementary School.[1] Because it was difficult getting American employers to recognize her two-year college diploma from Mexico, Vera earned a GED through Even Start, an innovative parent-child continuing education program affiliated with Bedford County Community College and Bedford Elementary School (see Gozdziak and Bump 2008), and took courses toward an associate degree at Bedford County Community College.

Because Vera had lived in urban areas in two traditional immigrant gateway states, Texas and California, I was curious to know what she thought about life in the rural South, and whether she had plans to stay or eventually leave. Overall, she reported liking the region and had no plans to move. To her, not only is eastern North Carolina less crowded and safer than California, but its public schools are also "a lot better" and its police more "trustful." She even said it feels more like home to migrants like herself who come from small villages abroad. Therefore, even though Vera still has family in California and acknowledged that her wages might be higher there or in other big cities, she preferred the "country" lifestyle for its peacefulness, beautiful natural landscape, and safety for children:

Vera: People from California want to know why I live here. My cousins say, "How's the life there?" I say, "Oh, it's kind of country life." "And you like that?" they ask. "Of course, I like that! I don't like to live around crime and all of that stuff. I'm diabetic!" [*laughs*]

Interviewer: So they don't understand it?

Vera: No, they don't understand. They make fun of it, and way the people talk. But I say I like it better than California, New York, or those places. I even brought my sister here, because I didn't want her to go to California. I told her to come to live here because it's better now that we're thinking about our kids. That's the main thing. I might get more money for what I do, a better house, a Mercedes Benz car, a restaurant or something, a better life, but the community there is wild. Especially the Hispanics. They've got the *Vatos Locos Forever* [a predominantly Mexican street gang], and I don't want that for my daughter. I could even go to Raleigh to make more money for my work, but I don't want to live in Raleigh. Big cities stress me out. And another one of the reasons that I stay in this state is because it's beautiful. The forest and all of that stuff. It's quiet, nice, and . . . it's like home! Yeah, you can adapt here like home. So people make fun of it here, but it's a good life!

By contrast, Silvia is a Puerto Rican American from Spanish Harlem in New York City who married a man whose parents are originally from Bedford County. In the early 2000s, Silvia and her husband, with their daughter in tow, relocated to Bedford to be closer to his aging parents. When I interviewed her in 2003, Silvia was still undergoing both North-to-South and urban-to-rural shocks from the transition. Initially she was hesitant to admit it, afraid of possibly upsetting her new friends and colleagues, but she was extremely homesick for New York, a place where she said Americans have more knowledge of life outside a "black and white" box, and where they are "less close-minded" toward different cultural, ethnic, and religious practices. For Silvia, making friends and being accepted in the rural South is harder than she expected. For the first time in her life, she finds herself "confused" and "constantly defending my American identity," because "being Puerto Rican just doesn't make sense to other people down here." With the potential exception of one "open-minded" white colleague in the local school system where she works, Silvia has had trouble befriending locals, many of whom she feels are close-minded and, because of being from a small town, "very stuck on their old ways." Finally, her daughter, who was enrolled in challenging parochial schools in New York City, is bringing home stellar grades of 100+, leaving Silvia worrying that the educational environment in Bedford Middle School is not sufficiently challenging.

Silvia's feelings about life in the rural South compared to that in a traditional immigrant gateway city are the polar opposite of how Vera feels about living there. When I asked Silvia if there was anything she did not miss about New York, she responded with an emphatic "No!" Silvia missed her extended family, the food, the "open-all-night" buzz of the big city, and, most important, having friends and neighbors of all stripes and colors. The things she used to complain about when she lived there—traffic, pollution, and delayed subway rides—she misses now. "If it was just me," she told me quietly, she would go back in a heartbeat, but she also loves her husband and thinks that Bedford could ultimately offer a better life for her daughter. So she has learned how to put up with the strange looks she gets from passersby when she and her husband walk down the street, with the parents of her daughter's soccermates who subtly ignore her on the sidelines at games, with the unwelcoming treatment from a local hairdresser, and even with the colleague whom she once had to correct for calling her "Yankee" instead of by her first name. Silvia is even steeling herself for the day her daughter will attend the local high school, ardently telling me that "she will not be competing" in the segregated, binary homecoming queen pageant there:

Silvia: I told her, "I don't care if they vote you in and you get all the votes, you're not going to be a part of that." Because I teach her that you don't look at people's skin, you just make friends with whoever you feel comfortable with, and who you think is a good person.

.   .   .

How are we to make sense of such opposing viewpoints regarding the influence the rural South has on Hispanic newcomers in the United States, including their perceptions of opportunities for incorporation and mobility and their intergroup relations with American natives? Vera thought the rural South makes life better and less stressful and facilitates positive interactions with mainstream Americans (especially whites), even though it might not lead to as much economic success. By contrast, Silvia thought the rural South makes being accepted by both mainstream whites and blacks (especially whites) more difficult, and she still felt economically unsteady despite her and her husband's lower-middle-class jobs. Of course, both women acknowledged the ambiguous or contradictory nature of living in the rural South, which involves economic tradeoffs and emotional bargains (on ambiguity and contradiction in rural areas, see Torres, Popke, and Hapke 2006). Yet Vera ultimately concluded that rural space is the deciding contextual factor, while Silvia argued the opposite, saying, "It's a southern thing. I think if Hispanics go to Raleigh, which is the biggest city, or Charlotte, they're still gonna feel the same way as I do."

In this chapter, I paint a picture of the ambivalent and contradictory ways in which both Hispanic newcomers and natives interpreted the influence of the rural South on Hispanic newcomers' lives. Respondents frequently conflated the two contextual effects—that of the southern region with that of rural space—and they also differed in their evaluations of the mechanisms behind and consequences of each one. This complexity may not be surprising; a rural and agricultural character has historically distinguished the South, making it difficult to isolate one effect from the other. Yet ultimately I identify rural space as the dominant influence on the Hispanic newcomers' American experience. I also show that its most positive effects emerged for lower-status Hispanic newcomers from rural origins (like Vera), while its most negative ones emerged for higher-status Hispanic newcomers from urban areas (like Silvia). These differences carry important implications for Hispanic newcomers' differential prospects for incorporation and assimilation as they disperse throughout the country.

Characteristics and Stereotypes of the Rural American South

To understand how the rural South might influence Hispanic newcomers' experiences, we first need to identify the salient characteristics and stereotypes of both rural America and the American South. Let's take rural America first. The significant convergence between nonmetro and metro areas since the mid-twentieth century (Albrecht 2006; Friedland 2002) has caused considerable decline in the many once-salient metro-nonmetro differences in America, such as educational level, income, family size, and birth rate. Nevertheless, metro areas still tend to exhibit more diverse employment structures, more numerous higher-level positions in their employment structures, higher income, and less poverty. By virtue of their physical location, these areas have more advantaged access to markets and consumers and higher property values compared to nonmetro areas, both of which can facilitate wealth accumulation (Albrecht 2006; RSS 2006a, 2006b).

This set of relative *economic* costs of rural life may have a negative impact on Hispanic newcomers' lives. At the same time, the recent restructuring and relocation of low-wage industry to nonmetro areas may counter this with greater job opportunities, as may the lower cost of living in nonmetro areas (Fraga et al. 2010; McConnell and Miraftab 2009; Torres, Popke, and Hapke 2006).

Next, major improvements in communication and transportation since the mid-twentieth century have also reduced metro-nonmetro cultural differences by lessening the cultural isolation of nonmetro residents (Albrecht 2006). Nevertheless, rural residents continue to be associated with cultural isolation, parochialism, traditionalism, moral and political conservatism, and intolerance for diversity and ambiguity, including intolerance for racial and ethnic minorities (Albrecht 2006; Saenz 2000). This set of *cultural* costs of rural life may influence Hispanic newcomers' lives negatively by slowing their acceptance (Fennelly 2005; Fennelly and Federico 2008).

Third, nonmetro areas are distinguished by their lower population size and density, which scholars argue reduce the total number of social contacts, allowing rural residents to become acquainted with one another on a personal level—that is, in terms of primary as opposed to categorical and secondary relationships—more easily than urban residents can (Albrecht 2006). On the one hand, this *ecological* factor of rural life may have a negative impact on Hispanic newcomers' lives by leading to more exclusionary attitudes, values, and behaviors among natives. On the other hand, it may affect Hispanic newcomers' lives positively by widening opportunities for primary-level social contact with mainstream American natives who have strong community networks (Cuadros 2006; Dunn, Aragonés, and Shivers 2005; Erwin 2003; Kandel and Parrado, 2006; Silver 2009).

Other ecological characteristics of rural life, such as closeness to nature, peacefulness, and safety, may also influence Hispanic newcomers' lives positively, and potentially balance out some negative ecological effects such as those wielded by lesser racial and ethnic diversity (K. M. Johnson 2003) and a less developed public transportation infrastructure (Atiles and Bohon 2003; Barcus 2006; Bohon 2008; Lacy 2007, 2008b, 2009; Odem 2009; Verdaguer 2008). Comparatively lax immigration enforcement may also shield many newcomers (especially unauthorized ones) from heightened institutional scrutiny in rural compared to urban areas (Lacy 2009; McDonnell 2008; H. A. Smith 2008; Torres, Popke, and Hapke 2006), although some scholars argue that immigrants may be more visible, not less, in sparsely populated communities, at least to community residents and local law enforcement authorities even if not to federal immigration officials (Winders 2008b; Zúñiga and Hernández-León 2005a).

Moving on to characteristics and stereotypes of the American South, and considering economic characteristics first, we find that the traditional South still exhibits the country's highest poverty rate, lowest unionization rate, and weakest labor movement arrangements in the country (Bauer and Reynolds 2009; Cornfield 2009; Eckes 2005; Fink 2003; Smith-Nonini 2009), all of which may have a negative impact on Hispanic newcomers' lives. However, because the South has also emerged as "the nation's most racially integrated and economically dynamic region" since the mid-twentieth century (Cobb and Stueck 2005: xi), the economic effect of living in the region is no longer clear, nor solely negative.

As part of the great economic "harmonization and convergence" of American regions since the mid-twentieth century, major improvements in communication and transportation have also reduced southern-nonsouthern cultural differences by reducing the cultural isolation of southern residents (Eckes 2005). Nonetheless, southerners continue to be associated with the same characteristics as ruralites—cultural isolation, parochialism, traditionalism, moral and political conservatism, and intolerance for diversity and ambiguity, including intolerance for racial and ethnic minorities (Griffin 2006; Mantero 2008; Reed 1986, 1993; Saenz 2000).[2] Although some of these cultural attributes of southern life may influence Hispanic newcomers' lives negatively (Duchón and Murphy 2001; Griffin and McFarland 2007), others—particularly hospitality and traditional family values—may do the opposite.

Finally, *ecological* characteristics of southern areas, including warm climate, may have a positive impact on Hispanic newcomers' lives, and potentially balance out negative effects such as those wielded by less racial and ethnic diversity and lower-quality community services.

Southern Region: Ambivalent and Contradictory

In some ways, the southern regional context exerts discernible economic and noneconomic effects on Hispanic newcomers' experiences in eastern North Carolina, although they range from negative to positive. Like Vera, Stephanie, a legal permanent resident who originally migrated illegally to California from Guanajuato, Mexico, in 1991 before settling down in North Carolina with her husband in 2001, felt her economic opportunities are more limited in the traditional South. Having lived previously in California, Indiana, and Nebraska, she hoped to move back to California so that her husband "can find a job for more than $15 an hour. It is very hard for him to find a job here that is well paid." Similarly, Muriel, a Puerto Rican American who was born in Lowell, Massachusetts, grew up in Florida, and migrated to Wilcox County in 1997, argued that Hispanic newcomers experience more racial or ethnic profiling by law enforcement officers in the traditional South than elsewhere, including Florida and Texas:

Muriel: I see more racism here, especially when you get to Alabama and Georgia and stuff, and all the places that are like that. For example, I can't remember what part of the United States we were driving in, but I want to say Alabama because we were going to Texas. Some highway patrolmen stopped us on the side of the road and asked for my [Mexican immigrant] husband's driver's license, and he gave his license to one of them. Then the patrolmen made us follow them to some kind of building thing. They looked in our truck, searching for drugs. And they broke our gas thing where they were putting metals and stuff in there. The doors, they messed them up. They wanted us to undress at one point, so they could check us. I said, "No, I will not undress unless there's a female to do that." "Well, do you want to go to jail?" "Well, I'll go if I have to because I'm not going to undress for you." So we didn't have to undress or anything, but they treated us real, real bad. And it was for nothing, because we weren't even doing nothing. We were just driving. And that was real wrong of them.

Like Muriel, Alvaro, a formerly unauthorized immigrant from the city of Saltillo in the state of Coahuila, Mexico, who migrated directly to North Carolina in 1990 and then became a legal permanent resident in 1997, thought that Hispanic newcomers suffer from greater prejudice in the traditional South. Alvaro suspected that this stems from two of southerners' cultural characteristics—higher religious fundamentalism and greater intolerance for racial and ethnic minorities—and ultimately he felt that such prejudice limits Hispanic newcomers' upward economic mobility:

Alvaro: Being a foreign or Hispanic person living in North Carolina, I feel a lot of pressure to succeed. Because there's a lot of people who are prejudiced, and they probably don't let you move your life at the speed or in the way you want.
Interviewer: Is there something unique about North Carolina when it comes to this kind of racism and prejudice?
Alvaro: I think yeah, well, because you know according to the history in North Carolina and the religious belt, which is this area, that's the places where you can see this racism is stronger. You can see it more often. Because if I lived in Los Angeles or in Miami or Chicago, I could probably compete with other Hispanics for higher positions. But right now, one of my big obstacles is racism.

Some respondents also singled out two ecological characteristics of the traditional South—less racial and ethnic diversity and lower-quality community services and resources—although they frequently conflated them with the same ecological characteristics of rural areas. For instance, Carmen, a Hispanic American of Puerto Rican, Panamanian, and African American ancestry, thought that the traditional South's weak immigrant history and lack of familiarity with Hispanic culture help account for fewer services being available to Hispanic newcomers in the region, especially in rural areas (Bohon, Macpherson, and Atiles 2005; Wainer 2004). Having lived previously in Pennsylvania and Miami, Carmen felt that the region's dearth of services might explain the greater cultural shock she sees among Hispanic newcomers in the South:

Carmen: We in North Carolina do not have the history, especially in the rural South, of dealing with Hispanic culture, language, it's just is not here. Miami has been a product of immigration for the past 20-something years. California, you know, they're over there by Mexico. Thanks to that, they have that understanding. We do not. Immigration was not a common thing here for some time. If it was, I think we would have more bilinguals or more facilities available.

Carmen was joined by Ignacio, a Nicaraguan American originally from South Carolina who migrated with his family to North Carolina as a teenager, and who, like Silvia, tied the region's ecological lack of immigrant history to rural southerners' greater cultural intolerance of outsiders:

Ignacio: North Carolina isn't known for its diverse population to begin with. There is a real lack of cultural awareness about other people's cultures, other people's lives. So I do believe that there is a major difference. If someone from Colombia comes to New York City, that person is one in nine million people. He can't walk down the street without passing five people from five different backgrounds. It's not out of ordinary. But a family coming from the Sudan to Wilcox County, it will be a whole different experience. There are probably a good number of American people here who don't even know where the Sudan is. They couldn't find it on a map. It'd be, "You ain't from around here, is ya?"

Together, these respondents sensed something peculiar about the traditional South that makes the encounters Hispanics have with mainstream Americans, and Hispanics' own integration into American life, more difficult there than it would be elsewhere, especially in traditional immigrant gateways. For them, southern region matters, and the explanations why revolve around the region's comparatively lower wages (which decrease the opportunities for economic mobility despite proliferating low-wage jobs), its residents' lack of cultural familiarity with foreigners (which increases prejudice and exclusion from mainstream Americans), and its historical lack of diversity (which translates into an ecological lack of services and resources). Even some middle-class Hispanic respondents who did not perceive the first, economic cost to living in the South did perceive the second two, noneconomic ones. For instance, even more so than Alvaro, Isabel, a naturalized citizen from Buenos Aires, Argentina, who lived in Chicago and South Carolina before migrating to Bedford County in 1987, felt marginalized by cultural values that continue to structure modern southern social life—particularly religious fundamentalism, the importance of membership and participation in a church, and moral and political conservatism:

Isabel: The way of thinking of people who are very religious here [has been hard]. People that are fundamentalist. In Argentina, most everybody's Catholic. And when I came here, I started hearing all this, "You don't drink . . ." or "To be saved . . ." And all these things that are very, very strange to me. It's very difficult for me to identify with people who think like that. So I have lots of problems with that part of the culture that is extremely religious to the right. Not their moral beliefs, but it's like they think that if you are not saved, you're going to hell and that you will have no chance to take the Lord in your lifetime. How can a person in the Amazon [be judged by that]? Things like that are hard for me.

Interviewer: Do you find more of that here in the South than in other parts of the country?

Isabel: Yes. And I feel very . . . I don't even say what my beliefs are for fear of rejection. So I keep my religious beliefs very much to myself. And I don't like that. Because I know that if I tell my American co-workers what I believe, they would be like, "Hmm . . ." [*sticks up her nose in a gesture of disapproval*] I have some friends from other places, like Pennsylvania or Chicago, and I feel that I identify more with them.

On the other hand, some Hispanic respondents sensed something positive about the traditional South's influence on their lives. Very few did so in economic terms, since few earned more than they might elsewhere; instead, they focused primarily on key cultural and ecological characteristics of the region. For example, Angela, a naturalized citizen from Peru who migrated to North Carolina in 1987 after living in various Latin American countries, Chicago, and Florida, believed "friendly" southern culture increases Hispanic newcomers' sociocultural incorporation:

Angela: For me, discrimination is universal. You see it in every part of the world— in Venezuela, Peru, Argentina. To be honest with you, when I came here to

North Carolina, I felt so welcome. People asked me, "How can I help you, Ma'am?" You know, the southern culture is very well known for welcoming people!

Similarly, Laura, an immigrant from Chihuahua, Mexico, who migrated to eastern North Carolina in 2001 via Texas and New Mexico, reported that the friendly southern atmosphere of hospitality (Striffler 2005a: 141) encouraged better intergroup relations with natives in North Carolina than in Utah, another new destination state she has visited:

Laura: Just now I went to Utah to visit my siblings. And I noticed that when you go to the stores, it's not like here. Here it's very common for the people to greet you and say, "Hello" or "How are you?" to you or whatever. It's very common here, and there it's not. The people there leave you in your status there, in the place where you just arrived.

Additionally, a small but theoretically significant set of Hispanic respondents saw other southern values in a positive light. Ramiro, an immigrant from Cuenca, Ecuador, who lived in New Jersey for three years when he was in elementary school, had a hard time understanding southern accents and relating to large populations of rural African Americans when he first moved to Bedford County in 2002. He reported having adapted positively over time; in fact, he now appreciated southern values and worldviews, which he described this way: "family, patriotism, and probably the love for the land. And I don't know about religious values but maybe we can include them. I think they are stronger here in the South than in any other places that I've been in the United States before." For Ramiro, living in the rural South provides better understanding of "middle America" and also makes adapting to American life easier, when newcomers "share some of the values that the South exhibits when facing big cities and the North." These positive interpretations suggest that, as some scholars of the South have argued, newcomers may have more rather than less incentive to identify with native southerners, as they recognize their shared characteristics as members of conquered "societies throughout the world that have seen themselves as reservoirs of tradition more than as engines of transformation" (Peacock, Watson, and Matthews 2005: 4–5; see also Cobb 2005; Mantero 2008; Watson 2005; and Woodward 1993).

However, couched among these negative and positive interpretations of the southern region contextual effect were numerous neutral responses demonstrating a larger theme: Hispanic newcomers' lack of knowledge or ambivalence about its effect on their lives. Most Hispanic respondents—especially those who are direct migrants from abroad, recent arrivals, poorly educated, or some combination of the three—did not know much about southern history or culture. Josefa, an unauthorized immigrant who migrated directly to Wilcox County from San Salvador, El Salvador, to reunite with her husband in Poultry Processing Plant, was typical of most direct migrant respondents who have no experience living elsewhere in the United States and so did not notice anything peculiar about the rural South:

Interviewer: Have you ever heard anything about the history or culture of the South of the United States—like about places like North Carolina, Georgia, Mississippi, or Tennessee?

Josefa: Very little.

Interviewer: Like what?

Josefa: No history, nothing like that. Just what they plant, what North Carolina has produced. For example, the turkey businesses, the hog farms, the chicken plants. The cotton harvest, tobacco, cucumber. Mostly production. But not history.

Interviewer: In your experience, are there any differences you see or have heard of between Americans who live in the South of the United States and Americans who live in other parts of the United States?

Josefa: I haven't had the opportunity to compare differences. This is the only place I have lived.

Interviewer: Do you think that Hispanics or immigrants have a similar or different experience in the South of the United States, like here, as they have somewhere else like California, Texas, or New York?

Josefa: I think it's the same. Similar.

Interviewer: Why?

Josefa: [*long pause*] . . . [*doesn't know*]

Interviewer: That's OK.

Josefa: No, it's because of the same thing. I don't know any other state, so I don't know if they are different.

This lack of knowledge was also evident among several Hispanic respondents who did have experience living or traveling elsewhere in the country, including Luís, an unauthorized immigrant from Chiapas, Mexico, who first migrated to San Francisco, returned to Mexico, and then migrated again to Bedford County via Florida in 2002 on the agricultural circuit. Despite having lived in at least three states, including two traditional immigrant-receiving ones, Luís thought this region has a negligible effect on Hispanic newcomers' experiences, reporting, "From what I have seen, everything is the same." Neida, an immigrant from Michoacán, Mexico, who traveled for a long time throughout the United States on the agricultural circuit with her parents before settling down in North Carolina in 1988 and later naturalizing as a U.S. citizen, agreed, noting that she has had insufficient opportunity to interact with mainstream Americans in any of these states to learn about their distinctive cultures and histories:

Neida: Well, I wouldn't know how to answer that. Because when I was in Michigan, picking apples, strawberries, cherries, and cucumbers, when I was in Florida, and here in North Carolina, too, I never lived with [white] Americans or blacks. I have always lived with all Hispanics, because we worked in the fields. We even ate only with Hispanics, and we didn't share that time with [white] Americans, nor with blacks.

These quotes demonstrate that Hispanic respondents, especially foreign-born and lower-status ones, often perceived southern region to be unimportant because they do not consider southern history and culture to be as distinctive as many lifelong southerners do (Smith and Furuseth 2006b; Watson 2005). This is partially due to these newcomers' less prolonged residence within the South, which decreases their identification as southerners (Griffin, Evenson, and Thompson 2005). But it is also partially due to newcomers interpreting their experiences primarily within the framework of their home country and ethnic culture (which, understandably, exert the strongest influence on their lives) and secondarily within the framework of the United States as a national whole (in which they see Hispanics having largely similar economic and policy needs, regardless of where they settle), not necessarily within the framework of internal American regions. Yet even U.S.-born and more educated Hispanic respondents, who demonstrated greater knowledge of southern history and culture, displayed a noticeable lack of knowledge about, ambivalence toward, or discounting of its contextual influence. For example, Santiago, a college-educated immigrant from Bogotá, Colombia, who had lived in Mexico City and Texas before migrating to Wilcox County in 1998, had some knowledge of southern history (notably North Carolina's and Georgia's participation in the Civil War). Yet he discounted its effect by arguing that regional differences are something from the past "that is forgotten," and that Hispanic newcomers' experiences in the South are similar to those elsewhere in the country.

Ambivalence is even illustrated by several white and black native respondents. Some argued that the South's weak immigrant history and lack of familiarity with Hispanic culture makes natives less accepting of Hispanic newcomers; others thought that southern hospitality makes natives simultaneously more accepting of them. Jan, a white American line supervisor/manager at Textile Mill in Bedford County, demonstrated this ambivalence internally:

Interviewer: Do you think that Hispanics have a similar or different experience in the South than they would have in other places, like New York or California or Chicago?

Jan: Well, I don't know, because in New York you've got so many different kinds of people. I think they don't really focus on [cultural diversity] like southern people do. But then I think in a sense, that maybe southern people would be more open and accepting. Well, I don't know—that's a tough one for me to answer. Because like in New York, I guess anything goes. You know? You see so much diversity. Where here, I think . . . I don't know, I just think the South is more receptive, I guess.

In sum, several respondents considered the influence of southern region on Hispanic newcomers' American experiences to be negative, a few others considered it to be positive, and most important, many Hispanic respondents considered its influence nonexistent or irrelevant. Taken together, their disagreement reflects the ambiguous or contradictory nature of the rural southern immigrant experience in the mid-2000s. Nonetheless, it is telling that when respondents did acknowledge a contextual regional effect, they did so most strongly in *noneconomic* terms. This does not mean that regional economic distinctions are unimportant. Rather, it may simply reflect greater concern about and disagreement over the role that cultural and ecological characteristics continue to play in modern southern life, while economic convergence and harmonization since the mid-twentieth century has potentially reduced the salience of the region's economic disadvantage (Eckes 2005).

Rural Space: Also Ambivalent and Contradictory

As with southern region, rural space also exerts discernible economic and noneconomic influences on Hispanic newcomers' experiences in eastern North Carolina, and influences again they range from negative to positive. Like Vera, Paulina, an immigrant from Tamaulipas, Mexico, who crossed the U.S.-Mexico border illegally in 1996 and came directly to Bedford County to reunite with her husband and his family, felt that larger cities offer Hispanics better employment opportunities, even though rural areas and small towns may be easier places to live in for other reasons. In her view, this is especially the case for unauthorized immigrants like herself, who find it easier to escape detection and "get by" outside of large gateway cities:

Paulina: We've thought about moving from here. To a bigger city, like Raleigh, or another place out there. It's more populated there. It's a bigger city where things catch your attention. Because here it's a small place, and there's not a whole lot of work here.

Interviewer: So you might like to move to another place in North Carolina?

Paulina: Well, I would like to go to Florida. And my husband would, too, because he also has family there. We've thought about it, but it's not something that we're going to do.

Interviewer: Why not?

Paulina: Because it's a little more difficult to live in Florida. We don't have our [immigration] papers yet and so things are more difficult there, to get a driver's license, to do everything. Here it's not as difficult.[3] There are many little things that are easier here than there.

Viviana, a Colombian immigrant who migrated with her husband, Davíd (whom we will get to know more intimately in Chapter 2), directly from the large city of Medellín to Bedford County in 1999, also argued that Hispanic newcomers experience more social discrimination in rural areas and small towns, because rural residents have less exposure to foreigners:

Viviana: Maybe because of what people I know who live in other places say, I believe that there is more discrimination against immigrants here than in the big cities. I don't know why, but maybe because it's a small town and it's something new. Immigration has been in the big cities since a long time ago. And I believe that it's something new here. Some people need to get used to that.

Interestingly, white and black natives agreed; Wilcox County commissioner Bruce speculated that it may be more difficult for Hispanic newcomers to be accepted into rural and small-town societies than large cities, because rural residents tend to be more skeptical of newcomers. Although he initially thought the difference might be due to southern region, after careful consideration he opted for rural space instead:

Bruce: The South is not as familiar with immigrants as say the North would be. Up there they don't look twice, and in the South we do. That's the nature of our people.

Interviewer: So it's somewhat harder for newcomers here?

Bruce: Yep. And it must be tougher in the rural and less-populated areas, because of the "This is my territory . . ." feeling. Things are more simple here, as opposed to in New York or Los Angeles or somewhere like that, where immigrants would integrate into the society and they'd never notice it perhaps. Well, I won't say that they'd never notice it, because they might. I assume probably in New York or Chicago they wouldn't. I'm not sure of that, but it's what I think.

Interviewer: Do you think these differences are more due to being in the South or to being in a rural area or small town?

Bruce: Probably being in a small community is more related to that. Being in small towns and rural areas, yeah.

Some respondents also singled out the same two ecological characteristics that we saw others mentioning earlier with regard to southern region—less racial and ethnic diversity and lower-quality community services and resources—this time with regard to rural space. For instance, Ashley (a pseudonym), then director of the foreign-language interpreter certification program run by North Carolina's Administrative Office of the Courts (NCAOC 2005), thought that Hispanic newcomers are at a distinct disadvantage in rural eastern North Carolina, where there is a dearth of certified court interpreters compared to the dense metropolitan areas in the central piedmont region of the state. Indeed, as of 2003–04 only one state-certified Spanish interpreter resided east of Interstate 95; Ashley maintained this is because the rural east has fewer "qualified" bilingual people to become certified, and also because the certification program is only offered in Raleigh. Either way, there are far fewer resources for newcomers, including immigrant advocacy groups, in the rural east than the urban piedmont, a resource disadvantage that other scholars of rural immigrant destinations uphold in various service arenas.[4] Notably, such resource disadvantages can grow out of rural areas' weak immigrant histories even when there are no longer any significant rural-versus-urban differences in ethnic diversity (Kandel and Parrado 2006).

Indeed, I frequently heard the complaint—whether in local workplaces, school systems, political systems, or legal systems—that rural areas and small towns "just do not have the same ability to compete" with bigger cities for resources that would assist their Hispanic (not to mention their native) populations.[5] Thus, reinforcing Ashley's observations, a variety of local institutions were having trouble hiring bilingual personnel to assist their Hispanic clients, as John, a bilingual white American lawyer in Bedford County, illustrated among police personnel:

John: And we had another [bilingual] guy here who was a Bedford police officer. But once he got his police officer certification, and became a real officer, he was gobbled up by Raleigh, or Winston-Salem, or Charlotte or somewhere they have a real problem [with needing interpretation services in law enforcement]. Bedford just cannot afford someone like him. Especially if you speak Spanish. He was being paid $26,000 or maybe $30,000 or $36,000 here.

Together, these respondents sensed something peculiar about rural areas that makes the process of meeting and interacting with mainstream Americans more difficult there than it would be elsewhere. For them, rural space matters, and the explanations why revolve around rural areas' comparatively lower wages, rural residents' lack of cultural familiarity with foreigners, and rural areas' historical lack of diversity, just as they did with regard to southern region.

On the other hand, just as many respondents sensed something positive about rural areas' influence on their lives. Here they did so in both economic terms, focusing on lower cost of living or higher relative value of wages in rural areas, and noneconomic terms, focusing on key cultural or ecological characteristics of rural areas and small towns, such as slower pace, more close-knit and receptive communities, "friendly" employers and neighbors, and respite from intense immigration enforcement and other negative aspects of urban life, notably crime, gangs, drugs, noise, traffic, and overpopulation.[6] For example, like Vera, many considered rural areas to be less congested and difficult to live in. Even Josefa, who I showed did not perceive southern region to have any noticeable impact on her American experience, identified a strong rural contextual one this way:

Josefa: For me, it's better to live in a rural place, like in a small town like this. Cities are more complicated, more expensive. With housing, more than anything. And because of the traffic. I like living in a rural place. I like living here very much. Like just recently, I went to Raleigh! And it's a more difficult place.

Likewise, Fausto, an H-2B temporary contract worker, highlighted safety as a key benefit of rural life. Having left behind what he called an unsafe and crime-ridden environment in his home city of Buenos Aires, he planned to stay "in a little town, maybe in Walton or around the area here." Fausto did not want to settle in an immigrant gateway city of the United States, because he thought he would just "feel the same as back home, unsafe. Especially now that we had a little baby, so we want a slow pace. And around here we have one." In fact, coupled with the perception of greater support from mainstream American employers in rural areas, these factors convinced Elva, an unauthorized immigrant from Guerrero, Mexico, who had migrated to Wilcox County in 1988 to work in agriculture and reunite with some of her family members but then moved to Chicago to try her luck working there, to return to North Carolina, a sentiment worth quoting at length:

Elva: I was here in Wilcox County before. And when I thought that it got very difficult, that the work was too hard for me on the farms and in the fields, I wanted to go to a city. So I went to Chicago. And I got a job there in a factory where they made pieces of plastic silverware to use in restaurants. And then the rent there was $500 per month. The wage that I got was the same that I had here. But my work there was only 8 hours per day, so 40 hours per week. That was all we could work. So I only earned like $350 every two weeks! And here, at 70 hours per week, I can earn $350 per week! And I cried and I cried, and I decided to return to North Carolina. I called up the office of Poultry Farms [a pseudonym] and I spoke with my former supervisor. He let me return, and he gave me back my job and my trailer back, too. He said, "Of course we'll be glad to have you back. Come back! Your former home is yours. Your job is yours. And we want you to know you haven't lost anything. You are good at your work." I had been gone three months, and they were still here waiting for me. "You are an excellent worker, come back." And I asked them, "Could you loan me money to come, because I don't have any!" And they sent me $500. They told me to get on a bus, and come back with my children. When I got back here, I continued paying my bills, and I bought a small piece of land to live on. They put a trailer there for me. And I put up another one, and I started renting it out. That's how I managed my little business, like that! So they were wonderful to me. They instructed me, too, when I was buying my land. I didn't know how to put in a septic tank, how to install all the lines. They brought me here and told me what to bring. They helped me a lot. I learned how to do all those complicated things, thanks to them. And so I have found a lot of support from Americans here. For me, they are wonderful. And I thank them. The difference between rural versus urban areas is that in rural areas they give you the opportunity to establish yourself, even on a low wage. Stability. I have also had a way of purchasing land economically. The prices aren't so high. That's something that we, with few resources, have been able to buy. And so there isn't . . . how do I say it? Food is not so expensive. It's more economical. There are more forms to make a little more money, to save. It's calmer even in terms of drugs.

Other Hispanic respondents also cited better intergroup relations with mainstream natives in rural areas than big cities. One rationale for this, offered by Lucas, a Mexican American who migrated from Harlingen, Texas, in 2003 to work as an ESL teacher in Weakley Elementary School, is that shared family and religious values help bind Hispanic newcomers closer to rural natives than urban ones:

Lucas: The area we're in here has really embraced a lot of the Hispanic community. And it has to do a lot with the kind of values that the people have around here. They're very similar with the kind of values that people have in that part of the U.S. where I'm coming from, from South Texas and from northern Mexico. Where it's family-oriented, where everybody tries to help out as far as the family goes. Since the Hispanic community has felt embraced by the same values, that's why they're flocking into this part of North Carolina.

Interviewer: So you think it's a rural thing?

Lucas: Yes, definitely. Because of how we Hispanics were also brought up in that kind of same environment, not much of seeing the big buildings and highways. But it has a lot to do also with the religion part. Since over here you see a lot of churches on every other corner. That has a lot to do with where we're coming from, too.

Another rationale was offered by Inés, an unauthorized immigrant who migrated directly to Bedford County in 1992 from Medellín, Colombia, in order to reunite with her husband, who had settled there two years earlier. She said close personal contact between Hispanic newcomers and natives in rural areas improves intergroup relations compared to more anonymous social life in big cities. Although Inés admitted that small-town life can be boring, especially compared to a "very big city with a lot of technology and many things to do and see" like Medellín, she still appreciated the openness and friendliness of her new Bedford neighbors:

Inés: Since the moment I arrived here to Bedford, I loved it. The town fascinated me. I loved that on the first night I was here, we could leave the doors open! In my country, you can't do that, because you get robbed. And here, everything was open. The people came in and went out, and there wasn't any problem. So I loved that, and the town itself. The people are so nice. Everyone said hello to me, and no one knew me yet.

Interviewer: Are there any differences you see or have heard of between Americans who live in the South of the United States versus other parts of the United States?

Inés: I would say it's the fact that this is a small town. Because I've been in New York, in Florida, Missouri, New Orleans, Nevada, and California. And what I have seen is that here people wave to you. Here they get to know you, they look at your face! They show you their face, and they say hello to you. Not in other states. You don't matter! Nothing! You just pass right by them. There isn't this cordiality among the people. Like this receiving you, this warmth. Here in Bedford, there is. And I think it's that Bedford is a small town, because you can even note a difference between people in Raleigh and people here in Bedford.

Of course, other respondents disagreed with Inés and said that Hispanic newcomers are more segregated from, rather than integrated with, natives in rural new destinations—such as on farms or in trailer parks, where some scholars even describe them as being "ghettoized" in "Little Mexicos."[7] Yet even some white and black natives saw a positive and integrative effect of rural space on Hispanic newcomers' experiences, including two white employers:

Bob: I think a lot of people from Mexico would probably fit in better in a small town than in a bigger town. Because again, it puts a face on it with a name, versus just faces in a crowd. And once you've got a name with a face, then, you know, people adapt easier. (Bedford County, Textile Mill)

Joseph: I really think in the rural areas immigrants will work into the culture and fit with natives better and quicker—in fewer generations, or less decades or whatever—than they will in New York. Or in Philly, or Atlanta. Because I mean, in cities they tend to have an area. You know, you've got Chinatown or Little Italy or I don't know what the Puerto Ricans call themselves in New York, but whatever those neighborhoods are. Here when you get rural, you're dispersed to a great extent. You learn to live with each other, work with each other. And I think that the cultures will mix a lot quicker. Both groups will change faster. They'll come to some midpoint. (Wilcox County, Poultry Processing Plant)

In sum, respondents were divided in their views of the influence of rural space on Hispanic newcomers' mainstream experiences as either negative or positive. Taken together, their disagreement continues to reflect the ambiguous and contradictory nature of the rural southern immigrant experience in the mid-2000s, and it may help explain why researchers have uncovered a variety of positive, negative, and neutral responses to immigrant newcomers in new destinations that do not neatly align across an urban-rural divide (Gouveia, Carranza, and Cogua 2005; Kandel and Parrado 2006). Nonetheless, most intriguing about rural space, compared to southern region, is that most respondents perceived both its economic and noneconomic aspects as highly salient in Hispanic new-comers' lives. Rural space thus emerges as the more influential of the two geo-graphic contexts, even though some southern effects surely exist.

Rural Space: More Salient than Southern Region

There are several ways to see how rural space was the more salient of the two geographic contexts in Hispanic newcomers' lives in eastern North Carolina in the mid-2000s. First, as I have done thus far, we can examine where respondents mentioned either effect, in order to gauge its salience and strength. Second, we can examine where rural space united the experiences of Hispanic newcomers across different regions of the United States. For instance, Gloria, a temporary Guatemalan "nonimmigrant" tourist whom I met informally during the course of my research, had a sister who was living in South Dakota and working with the Hispanic community there. Gloria commented more on the similarities between South Dakota and eastern North Carolina, as rural places where Hispanics are "living poorly," than on their location in different states or regions:

Gloria: I was comparing North Carolina with South Dakota, and they are almost the same. Because if you take a highway—you drive and you drive and you drive and you don't find anything or anyone! It's the same! And for Latinos there, it's almost the same as here. They give jobs to Latinos because they know that they work well and hard. And the way of life there is almost like here, because Latinos here are living poorly. That's what I have realized with the few families that I have met. It's the same here as it is in South Dakota. They don't want to learn English! [*laughs*]

Third, we can examine where rural space differentiates the experiences of Hispanic newcomers across the rural-urban divide within the same region or state—here, North Carolina. To illustrate, Russell, a bilingual lawyer in Bedford and Alexandria Counties, feared that Hispanic newcomers will make slower economic progress in rural eastern North Carolina compared to the urban piedmont, since this has been the case historically among natives. Vicente, a Mexican American whose family migrated from Florida to Wilcox County around 1980, on the agricultural circuit, also argued that Hispanic newcomers in the rural east will be more weakly represented politically, because state-level politicians centered in the urban piedmont do not pay them much attention:

Vicente: Reports show that Wilcox County has the highest proportion of Hispanics in the state. But I haven't been impressed with the Hispanic representative of the N.C. Governor's Office of Hispanic/Latino Affairs that's in Raleigh at all. I don't know why he hasn't come and at least met with officials in the county. I don't know if it's because he doesn't think that he has time, or if he hasn't seen the reports, but I haven't seen him do anything for Wilcox County or the surrounding counties. If we're supposed to be the number one in the state, where are your Hispanic advocates and the leaders?

Interviewer: So you feel like you don't have the kinds of resources here that are in the middle of the state?

Vicente: Yeah, like for example in Raleigh, you'd probably see a Hispanic representative on some of your boards—like your education board and DMV board. Here you don't have that many.

Finally, we can examine where respondents highlighted both southern regional and rural space contextual effects but then explicitly argued in favor of the latter. Bruce did this earlier, and he is joined by many other respondents, among them Mary, executive director of federal programs in the Bedford County public schools. Although Mary thought that there is something "cultural" about living in the rural South that affects all newcomers, including Hispanics, after careful consideration she argued that rural space is more important since it "bound communities closer" through close personal contact. She even saw it doing this for Hispanic newcomers in Bedford County, by helping them gain access to better school and job information through more tightly knit social networks compared to their counterparts in neighboring metropolitan Dickens County:

Mary: I think the South is just peculiar anyway. [*laughs*] You know, it's cultural. And within the South, whether you're in eastern North Carolina or anywhere else, it's regional. So in the South not only do you experience the southern culture, you also experience regional and community cultures that are very different from one another. And I think that there's a big clan influence. You know, it comes through generations of families that have been bound together through marriage, or proximity, through church, that tend to over the generations continue that same affiliation whether they're bloodlines or not. I think rural areas also bound the communities closer. The Hispanic community in Bedford is closer, tighter, more knowledgeable of each other than the one in our neighbor Dickens County is. Because Dickens County is much more metropolitan as far as its size. And that's the case in all small communities. I've worked in Bedford County for 25 years. I've lived in Dickens probably as long. I had a few years that I lived in Bedford. I know more people and more people know me in Bedford County than they do in Dickens County. And it's because it's rural. It's because I'm here, I'm visible, and people have forgotten that I'm not from here. So you can integrate into this society here, even if you don't live here. And I think the ruralness is part of that. You don't have the transience. We have a lot of migrants that come and stay, and I tell Elisa and Marco [two prominent bilingual Hispanic school employees in Bedford County] that they're their own Employment Security Commission because they help a lot of Hispanic people find jobs.

Arlene, a naturalized citizen from Cuba who lived previously in Puerto Rico and Los Angeles before moving to eastern North Carolina in 1979, argued precisely the opposite: that the rural South affects Hispanic newcomers negatively rather than positively. Still, she joined Mary in identifying rural space as the more important of the two geographic contextual factors. Although she originally argued that Hispanic newcomers have less opportunity to integrate and achieve upward mobility in the South compared to other American regions, since many of them start off with less education and are more residentially segregated from natives, ultimately she decided this may be due to rural space, because she also saw differences between rural and urban North Carolina:

Arlene: Hispanics probably have a different experience [in the South]. In Los Angeles it's different. Here [in eastern North Carolina] the Hispanics come in and they're isolated. They turn their television on in Spanish, they're in the middle of a trailer park with all Hispanic people, or maybe out in the middle of a field with nobody around, and so what do they learn? They're in a world by themselves. That hinders them in learning the culture, in assimilating to the country, and in learning the English language. Where[as] if you put them in the middle of a city—like Glendale, California—where you have your neighbors in close proximity, some of whom may speak Spanish, others English, they learn from one another, and they rub elbows with people. Literally! Here they're just isolated in many ways. The place they live in makes a big difference, I think.

Interviewer: Would you say that this is mostly a regional thing or a rural thing?

Arlene: [*sighs*] It might be a rural thing. When you drive up into Raleigh, I don't think you have this kind of [segregation] problem with Hispanic families like you have here. And I know in [a nearby urban military base], the children arriving there learn the English language faster. Because, again, it's the same situation as in Los Angeles. So it might be a rural thing in a way. Because here you're sending people out in the country. You know, I never even really thought about it, but it could very well be just a rural thing.

Together, these quotes demonstrate how the economic and noneconomic aspects of rural space are highly salient for many respondents, so much so that they frequently united the experiences of Hispanic newcomers in rural areas across different American regions and states, differentiated the experiences of Hispanic newcomers in rural and urban areas within the same region or state, and in a few notable cases explained away the perceived effects of southern region entirely.

Interactions Among Class Status, Geographic Origins, and Geographic Destinations

Yet Hispanic newcomers' own class and geographic origin characteristics are also important. Among the 88 Hispanic respondents in my sample, social class is conflated with (non)metropolitan origin, such that many lower-status Hispanic respondents hail from rural areas and small towns or villages in Mexico or Central America,[8] while other higher-status ones hail from larger cities in Latin America and the United States.[9] It is the former who perceived the greatest emotional benefits of living in rural eastern North Carolina. In other words, even though foreign-born Hispanic respondents of rural origins are the most likely to be current or "settled-out" migrant farmworkers, as well as to be poorly educated and of low socioeconomic status—thus experiencing multiple objective hardships, including constrained access to services—they are simultaneously the least likely to report problems adapting to rural southern life. In fact, like Vera, they frequently compared life in eastern North Carolina to life in their hometowns and villages, saying it "feels more like home" than do traditional immigrant gateways or other large cities.

To illustrate, Paco, a formerly unauthorized immigrant from Jalisco, Mexico, who migrated to North Carolina in 1992 after spending 10 years on the agricultural circuit between Florida and New York, and who then became a legal permanent resident and crew leader for other Mexican migrants working on what I call Tobacco Farm (a pseudonym), preferred American life in "the country" to that in the city. In rural Bedford County, he reported that he lives and works on his own small plot of land, just as he did in Mexico:

Paco: I like it here. I like it here in North Carolina because it's more or less the same climate as where I'm from in Mexico. And so they seem pretty much equal.

Interviewer: And would you like living in a city more?

Paco: No. [I prefer] the country. I've always lived like on a small farm, like with a small plot of land.

Similarly, Elva and her sisters from Guerrero, Mexico, also perceived the "tranquility," "solitude," and "life" emanating from the farms and forests of rural North Carolina positively in comparison to other, urban places where they had lived:

Elva: Because my sisters lived in Florida before, and they said that here [in North Carolina] they had found more tranquility. And in fact, it was also very pretty. I like the solitude of North Carolina. The places on the farms. It fascinated me to walk around in the forests. The pine trees that seemed to have so much life. They seemed to be . . . I don't know, but very alive. That's what I felt here. That smell seemed very pretty.

This mirrors the findings of other scholars, who also document lower-status newcomers from rural areas in Latin America preferring "smaller communities" in the United States and being willing to endure their less-than-ideal conditions, especially severe organizational resource disadvantages, in exchange for a more *tranquilo* and less frenetic lifestyle that better approximates what they knew in their country of origin (Cuadros 2006; Kandel and Parrado 2006; Schoenholtz 2005; Torres, Popke, and Hapke 2006; Torres et al. 2003; Zarrugh 2008). In my sample, it is these respondents who expressed greatest appreciation for the emotional as well as practical benefits of rural life, notably being able to interact with rural Americans, whom they perceived to share more of their history, values, and outlooks than urban Americans.

By contrast, Hispanic newcomers of urban origin, whether in Latin America or the United States, expressed greater initial shock and more numerous problems adapting to life in eastern North Carolina. Like Silvia, they often endured rough urban-to-rural transitions, going into nostalgic detail when comparing their new home to where they came from. For example, even though he is originally from a rural area in Ecuador, Tomás reported some initial difficulty adapting to life in eastern North Carolina. He attributed this to having spent several years in metropolitan Quito before he migrated to the United States in 1993:

Tomás: I came directly from Quito to Bedford. That's a tremendous shock, you know? When I came, I came to Miami. I thought, "Oh, Miami—how cool! This is the United States!" I stayed about half a day in Miami, and I caught a plane from there to Washington, D.C. I thought, "Oh, how cool here, too! I am going to live here." And then my stepfather picked me up in a car as soon as I got to the airport and said, "Let's go." "Okay." I got in the car, and several hours on I-95 without even knowing where I was going. And when we arrived here in Bedford, it was around 11:00 p.m. at night. I hadn't seen anything. I thought it was going to be a big city. But then I saw that we were not just here in the middle of Bedford—we were out in the wilderness! It was about five miles outside of Bedford, and when I got up in the morning, I was hoping to see tall buildings, highways crossing one over the other, and a lot of traffic. And when I woke up all alone in a house in the middle of a field? And the only thing there was some corn being grown, some soybeans, some tobacco. I wanted to turn right around! I wanted to grab all my things that I had right then, and leave, and go back home! [*laughs*] I was homesick. And that was a terrible experience, and with not knowing English it was even more difficult.

Immigrants from larger cities in Mexico also reported difficulty adapting to rural life. Alvaro, for instance, thought that his relatively high level of education and urban origin in Mexico impede the quality of the social relationships he can develop with other Hispanics in eastern North Carolina, who mostly "come from the country in Mexico, in small towns" and "don't have much education—or they have just elementary or maybe high school." Consequently, Alvaro said that most of his social relationships are restricted to family members, whereas he thought he would probably spend more time with friends and acquaintances in Mexico or in a larger city in the United States. Similarly, Dolores, an unauthorized immigrant from Puebla, Mexico, who migrated directly to Wilcox County in 1996, described many good things about life in eastern North Carolina, including the recent proliferation of jobs and the hospitality many natives show to Hispanic newcomers. However, she also thought that rural living conditions shock many Hispanics who either hail from large cities in Latin America or have visited larger places in the United States. Dolores went into great detail describing what it felt like to undergo such a dramatic urban-to-rural transition, and also how emotionally draining it is to justify to family members her decision to stay in rural North Carolina:

Dolores: I think that it's very different [in rural areas], Helen. I think that we live very differently here. I never—do you want to know why my cousins didn't want me to stay here in this tiny town? It's because where I come from in Mexico, Helen, there are huge cities, ones that put Raleigh to shame. Where there aren't any [public] transportation problems, where we travel in buses, where there are restaurants, where I had a lot of friends and movies. It's very different, and so my cousins said that here I couldn't do anything. But I disagree, I guess—I think I can find better options here. But yes, it's different than living in a city. Because I've been to Chicago, and Chicago is so different from here!

There is also a huge Hispanic population there, but they live very differently
there, too. The Hispanic people there have their houses—they don't even know
what "trailers" are there! [*laughs*] My parents never saw any trailers in California
either when they went there, Helen.

Interviewer: And so why do you stay here?

Dolores: Oh. I am here because I have a job, and I have better options. And because
even though it's a small town, I like it that way. Because I have the opportunity
to be able to work and make money. And also because it gives me so much
satisfaction when I can help someone out. I feel so happy and content working
here with the children in my church, which is my free work for God. And that's
why I'm here. Even though it's small and everything, I like it. And my cousins,
when they came here from Mexico they were already crying when they drove
in on the highway. Crying, Helen. Crying and asking me, "What are you doing
here again?" And they said they would never even come back here, and they
left. There are people who have come here and stayed for a while but then they
go home, because it's a totally different world from what we live in. But my
husband shows so much courage when someone says, "Gosh! We're coming to
Worthington, N.C. again." He says, "You should be proud and thankful. Because
Worthington is small, but it has provided you a lot of satisfaction. It is offering
you peace and tranquility. It is offering you money." And my husband is happy
here in Worthington, Helen! And I am happy. Even though my parents don't
like it—well, whatever! [*laughs*]

In my sample, it is these respondents who, like Silvia, were the most apt to
describe the rural South as unwelcoming. For Felipe, a 1.5-generation youth
from Oaxaca, Mexico, their hardship stems from key cultural and ecological
characteristics that make rural areas more "boring" and their residents more
close-minded than is the case in urban areas such as Chicago, where he and his
family lived for a year before this:

Felipe: [In Chicago] it was great! I lived downtown and I was working, you know,
it was awesome. And then when we moved to North Carolina, we were like,
"Wow." Everything was dark. Even recently, I had a cousin who's an American citizen who grew up his whole life in Chicago, and he came here and we
went out one night, and he said, "Wow! How can you guys drive? It's so dark!"
[*laughs*] It was funny. Yeah, it's boring here. I mean, why do you think I want
to move to Raleigh? Like, I know life is what you make of it, but it's a lot harder
when there's nothing else around, you know? People are a little close-minded,
too, in small towns. I don't think people mean bad, it's just what people in

a small town are like. They are afraid to change. They don't really welcome change that good.

In these ways, Hispanic newcomers' class status and geographic origin interact to structure their emotional experiences adapting to life in the rural South. Generally speaking, matching rural origins and destinations facilitate their adaptation, while conflicting urban origins and rural destinations complicate it, as Salvador and Olivia, a Costa Rican immigrant couple who spent 10 years living in Miami before coming to Wilcox County in 2000, explained:

Salvador: The experience here [in eastern North Carolina] is very different. Because in California, Miami, places like that, it's too agitated a life.

Olivia: You live with more stress.

Salvador: Here it's calmer. And if Hispanics come from a small town in their country, they adapt better.

Olivia: They adapt faster.

Salvador: Yes, I think it has a lot to do with where Hispanics come from. If a Hispanic from the city came to live here . . .

Olivia: [*laughs*] He wouldn't do well! It would be very boring for him. But if a Hispanic came from a small town, he would really adapt easy.

Salvador: Like for example, I come from the city in Costa Rica. But because of the way I was brought up [with rural customs passed down from my parents], I don't feel [the same boredom]. I don't like living in a city.

Olivia: And I'm from a small town and I don't feel the change, because I'm a person who likes tranquility a lot.

Summary

In the mid-2000s, the contextual effects of southern region and rural space wielded ambivalent and contradictory influences on Hispanic newcomers' mainstream experiences. Nonetheless, rural space, in economic and noneconomic dimensions, flavored them more so than southern region. This does not mean that southern region is not important. The relocation and expansion of low-wage jobs throughout many parts of the traditional South gives Hispanic newcomers opportunities to find and keep jobs, compared to other regions undergoing greater economic stagnation (see Chapters 2 and 3), and the region's lack of immigrant history and large population of African American generate salient dividing lines between Hispanic newcomers and both whites and blacks (see Chapters 4 and 5). Furthermore, as I have shown in this chapter, several respondents *did* think that southern region influences Hispanic newcomers' experiences in the

United States. Yet overall, they thought that living in a rural area is more distinctive than living in the South, and they interpreted their experiences in eastern North Carolina accordingly. Significantly, rural space emerged as most positive for lower-status Hispanic newcomers, who were more likely than their higher-status counterparts to affirm an emotional or noneconomic benefit to living in a rural area, one that feels more like home to those who originate from rural areas or small villages to begin with.

These differences carry important implications for Hispanic newcomers' differential prospects for incorporation and assimilation as they disperse throughout the country. On the one hand, they are worrisome in that they suggest that adaptation into new rural destinations may be comparatively difficult for Hispanic newcomers who are better educated or have had previous experience living in urban areas. For these newcomers, the noneconomic characteristics of urban areas may be more conducive to successful incorporation, particularly by creating an atmosphere where the natives they meet are more tolerant of diversity and where there is a more developed social service infrastructure. Nonetheless, quite a few of these higher-status Hispanic respondents in my sample reported having adapted to rural life in Bedford and Wilcox Counties over time, and even having learned to appreciate some of its noneconomic characteristics, such as peacefulness, neighborliness, "the greenery" (to borrow Cuban respondent Arlene's term), and safety for their children. This suggests that rural areas may be conducive to these newcomers' successful incorporation into American life in some ways, yet perhaps not in others.

Nevertheless, these findings are heartening. They suggest that many of those lower-status Hispanic newcomers who are least well off socioeconomically—and who have been characterized in the literature as facing the greatest risk for downward mobility into the ranks of an excluded and jobless rainbow underclass in the central cities of traditional immigrant gateways (Gans 1992; Portes and Rumbaut 2001; Portes and Zhou 1993; Zhou 1999)—perceived that rural areas offer them benefits, particularly noneconomic ones, that can help to ease their adaptation into a type of American life they consider to be more familiar and more easily navigable than what they might experience in the context of larger cities. These benefits are both practically and theoretically important, because they show how immigrants' geographic dispersion into rural America is, at least in some ways, encouraging rather than impeding their economic and social adaptation compared to what would be the case in traditional gateways.

Economy

2 "The Americans Give You the Opportunity to Work and Grow"

Stability and Short-Distance Mobility
in the New Rural Southern Economy

IN 1993, Marta migrated from Hidalgo, Mexico, to Chicago to reunite with her husband, Rogelio, who had been working in the United States for several years. Although she initially crossed the border legally, she later fell out of status for several months by overstaying her visa. Fortunately, Rogelio was able to regularize his status and become a legal permanent resident through the Immigration Reform and Control Act of 1986, and once he applied for and received his U.S. citizenship they were able to successfully apply for legal permanent residency for her, too. In 1996, Marta and Rogelio made their next "big decision" to leave Chicago and relocate to Wilcox County in eastern North Carolina. One of Marta's cousins was living there, and he told her that jobs were plentiful in Poultry Processing Plant, a giant complex built in the seeming "middle of nowhere" that would, over the next decade, become the largest poultry processing plant in the world.

As soon as Marta and Rogelio arrived in Wilcox County, Marta's cousin put in an application for a job for her at the plant, while she applied for housing in one of the company's subsidized onsite trailers. After taking a physical exam and attending brief worker training classes—where human resources staff "told us about the policies, insurance, benefits, obligations," including "that they can fire us at whatever time they want to" and that "participating in what we call union strikes in Mexico is prohibited here"[1]—Marta started work immediately. Each morning she awoke before sunrise; carefully donned the thick goggles, steel-toed boots, and heavy plastic outerwear that make up the production line-workers' standard uniform;[2] and came in to begin her eight-hour shift "out on the line" in the Evisceration Department, working overtime every chance she could. After Rogelio stayed home for the first year to care for their two young children, who had been born in Chicago, he too landed a job in the plant. However, he worked over in the "harder" Live Hang Department, where the lure of higher wages attracts many men to move live birds off incoming trucks and literally hang them up for the killing (Bjerklie 1995; Griffith 1995a; Hall 1995).

Marta's experience poignantly demonstrates how, to quote anthropologist Steve Striffler, "poultry processing is a tough way to achieve upward mobility" (2005b: 156). In 2003, there were many things she did not like about her job in PPP. One was her inability, no matter how hard she tried, to rid herself of the thick stench of freshly killed meat, which still clung to her skin and clothes every night when she got home from work. Another was plant managers' refusal to approve paid sick leave for many workers who incurred injuries on the job (including three of Marta's friends, who hurt their fingers and legs yet were told to come right back to work). Still others were the "preference" for black production lineworkers over Hispanic ones, and strong anti-union pressure, that Marta perceived to come from plant employers and managers. But perhaps the hardest thing for her was realizing that even with a college education, background in computer science, previous experience working in a bank in Mexico, and legal permanent residency status in the United States, she was stuck working in poultry because she could not speak English fluently and her Mexican degree does not translate equally into the American labor market. Thus, although Marta felt she had adapted to the work for the time being and was even hoping to enroll in some English classes someday soon, she still suffered from some of the psychological stress that migration bestows on formerly middle-class individuals, and she dreamed of the day when "they might change the laws so I can work here in a bank or in something like that, using my career and degree that I had in Mexico."

Still, Marta admitted that their two production line jobs were affording them the means to maintain a lower-working-class lifestyle while they focused on advancing the two children's education, especially since they were bringing in a dual income and resided in a company-subsidized trailer to help minimize housing costs (McConnell and Miraftab 2009; Schoenholtz 2005; Striffler 2005a). And although her cousin had forewarned her that "Wilcox County is a poor agricultural area—just a bunch of fields and towns that are very different than the city of Chicago with its industrialized companies and businesses," he had also convinced her that "there are schools, hospitals, and everything here," and also that "the places here remind us a lot of where we are from in Hidalgo, where we also have warmer weather, farms, and animals." Marta and Rogelio came to agree with him that eastern North Carolina's like-home feel and lower cost of living has helped them achieve more economic stability than would have been possible in Chicago.[3] There, she remembered friends who earn less per hour and also spend more and save less:

Marta: Here maybe it's richer, because many people have their plots of land, their animals, their farms. So I think that you live a little better economically here, because you also spend less. In the city, there are more stores, there is more entertainment, and here not really. At least for me, we save more money here than in Chicago. There are more expenses there!

Most promisingly, Marta was recently encouraged by one of her supervisors to "move up" within PPP, to teach classes on occupational safety to other Hispanic production lineworkers. This was something she felt her lack of English language skills did not affect; she reported that her supervisor had offered her the task because he took notice of her "capability" to "do more" at work, telling her that teaching the class would not require speaking English. Marta was highly appreciative of this. She interpreted it as evidence that there is ample opportunity for Hispanic production lineworkers to take on more demanding tasks within the plant even though—she sighed wistfully—their lack of educational credentials and English language skills may still prevent them from moving into better jobs outside the food processing industry. She therefore faulted other lineworkers who do not move up in the plant for not displaying the necessary drive to take advantage of the available opportunities to do so:

Marta: So then I got the different helmet, and then afterwards they gave me the opportunity to teach some safety classes. And I feel that it's because of my desire to work, my capability. Not because we all try to succeed. They give us opportunity. I have seen that out where I work, there are some Hispanics that have been working there for 10 years, or five years. But it's like they aren't interested in working. They come in, and they just stay there, working along by themselves. And then machines come in, and for them, they don't want to learn to how to operate the new machines. But me, no, I see that the machines are useful. It's another form of transporting the product or something. And I will see that, and I will say to them, "Look here. That's not the best way. You can do it like this." And so the team leader sees the people's interests. He sees the quality of their work, of their production, and he compensates those people. That's what I have seen. Those who want to can succeed. And so therefore, then my supervisor asked me if I wanted to teach classes, and I said, "No! I've never taught." He said, "Just go get your book and study. Go to the classes.

And then afterwards be like that person, and teach the classes." And I said, "OK. For me, that's good. To take advantage of an opportunity." And yes. I did it. I taught the classes, three classes in one month.

By contrast, driving along the one-lane rural back roads over into Bedford County, I uncovered a very different story. Davíd had been a civil engineer in his home city of Medellín. After graduating from college there, he started working for a "wonderful" company in Medellín where, within less than two years, he had "about 15 civil engineers under my authority." Although he liked his job and the salary there was "perfect," the political and economic situation in Colombia had deteriorated so badly that he no longer felt safe. "I still wanted to do something with my life," he told me, "but the economic situation in my country was really bad, and it wasn't looking like it will get any better." So, given that he had always wanted to study English in the United States, plus he already had a visa to do so, Davíd convinced his wife, Viviana, to get herself a visa, and they migrated directly to Bedford County together in 1999, where they "knew somebody here and she helped us to settle down." Davíd and Viviana heard about Textile Mill "because it's a small town," and they put in two job applications soon after they arrived. In 2003—although he did not know if there was an official name for his position—Davíd explained that for his job to be performed well it required someone with experience in manufacturing/textiles and computers, or at least a college degree in industrial engineering. Nonetheless, though it offered him health insurance, 401(k), vacation leave, and enough salary to pay the bills, he was frustrated that it did not pay more.

Even more important, Davíd saw bleak opportunities for internal advancement in Textile Mill. Without meaning any harm toward his employers, whom he liked, Davíd expressed his great frustration that he would never have the opportunity to move higher than his midlevel supervisory position, despite his college education and extensive training:

Davíd: I know I can do a whole lot more than what I do here. I compare myself
    with people that are taking care of high-level administrative jobs, and I know
    well that I can do their job a whole lot better than they do. But I just don't have
    the opportunity to. And I know a whole lot of Hispanics have the same feeling.
Interviewer: Why? What keeps you back?
Davíd: I'm not American.

This was especially frustrating to him because most of the mainstream Americans he had met in Bedford County, even those who had graduated from high school, struck him as unimpressive. He was still confused why this was so, but he considered them to be lazier, less knowledgeable, not prepared, not creative, and inefficient compared to Hispanic newcomers. He even gave "thanks to God every single day that I was born in Colombia and not here. Because I am well educated. And for my knowledge, I'm glad they taught me what they did."

Finally, even though Davíd expressed interest in applying for U.S. citizenship and voting in a U.S. election when I interviewed him in 2003, by 2007 I learned from one of his former employers, Bob, that he and Viviana had returned to Colombia. Although I will never be sure as to why they decided to move back home, Bob gave me the distinct impression that it might have been because they got tired of dealing with how the U.S. government has continued to make life extremely difficult for Latin American immigrants. Such an explanation is certainly plausible; back in 2003 Davíd did express anger and frustration over the acute discrimination he saw Hispanics, particularly unauthorized immigrants, facing in this country:

Davíd: Just turn on the TV. You will find a discriminatory comment about immigrants every five minutes. I'm talking about the news and everything. Closing frontiers. They let you in here, but they won't let you—like if you're [an unauthorized] Hispanic, you can't get your driver's license. Or get your number for your taxes [ITIN]. I mean, it's incredible. But at the same time, the government doesn't do anything. They promise a lot, but they know they can't do it. And so this country will get even worse.

· · ·

What can Marta and Davíd's divergent experiences tell us about Hispanic newcomers' opportunities for economic incorporation and mobility in the rural South? These two are certainly not representative of the Hispanic newcomer communities in either Bedford or Wilcox Counties; indeed, I have chosen to present their stories because the two of them have higher educational credentials and more secure legal status than many other Hispanic newcomers I interviewed in the rural South. Of course, both were frustrated at the "occupational downgrading" they had experienced by leaving middle-class jobs in Latin America to come to the United States, where their foreign credentials are no longer recognized (Batalova and Fix 2008; Menjívar 2008; Redstone Akresh 2006; Sabogal 2005; Winders 2009b). Yet Marta thought the food processing industry in Wilcox County, despite its relatively low wages, offers Hispanic newcomers the chance to advance within an internal labor market. Compared to traditional immigrant gateways, she also thought that the like-home feel and low cost of living in the rural South helps Hispanic newcomers working in the food processing industry to achieve stable, lower-working-class lives, even if they might not be moving up. They might have to work hard, endure long hours and difficult parts of the job, and be willing to assert themselves to be recognized by their team leaders and supervisors, but in her opinion they can make it if they try.

David, meanwhile, lost all hope that Hispanic newcomers can achieve any kind of upward mobility in traditional southern industries such as routine manufacturing and textiles, and he was even more pessimistic about their prospects working in agriculture, where he saw many of them being "exploited" by American growers because they do not have the education or ability to fight back to protect themselves. By David's logic, if a Hispanic newcomer as highly skilled as himself cannot move up, who can? Moreover, why would Hispanic newcomers want to settle in the rural South in the first place, where it seemed to him that most mainstream Americans are neither educated nor interested in making something better of themselves compared to what he has heard of Americans living in the Northeast and West? David confided in me his fear about the potential negative ramifications of this, on his own limited prospects for upward mobility and on those of his new U.S.-born son: "If I can do a good job as a father, my son will go to college. But I'm afraid that his contact with the rest of the Americans here will make him not want to."

Because their divergent experiences capture something important, in this chapter and the next I highlight key structural and institutional factors that were facilitating lateral and sometimes also short-distance upward mobility among some Hispanic newcomers, like Marta, in Poultry Processing Plant. By no means were all Hispanic newcomers working there upwardly mobile, but their economic situation still compared favorably to those of other Hispanic newcomers, like David, in routine manufacturing and textiles, despite the fact that scholars have tended to emphasize brighter prospects for immigrants' upward mobility in manufacturing over food processing. Several Hispanic respondents, including Marta, even noted that their situation in low-wage food processing compared favorably to those of Hispanics employed in low-wage service-sector jobs in metropolitan areas, where they knew they would likely confront the economic and noneconomic burdens of urban life in situations characterized by limited mobility and high vulnerability (Bernhardt et al. 2009; Massey and Sánchez 2010).

My explanation for this difference between food processing and routine manufacturing and textiles lies in the structural distinction between the new and old rural southern economies. Construction, landscaping, tourism, and high- and low-end services are the key economic sectors attracting Hispanics and other immigrants into central city and suburban new destinations throughout the country),[4] but agriculture,[5] agribusiness and food processing,[6] and manufacturing and textiles[7] are the three key economic sectors attracting them into rural ones. And even with all of the latter sectors generally offering low wages to their entry-level workers, agribusiness and food processing has been *expanding* across the rural South as the industry responds to increased economic competition and changing consumer demands since the 1970s by pursuing strategies of consolidation, vertical integration, and geographic relocation into the rural South and Midwest. As Striffler (2009) phrases it, "Chicken, now bigger than cotton or tobacco, dominates the rural South" (132). By contrast, manufacturing and textiles has been *contracting* across the rural South over the same time period, leaving behind a trail of uncertainty and blocked prospects for upward mobility. This difference carries important implications for our understanding how food processing, the economic sector most closely associated with the rise of the "*nuevo* new South" (Fink 2003; Mohl 2003; Smith and Furuseth 2008), is shaping Hispanic newcomers' prospects for achieving economic stability, mobility, and assimilation as they disperse throughout the country.

Opportunities for Economic Stability in Food Processing Jobs

Armed with the pessimism that characterizes the literature on food processing plants (LeDuff 2000; Schlosser 2001; Sinclair 1985), I was prepared for the worst when I entered PPP in Wilcox County to conduct my research in July 2003. I expected to find the kinds of dirty working conditions that appall most middle-class Americans (Bjerklie 1995; Griffith 1995a). I also expected to see blatant and visible occupational segregation by race, ethnicity, language, and sex (Fink 1998; Griffith 1993, 1995a; Hall 1995; LeDuff 2000) and to find that these forms of segregation contributed to strained intergroup relations both inside and outside the plant (Gouveia and Stull 1997; Griffith 1993; LeDuff 2000; Stuesse 2009). Finally, I expected to find blatant and subtle anti-union sentiment, especially among plant owners and employers,[8] as well as serious problems regarding occupational benefits and injuries.[9]

Of course, I did uncover some evidence of these negative aspects of working in PPP. Most Wilcox County respondents, whether they were production lineworkers, employers and managers, or community residents outside the integrated poultry industry, agreed that processing line jobs are hard, dirty, and desirable only if someone needs to earn money badly enough to take them. A few respondents complained about eroded internal labor markets, seeing little opportunity for production lineworkers to move up the ladder within PPP over time at wages under $10 per hour. Many reported that workers are segregated by race and ethnicity in the plant, or that intergroup relations on the floor are sometimes strained. However, they tended to explain this ethnic segmentation primarily because the human capital skills required for different jobs in the plant vary, and many respondents perceived mostly positive interpersonal relations at work, thanks to dependence on one another in order to meet shared production goals (Marrow 2006; for a similar argument on mutual interdependence in the warehouse distribution industry, see B. E. Smith 2009). Some respondents also criticized the plant's health insurance package for being too expensive (Gouveia 2006; Grey 2006), complained that the plant does not give workers sufficient paid leave when they incur injuries on the job, or like Marta resented the fact that workers are hired "at will" (Schlosser 2001: 174). Finally, a few reported that plant employers and managers are interested only in "controlling" or disciplining production lineworkers as much as they can, by housing many of them in subsidized onsite trailers, by treating them poorly at work, and so on.[10]

Together, these negative comments illustrate the myriad problems associated with the food processing industry at the turn of the twenty-first century. Nevertheless, keeping them in mind, Hispanic respondents' positive depictions of their jobs were even more salient (see also Fennelly 2005). Consider Julio, an unauthorized immigrant who migrated from Chiapas, Mexico, across the Arizona border and then directly into North Carolina in 2001. With only a sixth-grade education, Julio found work in PPP's Further Processing Department, where there are several types of jobs involving specialized and repetitive cutting motions.[11] Julio did not think his job is hard, or at least he thought his job is not one of the hard ones that exist there, such as in the Live Hang Department:

Julio: The job that I have is easy. And perhaps I could have one that was more difficult, and I wouldn't like the work, and it would be very hard.

Likewise, Liliana migrated from Huehuetenango, Guatemala, to work in Florida's agricultural fields in 1989, and then legalized her status and moved on to other nonagricultural jobs in Georgia and North Carolina, where she earned approximately $7.15 per hour in PPP's Tray Pack Department in 2003–04.[12] Liliana agreed that other jobs in the plant could be harder than hers, particularly if their line speed is faster. But like Julio, she did not consider her own job bad, reported that the income it produces is sufficient to cover her bills, and liked it overall:

Liliana: Well, sometimes the work here is good and sometimes it's bad. There are times when the work is not so hard and they don't give you anything, and other times when the work is much harder. But, overall I like this job. In the area where I work, it is not hard work. But there are other areas [in the plant] where the work is very hard. And I'm not referring to those places, because I don't work there.

Interviewer: Why are those areas hard?

Liliana: I think that it is because the line moves very fast. And if it were a little slower, then people could do the work a little better. If it goes very fast, well, it's harder on the person.

Even seafood processing jobs were evaluated relatively positively. Vera, the immigrant from Querétaro, Mexico, whom I introduced in the beginning of Chapter 1, used to work in coastal North Carolina's crab processing houses in the H-2B program before moving to Bedford County, and she reported liking both her work and her white employer there:

Vera: 'Cause it was a nice place. There were a lot of ladies. It was a quiet place. So I liked it. All of us ladies that came to work there, we lived together in a big place that [the employer] had there. And I enjoyed working there. And all the people were nice with me.

To understand why this is so, I examine Hispanic newcomers' evaluation of their jobs, prospects for economic stability, and opportunities for what sociologists Richard Alba and Victor Nee (2003) call "short-distance" upward mobility in food processing in Wilcox County in this chapter, and then I compare them with the situations of Hispanic newcomers working in tobacco agriculture and routine manufacturing and textiles in Bedford County in Chapter 3. This comparison is important because it highlights the structural and institutional factors behind Hispanic newcomers' evaluation of their food processing jobs as "better" than other "worse" opportunities abroad and in the United States, as well as behind their perception of greater opportunity for economic stability, even if not upward mobility, in food processing than in routine manufacturing and textiles.

Relative Evaluation: Economic Opportunities in Immigrants' Sending Country

Consider Nadia, an unauthorized immigrant with a 10th-grade education who migrated from Mexico City directly to Wilcox County in 2000, where she got a job in PPP's Cut Up Department. Nadia netted around $16,640 per year in 2003 and 2004,[13] placing her approximately 30% above the official poverty line of \$12,490 for a family of two in that year;[14] her ex-husband had moved back to Mexico and she was supporting herself and her eight-year-old daughter on her own. Still, Nadia considered her salary sufficient to cover her bills and, like Julio and Liliana, hoped to continue working in PPP in the future if possible:

Interviewer: About how much you earn at this job?

Nadia: \$8. I don't remember!

Interviewer: Do you make enough to cover your bills?

Nadia: Yes.

Interviewer: It is difficult?

Nadia: Sometimes.

Interviewer: What types of benefits does this job offer? Like health insurance, housing, anything else?

Nadia: This job, for me, it's located close by. They offer you [health] insurance. And sometimes overtime.

Interviewer: Do you have plans to stay here, working?

Nadia: I hope so.

Likewise, although Victoria, an immigrant with a partial high school education who migrated from Veracruz, Mexico, directly to Wilcox County in 1994 when her friends told her "there was work here," had been studying to be a hairdresser before she came to the United States, she got used to her work in PPP; "I am packing chicken," she said, "and I like it." Even for Olivia, a legal permanent resident originally from San José, Costa Rica, who expressed a very negative evaluation of labor-management relations in the plant, "in PPP, the problem is not the jobs in and of themselves, it's the supervisors."

A first reason many foreign-born Hispanics such as Nadia, Victoria, and Olivia evaluated their food processing line jobs positively is that they frequently compared them to opportunities in their sending country, which were even more limited and for many of them shaped their decision to emigrate in the first place (Piore 1979). For instance, Julio, the immigrant from Chiapas, Mexico, quoted earlier, was earning \$8.00 per hour working in Further Processing and began his interview by saying:

Julio: I like this place. I would also like to become American, too! Yes, well, I have been working for PPP and I like the work a lot. And I don't know. I plan to work for a little more time here in this company, and then go back to my country. Probably I plan to come back again one day, because I like this place.

Interviewer: You mean forever?

Julio: Forever, yes. Here I work with my supervisor. His name is Rafael. Well, in my job when I entered it, we were shoveling meat from one place to another. And then a new supervisor came in. And he told me, "I want you to work for me." And I started making brine, and right now we are moving and weighing meat. That's what I do. And I like it. I like my job.

Once a chauffeur in Mexico, Julio reported having trouble finding stable work there—a central reason he liked his job in PPP:

Interviewer: And why is it that you like it?
Julio: Because in my country, where I am from, I wasn't able to find any work. And now I am. I like working for this company.

Juan, an immigrant from Guadalajara, Mexico, whom I will depict in more detail in the beginning of Chapter 4, elaborated further on this issue of relative evaluation, explaining that many foreign-born Hispanics tolerate hard and dirty working conditions in food processing jobs precisely because here they can earn so much more money than in their sending country. Although Juan later "realized" that the money is not worth the hard working conditions and limited chances for upward mobility he now sees in food processing, he explained how recent arrivals still view their situation as he originally did:

Juan: When I was working at Poultry Processing Limited [PPL],[15] I was single. I was 18 years old. I was a kid. Doing whatever I wanted. Working here I just thought in pesos. And you think that earning $5 per hour, or at night or in cold places, is OK. It's perfect. Because in Mexico, you earn that in one day. What you earn here in one hour you earn in Mexico in one day. Therefore, for lots of people who come here, they conform with those jobs that pay so little. And they kill themselves. Because they keep thinking in that peso mentality. Indefinitely.
Interviewer: How long did it take until you realized this peso mentality thing?
Juan: It took about a year, more or less. Because you live very closed off and don't know anyone. It's not until you begin to familiarize yourself with everything around here that you start to realize. So now I think more about my future and my health. Yet there are people who've been working there for 15 years, in the chicken plant, and they earn about the same amount, or they get a raise of 50 cents per year. But I guess they like it. It's not that they don't have vision.

These quotes demonstrate how many Hispanic newcomers compared their low-wage food processing line jobs with more limited economic opportunities in their sending country. In Juan's words, that they liked these jobs is not reducible to any lack of vision on their part, despite low pay and hard working conditions by American standards. Many Hispanic respondents saw a minimum starting wage of $7.00 (in 2003–04),[16] the opportunity to work relatively secure and nonseasonal hours indoors, and a chance to participate in several of the plant's benefit programs[17] as positive—not negative—aspects of working in PPP.

Still, key structural factors influenced their relative evaluations. Among foreign-born respondents, factors include the selectivity of migrant streams coming from different sending countries, as well as individual immigrants' pre-migration socioeconomic status and motives for migrating abroad. Therefore, not surprisingly, the most positive evaluations of food processing production line jobs emerged among lower-status Hispanic newcomers who have the fewest economic options elsewhere—those who are poorly educated and from rural areas or small villages in Mexico and Central America. By contrast, better-educated and formerly professional newcomers such as Marta, and many Asian contract workers—whom PPP was hiring through the H-2B temporary labor contract program during the time of my field research, primarily from Hong Kong and South Korea (see the Appendix)—reported having a harder time adjusting to the work.

To illustrate, according to plant employers and managers as well as Hispanic production lineworkers, the foreign-born Asian contract workers do not like their jobs because most of them are well educated, have a lot of money, were professionals in their sending country, and have migrated to the United States with the primary goals of reunifying their families and opening up small businesses. Lidia, a legal permanent resident from Oaxaca, Mexico, and then a director of housing, reported that the Asian workers "don't like the work here" and have a different experience than the Hispanics, "because the majority of the Asians are intellectual people, professionals" and, in plant president Joseph's words, endure a process of "hardening" as they struggle to adapt to the work. By contrast, respondents agreed that most foreign-born Hispanics working at the plant fit a general profile of lower-skill, lower-class labor migrants (Portes and Rumbaut 2006), even though they admitted that some, such as Marta, fit an entrepreneurial or professional profile too. Consequently, in Joseph's words, they are "happier" with the work[18] and see it as more permanent, while the foreign-born Asian contract workers work strategically and temporarily in PPP, for exactly 365 days in order to obtain a green card and move on to better jobs more commensurate with their skills.

Relative Evaluation: Economic Opportunities in the United States

A second reason many Hispanics evaluated food processing jobs positively is that they frequently compared them to other opportunities in the United States (Grey and Woodrick 2005; Stull and Broadway 2004; Stull, Broadway, and Griffith 1995). Consider again Liliana, who worked on the agricultural circuit in Florida, Georgia, and North Carolina before coming to PPP. Like other "settled-out" Hispanic respondents who have experience working in American agriculture, which is seasonal, labor-intensive, and insecure,[19] Liliana preferred her food processing line job for its steady work:

Liliana: I lived in Homestead, Florida, for five years.

Interviewer: And then where did you go?

Liliana: To Georgia. I stayed there for about a half a year. And then from there, I came here. And I stayed! Because here you don't have to work that hard. Many people come here to PPP from the fields. So I left the fields and came here because here there is a steady wage. And steady work. In the fields, if the weather is bad there's no work, but if the weather is good there is work.

Yet some respondents also considered their food processing line job to be better than other nonagricultural jobs, particularly one in the low-end services sector where hours are unstable and wages and benefits are also low. Hugo, an immigrant from Honduras who has a high school education and a work permit, is one such respondent; he evaluated his job in PPP's Distribution Department positively compared to the janitorial and painting work he performed in southern California on his first trip to the United States. Similarly, Santiago, a college-educated legal permanent resident who migrated from Bogotá, Colombia, to Wilcox County in the late 1990s, thought that jobs at PPP are "great." He argued that whereas natives "do not want to improve themselves" through their work and might see food processing jobs as a last resort, many Hispanics prefer them to worse jobs elsewhere in the American labor market:

Santiago: No, I don't think this is [a last-resort job]. The company's a good company, and it has great jobs for many people. And really, it's the people's way of thinking, right? Because many American people can say, "Well, this is my last opportunity, or my last chance to have a job." And we don't see it that way. I have been there for almost two years, and I have seen a lot of people coming and going. And one of the things that I'm surprised about is that whenever an American comes to the company, they work for one or two weeks, and then they quit and go out. And I have seen a lot of Latin American and Mexican people that are working there and for some reason they quit, but after some time they come back to the company. Because they know it's a good job.

In these ways, even higher-status Hispanic newcomers such as Santiago perceived production line jobs in PPP not as bad or worthless, but rather, like some of their white and black native coworkers, as "good fall-back positions" (B. E. Smith 2003) that are able to provide full-time work and a modicum of occupational benefits when better options are unavailable elsewhere. As one white native woman who had been working at PPP for 16 years confirmed, "If you need a job and you got to work, then it's a job, but otherwise don't you come knockin' around these doors" (fieldnotes, August 2003). Although certainly not enough to launch them into the ranks of the lower middle class, in the mid-2000s Hispanic respondents appreciated food processing line jobs for helping them stay afloat somewhere between the rungs of the working poor and the working class, despite the other drawbacks and dangers involved in the work. Like Marta, they saw food processing as an industry where they can achieve at least some limited economic stability, especially when that opportunity is unavailable or contracting elsewhere.

Furthermore, key structural factors also influenced Hispanic newcomers' relative evaluations of economic opportunities within the United States. Among foreign-born respondents, the main one is clearly legal status. Again, not surprisingly, the most positive evaluations of food processing line jobs emerged among unauthorized immigrants who have the fewest options elsewhere in the American labor market, while naturalized citizens, legal permanent residents such as Marta, and even temporary contract workers like the Asian H-2B workers were more disapproving.

To illustrate, let's revisit the distinction respondents often made between Hispanic and Asian H-2B temporary contract workers' evaluations of their jobs in PPP. Respondents explained that the Asian workers dislike the work not only because they are former professionals and have higher educational qualifications but also because they have the option to get a green card after their one-year contract is completed, which frees them up to move on to better jobs as legal permanent residents. By contrast, in 2003–04 there was no guarantee that unauthorized Hispanic immigrants would ever be able to become permanent legal residents or naturalize as U.S. citizens. As explained by Ramona, an unauthorized immigrant who migrated from Oaxaca, Mexico, to Wilcox County in 1996, and who left the agricultural circuit to settle out into a job in PPP's Cut Up Department (where she debones breast meat all day "so that the bones fall out clean and all the meat stays with the breast"), "It's different for a Hispanic. Me, I've been working here for five years."

In fact, Alejandra, an island-born Puerto Rican working in PPP's Human Resources Department for five years, argued that all workers' evaluation of their job in the plant has more to do with their relationship to American citizenship and immigration policy—and therefore, to their opportunity to obtain better employment elsewhere in the United States—than with the selectivity of migrant streams or individual immigrants' pre-migration socioeconomic status and motives for migrating abroad. Alejandra recounted that in the 1990s PPP personnel tried to recruit low-skilled Puerto Rican workers through a contract program similar to the one currently bringing in Chinese and Korean workers. However, it didn't work out well, because those Puerto Ricans, despite being low-skilled labor migrants from what Alejandra called "the worst part of Puerto Rico," were already U.S. citizens. Therefore, they could leave the plant anytime they wished to pursue better jobs elsewhere, while the current Asian contract workers must wait a full year to do so, and while unauthorized Hispanics such as Ramona, with few better employment opportunities in sight, must simply adapt:

Ramona: It's difficult because it's hard at first. Your hands hurt and go to sleep be-
    cause you don't know how to do the work yet. And so the work is very hard. But
    then you learn some more of the job and after two or more months of working
    there, you learn the job and it's not hard. It's easy. When you don't know it, yes,
    it's hard. But when you learn it well, it's easy like any other job.
Interviewer: And your hands don't hurt now?
Ramona: No. I've gotten accustomed.

Opportunities for Upward Mobility in Food Processing Jobs

The results presented thus far show that food processing plants offer relatively attractive initial opportunities for many Hispanic newcomers' economic incorporation, especially compared to other more limited job opportunities abroad and elsewhere in the United States.[20] But what about their opportunities for upward mobility in this new southern economy? Although immigration into rural new destinations is still too new to answer this question definitively, most scholars are pessimistic about the possibilities for lineworkers to experience any significant upward mobility, within the food processing industry or beyond it. This pessimism stems from several factors, among them a decline in the real wages of food processing workers since the 1960s (Erickson 1994; Grey 1995),[21] the industry's continuing pressure to increase worker productivity while keeping wages low in order to maintain profit margins (Bjerklie 1995; Broadway 1994; Fink 1998; Hall 1995; Striffler 2005a), and the high level of uncontested power that large food processing corporations have amassed over their workers in today's "post-Fordist" economy (Gouveia and Stull 1997; Griffith 1993, 2006; Stuesse 2009; Stull and Broadway 2004).

Indeed, Fennelly and Leitner (2002) worry that the concentration of immigrant workers in low-paying jobs, the absence of unions, and high turnover in the industry offer "few grounds for optimism" (8). Gouveia and Stull (1997) point out that food processing wages peak soon after arrival and are not indexed to cost of living or seniority; that internal labor markets are "almost completely eroded"; and that lack of English skills "effectively blocks many immigrant workers from supervisory jobs, for which Anglos and bilinguals are preferred" (102). Millard and Chapa (2004) even argue that Hispanics are as trapped in food processing as they are in agriculture, while prospects for upward mobility are better in light manufacturing (142). Solórzano (2005) concurs, reporting that Hispanic newcomers in Utah have "no possibility of economic or social improvement" working in low-wage, entry-level jobs in food processing, meat-packing, livestock, and crop production (188–89).

A few scholars have painted a more optimistic picture, yet even they remain appropriately cautious. Dunn, Aragonés, and Shivers (2005), for instance, document Hispanic newcomers in the Delmarva peninsula using food processing as a "first step on an employment ladder leading to work with better working conditions or pay," usually in construction and service work but also in self-employment (162–63, 179; Griffith 2005; Zarrugh 2008). In rural Arkansas, Striffler (2005a) also argues that although most Hispanics are "decidedly working-class," since the 1990s many have achieved relative stability, become permanently settled, and acquired the trappings of middle-class life by working hard, living frugally, and pooling multiple working-class incomes to support a single household. In his words, the shift to poultry work in the southern United States is "a story about upward mobility" for Hispanics, albeit one that comes at a "tremendous price" because it often exacts a huge emotional and physical toll on their health (101–10).

In PPP, respondents described noteworthy opportunities for upward mobility, as when workers move up from a position as a production lineworker to team leader, supervisor, and then line manager or higher-level administrative employee. Their reports of opportunity to move up within PPP suggest the continued presence of an internal labor market, even if it is not as strong as those operating in the food processing industry were in the mid-twentieth century.

Here, I show how four key structural and institutional factors were facilitating short-distance mobility within this internal labor market for some Hispanic newcomers, although as I show in Chapter 3 they certainly did not do so for all.

Growth of the Immigrant Labor Force

Since its opening in the late 1980s, the growth of the Spanish-speaking workforce on the floor in PPP has necessitated that more Spanish-speaking workers be placed in higher-level roles, mainly to ease communication and maintain high productivity (Erickson 1994; Stull and Broadway 2004: 93–94). For instance, Marisa, a light-skinned Mexican American who migrated from Laredo, Texas, to North Carolina after spending time in California and abroad, started working at PPP in 1988, before Spanish speakers arrived there in large numbers. Even though Marisa was a lineworker in one of the most basic jobs in the plant, she recalled rarely using Spanish on the job ("no one out here really even knew that I spoke it") because there were so few other Hispanic employees that "it was not really necessary to have interpreters and such."

But then Spanish-speaking immigrants began working in PPP in larger numbers. The growing Spanish-speaking population facilitated Marisa's occupational advancement by creating an "ethnic queue" (Jiménez 2010; López-Sanders 2009; Waldinger 1996; Waldinger and Feliciano 2004) in which U.S.-born and bilingual Hispanics began moving up into supervisory, translating, and clerical positions in order to recruit and assist incoming immigrants:[22]

Marisa: Well, while I was in Cut Up, on the line, we started getting a few more Hispanic or Latino lineworkers. And at the time, my supervisor [was] an African American gentleman so he didn't speak a lick of Spanish. And one day he's sitting here trying his best to get through to one of the Hispanic lineworkers what he's expecting of her, and it was just going over her head. She was looking at him like, you know, he might as well have been making faces at her! And I just happened to jump in and start interpreting for him and for her. And of course, his mouth dropped open. He said, "Now where did that come from?" You know, so after that happened, small changes started to happen. It got to the point where he was using me so much as an interpreter and things like that, that I wasn't on the line as much as I was at the beginning. And believe it or not, as much as he needed me on the line, he's the one that found out about the position in Health Services that I originally started out, in the office [translating and interpreting] for the lineworkers that came in there with problems and such. So needless to say, I got the position.

Once Marisa's African American supervisor realized she could speak Spanish, her ability to act as an interpreter for other employees increased her value to the organization. Later, Marisa took an interpreter position in the Wilcox County Department of Social Services, where she said the benefits were better than those offered in PPP. Then she came back to work at PPP as a human resources employee, when plant personnel made her an offer she "could not refuse." Several other Hispanic workers followed a similar trajectory; as the Spanish-speaking labor force in the plant grew, employers and managers found themselves in the position of needing bilingual workers who could help them maintain communication on the job and disseminate information and services to new workers.

Internal Job Posting System

Another factor behind the upwardly mobile trajectory of some Hispanic newcomers is an internal job posting system (Stull 1994). Santiago, the college-educated legal permanent resident from Bogotá, Colombia, who was quoted earlier as describing jobs in PPP as "great," described the structural benefit of this system. He started out as a production lineworker in the Live Hang Department, but he quickly moved up to a position in Human Resources, where he taught courses on occupational safety to Hispanic production lineworkers in 2003:

Santiago: Well, I began working as a Live Hanger, because I needed a job. And three weeks later, when there was an opening in another position, I applied for that, and I was changed to a training post, and then to Safety [in Human Resources], because all my experience is in Safety. So I've been here for around two years, more or less.

In less than six months, Santiago had moved out of his starting position as a regular production lineworker into higher-level jobs, twice. In 2003 he made more money than he previously did in the Live Hang Department and had future plans to continue moving up by joining management someday. Of course, like Marta, Santiago benefited from the fact that he has a college degree with training as an industrial engineer in Colombia, is bilingual in English and Spanish, and is a legal permanent resident of the United States (I address the issue of individual skills, legal status, and their effect on a worker's mobility path in Chapter 3). Yet Santiago credited his upward mobility not just to these factors or the growth of the plant's Spanish-speaking workforce but also to the fact that PPP advertises opportunities for promotion to its workers through an internal job posting system that gives first dibs to current workers, only later opening up the search to applicants outside the plant.

Other upwardly mobile workers, including ones with fewer skills and less English language ability, such as Hugo, the Honduran immigrant mentioned earlier, reiterated how important this internal job posting system is. Hugo started out in the Distribution Department earning $7.25, but within six months his hourly earnings had increased to $10.75:

Hugo: Fortunately I found a very nice place to work [in PPP]. So I'm trying to go up and up. Because I have experience in management, and I really, I would like to do a peaceful job! [*laughs*] And since I have a better position in PPP, the money I'm making is a lot better. Because I've seen that here are a lot of opportunities that you can get—better jobs, better money, and better positions. Because I started in PPP, as anybody else, in Distribution.

In fact, Hugo felt great esteem for this system, calling it a "democratic" way of helping workers with the motivation to improve their skills to move up into higher-level positions:

Hugo: You can move in the plant, to any department you want if you apply for it and if you're qualified for the job they are posting up, so. When there is an opportunity, what they do is they post it and they interview people. Because we apply for an internal application for that position, and then we go in a process of interviewing and demonstrating the abilities of what we are planning for. So it's real, real nice program they have there, I can say. Because if you, if you know something and if you apply for it, then they just do it, so. Actually, PPP has a lot of opportunities. But it's all up to the people who are looking for a job or a better future. Because if you wanna get something real good, you gotta be educated and prepared. Or you gotta have certain abilities to demonstrate that you can do a job. Or a better job. However, it's not easy if you don't learn the [English] language or you don't understand the rules of the company. And in my opinion, I can say that it's a real democratic system they have there. That everybody can apply when they post a job.

Finally, the internal job posting system was even working for some natives. Management workers in food processing plants often have previous experience working on the floor themselves (Erickson 1994). Margaret, an African American woman who worked as a finance specialist in 2003–04, started out as a production lineworker in PPP in 1988. Two years later, she moved up to a receptionist position, then on to an employment tech specialist position, and later an administrative position. Like Santiago and Hugo, Margaret placed special emphasis on the internal job posting system in describing her initial move from production lineworker to receptionist, and she reported being offered her current job as a finance specialist before ever applying for it:

Interviewer: How did you first hear of your receptionist job?
Margaret: A posting. One of the things that I love about PPP is that they always try to promote from within. They try to hire from within. So the job was posted on the bulletin board, and I saw it, so I came in and applied, and a week later they offered it to me.

Direct Encouragement by Superiors

Like Marta, many respondents reported that employers and managers actively encourage lineworkers to move up within the plant. Margaret went on to describe a general education reimbursement program at PPP through which workers can receive tuition reimbursement to take classes that teach them skills that will help them move up the ladder at work. More generally, respondents described the encouragement they receive from superiors at work as genuine rather than self-interested, pointing to various times when supervisors have encouraged them to learn important skills or gain more knowledge that will be helpful to them in the long run, not just be a short-term strategic tool to move up to the next job in the plant. The experience of Alejandra, the island-born Puerto Rican quoted earlier, is characteristic:

Alejandra: I knew about the Hispanic Leadership Course because our manager told us, and he came to my window and said, "Hey, Alejandra, I want you to take a leadership course. It's going to be in Spanish. It won't cost you anything. The only bad part is you have to take an hour out from your work [because I work the evening shift] and you won't be paid for it." And the first thing, I said was, "Yes." Why? Because even if I'm not going to receive any payment, I strongly believe that everything that you can get is good for you. Because it's going to be part of your knowledge. It's going to help you everywhere that you go. And I've always been—I like to be active in organizations and everything. And I like that.

Fausto, an H-2B temporary contract worker from Buenos Aires, Argentina, is another example. He moved from his first job in the plant (a human resources employee) to his current one (a line manager who oversees line supervisors and the production lineworkers underneath them) precisely because he was encouraged by his superiors to move up into a more demanding job through the plant's supervisor training program:

Fausto: I did Human Resources for eight months. Then they had this new supervisor training program going on, and they offered me a chance to apply, so I went through the interviews. And they accepted me to the program three months later, after I started. The program was more or less a 16- to 20-week program, where they have you going around the plant for those four or five months, trying to get the basics of the PPP process. So around two or three months after that, they pulled me out of the program and said, "Look, we have this need in the Distribution Department. And although you haven't finished even half of the program yet, the company needs this and you're here, so we're going to fill that spot with you." I said fine. And then I spent a year as a supervisor. And this opportunity was last year sometime in September that they had this Distribution manager position open, so I applied for it. A lot of people applied for it, but I got it. So that's what I've been doing since. So far so good. And I've been learning more about the plant, about the process.

In fact, there were two types of supervisor training programs in PPP. Fausto went through the *supervisor training program*, which was directed at current minority workers inside the plant to move up into supervisory positions, as opposed to the *supervisor apprentice program*, which was directed at minority college graduates outside the plant to come directly into interpreter, supervisory, or administrative positions.

As I discuss in the next section, by focusing on the internal promotion and external recruitment of minority workers, respectively, both programs exemplify the profound institutional changes that Alba and Nee (2003) note have occurred within American culture and its workplaces since the Civil Rights Movement, notably the rise in the legitimacy given to "diversity" in American culture and the increased cost of discrimination that workplaces face in an era governed by new institutional mechanisms for monitoring and enforcing the formal rules of state organizations. According to former PPP vice president Christopher, the purpose of the supervisor training program is to get minority production lineworkers to the supervisor level "because the upper management truly believes that the makeup of the supervisor group should represent or reflect the population of the hourly lineworkers." He even reported that plant management was getting ready to "start doing some testing on nominees" to the program "to try and preclude failures" since retention in that program had recently stalled at 40% "and it's really amazing to see how much confidence they get after going through it, how they begin to work and act." So perhaps Fausto would have made his way upward within the plant on his own. However, from his own account of his trajectory, having been offered the opportunity to enroll in the supervisor training program—and then, during that program, to exit early and take on a supervisory role in the Distribution Department—greatly reduced the time it took him to move up to a point where he could take advantage of the plant's internal job posting system and apply for an even higher managerial role in Distribution.

The importance of direct encouragement is further illustrated by Eduardo and Ramona, both of whom have a grade-school education, do not speak English well, and are unauthorized immigrants. Eduardo, who migrated directly to Wilcox County from Quetzaltenango, Guatemala, in 2000, recounted being encouraged by his American superiors to educate himself and move up within the plant:

> Eduardo: I like working there because I work in a place that is clean. I also like the work because the Americans help a lot. They give us a lot of courses, and they give us opportunity to work, to grow. And if you want to move forward, if one day you hope to be a supervisor, yes, you can do it. The company gives us the opportunity to educate ourselves.

When asked to elaborate on how his superiors encourage this kind of mobility, Eduardo reported being encouraged to take classes on occupational safety (to be able to teach it to other production lineworkers, like Marta), pursue English classes (to improve his language skills, because bilingual people can serve as interpreters at work), attend the Hispanic Leadership Course, and take advantage of the plant's supervisor training program (to train himself to move up from his current position as a production lineworker to a team leader, and then perhaps to a line supervisor after that).

Moreover, through these multiple forms of encouragement, Eduardo noted that he has learned valuable information that goes beyond his individual work goals—such as the importance of communicating with Americans and the U.S. government, treating everyone equally, participating in American civic and political life, and standing up for immigrants' rights, all of which he hoped to someday use to "help the Hispanic community" outside of work. Eduardo's experience illustrates that when production lineworkers are encouraged by their superiors at PPP to build their skills, what they acquire can translate into upward mobility within the plant and also into greater feelings of self-efficacy and acquisition of general knowledge. As Gordon and Lenhardt (2008) argue, even low-wage food-processing work can sometimes serve as a pathway to upward mobility and greater feelings of "citizenship as belonging."

Ramona is the unauthorized immigrant from Oaxaca, Mexico, whom I quoted earlier as having adapted to the work in PPP, because she had little hope of being able to legalize her immigration status and therefore of being able to move on to a better job elsewhere. She reported being encouraged by several supervisors (white, black, and Hispanic alike) to attend the Hispanic Leadership Course, and being encouraged by them to enroll in the plant's supervisor training program. Like Marta and Fausto, Ramona even reported that her superiors acknowledged her capability to do more at work; in fact, she had already become a team leader there, having moved up from the rank of production lineworker. Also like Marta, Ramona espoused an individualistic view of success and failure, arguing that opportunity for upward mobility in PPP is available to anyone willing to take it:

Ramona: I want to move ahead at my job. And when the [Hispanic] Leadership classes end, I am thinking of taking a program called the supervisor training program in the company. In PPP. To see what happens.

Interviewer: And this course gives you a little support to take that program at work?

Ramona: Yes.

Interviewer: How did you hear about the Hispanic Leadership Course?

Ramona: Lidia. And my supervisor. There are about four supervisors. Two are white Americans, and two are blacks. They sent me here. They said, "You have to go to take this course and think about this [supervisor training program] course that we are giving." They told me, "You are a good person, and you need to go there. Because you need to move up at work, and you can do it. You can do it, and you can move ahead. You have to go there to learn many things." And I learned many things, and I like it, and now we'll see what happens from here.

Interviewer: So are there a lot of opportunities like this in PPP?

Ramona: Yes.

Interviewer: Do you think that the majority of people there think this way—that they can move ahead, move up?

Ramona: I think so. I think if it's important to you and you make a goal for yourself, you can achieve it. If you do it.

Finally, like Eduardo, Ramona felt that the skills she has learned in the Hispanic Leadership Course can help her to "help the Hispanic community," although she has not decided how to do that yet.

In fact, both the internal job posting system and direct encouragement by superiors may have their strongest effect on the mobility paths of less skilled, non-English-speaking, and unauthorized workers in PPP—if and when they reach them—because it is these workers who have the fewest options elsewhere. Raquel, a 1.5-generation unauthorized youth originally from Honduras who dropped out of school after the 10th grade, reported being encouraged by her superiors to improve her English language skills and go back to school to earn her GED, to move up into a better position in the plant:

Raquel: I believe I want to take another class. Somewhere where I can learn more. I would like to get my GED, but if I get my GED here, it will be with my real name. And the managers that I work with are just like, "I need you to get your GED so I can put you in a better position."

Most interesting about Raquel's experience is that she was receiving this kind of direct encouragement despite one of her direct superiors knowing she is unauthorized and working in the plant under a false name.[23] It was precisely this encouragement that was fueling her drive to continue her education and move up within PPP:

Raquel: And I kind of explain to them. My manager knows. So how am I going to get my GED, with my real name?
Interviewer: So he knows you're working with a false name right now?
Raquel: Yeah. So he's like, "Oh yeah, you've got a point there, but you should get your GED somehow." And I want to get it. I actually want to get it because when I go back to Honduras, I want to get a better job. And after I finish my [Hispanic] Leadership class, I want to take a bilingual class. Where I can get certified and try to find a better job. And I don't care if it's with the name that I'm working with. Because that's what I want. Because it will help me out. Because if I get it on my fake name, they're going to be like, "Who is this? And who is this?" [laughs] So yeah, I kind of want to get a better education, that's all. I want to have something more than just . . . I want more for my kids. I want to be an example to them. I want to tell them when they're big that I was here and I learned this, and I had you and I had your brother. And I had my job and your father and I had to take care of each other and you, so.

Long-Term, Competitive Business Strategy

The results presented thus far counter the predominantly pessimistic outlook in the literature on food processing. To be sure, upward mobility with PPP has not translated into wage levels or benefits like those that existed in the industry before major restructuring took place in the 1970s.[24] But the fact remains that many Hispanic newcomers saw the opportunity for short-distance mobility and were experiencing some degree of it through structural and institutional mechanisms such as ethnic queues, internal job posting systems, and direct encouragement by superiors.

In this way, poultry processing appears similar to the low-wage fast food industry, which Newman (1999) describes as "healthy enough to open up many managerial jobs in the United States" and "committed enough to its workforce (and unpopular enough among outsiders) to open those opportunities to promising internal candidates" (173–74). On the one hand, food processing jobs have long been stigmatized by many Americans (Grey and Woodrick 2005). On the other, agribusiness and food processing have been *expanding* across the rural South since the 1970s. No matter what kinds of pressures PPP may have been feeling in the mid-2000s, there was still a large "NOW HIRING" sign posted out on the highway in front of the plant during the entire period of my research. Furthermore, although PPP posted an internal memorandum to all its administrative personnel in July 2003, announcing that because the world poultry market had fallen it would not be able to administer a general salary increase to its salaried associates for the first time in its history of operation, Marisa remarked, "Well you know, the market may be down, but we're still keeping our entire workforce" (fieldnotes, PPP, August 2003).

The combination of these two things has opened up space for Hispanic newcomers to move into and upward through the industry. Plus, following a period of intense negative media press covering racial strife and poor working conditions in other processing plants in the region—especially the Smithfield Foods pork processing plant in Tarheel and others near Siler City, North Carolina (not a pseudonym)[25]—PPP managerial personnel made a conscious decision to promote more minorities into the managerial ranks. As I have shown, this opened up more management opportunities for Hispanics and Asians, both those who were already working in the plant (via the supervisor training program) and college graduates outside of it (via the supervisor apprentice program).

Such changes reflect the power of emerging institutional mechanisms to monitor and enforce formal rules against discrimination in firms, corporations, and nonprofit organizations since passage of Title VII of the Civil Rights Act in 1964. Because the cost of discrimination has become more transparent in recent decades, workplaces—especially very large and heavily bureaucratized ones such as PPP (Waldinger 2001; Waldinger, Lim, and Cort 2007)—now work harder to enforce antidiscrimination rules, and an increasingly diverse labor force creates positive incentives for management to promote a normative climate of racial tolerance to avoid costly ethnic conflict and tension (Alba and Nee 2003: 55). According to former vice president Christopher, several of the "rough redneck" managers and supervisors who initially resisted these "diversity" changes were even asked to leave the company. This paved the way for further changes, such as institutionalizing a new "integration" policy through which plant managerial personnel actively attempt to reduce racial separation and conflict in order to enhance productivity:

Christopher: [At the management level] we did a lot of things around values, profile. We're not where we want to be relative to an ideal state, but we've made progress toward it. We're trying to hire people who are more skilled at managing people. We had some pretty rough redneck [supervisors and managers] in the group. And most of them are gone now. And we've done a number of training programs on harassment. Diversity is part of the orientation program. We have made a point—and I'm jumping down now to hourly hiring. I was a strong advocate of that you do not, for lack of a better term, "congregate" one department or place with a single ethnic group. I believe that that breeds discontent. The grass is always greener on the other side. So people have been able to move about the plant whenever they would like. Have you heard of the Smithfield Tarheel plant? I'm told they have certain departments staffed with African Americans, and most Latinos are in another area and are paid differently.

Interviewer: Was that the case here before you came into this plant?

Christopher: At one point, yes. They pretty much concentrated them. Now, when I got there, they weren't then. But they had very soon before then.

Indeed, Hispanic then director of housing Lidia argued that such reforms—including the two supervisor training programs, active integration of workers of different races and ethnicities across the plant, and a "zero tolerance" policy against discrimination—not only promote upward mobility among Hispanic workers but also strengthen the company's long-term competitiveness. She admitted that the opportunity for Hispanic workers to move up the ranks and get managerial and administrative jobs like hers is relatively new:

Lidia: We've only started seeing the company mobilizing employees and training Latinos for high-level positions in the past few months. I think now the company also sees it as a necessity to be able to compete against its competitors. Because when you're talking about such a diverse labor force, and when the majority are of Latino origin, it knows management personnel should be at that same level to be able to compete.

In this forward-looking context, as Newman (1999) found in the low-wage fast food industry, plant employers and mangers have "groomed" production lineworkers who have good credentials, show initiative and accept responsibility, display a "hint of leadership" or a "special spark," diversify the supervisory staff according to its new policies and business goals, and can be relied on in terms of supervising the workforce and smoothing over interethnic tensions that might impede high productivity (174–85).

Interestingly, all three upper-level employers I spoke with in 2003–04 (president Joseph, former vice president Christopher, and incoming vice president Thomas) reported wanting to encourage even more retention and upward internal mobility among the plant's minority workers. Christopher was frustrated that the plant has not been able to attract more well-educated workers through the supervisor apprentice program. He also wanted to work harder to find a way to make staying at PPP a more attractive option for the Asian H-2B contract workers who leave their production line jobs after their 365-day contracts are up, reporting that the "bottom line is be more proactive in retaining these people, to get those who have an education and can speak good English in management." Nonetheless, although he personally thought it was shortsighted and detrimental to the industry at large, he noted that the plant's more distant owners "have little incentive" to improve workplace conditions, labor-management relations, and opportunities for upward mobility because it will not produce direct financial returns for them. At the same time, Thomas disagreed, emphasizing that owners can be brought on board if they are presented with a good business strategy for improving worker loyalty, productivity, and the bottom line in a situation of dramatic ethnic change:

Thomas: It's just that you need to show the owners, the CEO, the board chairmen, a business strategy for it. Show them the long-term benefit of it, and really make the business case out of developing plant loyalty and a good relationship with these workers, who are really good. I believe there is a big possibility there, but they are not just going to do it because they want to be nice. It's got to make business sense. And in the long term, it is more than just learning about each other and cultural awareness. It's going to be something critical to the industry. By 2030, white males will be in the minority. Have you seen those figures? I mean, that's going to be a huge change. And don't you think then that the owners are going to wish they had treated these people better than they treated them? There is a real case to be made here.

Opportunities for Upward Mobility
Beyond Food Processing Jobs

Finally, some respondents noted opportunities for upward mobility outside the food processing industry, as when workers move out from positions in PPP to positions elsewhere, usually in county service agencies, school systems, and even county court and government systems. Earlier I showed how Marisa extended her upwardly mobile trajectory within PPP out into an interpreter position at the Wilcox County Department of Social Services. One of her sisters (Sofia) had also moved up to a position in the Benefits Department of PPP, and another (Magdalena) had gotten a "hot shot job" over in the Wilcox County Social Department of Social Services, of which Sofia was very proud.

Other Hispanic workers followed similar trajectories. Since I completed my research, Lidia, then director of housing, moved on to a position at a local community college coordinating continuing education courses for Hispanics across three rural counties, continuing her move up and out from her first job in American agriculture more than 20 years ago. Even Delmira, a legal permanent resident who migrated directly from Mexico City to Wilcox County in 1989 and who did not see any prospects for upward mobility at PPL, eventually applied for a job at the Wilcox County Health Department, which offered her a $3.00 higher hourly wage and a chance to move up. Looking back, Delmira admitted that the hands-on first aid work she performed while working at PPL helped her attain her new job working for the county:

Delmira: With the experience that I had gotten there, at PPL, being a first aid attendant, the [Wilcox County] Health Department was looking for an interpreter with medical experience in a way. And they had also lost a certified nurse-aide, an American CNA. And since I had the CNA certification and the bilingual Spanish-English, I guess they saw they could get two in one! So they hired me. I guess that's why they called me that same day. And so that's how I got there, to the Health Department.

In fact, that several Hispanics were moving out and on to other jobs was described as a "net loss" to the plant by PPP president Joseph:

Joseph: And we've lost some of our good bilinguals to Social Services, hospitals, emergency care, and legal and other areas that become quite attractive to them once they develop good communication skills. They can move on. They can sometimes move faster into another position there than we're able to move them here. Or they may be more qualified for that type of position rather than supervision.

Although these cases do not attest to widespread occupational mobility among Hispanic newcomers who start out in food processing, they do illustrate how some are using the industry as a stepping stone to blue- and white-collar jobs elsewhere (Dunn, Aragonés, and Shivers 2005; Griffith 2005; Striffler 2005a).[26] Hispanic population growth has even spawned a rapidly expanding immigrant entrepreneurial sector in Wilcox County by the time of this writing, which has facilitated upward mobility among several new business owners.

Summary

In the mid-2000s, key structural and institutional factors were facilitating lateral and sometimes also short-distance upward mobility for some Hispanic newcomers employed in Poultry Processing Plant in Wilcox County. Structural variables such as the selectivity of migration streams and individual Hispanic newcomers' socioeconomic and legal status shaped how they evaluated their jobs and prospects for both economic stability and upward mobility. Comparing their food processing jobs to other, worse employment options in their sending country and elsewhere in the United States, most notably agriculture and some types of low-wage urban service work, respondents tended to judge food processing positively—despite being well aware, as Marta demonstrated, of its drawbacks and dangers. Not surprisingly, lack of education, English language ability, and legal status produced the most positive evaluations of food processing work by limiting Hispanic newcomers' options for finding better employment elsewhere in the American labor market. Formally prohibited from working in the United States at all, unauthorized respondents were especially appreciative of the full-time work and steady income afforded by their food processing production line jobs. Even when these jobs did not generate enough money to cover all their bills, these unauthorized respondents often believed, as did Gabriel, a grade-school-educated and unauthorized immigrant who migrated from Chiapas to Wilcox County via Tamaulipas, Louisiana, and Florida, that there is "nothing but to look for a way" to make those earnings suffice.

Additional structural and institutional factors, notably growth of the immigrant labor force, an internal job posting system, direct encouragement by superiors, and long-term, competitive business strategy, were also generating what Lidia called a new landscape of upward mobility for Hispanic newcomers within the plant. Several Hispanic respondents moved up from positions as production lineworkers to team leaders, supervisors, and then line managers or higher-level administrative employees; in fact, Lidia reported that three Hispanics had been promoted in one week alone in September 2003 (fieldnotes, informal conversation). A few also "moved out" to positions or self-employment elsewhere. As I show in the next chapter, not all Hispanic newcomers were achieving this kind of short-distance upward mobility. Nonetheless, as the contrast between Marta's and Davíd's experiences highlights, those who were not moving up still felt more economically secure and better poised to achieve what sociologists Richard Alba and Victor Nee (2003) call "lateral" mobility and stability in food processing compared to routine manufacturing and textiles. This focuses our attention on the critical importance of, on the one hand, employment availability and job security to Hispanic newcomers' successful economic incorporation and, on the other hand, contraction of opportunity at the bottom of the American labor market and lack of legal status to their blocked mobility.

3

"It's Not Like If You Work in a Big Place and You Can Move up the Ladder"

Insecurity and Stagnation in the Old Rural Southern Economy

IN THIS CHAPTER, I extend my analysis from Chapter 2 into the life-worlds of Hispanic newcomers who were not experiencing short-distance upward economic mobility in the rural South, to further examine the individual and structural factors that they saw blocking their ability to do so. To return first to Poultry Processing Plant in Wilcox County, although respondents agreed that a lack of human capital skills and, even more important, unauthorized legal status impeded upward mobility in the plant, they also thought that "soft skills" such as personal ambition and willingness to put forth effort can assist even lower-status and unauthorized immigrants to move up. In this way, they interpreted Hispanic newcomers' opportunities for mobility in PPP in largely individualistic terms, not structural ones that would locate the source of blocked opportunities in the plant's failure to provide adequate opportunities for upward mobility. They bought into the American "achievement ideology" (MacLeod 1995), believing very strongly that anyone who works and tries hard enough will eventually be successful, and that anyone who does not can be faulted for not taking advantage of the opportunity to do so.

Turning next to Bedford County, we find that respondents in Textile Mill saw a much different future. For them, downsizing and restructuring in routine manufacturing and textiles have all but eliminated the notion of internal upward mobility and are even now threatening workers' prospects for what sociologists Richard Alba and Victor Nee (2003) call "lateral" mobility and economic security as well. Indeed, contraction of opportunity in this part of the old rural southern economy has made Hispanic newcomers' opportunities in food processing in Wilcox County appear even more precious. It showed them how the economic stability they can attain from being able to count on a full-time food processing job, no matter how limited, is crucial to avoiding poverty and to potentially achieving a lower-working-class lifestyle, from which they hope their children can make additional gains in the future.

Limits on Opportunities for Upward Mobility in Food Processing Jobs

Is the picture of internal upward mobility that I painted among Hispanic newcomers in PPP in Chapter 2 too rosy? Even a cursory view of the plant in 2003–04 revealed that those Hispanics who occupied supervisory and administrative positions are U.S.-born, well-educated, relatively good English speakers, and (if they are foreign-born) legal immigrants or naturalized citizens—statistics that square with research in the industry at large. Put differently, education, English language ability, nativity, and legal status intersected to produce a distinctive hierarchy or "ethnic queue" among Hispanic workers in the plant. Within it, Puerto Rican, Mexican American, Cuban, and some South American employees—including Marisa, the Mexican American from Laredo, Texas, whose bilingual ability and U.S. citizenship quickly propelled her up the ladder when more Spanish-speaking immigrants started arriving at the plant in the early 1990s—stood above Mexican immigrant, Central American, and other South American ones. According to Lidia, a legal permanent resident from Oaxaca, Mexico, and then director of housing, such differences in human capital and citizenship were reflected in Hispanics' different occupational statuses and also in the distrust they felt toward one another within the plant:

Lidia: There are differences, and sometimes [these groups] don't know how to relate. The people up in the Human Resources Department are more like Caribbean. And the people you've got working on the production lines, the majority of them are Mexican, Central American, and South American. There are a few who identify with them well, but there are others that don't. And sometimes that causes a conflict of trust between the lineworkers and the people in Human Resources. Because in the Department of Human Resources there is only one person who is Mexican. And the rest are all Puerto Ricans and Argentines.

Here, Lidia used the terms *Caribbean* and *Puerto Rican* to describe immigrants who migrate to eastern North Carolina with their U.S. citizenship in hand (Puerto Ricans) or with relatively easy access to refugee status and U.S.

citizenship (Cubans). Similarly, she used the term *Argentine* to describe certain South American immigrants who migrate to eastern North Carolina with better educational credentials than most contemporary Mexican and Central American labor migrants.[1] Indeed, although PPP was offering the opportunity for short-distance upward mobility to many Hispanic newcomers, respondents made it clear that not everyone working there will eventually move up. What factors explain who moves up, and who does not?

Hard and Soft Skills: Human Capital and Individual Ambition

In Chapter 2, I showed how Marta, Santiago, Hugo, Eduardo, and Ramona viewed mobility within PPP in largely individualistic terms. They praised Hispanic workers like themselves who are "on the way up" and faulted other Hispanic workers who are not, even while simultaneously attributing some of their own upwardly mobile trajectory to the influence of key structural and institutional factors. As other studies have shown, that structural and institutional factors shape immigrants' paths within the American labor force does not discount the continuing importance of immigrants' own human capital characteristics (Raijman and Tienda 1999). Respondents of all backgrounds and statuses within PPP most frequently associated lack of upward mobility with the lack of human capital, including not having the necessary educational training or English language skills to take on higher-level jobs. Eduardo, the grade-school-educated and unauthorized immigrant from Quetzaltenango, Guatemala, whom I introduced in Chapter 2, explained:

Eduardo: Those who work as Hispanic managers, I think it's because they
    speak English well. They probably got more education. And those that are
    working in there, the lineworkers who do the processing, they probably
    don't speak English. They didn't study enough to have that responsibility, or
    they haven't had a class or something. Or mostly because they don't speak
    both languages.

Some respondents even thought that individual workers' level of human capital helped account for different experiences in the plant as well as in the United States generally. Consider Salvador, who migrated from Cartago, Costa Rica, to Miami in 1988 and then later to Wilcox County in 2000. In contrast to his wife, Olivia, who expressed a very negative evaluation of labor-management relations in the plant and claimed that Americans treat Hispanics "inhumanely" and "like dogs," Salvador wondered aloud if his better English-language skills have allowed him to advance farther at work, be treated better by his superiors, wield more leverage to make his opinions and complaints known, and develop a better opinion about life in the United States:

Salvador: So far I really haven't had any bad experiences like hers, but we are in different departments. And my supervisor, he's demanding, but at the same time he rewards you when you do your work well. So there's a balance in that aspect. But really I haven't; because we're in different departments I haven't felt the same thing as she has. But maybe it might also be because I am more bilingual than she is. I don't know if that has helped me. Maybe they don't treat me the same way. And up to a certain point it is that way. When you are bilingual, or when you are in an administrative position and you are bilingual, you have the possibility of going to someone even higher up than you and being able to make your complaints known about whatever problem. And I imagine that that is part of why I haven't felt the same thing.

Just behind lack of human capital, respondents associated lack of upward mobility with inadequate individual ambition or desire to take on more responsibility in higher-level positions.[2] To illustrate, former vice president Christopher claimed that there is more opportunity for upward mobility within the plant than many Hispanic workers, especially female ones, are ready to assume:

Interviewer: Do you think there is opportunity for Latino workers to move up the ranks here, and do you think most Latino or immigrant workers will?
Christopher: Yes, there is a lot of mobility, more than most of them are prepared to take advantage of. Particularly Hispanic/Latino females.
Interviewer: How so?
Christopher: It is so difficult to get them to be willing to step up and try to improve themselves.

Plant president Joseph agreed, noting that one of the challenges of employing Hispanics in the plant is their unequal representation in higher-level positions. He thought this might have something to do with Hispanic newcomers' cultural attitudes toward gender, which in his view result in female Hispanic workers not trying hard enough to assume the kinds of positions that many male Hispanic workers do:[3]

Joseph: Hispanics have different attitudes toward gender than we do. And of course that becomes a challenge when you are dealing with the laws of our country with regard to equality and those kinds of things.

Similarly, Marisa thought there is quite a bit of opportunity for upward mobility within the plant. She emphasized lack of ambition or desire to move up, combined with low educational and English-language human capital skills, to explain why some Hispanic workers will never achieve the mobility that she has by being willing to make some sacrifices and put her best foot forward:

Marisa: There is quite a bit of mobility within PPP, yes. I mean, if someone wants it bad enough, and if they're willing to make some sacrifices, like take some courses. Like I went back to school for clerical training in order to do my job at Occupational Health. I mean, one of the main reasons I went back to school for the clerical courses that I took is because I went from the floor into an office job and I wanted to be able to do that job to the best of my ability. But if someone's not willing to put their best foot forward, you know, and make the sacrifices necessary to better themselves, there's always going to be someone else that is willing to make the sacrifice. And of course, they're going to ace 'em out of the good positions every time.

Interviewer: Do you think most Latino workers will move up in the ranks to get jobs like yours?

Marisa: I'll be honest with you. I don't think you could say "most." Because a lot of it goes back to the fact that a lot of them are illiterate. In order to be a line supervisor, you have to have some ability to read and write and do reports, and God knows what else they do out there. I mean, even the team leaders get responsibilities that takes [*sic*] them into a next level. *That someone is sitting there and they're illiterate—they never went past a certain grade and they just can barely write their name—they probably wouldn't even try for advancement. You know, because with them being unable to read and write and all this other stuff, if anything they don't have the confidence to try something new. You know, they just feel that, you know, it's like, "As long as I can do the job." You know, "my physical job."* But of the ones that are either bilingual or have had school-ing—even if they're not totally bilingual—they can read, write, and have a lot of understanding of certain things, yeah, I see them moving up and taking some important positions around here. As a matter of fact, I mean, we have examples out there all over the floor. Of Hispanics who started on the line, and now they're supervisors or managers or lead people. Heck, we've got a lot of Latino lead people. But see, they have to at least be able to speak enough English to where they can talk to their supervisor and the English-speaking people on the line. So even the lead people kind of—it helps if they're bilin-gual [my emphasis].

In sum, Hispanic newcomer and native respondents alike perceived that the "hard skills" of human capital—specifically education, training, and English language ability—are the most important determinants of upward mobility within the plant, whereas the lack thereof leads to occupational stagnation (Massey and Sánchez 2010). Nonetheless, respondents also agreed that strong individual ambition—a desire to take advantage of what opportunities are made available to workers, and, in Marisa's words, a willingness to "make the sacrifices necessary"—can sometimes lead to upward mobility even for those workers who may otherwise lack hard skills, whereas lack of ambition and effort is a sort of occupational death knell that all but condemns them to the bottom floor of the plant. As Lidia explained, whether or not Hispanics will be able to move up within the plant was perceived by most employers and employees of PPP to depend on how much they want to take advantage of the available opportunities to do so. When asked if most Hispanic workers will move up the ranks to get jobs like hers, she responded emphatically, "No. No. No. We're still missing a lot to be able to do that. That's going to depend on them, on the new ones that are coming in, to take advantage of the [supervisor training] program a little more."

Legal Status

Following these two dominant individual-level explanations for why some Hispanic workers do not achieve upward mobility within the plant, that they are deficient in either human capital or individual ambition, respondents also cited one main structural reason: the absence of legal status (Massey and Sánchez 2010). However, for the most part respondents faulted unauthorized immigrants for being fearful of displaying the soft skill of ambition to pursue more responsibility within the plant *because of* their unauthorized status, thereby mixing together structural and individualistic interpretations of how their status impedes upward mobility. To illustrate, Denise, an African American clerical worker in the Evisceration Department, agreed with Marisa that high education and English language ability lead to upward mobility for many Hispanic newcomers in PPP, while the absence of education and desire to move up lead to occupational stagnation for others. Yet even though Denise believed some Hispanic workers are simply not interested in moving up through the ranks, she also thought that others are inhibited by their unauthorized status, which, like low education, correlates with having little ambition to do more and "go for it" at work:

Interviewer: Do you think most Hispanic workers could move up the ranks to jobs like yours?

Denise: They may try. Like I said, it's just a few. But you know what? A lot of 'em
that I notice do move up in the ranks, to get office jobs, are born here [in the
United States]. But most of them that actually comes [sic] from another country or whatever, they don't usually go for it. It just basically comes down to the
education. I think that'll keep a lot of 'em from doing office work [although] I
wouldn't doubt that they have the ability to do it. And I mean, you know, a lot
of people come in under false names, and they're in a position where they're
not going to give out too much for what they need to.

As Denise explained, many unauthorized immigrants in the plant are not
likely to display ambition by doing something like applying for a promotion.
This is because the very act of doing so might require them to "give out too
much" information about themselves, thereby drawing unnecessary attention
that could potentially lead to their being fired if superiors discover they are
unauthorized. In this way, even though respondents readily acknowledged that
unauthorized status is the main structural barrier limiting Hispanics' chances
for upward mobility within PPP, it is because this status leads many Hispanics
to refrain from displaying more individual ambition than "what they need to,"
not because lack of legal status directly precludes moving up. In fact, in early
2004 Margaret, the African American finance specialist whom I introduced in
Chapter 2, thought this was something that might improve over time, if more
unauthorized immigrants realized they could assume higher-level positions
despite not having their papers, if they only put forth the effort.

Such a possibility did not seem far-fetched in the mid-2000s. As I showed
in Chapter 2, several unauthorized respondents reported receiving direct support and encouragement from their superiors to move up in the plant. Indeed,
although most native personnel at PPP did not consider employing unauthorized immigrants to be a desirable cost-cutting strategy or responsible civic
behavior on the part of employers and employees who otherwise consider
themselves law-abiding Americans, some openly argued that being prevented
from hiring "good" (albeit unauthorized) workers also creates undue problems.
For example, Shonda, an African American team leader in the Cut Up Department, argued that it disrupts smooth plant operation and production, not to
mention the livelihoods of unauthorized workers:

Shonda: I don't think it's fair to the Hispanics if they're being brought in and they
don't have papers, and then after they have worked this job they have to go. Or
they're being found out that they don't have papers.

Interviewer: What do you mean?

Shonda: I feel like as a standard formality of the job, that the company should know whether they have papers before they hire 'em. Because you get used to people, and they get used to working, and when something comes up, like their social security number is not right, and then you've lost that person. It's just so unfair. It's something that I just wish there was another way, or that it would be easier for them to just get papers. So they can just come and not have any worries about, "Oh, they might find this out or they might find this out, and I'm going to lose my job then."

Like many unauthorized respondents, these native PPP plant personnel placed the brunt of the blame for problems surrounding the hiring of unauthorized immigrants on the U.S. government and a flawed federal immigration policy, not on the individual shortcomings of unauthorized immigrants or, their least favored target, employer self-interest. Given the dependence of the plant on its immigrant workforce in the mid-2000s, this meant that in many cases unauthorized immigrants would be allowed to continue working there until employers were forced to terminate them.[4] In the meantime, given the dependence of the plant on its Spanish-speaking workers, supervisors, and interpreters, this also meant that in many cases unauthorized immigrants would be allowed (and perhaps also encouraged) to move up into higher roles. Thus, in the mid-2000s respondents agreed that lack of legal status did complicate many Hispanic newcomers' ability to move up in the plant, in large part because it depressed their willingness to display ambition and bring attention to themselves. Still, respondents did not think that their unauthorized status created an insurmountable structural barrier to upward mobility. They argued that if unauthorized workers could display the necessary motivation and drive, keep their legal status unknown, and earn the support of their supervisors, they could achieve upward mobility despite their status.[5]

Rising Economic Instability and Limits on Upward Mobility in Routine Manufacturing and Textiles

The contrast with the situation of Hispanic newcomers working in tobacco agriculture and routine manufacturing and textiles in Bedford County could not be starker, although perhaps in an unexpected way. Traditionally, scholars have emphasized brighter prospects for immigrants' upward mobility in manufacturing than in food processing. This is because manufacturing tends to offer higher hourly wages than either food processing or the low-end services sector, where rural sociologists have been worried about the growth of "bad" jobs that are part-time, temporary, low-pay, and devoid of meaningful benefits (Mc-Granahan 2003).[6] As Eckes (2005) writes, "Manufacturing generally pays well, far better than retail service jobs," and it "supports additional jobs in services, construction, and agriculture" (55). Accordingly, manufacturing is often portrayed as the most likely sector through which immigrants can enter the ranks of the American middle class, whereas food processing and low-end services are often portrayed as just the opposite. In their study of Hispanic/Latino newcomers in the rural Midwest, for example, Millard and Chapa (2004) argue that in communities where Hispanic newcomers are employed mainly in food processing they are "trapped," working in "the least desirable and lowest-paying" jobs where they "wash, chop, can, freeze, slaughter, and pack food under arduous conditions requiring physical strength and endurance" without adequate benefits. However, in communities where Hispanic newcomers are employed mainly in light industrial plants, mostly auto parts factories, they argue that Hispanic newcomers are building "lower-middle-class suburban communities" by bringing in dual-earner household incomes of approximately $44,000 per year with medical benefits (8–17).

Unfortunately, my research uncovered a less savory picture of Hispanic newcomers' economic trajectories in the core manufacturing industries of the old southern economy—what Falk and Lobao (2003) identify as textiles, apparel, furniture, metal working, rubber, and plastic. No matter what limits there might have been on Hispanic newcomers' opportunities to achieve economic incorporation and upward mobility in Poultry Processing Plant in Wilcox County, their opportunities were substantially worse in routine manufacturing and textiles over in Bedford County. In fact, although both native and newcomer respondents working on the production floor in Textile Mill in Bedford County reported higher hourly wages and somewhat better benefits than their counterparts working in PPP in Wilcox County, they also reported a far higher degree of uncertainty as to whether they would even remain employed in the plant in the near future, much less be able to move up in the mill over time.

To explain this difference, it is important to understand the contemporary situation of textiles and furniture manufacturing as declining rather than expanding sectors of eastern North Carolina's low-wage economy. Whereas high-technology manufacturing and service sectors have fueled much of North Carolina's recent economic growth at the state level, traditional manufacturing sectors such as textiles, apparel, and furniture have been hard-hit, experiencing severe contraction in the other direction. According to White (2004), North Carolina was already losing about a thousand jobs per month in these sectors as far back as the 1970s and 1980s. Between 1978 and 1997, it lost about 32% of its textile manufacturing jobs and 40% of its apparel jobs, followed by further hits in the range of 30 and 39%, respectively, between 1997 and 2001. Job losses from industrial restructuring continued apace into the twenty-first century, when employment in textiles and apparel fell by another one-third between 2000 and 2003, and when industrial restructuring also began to affect the furniture industry, where manufacturing employment fell by one-quarter. In fact, between 1994 and 2000 North Carolina accounted for nearly 40% of textile job losses nationwide, and it lost more jobs in textiles and apparels combined than did any other state (Cobb 2005). Between 2001 and 2005, it lost more manufacturing jobs than Michigan or New York, which have larger manufacturing workforces (Johnson and Kasarda 2009).

As in the rest of the traditional South, these losses have disproportionately affected the state's rural areas because of their heavy concentration of textile and apparel employment (Cobb 2005; Collins 2003; Falk and Lobao 2003).[7] While large layoffs and plant closings were still echoing through the central piedmont region of the state during the time of my research, one Bedford County resident remarked that "we were pretty much through being hit by then" (postfieldwork notes, Nov. 2, 2006). For instance, even before Pillowtex textiles (not a pseudonym) announced a massive 5,500-person layoff in July 2003—the biggest layoff in the state's history to date, most of which took place in central piedmont Cabarrus County (not a pseudonym)—the local Bedford Pillowtex plant had already closed in 2002, laying off around 170 workers (fieldnotes, local resident of Bedford County, August 2003). Even before that, part of Fabrico (a pseudonym for another local textile mill in Bedford County) had been bought out by Chinese investors in the early 2000s, and Household Equipment Company (a pseudonym for one of the staple manufacturing industries in Bedford County during previous decades) had closed down and relocated to Mexico in the early 1990s. "In this sense," Cobb (2005) writes, "job globalization seems to exacerbate the South's economic unevenness, because it tends to benefit metropolitan economies while decimating rural ones":

> East Alabama gleams with new auto facilities as West Alabama hemorrhages apparel plants. A strikingly international Spartanburg flourishes, while nearby, what had once been single-industry textile-mill towns are now effectively no-industry ghost towns. (3–4)

In North Carolina, although higher-end manufacturing and service businesses have expanded in metropolitan areas, local economic-development and political officials in disadvantaged rural counties such as Bedford and Wilcox have been left struggling to find cost-effective ways to draw in better industries despite the fact that their populations have characteristics, particularly low human capital, that do not make them competitive in doing so (McGranahan 2003).

It is within this context of rural economic restructuring and decline that Hispanic respondents critiqued their economic situations in Textile Mill and other nearby manufacturing plants. Most important, they singled out rising economic instability and job insecurity as a critical negative aspect of their jobs. María, an unauthorized immigrant who migrated directly to Bedford County from Huehuetenango, Guatemala, in 1998, to reunify with her husband, who was helping her become a legal permanent resident, had previously worked in two local routine manufacturing "factory jobs." However, she came to Textile Mill because neither of them offered her stable, full-time work:

Interviewer: When you arrived here, how was it that you learned about work here?

María: When I came here, I didn't have my papers yet. So I worked under another name. I worked in a toy factory. I worked there about two months, and I finished the work and I left. I spent a little time at home, and then I went to work in [another manufacturing plant]. It's over there near where the sheriff station is, near Fabrico. And I said to another sister in my church that I needed another job because there wasn't work all the time. And then our pastor's wife called me and told me that they are looking for people in Textile Mill. And then we came here and put in an application. And they said yes.

However, María's job at Textile Mill was still not secure. As the only hosiery mill left in eastern North Carolina in 2003, Textile Mill was locked in serious competition with cheaper foreign imports. Co-employer Bob Battle reported having had to downsize over the past few years and change business strategies toward producing "for niche markets rather than mass markets" (McGranahan 2003: 141) in order to remain competitive. He also reported having to conduct a large round of worker layoffs in 2002, during which the mill laid off approximately a third of the total workforce. This was something he had never been forced to do before, and he was worried he might face doing it again if the company continued having trouble maintaining its workers' wages and benefits while meeting buyers' ever-lower price points:

Bob Battle: We've had to downsize, because we have a lot of things that are going overseas. Customers we used to sell to say that we have to reach this price point. And to pay workers the amount that we pay them—they may earn upward of $9, $10, $11 an hour—and also pay them benefits and the health insurance, you know, covering everything for OSHA, covering everything for EPA, covering Family Leave Medical Act, covering everything for all the government requirements we have, all of that we basically have to incur as a cost. And at this moment we still pay 100% health insurance on each employee. And if they choose to insure a spouse or children then they pick up that cost. And it's very difficult to compete with [lower pay rates and government standards in China].

Interviewer: When did you downsize?

Bob Battle: About a year and a half ago. Basically we did away with a second shift of Boarding and went to a third and a first. We did away with a second shift of Sewing. And then basically it was cutting out some people throughout each department.

Interviewer: What do you foresee happening now?

Bob Battle: Well, what we're intending to do is basically trying to establish ourselves in more niche markets that are insulated from some of this overseas competition. Plus we're doing things with a lot of fashion-oriented companies who can't get what they want from overseas. They want things to be a little more flexible, and therefore we are able to maintain that business with 'em.

These large-scale changes in the routine manufacturing and textile industry have translated into fewer opportunities for workers in the rural South to find employment, owing to downsized work shifts and reduced job openings. Several Hispanic respondents reported having been laid off recently from area manufacturing or textiles jobs, including from Textile Mill; Fabrico, the nearby toy factory María mentioned; and an agricultural equipment-making company in Bedford County, as well as a hammock factory in neighboring Dickens county and a furniture-making company in Wilcox County. Yet even for workers able to find employment, it has translated into less leverage regarding hours, wages, and benefits, plus an almost constant threat of immediate job displacement (Collins 2003). For instance, Patricia, a middle-class Mexican immigrant who was recruited to work in Fabrico in 2003, told me that the plant had already eliminated its second shift and was considering cutting back even further on its hours of operation—staying open, for example, every other week instead of every week. Moreover, Patricia reported that the threat of immediate job displacement there was so strong as to be a daily topic of conversation among workers, native and immigrant alike; in her words, conversation "almost always" begins with, "Well, if I'm still working here in two months . . ." (fieldnotes, Bedford County, July 2003).

Within Textile Mill, Jan, a white American line supervisor/manager, described a similar climate of uncertainty produced by the movement of textile jobs overseas, reduced work hours, and increased layoffs:

Interviewer: Has your financial situation changed in any way recently?

Jan: Well, only that we don't work like a steady 40-hour week. Where you go like the first of the year, and really be on short-time, like working only 24 hours per week. And you've heard of people being laid off and this and that. And it's really quite scary. And then you hear about they're sending a lot of work overseas because there's cheaper labor. I think I've heard that we're losing our J. C. Penney account. It's going to Turkey. You know, that account's something we've had here all my life at Textile Mill. And it's just kind of scary.

Likewise, Antonia, a legal permanent resident who migrated directly to Bedford County from Veracruz, Mexico, in 1994, reported that "the economic situation has changed a whole lot. The work is a lot harder, and they had to lay off a whole shift."

Thus, despite the drawbacks of hard food processing work, Hispanic newcomers reported better prospects for achieving limited economic stability and lateral mobility in PPP in Wilcox County than their counterparts in Textile Mill and other local manufacturing plants did. Not surprisingly, because workers in these routine manufacturing and textiles plants were so focused on not losing their jobs, they were also less oriented toward long-term prospects for upward mobility than were those in PPP. For instance, Darma, a white American line supervisor/manager, explained how factory workers like her have little hope for upward mobility in companies as small as Textile Mill, especially ones undergoing such serious industrial restructuring and downsizing pressures:

Interviewer: In your opinion, do you think immigration affects how much people can earn at their jobs here?

Darma: Not here.

Interviewer: Do you think it affects the types of jobs people can get?

Darma: Not here. Because there's not really different jobs you can get here. You're sure not gonna get one of these offices! [*laughs as she refers to the conference room and offices of the employers*] I mean, it's not like if you work in a big place and you can move up the ladder, because you can't. Not here. And I don't think it's going to get better. Because the cost of living [is rising] and all the jobs here are leaving, and sooner or later jobs are going to run out. And like that line out there. If you can punch a computer button and put the sock up, well then you wouldn't need workers at all, you know?

Of course, if long-time native workers such as Jan and Darma saw few opportunities to move up in Textile Mill, unskilled Hispanic newcomers such as María and Antonia only saw fewer. Yet even Davíd, the highly skilled immigrant from Medellín, Colombia, whom I introduced in the beginning of Chapter 2, was extremely pessimistic about Hispanic newcomers' chances to move up and make something better of themselves working there.

Such critical statements are striking in comparison with those made by both unskilled and skilled respondents working in PPP. Despite reporting somewhat lower wages, somewhat leaner benefits, and decidedly more physically demanding work than their counterparts working in Textile Mill, low-skilled respondents in PPP expressed more appreciation for jobs they could count on for full-time work (and often overtime as well). As I showed in Chapter 2, several had even attained some degree of short-distance upward mobility there, moving into supervisory, administrative, or interpreter positions over time. Finally, higher-skilled respondents working in PPP, such as Marta, Fausto, and Santiago, displayed noticeably more optimism about their possibilities to move up the ladder compared to their counterparts in routine manufacturing and textiles, such as Patricia and Davíd.

Indeed, contraction of opportunity in this part of the old rural southern economy, and also in tobacco agriculture (see Hartch 2008; and Torres, Popke, and Hapke 2006), has made the opportunities Hispanic newcomers saw in food processing appear even more precious. One marker of the rising value of food processing jobs was that worker turnover in PPP had fallen to unprecedented levels in 2003–04. PPP president Joseph reported a turnover rate of 120–130% in the early to mid-1990s, but former vice president Christopher reported a much lower 20% in 2003–04. Both men readily admitted that 20% is "almost unheard of" in an industry known for extremely high turnover (usually upwards of 100–300% annually), where plant managers "*dream* of annual turnover rates of 36–50 percent" (Stull and Broadway 2004: 80, my emphasis; Bjerklie 1995;

Gouveia and Stull 1997; Grey and Woodrick 2005; Stuesse 2009). On the one hand, they attributed part of the reduction to recent changes in the composition of the immigrant workforce (which has become stabler and more permanent as women and children join adult male workers in the region) and to internal changes implemented by plant personnel to improve worker retention (including "addressing management issues in order to make the plant a better place to work"[8] and implementing various "screening processes," such as trying harder only to hire "legals," doing background checks on native workers to weed out applicants who are felons, and offering applicants a chance to tour the plant before they sign up to work there).

On the other hand, they also attributed part of the reduction to downsizing and restructuring in other traditional local industries. For instance, they reported that more workers—especially white and black natives—have been coming into PPP to search for jobs after being displaced from tobacco agriculture or furniture manufacturing and textiles factories.[9] According to plant president Joseph:

> As a percentage of the workforce, the Latin group has actually decreased a few
> percent in the last few years. And you know, this may have something to do
> with the economy and the number of jobs available. Because we have people
> that have been displaced in other industries coming here for work, who are
> [white or black] native.

Similarly, according to former vice president Christopher, "Primarily Caucasian Americans, who have a pretty simple lifestyle," have been coming into the plant to apply for jobs because

> you've also had a dramatically changing economic base taking place in North
> Carolina over the last five years, which has accelerated in the last 24 months.
> You've had a very strong furniture industry, a very strong textile industry, and
> both of those virtually are gone. And you do not have the type of industry
> coming in behind them where a lot of these people can work, because so many
> of them do not have high enough or good enough educations.

Eleanor, a white American migrant tutor at Weakley Elementary School, confirmed their observations from outside the food processing industry, noting that "as far as farming goes, a lot of folks recently have switched out of tobacco to be more diverse. They realized they needed to get into other things as tobacco has been getting harder."

Christopher even reported that "because of the change in tobacco especially" more Hispanic workers have been holding on to their poultry processing jobs instead of moving seasonally between food processing and agriculture (see Griffith 1995a), as "about 50 lineworkers" used to do during the "green season when the weather changed." In this way, not only have downsizing and restructuring in traditional local industries led many native workers into food processing, where they consider their prospects for finding stable and full-time employment to be more favorable. It has also made the workers who already have production line jobs in PPP feel lucky and appreciative of them. Fausto, the H-2B temporary contract worker from Buenos Aires, Argentina, whom I introduced in Chapter 2 and who worked as a line manager in the Distribution Department, put it most succinctly:

Fausto: I know that the unemployment rate has risen over the last couple of years. So somehow, I'd say that the people who have the jobs around here have to be lucky that they've got one.

The Dilemmas of Rural Economic Development

These findings call for a more nuanced and cautiously optimistic understanding of how food processing, the economic sector most closely associated with the rise of the *nuevo* new South, is shaping Hispanic newcomers' prospects for achieving economic stability, mobility, and assimilation as they disperse throughout the country. That many Hispanic respondents saw an opportunity to move up the ranks into lower-middle-management positions in PPP lends support to the argument that low-wage yet expanding "growth industries" sporting internal labor markets may offer better opportunities for upward mobility to their entry-level workers than do low-wage industries in decline (Newman and Lennon 2004). By contrast, what remained of routine manufacturing and textiles in eastern North Carolina in the mid-2000s was neither large nor strong enough to offer Hispanic workers the same kinds of avenues. For instance, although several Hispanic newcomers in Bedford County were employed full-time and earning relatively high wages in Metal Company (a metal and steel fabricating company) and Tractor/Trailer Company (an agricultural equipment–making company), both were small; Metal Company employed fewer than 20 workers, and demand for Tractor/Trailer Company products had fallen drastically since the days when it employed 500 to 600 workers.[10] Moreover, like local construction companies in the region, both factories hired almost exclusively men, whereas PPP hired and also promoted (according to my female respondents) women and men.

Taken together, these findings focus our attention on the importance of employment availability and job security to Hispanic newcomers' successful economic incorporation. The distinction often made between undesirable food processing jobs and more desirable light and routine manufacturing jobs is largely based on differences in wage and benefit structures. Nonetheless, sociological research shows that simply being able to participate in the labor force at all is a vital first measure of economic incorporation. It also shows that being able to count on continued participation in the labor force shapes workers' reports of satisfaction on the job;[11] in one survey, a 10% increase in the expected risk of job loss in the next two years reduced a job's rating as much as did a 10% pay cut (Jencks, Perman, and Rainwater 1988, quoted in Tilly 1996). For these reasons, taking employment availability and job security into account alongside wage and benefit structures helps to explain why many Hispanic newcomers evaluated their food processing line jobs positively. According to Elva, the unauthorized immigrant from Guerrero, Mexico, whom I quoted at length in Chapter 1, "stability" even makes jobs in the food processing industry better than those in some higher-paying agricultural and urban manufacturing jobs:

Elva: The first person in my family to work with Poultry Farms was my brother. And he did a lot of things for them. Like me, he liked to work a lot. He worked at night, and he did all of his work. And so he said that he got paid very well. Like before that he got paid $400 per week in the fields. At Poultry Farms he was earning $350—so it was $50 less. But he was stable in one place. And his job was secure. And so it was about the security of the job. What he appreciated most—the job security, that it was stable here.

In this sense, that Wilcox County had a large and expanding food processing industry—one capable of absorbing and providing "fall-back positions" to low-skilled workers laid off from other traditional local industries—helped to ease the harsh blows of downsizing and industrial restructuring its residents were feeling in the mid-2000s. Of course, compared to Bedford County, where economic-development and government officials rejected a proposal to construct a large pork processing plant in the 1980s out of concern about the potential for "horror story" environmental and quality-of-life impacts, Wilcox County faced many pressing policy concerns. Chief among them were the environmental stress being placed on local resources by expansion of a large industry and the fiscal and social stresses being placed on local service-providing institutions and intergroup relations by rapid population increase (Stull and

Broadway 2004). At the same time, in choosing to go the food processing route, by the mid-2000s Wilcox County appeared to have been moderately more successful than Bedford County at counteracting rural population decline[12] and holding down local unemployment and poverty.[13] As Bedford county commissioner Don attested, the major downside of defeating a proposal to construct a large slaughtering operation is that "you know that you are losing jobs and the people need work regardless of the quality of jobs." Bedford's website agreed: "The most recent Census numbers indicate that Bedford and Bedford County have declined in population, one of only three counties in the state with projected future losses. Unless there is growth, our community will surely wither and die" (last accessed May 2, 2005).

To be sure, local officials in both counties are well aware of the need to educate and train their local workforces (including Hispanic newcomers) to make them more capable of vying for better jobs. They are also well aware of the need to diversify their local economic development strategies so as not to remain dependent on declining traditional industries, or in the case of Wilcox County a new low-wage agro-processing industry instead (Gouveia and Stull 1997; McGranahan 2003). Specifically, these officials see attracting higher-end manufacturing and services jobs as the key to giving their local residents better economic opportunity in the long run; consequently, their sights are set on drawing precisely the kinds of light manufacturing industries described by Millard and Chapa (2004), such as auto parts plants, into local industrial parks (Cobb 2005). Even so, economic development in rural counties such as Bedford and Wilcox is complex (Brown and Swanson 2003). With only 8.5% of the population age 25 and older in Bedford County being college educated in 2000, and only 10.5% in Wilcox County,[14] it was proving extremely difficult to successfully attract companies that could offer good jobs on favorable terms. To do so, Bedford County commissioner Don lamented, they had to engage in ruthless "incentives games" simply to "survive":

Don: Survival is my top objective. In Bedford County or rural eastern North Carolina, rural areas throughout the country are losing jobs. We've lost jobs, we think, to NAFTA. We've lost jobs to the tobacco industry. Farm employment is dropping. Now young people leave Bedford County and most do not return for lack of opportunities. I see a decay in way of life in Bedford County, and I wish we could reverse it. We've been extremely aggressive on trying to recruit industry to Bedford County. The incentives games that we have to play to bring in jobs. To bring in jobs anywhere, but particularly to rural areas. I call it corporate welfare, and it's next to criminal. Industries basically want governments to build 'em new plants and hold jobs to competition in various towns and counties and states. It's pure bribery. Extortion.

In such competitive situations, even the ultimate benefits of bringing in light manufacturing jobs remain unclear to these officials, just as they do to many frustrated rural midwesterners who describe their new jobs in electronic and plastic automobile component production as "low-paying" (Millard and Chapa 2004: 143–45). Unfortunately, if rural areas are to succeed in their dual goals of attracting higher-paying and less strenuous jobs and educating and training their local workforces (including Hispanic newcomers), they will need a lot more external resources to do so. Even though Bedford County officials decided against construction of a large pork processing plant in the 1980s in the hopes of attracting better jobs instead, continued population decline and higher unemployment, poverty, and economic polarization compared to Wilcox County attest to currently unrealized dreams.[15]

Summary

Opportunity for advancement in the contemporary food processing industry is clearly stratified. As Gabriel, a grade-school-educated and unauthorized immigrant from Chiapas, Mexico, explained, although "there are some [Hispanic] people who have overcome a lot, people who have moved up at work, and who have stayed here and moved ahead," there are also "others who haven't." A large body of research shows that, more often than not, the latter group of workers has low educational and weak English language ability, does not have U.S. citizenship or legal status, and toils in the most difficult and least well paid jobs at the bottom of the industry. Nonetheless, in the mid-2000s even these lower-status Hispanic respondents expressed a relatively hopeful vision about their jobs and futures. Importantly, they did not consider the food processing industry to have condemned them to bad jobs and lives of permanent poverty. Almost uniformly, they agreed that acquisition of greater human capital can still lead to internal advancement in PPP, and furthermore, that personal ambition and willingness to put forth effort can help compensate for the major mobility impediments regarding human capital and legal status. They also expressed appreciation for the modicum of economic stability afforded by available, full-time food processing work, and they saw opportunities for their children to get a good education and acquire better jobs outside the industry in the future.

Thus, even though Hispanic newcomers were clearly not on the verge of achieving rapid incorporation into the economic mainstream by starting out in low-wage food processing jobs—at least not if that mainstream is defined in traditional middle-class terms—neither was the new rural southern economy destining them to the ranks of an excluded and jobless rainbow underclass along the lines hypothesized in the central cities of traditional immigrant gateways (Gans 1992; Portes and Rumbaut 2001; Portes and Zhou 1993; Zhou 1999). Rather, in the mid-2000s the food processing industry was affording many Hispanic newcomers limited yet much-needed economic stability, which, combined with several other positive aspects of rural life (cited most strongly by lower-status newcomers of rural origin themselves; see Chapter 1), was helping them set the stage for their children's upward incorporation into a distinct sort of rural working class.

This point bears emphasizing. Both lateral and short-distance mobility into the American working class are empirically distinct from downward mobility into a disadvantaged underclass, and neither categorically precludes the potential for long-term upward mobility into the American middle class over time or generations (Alba and Nee 2003; Waldinger and Felicano 2004; Waldinger, Lim, and Cort 2007). In addition, that many mainstream natives in eastern North Carolina also have relatively little education, have an appreciation for rural lifestyles and occupations, and are also feeling the brunt of industrial restructuring and downsizing (to the point that several were coming back into food processing in 2003–04) demonstrates how Hispanic newcomers' short-distance mobility in food processing is, at least in some ways, facilitating rather than impeding their entry into the economic mainstream compared to what would be the case in traditional gateways. To complete Steve Striffler's seminal quote, "Poultry processing is a tough way to achieve upward mobility, *but that is precisely what these jobs represent for most immigrants*" (2005b: 155–56; my emphasis).

If anything, my research uncovered that Hispanic newcomers' successful economic incorporation is most seriously hindered not by the internal opportunity structure within PPP but rather by contraction of opportunity at the bottom of the American labor market more generally and by unauthorized legal status. Regarding the former, downsizing and restructuring have reduced the opportunity for participation and mobility in the old rural southern economy, for natives and newcomers alike. As Guatemalan immigrant María explained, when her Mexican immigrant husband "first came here there were a lot of jobs to enter in the companies and factories and everything. But now, work is more scarce. There's not much work." Second, compounding this contraction of opportunity are increasingly stringent requirements enacted by local routine manufacturing and textile factories against the hiring of unauthorized immigrant workers, especially after the September 11, 2001, terrorist attacks. When I interviewed him in Bedford in 2004, for instance, Mauro, an unauthorized immigrant who migrated to Bedford County from Guatemala City in 1999, after working on the agricultural circuit in Florida, had recently been laid off from two routine manufacturing jobs for not having a valid social security number; further, his applications for jobs in other local factories (which he was determined to complete without using false papers) were going nowhere.

Even in the expanding food processing industry in Wilcox County, increasingly restrictive government laws against hiring unauthorized immigrants posed a grave threat to the livelihood of many Hispanic newcomers. Unauthorized status limited the ability for many of them to move up and out of the industry into better jobs (as Asian contract workers could do after acquiring their green card). It also subjected whatever economic stability they had managed to attain thus far to the constant threat of immediate repeal; they knew that at any moment they could be fired from their job and lose all of their accrued earnings and benefits.[16] In several notable cases, their unauthorized status even obstructed some supervisors' efforts to keep them employed or grant them a promotion.

What happens to these unauthorized Hispanic newcomers after they get laid off from a job? Government strategies of interior enforcement in the workplace are carried out with the goal of giving unauthorized immigrants an incentive to return to their sending country. Some unauthorized immigrants may indeed return home, but my research uncovered that most have instead stayed put, moving back into "worse" agriculture, agribusiness, or low-level service jobs (especially in domestic and janitorial service),[17] often with the assistance of false documents they can easily purchase in a well-organized and expanding black market. Others, like Mauro, have remained persistently unemployed, especially if they wanted to "do the right thing" and find nonagricultural work without using false papers. Almost all have seen their opportunities to achieve economic stability and upward mobility shrink, although the more fortunate among them have been able to use social networks to land a job in Wilcox County's larger immigrant entrepreneurial sector.

This calculus was not lost among the unauthorized Hispanic newcomers still employed in food processing in the mid-2000s. In fact, some continued working in PPP, despite their unauthorized status directly prohibiting them from earning the full value of their weekly paycheck.[18] Many had bought what they called "hot papers" (an unknown person's social security number) to satisfy the plant's requirement of showing sufficient documentation to gain employment. However, buying such a number is extremely risky; it cost approximately $1,000 in 2003–04, and the buyer could only hope that it would turn out to be good. In many cases it did not, and the owner would grudgingly watch as a portion of his or her paycheck was automatically deducted every week to cover child support payments owed to the U.S. government by the American citizen to whom the hot social security number truly belonged. Other more serious cases also existed, as when a Hispanic newcomer in Bedford County was arrested a week after he began working in a local textile mill because his hot social security number was linked to an American citizen with a felony conviction. In 2003, this Hispanic newcomer was reported to be housed in the Bedford County jail, at a cost of about $40,000 per year to American taxpayers, too scared to tell local law enforcement officers that the social security number is not truly his (fieldnotes, informal conversation with Marco after Hispanic Assistance Council meeting, Dec. 3, 2003).

In these ways, the structure of the contemporary low-wage food processing industry may have indeed made it more difficult to achieve upward mobility than was the case several decades ago. Yet unauthorized status—which has been intentionally produced by American immigration law and border enforcement policies over the course of the twentieth century (Cornelius 2009; Cornelius and Lewis 2007; De Genova 2005; Hincapié 2009; Massey, Durand, and Malone 2002; Ngai 2004) and exacerbated by recent increases in interior enforcement (Hincapié 2009; Massey and Sánchez 2010; Terrazas 2008)—has the power to eradicate an even more basic measure of immigrants' economic incorporation: mere participation in the labor force.[19] Going another step further, unauthorized status also presents the greatest barrier to the prospects for Hispanic newcomers' children to find upward mobility. Across my interviews, respondents reported that Hispanic youths "do not want to work" in agriculture or food processing in the future. Even though respondents were generally optimistic that most of these youths will acquire the education and English language skills to progress on to better jobs (Allegro 2008; Morando 2009; Silver 2009), they did worry about the prospects of generation 1.5 unauthorized Hispanic youths, who were brought to the United States by their parents at a young age and whose access to higher education and employment is formally restricted by the government.[20] According to key respondents in both counties' educational systems (including Armando, a naturalized citizen originally from Monterrey, Mexico), some unauthorized young people are already frustrated with their inability to acquire higher education or find good employment opportunities, and several are considering gang activity or the illicit drug market instead:

Armando: I think that if they would give Hispanics an opportunity to be able to go to college, regardless of their [legal] status, it would just make it so much better. Because it's so easy to point the finger at drugs or drug dealers, and most of the time, you see them being Hispanics or blacks. And lately, here, it's been Hispanics. You know, you open up the paper, and they're selling this, selling the other, selling drugs, dealing drugs or whatever. And I know that I've heard a lot of people comment on guys or girls who they know that are not able to go to school because they are not legal, and they have just turned themselves into the easy money. As far as being able to make a living, they don't want to go work in poultry plants, they don't want to go work in hatcheries, or whatever other kind of job they're able to do. Because I guess they figure that they can make more money that way, with drugs. But I think that if, if they were given the chance to be able to go to school, I think then we wouldn't have such a big dropout rate.

Armando's concern highlights the still serious potential for restrictive government policies against hiring unauthorized immigrants to curtail not only the trajectories of adult Hispanic newcomers—by directly cutting them off from participation in the American labor force, or by indirectly encouraging them to refrain from displaying more ambition than what they need to show in order to move up—but also the ability of unauthorized Hispanic young people to build on their parents' limited economic stability and short-distance mobility to achieve even longer-distance mobility.[21] Without sufficient opportunity to pursue higher education or economic opportunity outside the food processing industry, these unauthorized youths are the most at risk for becoming downwardly mobile should they become frustrated with their situation of collective disadvantage (Gans 1992) at the same time as the "ambiguous role of time" brings about what Portes and Rumbaut (2006) call "a progressive weakening" of their original immigrant drive to succeed (282). One early analysis of second-generation Hispanic youths elsewhere in rural North Carolina finds little support for dire predictions of downward mobility, arguing that the safety, absence of inner-city gangs and street violence, and strong social networks characteristic of rural and small-town new destinations facilitate upward educational mobility even among those youths who lack legal status (Silver 2009). However, the same study offers an important cautionary tale, showing that North Carolina's post-2008 policy of barring

unauthorized youths from enrolling in degree-seeking programs in its community college system—something I discuss further in Chapter 6—has had an
immediate blocking effect on this positive trend. In other words, even though
the new rural southern economic context of reception shapes Hispanic newcomers' opportunities for economic incorporation and mobility in several
positive ways, restrictive government policies are powerfully offsetting them
for the worse.

The Look and Feel of Eastern North Carolina in the Mid-2000s

The "new" rural southern economic landscape, dotted by chicken and turkey feathers, taken from a rural public highway in Wilcox County (a pseudonym).

The "old" rural southern economic landscape, with the tobacco harvest, taken from a rural public highway near Bedford County (a pseudonym).

Helpful linguistic accommodations made by personnel at a Wilcox County public middle school for the parents of its Hispanic students, taken from the school's main driveway.

Hispanic elementary schoolchildren being included in an important public event— the annual Christmas parade—in Bedford in 2003.

Hispanic Entrepreneurship

Hispanic newcomer family standing proudly in front of their restaurant (now closed), taken from the parking lot of the local mall in my hometown of Tarboro, North Carolina (not a pseudonym).

"Latino Park" Road, taken from a rural public highway near Wilcox County. This photo illustrates how Hispanic newcomers are sometimes able to name their own neighborhoods, trailer parks, or streets in eastern North Carolina, since rural areas often have less strict zoning laws than do densely populated cities.

Hispanic youths vying to carry the American flag in the "Parade of Nations," held during the First Annual *La Raza* Festival at a public park in Wilcox County in 2003.

Hispanic child watching a native white family hesitantly trying tacos and gorditas for the first time during the First Annual *La Raza* Festival, held at a public park in Wilcox County in 2003. This photo marvelously captures the mutual ambivalence that often characterized white-Hispanic relations in the mid-2000s, as rural white natives and Hispanic newcomers began to come into contact, get to know one another, and make initial attempts to cross the boundaries that divided them.

(Disclaimer: no one pictured in any of these photographs was an interview subject or informal contact in my research.)

III

Race and Citizenship

4

"The Blacks Don't Like Us, and It's Worse Than with the Whites"

Class Structure, Black Population Size, and the Threat of Social Leapfrogging

WHEN I MET JUAN, a 22-year-old immigrant from Guadalajara, Mexico, in 2003, he had been living in North Carolina for four years. As was true for many Mexicans who crossed the U.S.-Mexico land border illegally in the late 1990s and early 2000s, new U.S. policies of border militarization had deterred Juan from attempting to cross over one of its more heavily policed sections in southern California (Cornelius 2001; Cornelius and Lewis 2007; Durand, Massey, and Capoferro 2005; Massey and Capoferro 2008; Massey, Durand, and Malone 2002; Orrenius 2004). Instead, in the spring of 1999 Juan took a bus up from Guadalajara to San Luís Rio Colorado in the Mexican border state of Sonoma, where he paid a professional smuggler (*pollero* in Spanish) $1,000 to help him cross the border through a more remote section of Arizona.[1] The *pollero* led Juan and a group of approximately 30 other migrants through the desert, where they were caught by INS officials on the fifth day of their journey and returned to Mexico. They set out again the next night, only to meet the same fate, but on their third attempt, most were able to get away from INS officials and escape into the arid desert night.[2] Unfortunately, they also got lost from their *pollero*, who was "the only one who knew his way," and so they spent the rest of the week walking alone through the dangerous terrain. According to Juan, some in the group never made it; they died along the way because of the heat or "losing their feet in the sandholes" or wild snakes.[3]

But Juan was lucky. Seventeen days after his initial departure from Guadalajara, a friend picked him up in Arizona and drove him by van to Wilcox County, eastern North Carolina, where several of Juan's immediate and extended family members lived in a trailer, and where several more would join them by 2003.

Because Juan had stopped going to school in Mexico in the ninth grade in order to work to support himself and his grandmother, he initially took low-skilled jobs on the chicken line in Poultry Processing Limited and on the night shift in a nearby poultry farm (see Chapter 2). Although both jobs were "terrible," they helped him pay off the additional $500 debt he had accrued to his *pollero* for the false social security number that allowed him to find work in the United States. Also, by 2003 Juan had studied for and received his GED through an agricultural worker program offered in Raleigh, taken several adult math and ESL classes in Wilcox and neighboring Union and Van Buren Counties in order to "move ahead more," started working as a self-employed retail salesman, and even enrolled in the Hispanic Leadership Course offered by Wilcox Community College in the fall. In other words, Juan was solidly working-class and upwardly mobile (he even built his grandmother a house in Guadalajara and was still sending her approximately $100 a month). He had also "gotten more involved in everything" and "made more decisions about what it is that I am going to do" now that he had decided to stay in Wilcox County for "all of my life." In 2003, for instance, Juan was busy collecting signatures to request that the Wilcox County Community College begin offering a series of tiered ESL courses, so that Hispanics who complete beginner-level classes might finally have the option to take more advanced ones (Gozdziak and Bump 2008).

Juan credited his new civic-minded activity to two things: first, the fact that he has always read a lot, and second, that he recently joined a church, where he met Armando, a naturalized citizen from Monterrey who invited him to join the Association of Mexicans in Wilcox County, which in turn exposed him to the Hispanic Leadership Course. "Basically," Juan told me,

> my biggest goal is to get more involved with the Hispanic community and to do more to inform them so that they know that they can do it. Know that they can arrive here and go to some meeting, even with the town mayor, and tell him what they want here. Most Hispanics don't know that they can become a part of helping the authorities know what problems Hispanics are having. Like, by law the community college has to [offer ESL classes] if the people request them. So I want Hispanics to know that. That it's a decision that's up to them, if they want to learn.

Because Juan was a low-skilled Hispanic newcomer who had started off working in the food processing industry, an emergent local Hispanic entrepreneur and political leader, and a resident of the heavily African American western part of Wilcox County all in one, I was curious to know how he would characterize intergroup relations among Hispanic newcomers, whites, and blacks there. On the one hand, he reported that Hispanics have more interests in common than in opposition with blacks, primarily because "whites have more money and better jobs" than do blacks and Hispanics, who are more likely to be found working the night shift and to be mistreated in shops or car dealerships for "not having good credit." As Juan went on to explain, "The majority of black people that I know, it's like they know what it is to be discriminated against" and so "they don't bother us Hispanics." Importantly, Juan's perception that Hispanic newcomers share interests in common with blacks was buttressed by his participation in the Hispanic Leadership Course. Several African American community leaders had been instrumental in extending this eight-week leadership training course, organized by the Wilcox County Center for Leadership Development (a pseudonym) and offered through the Wilcox County Community College, outward from its original focus on the underrepresented African American population to the growing Hispanic population. Juan appreciated their support.

On the other hand, he also reported that whites "like Hispanics more" than blacks like Hispanics. In fact, he could only think of one African American person he had ever considered to be a good friend, and even this man eventually "run me out of my job" because of anger that Hispanics don't pay income taxes. Juan thought that this fiscal misperception is stronger among blacks than whites, and moreover that it arises from a combination of blacks' "lack of information" and "error":

Juan: Blacks have that foolish idea that we Hispanics don't pay taxes. We pay taxes whenever we buy gasoline and on everything that we buy here. My friend was referring to us not paying taxes on our paychecks, but they take our income taxes out of our paychecks. It's doesn't matter if we have a good or bad social security number, they take out taxes from it either way! So I don't know, but almost all blacks have that idea that we don't pay taxes.

In the meantime, Juan reported that as good workers, Hispanics are winning over many whites in Wilcox County, primarily as employees and also sometimes as friends. In his words, the rise of Hispanic immigration is threatening to many blacks because whites prefer Hispanic over black workers, which leads "Hispanics to come to do the jobs that the blacks used to do, without necessarily wanting to [replace them]":

Juan: What happens is we win whites over. Hispanics like to work, some out of necessity, others whatever. And so I think white Americans think Hispanics are maybe responsible people who arrive on time to work and who like the work that we do. I know many who say that Hispanics are good workers, in the sense of that they work themselves "to death," very hard. They even like to do extra. And many times whites make that comparison. If a black arrives to work, and the white asks him, "Can you do this?" and the black says, "How much am I going to earn? When am I going to get to leave?" Versus if a Hispanic arrives and says, "What do I do?" [*laughs*] That's the comparison that whites make. They think that blacks take advantage of the rights that they have as a minority a lot, which is something that Hispanics can't do. Because if you pay a black $5.15 per hour, he has the backing of the government, but many Hispanics don't, because they don't have their [immigration] papers. So there is both tension and cooperation between Hispanics and whites. I know that many white Americans prefer Hispanic workers on their farms than black ones. It's just that sometimes they can't hire Hispanics because they are scared that it will bring repercussions from the INS. It's logical that they're in favor of Hispanics, because they make money off them. But I have heard more than once that they don't want to say anything and support those people who want to give Hispanics more voice and vote, because of fear that it might bring repercussions on them.

Interviewer: So you think there would be even more cooperation if it weren't for this fear?

Juan: Yeah, I think so. Around here, the majority of white people I know like how Hispanics work. They like them because they are earning off them.

Over in Bedford County, intergroup relations emerged as similarly mixed. Yet there, the reports of black-Hispanic competition, blacks mistreating Hispanics, and whites preferring Hispanics over blacks were even stronger, despite a few notable counterassertions that blacks and Hispanics have some interests in common. Consider Nina, for example, an immigrant student who migrated from Cali, Colombia, to New Jersey in 1986, became a naturalized citizen in 1994, and then migrated to the county seat of Bedford in 1997 when she received a job offer to teach Spanish and ESL courses in Bedford Middle School. As a middle-class, graduate-educated woman who has since worked with Hispanics in a variety of local educational institutions, nonprofit groups, and medical services agencies, Nina was well positioned to observe their relations with whites and blacks, and to evaluate and interpret the variety of factors she saw to be producing intergroup hostility there.

Nina reported the same thing that Juan did in Wilcox County: that Hispanics have both good and bad relations with both whites and blacks.

Nina: There are people in both communities who don't care and never will. They say, "Well why are you in this country?" "If you are in this country, why don't you learn our language?" And "Why do we have to provide services for you?" They are very negative, very mean. But on the other hand, we have some really positive reactions from both communities, too. There are people who will open their arms to you, and even people who will go out of their way for you. They want to learn a little Spanish, to help, to try our food. And we've even had people who want to go visit our countries.

At the same time, Nina thought that Hispanic newcomers' relations with blacks are more tense than are their relations with whites. She agreed with Juan that a major cause of such tension is blacks' "jealousy" that Hispanics are moving ahead of them socioeconomically—a jealousy she too saw developing in the context of strong economic competition at the bottom of the rural southern labor market, where both groups are disproportionately located. However, Nina went even further than Juan to argue that such competition extends outward from the workplace and into local schools, neighborhoods, and politics, too:

Nina: Children in school start teasing Hispanics and telling them that they don't belong here and that it's not their country. And Hispanic children want to assimilate, so they learn English and they stop speaking Spanish, because they are embarrassed of Spanish, of where they came from. So by the time you hit middle school, Hispanics are only friends with Hispanics, blacks are only friends with blacks, and whites are only friends with whites. It's really sad. And there is a lot of black-Hispanic tension, and I've heard a lot about it. You know, really a lot of it comes from the fact that in the African American culture here you don't have a lot of students getting really high grades. It's not a part of the culture. There's some bad feelings on the part of African American students when Hispanic students start doing very well, which a lot of them already are. . . .
Interviewer: Jealousy, you mean?
Nina: Yes. Like I know one little [Hispanic] girl who was doing really well in school. She was getting 3s and 4s in everything [on her end-of-grade tests]. And she was beaten up by a black student in school. I really do think there is some jealousy. Of African American students feeling that these people are not even from here, they are only recently arrived, they don't even speak the language. And here they are, and doing better only after a little bit of time.

They are doing well. And that's hard on African Americans. And I kind of see the same tension with the adults. You know, a lot of adults say that Hispanics are here to take their jobs and work for less. They say, "They're taking all of our jobs." And it's not really like that, but that's the feeling. The feeling of jealousy of having these people be new, being undocumented, not being from this country, and having their jobs. And so I do see conflict between Hispanics and African Americans. African Americans are not going to do a certain job unless they get paid a certain amount. Like if you pay an African American $10 to do a certain job, you might pay the Hispanic $5 to do a job. Because all Hispanics care about is working, they just want a job. They don't care how much they are getting paid as long as they are getting paid and as long as they can provide for their family. And that creates tension.

Finally, Nina pointed to another problem rooted in what she described as blacks' and Hispanics' mutual tendency to distance from one another. "You know," she told me, "blacks in this community are not really affected by other groups. They don't have a lot of relationships with other groups. And at the same time Hispanics come here to this country and want nothing to do with blacks. We don't want to socialize with them and be part of that world. Even in our own countries, we learn this. We learn we don't want to be a part of their community."

·   ·   ·

What can Juan and Nina's responses tell us about how Hispanic newcomers might become incorporated into, and potentially transform, the heretofore binary rural southern racial hierarchy? Both illustrate that although cooperation and conflict coexist in Hispanic newcomers' relations with whites and blacks, often in ambivalent and contradictory ways (Fraga et al. 2010; B. E. Smith 2009), black-Hispanic tensions frequently outweigh a sense of shared racial solidarity vis-à-vis whites. Together, Juan and Nina highlighted class structure as a central factor influencing such tensions, noting that many low-skilled Hispanics and African Americans vie for jobs, resources, and social status on the bottom rungs of rural southern society, while whites tend to occupy more advantaged positions, especially as the primary employers of both minority groups. Nina also illustrated how black-Hispanic tensions are much stronger and more pervasive in majority-black Bedford County, whereas Juan and other respondents in majority-white Wilcox County were more likely to highlight cooperation as well as conflict.

Going further, we see that both Juan and Nina illustrated how Hispanic newcomers often perceived worse treatment from blacks than from whites. Although neither went so far as to call such mistreatment discrimination, several other Hispanic respondents did. For them, discrimination is not just something racial that nonwhites experience only from whites. It is also something nonracial that all people "from somewhere else," who are easily marked by characteristics such as foreign nativity, lack of English language ability, and even nonwhite or nonblack racial status, experience from both whites and blacks, as the rural South's long-time insiders. And even though many Hispanic newcomers told me they were prepared to experience some of both types of discrimination from whites, they were unprepared for the nonracial discrimination they encountered from blacks. The latter challenged their sense of moral order, in which they thought that hardworking and virtuous Hispanics should be positively—not negatively—distinguished from "lazy" and entitled African Americans, who are often portrayed in American society as having failed to achieve.

Of course, some Hispanic respondents, especially emerging community and political leaders such as Juan and Nina, resisted such an overly simplistic and pernicious distinction. Instead of seeing the main difference between unauthorized Hispanic immigrants and African Americans as revolving around the former's better work ethic or moral superiority, Juan and Nina explained how unauthorized Hispanic immigrants, as "target earners," have a different metric than do blacks for judging their self-worth in the low-wage American labor market—and also, as noncitizens, how they lack African Americans' power to resist what they see as unjust working conditions (Gordon and Lenhardt 2008; B. E. Smith 2006, 2009; Stuesse 2009; Waters 1999). Nonetheless, other Hispanics did internalize what sociologist Robert C. Smith (2006) calls the "immigrant analogy," embracing moral and cultural deficiency as an easy way to explain why so many African Americans around them are still poor, and differentiating and distancing themselves from African Americans in order to fashion a more positive image as upwardly mobile immigrant newcomers deserving of full inclusion and citizenship.

To be sure, Juan and Nina's responses are controversial. But because race and citizenship are critical to the story of new Hispanic immigration in the rural South, in this chapter and the next I address two main patterns that emerged from my research head on. First, despite the rural South being a region well known for its historically intolerant white population, in the mid-2000s Hispanic newcomers reported better interpersonal relations with whites than with blacks, and many also perceived greater discrimination from blacks than from whites, especially in majority-black Bedford County. Second, despite being indebted to

African Americans for providing them with a model with which to resist racial discrimination by whites, many Hispanic newcomers had already begun to distance themselves from blacks and blackness.

My explanation for these patterns stresses the confluence of key structural factors, notably class structure, black population size, citizenship, and the institutional arenas in which groups were interacting. The interaction between race and class structure in the lowland rural South is particularly important. It places Hispanics and blacks in a more competitive situation, at the individual and group levels, than it does Hispanics and whites, which in turn heightens black-Hispanic conflict. Moreover, the interaction of racialized class structure with large black population size in places such as Bedford County further elevates blacks' feelings of socioeconomic (although, interestingly, not necessarily political) threat in the face of what many perceive to be sharp incoming material and symbolic competition, intensifying black-Hispanic tensions in workplaces, neighborhoods, and schools in turn.

At the same time, citizenship also plays a key role, because it creates lines along which Hispanic newcomers perceive blacks as well as whites to be acting as agents of nonracial discrimination against them. Importantly, Hispanic newcomers' perceptions of nonracial discrimination and horizontal exclusion in relation to blacks combine with the two other mechanisms typically identified in the scholarly literature on immigration—immigrant newcomers' own antiblack stereotypes and whites' preference for immigrants over African Americans—to facilitate racial distancing from blacks and blackness. Together, these findings carry important implications for our understanding of how the contours of race relations are changing in the rural South today, and also of how Hispanic newcomers are fitting into, and potentially challenging, the rural southern color line.

Black-Hispanic Conflict: The Importance of Class Structure

The overall picture of intergroup relations and responses to Hispanic newcomers that I uncovered in eastern North Carolina in the mid-2000s, as Juan and Nina illustrated, is mixed. In this sense, it accords with the broader literature on intergroup relations, where studies conducted at the national level and in traditional immigrant gateways uncover both cooperation and conflict among members of all the major American racial and ethnic groups (Bobo and Johnson 2000; Hochschild 2007), including between blacks and Hispanics, among whom relations often appear most hostile.[4]

Even so, Hispanic respondents in Bedford and Wilcox Counties reported better interpersonal relations with whites than with blacks. Alvaro, a formerly unauthorized immigrant from the city of Saltillo in the state of Coahuila, Mexico, who migrated directly to North Carolina in 1990 and then became a legal permanent resident in 1997, aptly expressed many Hispanic respondents' view that whites react to them in more bifurcated ways than do blacks, who react to them more negatively overall:

Alvaro: I would say that 50% of whites, they have a good attitude to the Hispanics. But the other 50%, that's where I would say that it's a bad attitude to the Hispanics. It's like everybody says, there are bad apples and good apples. But at least to me, it's a kind of half and half. I see more white people, Caucasians, doing or trying to do positive things to the Hispanic community versus the African American people. With a better attitude, with a better approach. Whites are being more kind. I can't say [the relationship between Hispanics and blacks] is good. Because my opinion is that a big part of the African American population, they really doesn't [sic] accept the Hispanic community. We are intruders. Just a small part, probably one quarter of the population, they are the ones who realize or can see us as allies.

In fact, Alvaro's view that roughly 75% of the local African American population "really doesn't accept the Hispanic community" is consistent with anecdotal and scholarly reports of black-Hispanic conflict throughout the South, despite some recent improvements in elite-level coalition building since the early 2000s.[5]

Going another step further, many (though certainly not all) Hispanic respondents perceived that Hispanics are discriminated against more by blacks than by whites (see also Griffith 2005; and Rich and Miranda 2005). Here, Alvaro was joined in his perception that blacks "don't accept" and even discriminate against Hispanics by several other respondents, including by Delmira, another formerly unauthorized immigrant from Mexico City who migrated directly to North Carolina in 1989 and then became a legal permanent resident in 2003; and by Ricky, a Mexican American from McAllen, Texas, who followed his father around on the agricultural circuit before settling down in North Carolina in 1996:

Delmira: Blacks still have that "for years we've been discriminated and discriminated against" [mentality]. And sometimes it's the opposite sometimes. They discriminate against Hispanics.

Ricky: Blacks feel threatened. They think that Hispanics going to take something away from them, and they have tendency to treat Hispanics a little bit wrong.

Why Hispanics perceived more negative treatment—which they often interpreted as discrimination—from rural southern blacks than from whites may seem counterintuitive, given the legacy of white-on-nonwhite discrimination in the traditional South, the larger gap separating the material positions of Hispanic newcomers from whites than from blacks in the region,[6] and the relative lack of resources with which rural black southerners can truly discriminate against other groups. Yet one reason is that rural southern blacks and Hispanics have met under more competitive structural conditions than have rural southern whites and Hispanics. This is due to how race and class structure continue to interact in the lowland rural South. In other words, Hispanic newcomers perceived that education and class strongly structure natives' responses to their presence, with better-educated and higher-class natives responding more positively than less-educated and lower-class ones (Fennelly 2008; Hernández-León and Zúñiga 2005; Mindiola, Niemann, and Rodríguez 2002; Vallas and Zimmerman 2007).[7]

By this class-based logic, since blacks in eastern North Carolina are poorer than whites, at the group and individual levels,[8] Hispanic respondents perceived that blacks' reactions to newcomers are more negative, as African Americans respond to greater fears of being displaced or "leapfrogged" by Hispanics, not only economically in low-wage workplaces but also socially in lower-class neighborhoods and public schools. As expressed by Alicia, an immigrant from Santiago, Chile, who migrated directly to Bedford County in 2000 and was currently in the process of naturalizing through her white American husband, class status mediates intergroup relations in such a way that discrimination is perceived to come mostly from black Americans and poor white "rednecks." Although the term *redneck* denotes elements of cultural orientation as well as social class (Cady Hallett, in progress; McDermott, in progress), Alicia nonetheless associated the cold reactions she has received in eastern North Carolina with the lower-class status of many black and white natives. Moreover, as I explore further in Chapter 5, such associations exacerbated her negative judgment of blacks as both the moral ("vulgar") and cultural ("fairly aggressive") inferiors of whites and Hispanics:

Interviewer: Have you ever been discriminated against for being Hispanic or being an immigrant in this country?

Alicia: Yes, I think everyone feels it.

Interviewer: Can you give me an example of this?

Alicia: At the post office. I go to the post office every day. I get the mail every day. And there are a lot of African Americans. [*Whispers quietly*]. And they are, well, fairly aggressive, vulgar. I mean, it's very difficult to say if it's because I'm Hispanic or just because they don't like me. It's very difficult. But because I'm Hispanic, I see it from that point of view. Do you understand? And sometimes here in the office, there are people I know who don't like Hispanics. And I get a feeling from them . . . how would I explain it you? Very cold. And so they think that I am a person who, that Hispanics are people who are worth less. But I also have a conception of them . . . how would I explain it to you? The fact that someone can't treat me or anyone else well, or is vulgar. I think we have to make those people understand that we are not strangers to them. We have to give them the possibility of some time to get to know us.

Interviewer: Does this happen more with white Americans or black Americans?

Alicia: More with black Americans.

Interviewer: How come?

Alicia: Well, and like, with the white people that here you call "rednecks." It's social class that accounts for it.

That Hispanic respondents in both Bedford and Wilcox Counties frequently relied on class structure to portray white-Hispanic socioeconomic relations as more positive than black-Hispanic ones demonstrates how, as other studies of both the rural and urban South have shown (Griffith 2005; Mantero 2008; McClain et al. 2003, 2006, 2007; Rich and Miranda 2005; Studstill and Neito-Studstill 2001), elements of both individual and group-level socioeconomic competition combine to produce black-Hispanic tensions.[9] On an individual level, the broad socioeconomic differences between whites and blacks in these two counties (regardless of their causes) mean that blacks are disproportionately underrepresented as both employers and skilled workers. Consequently, many whites and Hispanics perceive incentives to relate to one another in complementary ways—for example, when white employers want to hire Hispanic workers. By contrast, many blacks and Hispanics perceive incentives to relate in more competitive ways—for example, when they vie to obtain jobs in a region where employers are predominantly white (Alvarado and Jaret 2009; Gordon and Lendhardt 2008; McDermott, in progress; Mohl 2002, 2003, 2009; Stuesse 2009).

A Mexican immigrant in rural Georgia expressed this in less technical terms when he remarked that he had not yet met "a single Latin who works for a black man" (Studstill and Neito-Studstill 2001: 78). Likewise, Eduardo, an unauthorized immigrant who migrated directly to Wilcox County from Quetzaltenango, Guatemala, in 2000, described poor relations between black and Hispanic lineworkers in PPP. Eduardo attributed conflict there to strong perceptions of direct and indirect economic competition over jobs and wages between lower-class black and Hispanic workers. At the same time, as Juan did, Eduardo noted that many higher-status white employers and managers respond more positively to Hispanic lineworkers, primarily out of economic self-interest:

Eduardo: The white American race likes Hispanics a lot. And the black race does not, does not like Hispanics very much.

Interviewer: Why not?

Eduardo: Because they think that we are taking away their jobs.

Interviewer: And how come?

Eduardo: Because they say that because of us, they earn less. And the white American race likes us because we do the work like they want.

Interviewer: So white Americans like Hispanics to do those jobs? And the African Americans are scared that Hispanics are going to do their jobs, or are going to take away their jobs?

Eduardo: Or like, well, they don't like that, because of us, they don't raise their wages.

Interviewer: So you think that the majority of Hispanics have better relations with American whites than with American blacks?

Eduardo: Yes, because they have more communication because whites say, "Do you think that you can do this job?" And so we tell them, "Yes." And blacks say, "No, it's very hard." So because of that, at work white Americans always talk with Hispanics, if it is possible for them to do the work. And Hispanics will, because we like to work. They give us things, and Hispanics are going to do that work. And I think that white Americans always talk to Hispanics.

Even when not singling out specific instances of individual-level socioeconomic competition, Hispanic respondents in both counties perceived that blacks are more likely than whites to perceive Hispanics as a socioeconomic threat to their group as a whole. Significantly, their perceptions were shared by many white and black native respondents. One was Don, a white Bedford County commissioner, who mused, "Oddly, I think there would probably be more tension between blacks and Spanish immigrants than white and Spanish immigrants. And it's just a perception. I tend to feel like many blacks feel like that the immigrants are taking their jobs." Others are Tyrone and Quincy, two lower-class African American truck-tractor drivers at Tobacco Farm in Bedford County, who despite not having been displaced from their own jobs still expressed an acute sense of declining African American socioeconomic worth and power relative to Hispanic newcomers there. In fact, when I asked them to describe the political situation of African Americans and Hispanic newcomers in Bedford County, Tyrone and Quincy responded by expressing their concern about how Hispanics are gaining in socioeconomic power over African Americans instead:

Interviewer: Do you feel that African Americans have sufficient political power in your area?

Tyrone: Ah, we ain't got no power left! [*both of them laugh*] Blacks ain't got no power left. We just make it by. Especially on this farm anyhow, we just make it. Like I said, like I said, you know, it's all about the white person here. Whites going to take over this farm here. The black ain't gonna have no chance over here. The white and the Mexican. They going to take over, 'cause it's hard on the black on the farm, like I said.

Interviewer: And what about Hispanics? Do you feel that Hispanics or immigrants have sufficient political power?

Quincy: They doin' all right [economically]. From what I seen doin' all right.

Tyrone: After a while we get enough Spanish down here, they gonna run the white out! [*laughs*] I really believe that. They gonna run the white out. They get enough of 'em over here, they gonna try to run 'em out. After a while this place might end up turnin' to Mexico. Gonna have 'em all down, family and all of 'em. But they good people, but they come down every year, you know, come down every year and work and get dream cars and stuff.

Such interpretations, where respondents focused heavily on job competition between Hispanics and African Americans at the lower end of the employment structure, are compounded by others, where respondents focused more on emerging social tensions in neighborhoods and schools. The latter demonstrate respondents' recognition that Hispanic newcomers might be displacing or leapfrogging blacks in a larger social (and not just economic) sense. In other words, regardless of whether or not Hispanic newcomers are actually threatening the individual economic positions of blacks in eastern North Carolina—a question that is hotly disputed in traditional[10] and other new immigrant destinations alike[11]—the symbolic threat that Hispanic newcomers pose is indeed greatest for blacks; this is due to their more disadvantaged position in the local class structure. Rich and Miranda (2005) concur, pointing out that the threat posed by Hispanic newcomers to blacks and working-class whites in Lexington, Kentucky, is largely noneconomic, involving concern over the potential loss of territorial and cultural space, not just concern over jobs and wages (Dunn, Aragonés, and Shivers 2005; Erwin 2003; Hernández-León and Zúñiga 2005; H. A. Smith 2008; Weeks, Weeks, and Weeks 2007).

To illustrate, in the mid-2000s black-Hispanic tensions in eastern North Carolina were evident not just in several industrial and occupational sectors, where Hispanic newcomers had begun working in jobs that either tradition-ally hired (agriculture and food processing) or traditionally excluded African Americans (construction and some manufacturing sectors). Black-Hispanic tensions were even worse *outside* local workplaces, especially in several formerly black neighborhoods and trailer parks where Hispanic newcomers had recently moved in or established small businesses, and in local public schools (especially middle schools). Quincy illustrated these underlying social tensions when he explained how white rental agents now prefer Hispanic over African American tenants in local trailer parks, to the point that some African American tenants have even been told that they must "pay the bills" or they "got to go":

Quincy: I think we got a real population though, it's Hispanics now. Years ago we didn't even see none of 'em, but now, boy, they're everywhere! We got housing developments now, where it used to be blacks. Now it ain't nothing but Mexicans.

Interviewer: You mean like whole neighborhoods?

Quincy: Trailer houses, trailer parks. I betcha there ain't three or four of colored ones [i.e., African American families] left out in the park. All of 'em are Hispan-ics. The park up there in Bedford, that one's full of Hispanics. There's a bunch of 'em everywhere. 'Cause whites would rather have Hispanics in there than African Americans, 'cause Hispanics pay 'em.

Interviewer: So what happened to the black people who used to live there?

Quincy: They had to go. Whites said they don't pay the bills like Hispanics do. They tell you that you got to go, be a certain time to go.

Even in several elementary schools, some Hispanic students were making such rapid academic progress that local teachers and administrators had begun to wonder why African American students—their historical minority group—are not keeping pace.[12] Vice principal Randy described a strong degree of re-sentment among African American teachers and administrators at Bedford Elementary School, in response to their feelings that Hispanic youths might be displacing or leapfrogging African American students in terms of educational progress (see also Wainer 2004):

Randy: We are aware that a number of our Hispanic children do well on their coursework, as well as their end-of-grade tests. Only in conversations with black colleagues and community members, they're feeling . . . I'm not sure what the feeling is. They're feeling threatened. They're feeling some anger. Resentment. But I don't know that they themselves can put their finger on why. I don't know that they have really thought through and analyzed. But they do know these people who they consider as foreigners have come in, and are now being successful in their school system, where a lot of their people are not being as successful. So there is a resentment there. I mean, you know, you can look at our test scores, and we can point out where some of our Hispanic children have been and where they are now, and how they are becoming more and more successful.

All of these quotes show how the structural conditions affecting Hispanic newcomers and blacks in the lowland rural South create a context where Hispanics' interpersonal relations with blacks are more heavily shaped by symbolic, even if not actual, socioeconomic competition (Dunn, Aragonés, and Shivers 2005; McClain 2006; McClain et al. 2007; McDermott, in progress; Rich and Miranda 2005; Stuesse 2009). Agreeing with Hernández-León and Zúñiga's argument (2005) that interethnic interactions in the American South do not develop separately from class relations, Hispanic and white respondents alike singled out African Americans' lower-class status relative to that of whites as a primary reason blacks are responding more poorly to Hispanics, not only in local workplaces but also outside them.

Importantly, in such competitive situations the negative tensions between minority groups carry great potential for misinterpretation as group rejection (Rockquemore 2002) or even as discrimination (Kasinitz et al. 2008; Waters 1999). Such is the case for Eduardo, the unauthorized Guatemalan respondent quoted earlier, who told me that this thing "you could even call racism, right?" makes him feel "humiliated" and "made fun of" by some blacks. In fact, black-Hispanic socioeconomic tensions were such a serious concern in the mid-2000s that several employers and employees at a local milling company where I almost conducted some of my workplace interviews laughed at me when I told them I was interested in investigating black-Hispanic relations there. They reported that there was "nothing but bad blood" between the two groups and suggested that "investigating part of the issue of Hispanics becoming the more prominent minority group [over blacks] might be interesting for me to do" instead (fieldnotes, June 23, 2003).

In these ways, to fully understand black-Hispanic tensions in the rural South we must understand not only African Americans' and Hispanic newcomers' objective economic deprivation. We must also understand African Americans' subjective sense of diminishing economic and social status vis-à-vis Hispanic newcomers (Gay 2006; Oliver and Wong 2003) and how this violates African Americans' historically developed judgment about how they, and not Hispanic newcomers, should be "next in line" to experience the upward socioeconomic mobility that 150 years of formal American citizenship has promised but not yet delivered (Gordon and Lenhardt 2008).[13]

Perhaps the clearest example of this perceived threat to African Americans' socioeconomic standing can been seen in a question posed by an African American businesswoman to Alexandria County Democratic congressional candidates in Archer Bluff in 2004: "She asked directly—even bluntly—what black constituents could expect for their votes from the candidates as a quid pro quo, in terms of economic development, reparations for slavery, and the effects of Latino immigration on the standard of living for blacks in the district" (*Archer Bluff Times* [a pseudonym], June 13, 2004). As this woman made clear, many African American residents of Bedford and Alexandria Counties were concerned about their "declining standard of living," and some were even drawing a connection between rising Hispanic immigration and the stagnation in African Americans' larger struggle for socioeconomic justice.

Black-Hispanic Conflict: The Compounding Roles of Black Population Size and Institutional Arena

As shown in the Introduction, Bedford and Wilcox Counties lie in the same generally impoverished eastern region of North Carolina and host African American populations large enough to be characteristic of the racially divided rural South. Still, one of the central differences between them is that the proportion of Hispanics in majority-black Bedford County (only 3% in the 2000 U.S. Census) remains far lower than the very high proportion of African Americans there (58% in the 2000 U.S. Census), while the proportion of Hispanics in majority-white Wilcox County (15% in the 2000 U.S. Census) is much closer to that county's smaller African American population (29% in the 2000 U.S. Census). Considering how the rural South's racialized class structure intensifies black-Hispanic tensions in both counties, I wondered how black population size might further shape the contours of Hispanic newcomers' interactions with natives across both counties.

Black Population Size and Socioeconomic Threat

I quickly discovered that black-Hispanic socioeconomic relations were more tense in majority-black Bedford County than in majority-white Wilcox County. Reports of black-Hispanic tensions in Bedford were stronger and more prevalent than in Wilcox. As mentioned, they were also disconcerting in the arenas where they were cited most frequently: lower-class neighborhoods (mostly local trailer parks) and public schools (mostly middle schools). To illustrate, although several white and Hispanic respondents in both counties expressed common negative stereotypes of African Americans as loud, violent, lazy, uneducated, dependent, or lacking in family values, I had a hard time locating any descriptions of black-Hispanic tensions in Wilcox County that could rival those I heard in Bedford County. Like Juan, most respondents in Wilcox County identified cooperation as well as conflict. Or, like Josefa, an unauthorized immigrant who migrated directly to Wilcox County from San Salvador, El Salvador, to reunite with her husband in PPP, they discussed intergroup relations in more muted and neutral terms:

Interviewer: In general, how would you describe the relations between Hispanics and American whites?

Josefa: Well, at work we have a daily relationship. When we're not at work, we go to the stores, or we meet someone and we say hello.

Interviewer: In general, how would you describe the relations between Hispanics and American blacks?

Josefa: There isn't any problem between the two races.

Interviewer: Do you think that having more Hispanics or immigrants here affects the way blacks think about their race—about what it means to be black here?

Josefa: I think right now it doesn't have anything to do with that. Probably maybe a long time ago, in the time of slavery. But right now, I don't think there is any problem.

Similarly, even though some schoolteachers and administrators in Wilcox County expressed concern about the balance between Hispanic and black students' educational progress at the elementary school level, their concerns were less heated than those of Bedford educational officials during the time of my research.

To probe this difference further, I began asking Wilcox County respondents who did not note much black-Hispanic conflict in the eastern part of the county (which is heavily white and Mexican) or in Weakley Elementary School (which is predominantly white and Hispanic) whether they had heard of any in the western part of the county (which is heavily African American and Honduran) or in schools other than Weakley Elementary (where more African American students are enrolled). Still, nothing came close to the extremely negative reports I heard in Bedford County. Even Jaime, a bilingual and North Carolina–born respondent who identified himself as "American of

Spanish origin, Hispanic Caucasian," reported that his eldest daughter had not experienced any conflict with African American students at her predominantly black local high school, even though he had been prepared to confront that when she first enrolled there:

Jaime: The oldest [daughter] is 17 years old. She'll be going to Governor's School
this year. She turned down the N.C. School of Math and Science because she
did not want to leave her high school. She enjoyed it so much there.
Interviewer: Which school is that?
Jaime: Wilcox High School. She loves it there. It's supposed to be one of the worst
high schools in the county as far as blacks and racism and gangs, but she's the
drum major. She's on soccer, she's on volleyball, she's on every committee that
comes through there. She loves it. And her lowest grade that she's ever brought
home was a 94.

Similarly, Eva, an H-1 temporary contract worker from Buenos Aires, Argentina, who taught ESL classes at Wright Elementary School and Wilcox High School before coming to Weakley Elementary, agreed that "it is very different on the other side of Wilcox County," where there are more African Americans and the towns are poorer than those near Weakley Elementary on the eastern side of the county. But even at those two schools, which have more African American students than Weakley Elementary, Eva reported that most conflict "was more between the immigrants," not between African Americans and Hispanics.

These more neutral depictions of black-Hispanic relations in Wilcox County contrasted starkly with decidedly negative reports in Bedford County, including ones regarding African American students harassing and picking on Hispanic students in local middle and high schools and on school buses, "diversity" problems concerning African American schoolteachers not treating their Hispanic students or coworkers well, serious problems concerning robberies committed against Hispanics by African Americans in local trailer parks (to the point where Marco, a prominent bilingual Puerto Rican school employee, had contacted a local Bedford police officer and the Bedford County sheriff about starting a community watch program in one trailer park; fieldnotes, Mar. 3, 2004), and accusations that local African American community groups are not being 100% forthright in their efforts to reach out to Hispanics when and where such efforts are made. There are too many of these negative reports to present here, but two will illustrate the seriousness of black-Hispanic tensions in majority-black Bedford County.

First, Anita is an unauthorized immigrant from the city of Uruapan in Michoacán, Mexico. In 1996 she crossed the U.S.-Mexico land border illegally on her way up to Riverside, California, to reunite with her husband. A year later she accompanied him to Bedford County, when a friend told them "there was work" available in North Carolina. Anita expressed the perception, shared by many Hispanic respondents in Bedford County, that either they or their children are more discriminated against by blacks than by whites:

Anita: There's another case, too, with my oldest daughter. When she goes to Bedford Middle School, she wears her gold necklace. She said that some of the black students pick on her a lot, and they even tried to grab her necklace to try and take it off her. And she spent a couple of days scared. And her father told her, "Just ignore them, because if they go to school and don't show respect for other people, well, you can't do anything about it. And sometimes it's not worth worrying about it, if they can't hold themselves back. But if they demand it from you, then there will be problems." And honestly that's what you have to do.

Interviewer: And how do we find a solution for this conflict between blacks and Hispanics?

Anita: Well, it's difficult because you're always hoping that your children leave and come home OK. When it's time for my daughter to come home and she hasn't come home, I worry. It's not because I want something to happen, it's because with those [black] boys you never know what can happen [and so] you try to protect your children. Because you are conscious that the blacks are people who sometimes don't hold themselves back or don't think about what they are going to do, even among themselves.

This quote shows how Anita felt distant from and fearful of blacks because of specific negative interactions that her children have had with their African American peers in Bedford Middle School. Such competitive encounters in turn intensified her antiblack stereotyping, as she, her husband, and her children now talked openly about African American men as "disrespectful," "unrestrained," and "dangerous."

Second, Elisa is a naturalized citizen from Tamaulipas, Mexico, who worked as a Migrant Education Program recruiter and parent facilitator in the Bedford County public school system. In her interview, Elisa expressed frustration with her African American colleagues, whom she and several other white and Hispanic educational officials also criticized for not treating Hispanic staff and students well. For instance, Elisa felt that her African American colleagues do not adequately assist her in attempts to provide support to disadvantaged Hispanic students or to collect donations for needy Hispanic migrant workers. Likewise, she thought they do not adequately include Hispanics as equal partners in planned community events. In fact, she recalled once even having to confront an African American school bus driver upon finding out he had not intervened when several male African American students touched a female Hispanic student inappropriately on the bus. But her experience encountering multiple forms of resistance to her action—from the African American bus driver as well as from other African American school personnel, including the then principal of Bedford Middle School—has reinforced Elisa's feeling that Hispanics are more discriminated against by blacks than whites. Moreover, it has led her to think that black school personnel tend to "side with their own group" rather than support and protect Hispanic youths in need:

Elisa: And I did talk to the bus driver, because the bus driver had laughed when the guys handled the girl. Like, you know, what do you do? Do you take it to the principal? Who's probably going to side with his group? The black students. The principal and the staff in the school, and the counselor, they're black. And the kids that were doing this to her, they were black. So I told the principal, "I'm just doing what I'm supposed to be doing. Letting Hispanics know that I'm here for them even though they do not know English." And I wasn't afraid.

Perhaps what is most interesting about Elisa's frustration with African Americans is that elsewhere in her interview she also noted commonalities between the experiences of contemporary Hispanic migrant farmworkers and past African American field slaves:

Elisa: I was watching this program on the TV last night. I fell asleep on it. But it was about a lot of slaves, how they used to be maybe like 50, 75 years ago. It reminded me of what the migrants are going through now.
Interviewer: How so?
Elisa: How the slaves used to be in the fields and exploited. And they were talking about how farmers would buy this black guy and say, "This is what's expected of you. You either do what I expect of you to do or leave." And it's just like with the [Hispanic agricultural] crew leader today. You know, they bring the people in here and say, "This is what's expected of you, and if you don't like it . . ." You know? I don't think that they treat 'em that well.
Interviewer: So there are some similarities that are important? Maybe some lessons to be learned?

Elisa: Oh yes, yes. They used to live, like a lot of the slaves, working in the fields.
And were expected to do it for very little pay. And it's because of how they
were bonded, or how you met when your crew leader came and brought you.

Thus, as a Hispanic closely tied to the plight of migrant workers in North
Carolina, although Elisa demonstrated some potential to develop a sense of
racial solidarity, or "linked fate" (Dawson 1994; Kaufmann 2003), with African
Americans on the basis of common experiences of nonwhite racial minority
status and exploitation vis-à-vis whites, her other negative personal experiences
with African Americans have so far mitigated against this. In fact, she hoped
that Hispanics will not "carry resentment to the next generation" as she thought
many African Americans now do, when they target Hispanic newcomers for
taking their jobs. Finally, Elisa was skeptical that black school and community
leaders truly want to include Hispanic newcomers as equal partners in planned
community events, even though, in her view, they have tried to make it look as
if they want to:

Elisa: And also, once over in Broward, I was invited to come speak at a gathering
that they were holding. They wanted the black and the Hispanic communities
to be there. But I don't know, I guess they had canceled the gathering at the last
minute. But they didn't tell me! So I showed up, and nobody was there. And
then I guess they also rescheduled the gathering for the next week. But they
didn't tell me about that either! They went out of their way not to tell [me]
they had canceled one meeting and rescheduled another. So I felt like they
didn't really want us there. I had wanted to bring some of the Hispanic community, to get them to show up. I even took pictures. I always have my camera
on me, you know to take my pictures everywhere, and I took some pictures of
everything here and there. Just to show, you know, that I didn't forget about
it and that I really did show up. I don't know how the gathering went the next
week, because I didn't know about it, but there were no Hispanics there.

Overall, these more negative depictions of black-Hispanic relations in Bedford County suggest that Bedford's large black population size has intensified
rather than smoothed black-Hispanic socioeconomic conflict, compared to what
is documented in the literature elsewhere. In Bedford County, Hispanic newcomers reported strong tensions with blacks in workplaces, neighborhoods, and
schools, and they attributed them in part to the large number of disenfranchised
blacks feeling threatened by incoming material and symbolic competition. In
fact, Davíd, the immigrant from Medellín, Colombia, whom I introduced in the

beginning of Chapter 2, argued that large populations of African Americans mar Hispanic newcomers' experiences across the South, because "the blacks don't like us, and it's worse than with the whites." Lending additional support to this explanation is the fact that other demographic and structural factors, including local Hispanic population size and local political structure, cannot account for the more negative black-Hispanic relations that I uncovered in Bedford County. African Americans constituted 58% of Bedford County's population in 2000, while Hispanics constituted only 3%, a large gap suggesting that full socioeconomic displacement was still a long way off for blacks in Bedford County in the mid-2000s. Moreover, by demographics alone, we should have found evidence of greater socioeconomic threat among blacks in Wilcox County, where they constituted 29% of the local population and Hispanics were a closer 15%, yet the reverse is the case. Finally, both counties have similar political structures; they operate on a county manager form of government and have a group of six or seven elected county commissioners, each representing one of the county's electoral districts.

Of course, these findings should not be interpreted to mean there are no efforts to build coalitions between blacks and Hispanics in Bedford County, nor that there are no examples of individual-level cooperation between blacks and Hispanics in workplaces, schools, or neighborhoods there. Such efforts are indeed present, but the interaction between racialized class structure and large black population size has produced a situation where black-Hispanic conflict simply outweighs black-Hispanic cooperation, at least for now.

Black Population Size and Political Threat

In contrast, black-Hispanic political relations were less tense in majority-black Bedford County than in majority-white Wilcox County. In the political arena, Bedford County's larger proportion of African Americans afforded them some protection, through strength in numbers, from feelings of heightened political competition and threat from incoming Hispanic newcomers. To illustrate, African Americans in Bedford County were reported by whites, blacks, and Hispanics alike to wield substantial political power at the local level, and as Clarence, Bedford's African American county manager, pointed out, this power rests squarely on their large population size and concentration:

Interviewer: Do you feel that African Americans have sufficient political power in this area?

Clarence: I would have to say yes.

Interviewer: How come?

Clarence: Well, you have African Americans in quite a few leadership roles. One of the things that I've said more than once is that African Americans have not participated in the political process long enough to "know how to play the game." But I think that in this area, with the population of the county being [nearly] 55% African American, that there is a good representation of African Americans. There are some wards and districts that have been great for African Americans' participation in the political process. Before that time, you could look at boards and commissions, and all of their representatives were basically living in one neighborhood or one geographic area. And by splitting everything up into wards and districts, you almost assure yourself of having a diverse group of people being political leaders.

Interviewer: You mentioned that the African American population here is 55%, which is much higher than the national average. Do you think blacks have sufficient political power at the national level?

Clarence: Blacks? No.

Interviewer: So you think it's better for them here?

Clarence: Oh yeah. Yeah.

Interviewer: Do you think that having more Hispanics or immigrants here affects the way that blacks think about their race?

Clarence: No.

Interviewer: Why not?

Clarence: Why not? Because we have not been significantly impacted by Hispanics being here in this county. I mean, the groups of black people I've been around in general don't sit around and talk about or perceive the Hispanic population as being threatening.

The feeling that Hispanics are not yet challenging African Americans' formal political power in Bedford County because they lack similar organization and numbers at the local level, even though Hispanics may be making great political strides at the national level, was also expressed by some white natives, among them Don, the white Bedford County commissioner quoted earlier:

Don: My understanding is that the Spanish community is already the largest minority group in the country. And as I hear political debate and strategies, I hear 'em going after the Latino vote and so forth. So I think certainly on a national level it's a recognized stronghold of potential votes, much more so than, than, as I say here on a local level. And I think when you think of it nationally, they are probably a lot more organized than they are on a local level.

Interviewer: Do you think that African Americans have sufficient political power in this county?

Don: Definitely.

Interviewer: How come?

Don: Well, they have fought for it and they've been successful. In Bedford County, they are a majority in reality. The majority voters in Bedford County are black. They have control of the city council in Archer Bluff, majority control. They have had majority control of the Bedford County commissioners, so they have shown that when they get united behind an issue that they can carry, they will. And they are well represented, I think, although I'm sure some black communities would disagree. They're well represented on all of our elected boards and appointed boards. I think the two communities [white and black] are trying to work together, and certainly their voice is heard strong on every issue. That certainly is not true in the Spanish community.

As both Clarence and Don attested, African Americans' political power in Bedford County was considered relatively secure in the mid-2000s. Consequently, African Americans have engaged in few organized efforts to promote black-Hispanic political cooperation or coalition building, despite more acute black-Hispanic socioeconomic tensions than in Wilcox County, because such efforts have not been considered necessary in terms of numbers yet.

Even the sense that African Americans might someday be displaced or leapfrogged by Hispanics in electoral politics—either because Hispanics might make political progress faster than African Americans did, by drawing on and learning from African Americans' Civil Rights Movement gains, or because Hispanics' more conservative ideologies and more divided partisan attachments might put them up for grabs to both major political parties in a way that those of African Americans currently do not (DeSipio 2006)[14]—was weaker in Bedford than in Wilcox County. In fact, only one political leader respondent—Benjamin, a white Republican who represented part of Wilcox County in the North Carolina House of Representatives—explicitly acknowledged the possibility that Hispanics may become a potent political force at the local level, and therefore that their support will need to be fought for and won competitively at the local level as well:

Interviewer: There is a lot of talk today about Hispanics' population growth— them becoming a bigger group than African Americans.

Benjamin: My understanding is that it already is.

Interviewer: Right, and what that will mean for both conflict and cooperation between African Americans and Hispanics. What do you think about this as it pertains to this county and the population here?

Benjamin: On par, I think Hispanics will have greater influence on local politics, and on statewide politics for that matter, too. The problem as I see it is that African Americans have been such a huge and loyal voting bloc for Democrats that most Republican politicians won't even court them anymore. And you'll probably see these Republican politicians seek out Hispanics, you know, to balance out, and so Hispanics will have more influence that way. So African Americans' power level is going to decrease. I think they'll be isolated to one party, who takes them for granted. In fact, I think they already are.

By contrast, the only political leader respondent in Bedford County who acknowledged a similar possibility—Steven, a white Democrat who represented part of Bedford County in the state House of Representatives—did so primarily at the state level, not the local one:

Steven: Yeah, and I think that's why [Democratic] Governor Easley has really made an effort to put some Hispanics in the state legislature and to try to start looking at their issues. He's been trying to go ahead and have the Democratic Party begin looking at their needs. And I think that's where we will see some potential conflict in the future, when blacks start seeing Hispanics making some inroads faster than they did or have been able to. That's why we need really good leaders from all the groups, to address those issues and make sure that doesn't happen.

Thus, even though some political leaders in both counties were attuned to the possibility that Hispanic newcomers might become a future political force, perhaps so much so that African Americans may feel displaced or leapfrogged by them as they gain in formal political power (Morris and Gimpel 2007), in the mid-2000s this possibility was more imminent at the local level in majority-white Wilcox than it was in majority-black Bedford County. In the latter, although such a possibility was sometimes acknowledged at the national and state levels, it was still perceived as locally remote because of the combination of African Americans' majority status and relatively secure formal political power, as well as Hispanic newcomers' still small population numbers. Put simply, Bedford County political leaders lacked a local demographic incentive to develop formal political coalitions with Hispanic newcomers, and this was perhaps even more the case among its black than white political officials, given African Americans' majority status and political power there.

Another indicator of the difference in how political leaders in the two counties viewed the potential threat of Hispanic newcomers to African Americans' political power is that I observed more instances of formal political black-Hispanic coalition-building efforts at the North Carolina state level (where African Americans constituted 22% of the state population in the 2000 U.S. Census) and in Wilcox County (29%) than in Bedford County (a larger 58% of the county population). For example, at the state level, black-Hispanic coalition building was one of the principal goals of the North Carolina Coalition on Black and Brown Civic Participation, a state-level subsidiary of the National Coalition on Black Civic Participation, formed in 2003 to foster black-brown coalition building and promote long-term voter registration and education projects at the state level (with the goal of networking down to the local level).[15] In Wilcox County, the most visible example of formal, local-level, black-Hispanic coalition building to date was the Wilcox County Center for Leadership Development's use of external grant money to expand the Hispanic Leadership Course outward to the new Hispanic community in Spanish, beginning in 2002 and repeated through 2005. I did not locate any formal efforts of this sort in Bedford County,[16] although Regina, an African American Bedford County commissioner, told me that black-Hispanic coalition building was "on the agenda" at the Bedford County Chapter of the NAACP, where she was also a member (I was unsuccessful in contacting NAACP leaders in Wilcox County).[17]

Thus, even though black-Hispanic relations in both counties are strongly shaped by class structure, they also diverge in interesting ways across the two counties. On the one hand, in the local socioeconomic arena the large presence of African Americans in majority-black Bedford County has intensified black-Hispanic tensions by elevating more African Americans' sense of socioeconomic threat. Perhaps this is because, as Barreto and Sanchez (2009) argue in their analysis of 2006 Latino National Survey data, perceptions of black-Hispanic competition in the South rise in a curvilinear fashion relative to black population size. That is, although Barreto and Sanchez find that Hispanics/Latinos who live in southern counties with almost no black presence perceive little black-Hispanic competition, perceptions of competition rise in medium-density black southern counties before dropping back down again in high-density black ones. At 58% African American, Bedford County may well represent the type of medium-density black southern county where black-Hispanic socioeconomic competition is strongest.

On the other hand, in the local political arena the higher proportion of African Americans in majority-black Bedford County has smoothed black-Hispanic tensions by protecting African Americans from an elevated sense of political threat through strength in numbers. Nonetheless, this political security has led to fewer coalition-building efforts than is the case in Wilcox County, where African American political leaders and civil rights organizations sensed a stronger strategic need to engage proactively in building relationships with Hispanic newcomers. Put differently, African Americans are considered to be socioeconomic and racial minorities in both Bedford and Wilcox Counties, but their majority population size has translated into more formal political power (and therefore less of a political minority status) in Bedford County, and this has in turn depressed blacks' efforts to reach out to Hispanic newcomers there. By contrast, at least some leaders in Wilcox County (notably in the Wilcox County Center for Leadership Development) have begun to envision local Hispanics as a political minority group in a similar position to African Americans.

The situation in Wilcox County resonates with that in Dalton, Georgia, another new immigrant destination, with about 28,000 residents in the 2000 U.S. Census, only 8% of whom were African American. Even though African American responses to Hispanic/Latino newcomers in Dalton have been varied and not always smooth, black and Hispanic leaders have organized meetings to find a common political agenda, including beginning a drive to register new Latinos within the local chapter of the NAACP. According to Hernández-León and Zúñiga (2005), this partially reflects African American leaders' feelings that blacks are at risk of becoming "irrelevant" in the face of massive new Hispanic immigration (267), and consequently, they have started to view "Latino immigration as a way to overcome their marginal status" (267). As in Wilcox County, and in contrast to majority-black Bedford County, small black population size in Dalton seems to have encouraged black-Hispanic coalition building in the political arena for strategic demographic reasons, not just perceptions of shared minority status or linked fate.

At the same time, it is worth noting that several Hispanic political and community leaders in Bedford County were showing signs of frustration over what they perceived to be a lack of attention from black political leaders during the time of my research, even though they were not actively voicing it yet (field-notes, Mar. 3, 2004, informal conversation after a Hispanic Assistance Council meeting). These feelings are significant because, as McClain and Tauber (2001) argue, intergroup political competition often arises "when the size of one group obviates the need to form coalitions with other minority groups" (115). Thus, perhaps black-Hispanic political competition in Bedford County will emerge in the future, after the current period of security because of strength in numbers, as Hispanics become more politically organized and begin to vie for formal political power with the local African American as well as white political establishment. Such a possibility does not seem far-fetched, given what has occurred in other majority-black locales witnessing new immigration, such as Compton, California, where it has taken heated black-Latino conflict to bring to light Latinos' concerns over their absence of representation in local politics and their limited access to institutional resources (Camarillo 2004). And it underscores the need for proactive black-Hispanic coalition-building efforts, even in rural southern new immigrant destinations with large and politically secure African American populations.

Summary

Despite a predominantly mixed picture of intergroup relations, one characterized by both cooperation and conflict with whites and blacks, in the mid-2000s Hispanic newcomers felt more excluded and discriminated against by blacks than by whites. I have begun to explain this pattern by focusing on the interaction of key structural factors, namely class structure, black population size, and the institutional arenas in which groups were interacting. Racialized class structure is a critical feature of the rural southern context of reception shaping Hispanic newcomers' interactions with American natives in the early twenty-first century. By no means does it explain the entirety of black-Hispanic conflict and racial distancing, as I show in the next chapter. Yet it is fundamental because it places Hispanics and blacks in more competitive situations, at both the individual and the group levels, than it does Hispanics and whites. Consequently, Hispanic and white respondents alike noted that rural southern blacks perceive, in academic parlance, greater socioeconomic and symbolic "threat" from Hispanic immigration than do rural southern whites. In response to this threat, these respondents perceived the reactions of African Americans to Hispanic newcomers to be more negative than those of whites, exacerbating black-Hispanic tensions in Bedford and Wilcox Counties.

Furthermore, black population size and institutional arena interact with racialized class structure to shape Hispanic newcomers' interactions with natives. As Morawska (2001) notes, Civil Rights Movement gains have given African Americans a significant "competitive edge in the public and political arena" (61) that they do not enjoy in the low-wage private sector, especially in the rural South, where the black middle class remains weak. By contrast, even unauthorized immigrants in Bedford and Wilcox Counties contrasted their greater ability to work hard with automatic exclusion from electoral political participation. These differential loci of power—greater for African Americans in politics and greater for Hispanic newcomers in the workplace—have made Hispanic newcomers' presence less immediately threatening to blacks' political position (as opposed to socioeconomic position) in both counties. But this is especially the case in Bedford County, where large black population size has created a sense of political power and security unmatched either in Wilcox County's political arena or in either county's economic arena, where blacks continue to occupy the bottom rung of a heavily racialized rural southern labor market. In this way, the interaction of racialized class structure with black population size has elevated black-Hispanic socioeconomic conflict in Bedford County, where a larger number of disenfranchised African Americans have begun to feel their economic standing threatened by the entry of Hispanic newcomers. By contrast, it has generated more political tension—but perhaps also in consequence earlier efforts to promote black-Hispanic coalition building—in Wilcox County, where a smaller number of African Americans have begun to feel threatened with political "irrelevance."

5

"The White Americans Have Always Been Very Friendly"

Discrimination, Racial Expectations, and Moral Hierarchies in the Black-White Binary

IN THIS CHAPTER, I augment my analysis from Chapter 4 with a detailed examination of Hispanic newcomers' multiple interpretations of the meaning of discrimination, expectations about blacks, and racial and ethnic identifications to explain why many perceived greater black-Hispanic than white-Hispanic tension in eastern North Carolina, and why many had also begun to distance themselves from blacks and blackness. Even though the structural factors of class structure, black population size, and institutional arena of interaction go a good way in helping to explain these patterns, they in no way constitute a complete account. Another central factor is citizenship. It creates lines along which Hispanic newcomers perceive blacks as well as whites to be acting as agents of nonracial discrimination against them. Indeed, Hispanic respondents interpreted discrimination predominantly in terms of characteristics associated with their "outsiderness" (particularly noncitizenship), not race or skin color per se, and they were particularly surprised to encounter it from blacks, whereas they had expected some racial and nonracial discrimination from whites. Ultimately, I show that Hispanic newcomers' perceptions of nonracial discrimination and horizontal exclusion in relation to blacks combine with two other important mechanisms typically identified in the scholarly literature on immigration—immigrants' own antiblack stereotypes and whites' preferences for immigrants over African Americans—to facilitate racial distancing from blacks and blackness.

Racial Discrimination and the Minority Group View

There are several reasons to think that Hispanic newcomers might experience discrimination in the traditional South in ways reminiscent of African Ameri-

cans' historical experience, and therefore that they might interact with and identify more closely with African Americans than with whites. Elsewhere in the
United States, researchers have speculated that whites's discrimination against
Hispanics, as "nonwhites," will lead the latter to develop interests and outlooks
more in common with African Americans than whites over time, as Hispanics
start to confront the various barriers to economic, social, and political incorporation that African Americans confronted in the past. This perspective is usually referred to as the "minority group" or "rainbow coalition of color" view,
since common experiences of racial discrimination are envisioned as the basis
on which various groups of nonwhites can unite despite their other internal differences (for concise overviews, see Lee and Bean 2007; and Rogers 2004). In this
view, the growth of a new subordinate group (here, Hispanics) is predicted to
activate threat among the superordinate group (here, whites), such that the latter will begin to react negatively toward the former, as has been African Americans' historical experience relative to whites (Fossett and Kiecolt 1989; Glaser
1994; Key 1984; Taylor 1998).

In the traditional South, especially in its rural areas, such speculations are
compounded by the tenacity of the region's adherence to the racial binary and
its ugly history of racial discrimination and conflict (Saenz 2000). As Duchón
and Murphy (2001) phrase it, we would probably expect immigrants to have
a hard time in the South because "after all, the South has a history of racial
intolerance, xenophobia, and poverty" (2) that might work to keep Hispanic
newcomers on the nonwhite side of the color line, alongside blacks. Such speculations are also supported by similarities between African American and Hispanics' low socioeconomic positions in the region relative to those of whites
and Asians (see Chapter 4). These might give African Americans and Hispanics
in the rural South—especially Mexicans and Central Americans, who are both
the largest in number and most socioeconomically disadvantaged among them
(see Chapter 3)—a set of common experiences through which to filter and interpret their experiences of racial discrimination.

Indeed, some Hispanic respondents did recount instances of mistreatment
by whites based on race or skin color. And when they recognized such discrimination—whether against African Americans or themselves—as racial, it could
serve as a powerful tool for developing a sense of nonwhite identity or racial
solidarity with African Americans. Two examples illustrate this potent force,
the first stemming from an instance of explicit white-on-Hispanic discrimination interpreted partially in racial terms, and the second from an instance of
explicit white-on-black racial discrimination.

First, in October 2003, in Alexandria County (an immediate neighbor to Bedford County), a white county Board of Education member whom I will call "Michael" incited great controversy at a local school board meeting by making a recommendation to separate the English- and non-English-speaking students in a small rural elementary school. Located in a rural portion of Alexandria County heavily dependent on migrant agricultural labor, by 2003 Alexandria Rural Elementary School had seen its non-English-speaking student population grow to more than one-third of the school populace, the great majority of whom spoke Spanish as their primary language. Two Hispanic officials affiliated with the Alexandria County school system—Isabel, the Hispanic ESL program coordinator, and Esperanza, the Migrant Education Program recruiter/parent facilitator in the Alexandria–Archer Bluff municipal school system—quickly responded to Michael's comments, calling them "ignorant" and "racist." Isabel called them ignorant because she did not think Michael acknowledged how much progress non-English-speaking students are making in learning English at the school, something she argued was assisted by contact with (not separation from) English-speaking students. Isabel also called them racist because she thought Michael's call for "segregation" of the English- and non-English-speaking students violates the federal Equal Educational Opportunities Act of 1974 (which "prohibits specific discriminatory conduct, including segregating students on the basis of race, color, or national origin") as well as North Carolina state law (in which "each school district must ensure that limited English proficiency students are 'educated in the least segregative manner based on the educational needs of the student'"; *Archer Bluff Times*, Oct. 23, 2003).

Both Isabel and Esperanza acknowledged that Michael's intentions toward the non-English-speaking students may have been misguided rather than intentionally racist—and also that separating students by language ability is not necessarily equivalent to separating them by race, color, or national origin—but both held firm in their view that he would not have called for separation of these two groups of students if he were truly concerned about the linguistic progress of non-English-speaking students. Instead, the two thought that the terms "English-speaking" and "non-English-speaking" became code words for "whites" and "Hispanics," and that his recommendation to separate the two groups concerned not the latter's English language ability but rather the racially exclusive interests of white students at the school (including his own son, whom he had already transferred to another school).[1]

Consequently, through this experience both women developed a deeper sense of connection to African Americans. In fact, Isabel reported that their

African American coworkers stood in coalition with them against the recommendation, at least in private,[2] interpreting it as a white attempt to exclude Hispanic students from full participation in the public school system in a way that reflected their own historical experience:

Isabel: I realized that I had a problem here with the Board of Education member, because the blacks were like, "Oh, good for you! Thank you, thank you." They were thanking me. Because they felt attacked when Michael attacked me. Because he really did. The black people felt that, too. Because they were like, "You can see the way whites treat us, because they're treating you the way they treated us so many years ago."

Interviewer: So in a sense they're seeing similarities in whites' treatment of blacks and Hispanics?

Isabel: Mm hmm.

Interviewer: And so you felt a lot of support from them, in terms of this incident?

Isabel: Mm hmm. A lot. A lot of support.

Likewise, Esperanza has come to sense a connection between whites' ability to exclude Hispanics from full participation in American public schools and their ability to exclude other racial minority groups and low-income students in general. The incident has helped her develop a sense of nonwhite identity and racial solidarity with African Americans that is informed by class as well as racial exploitation (Guinier and Torres 2002; Jennings 1997; B. E. Smith 2009).

Such solidarity can also be encouraged by clear examples of white-on-black racial discrimination. Horacio, an outgoing man from Honduras who attended the Hispanic Leadership Course in Wilcox County in fall 2003, recounted a troubling experience at work when his direct white superior actively tried to "divide and rule" black and Hispanic construction workers on the job by using Hispanics as a tool to intimidate African Americans:

I work in construction, doing soldering and bricklaying in Warner, and there were five of us Latinos there. I came back from lunch, and I saw the [confederate battle] flag hanging there. This white guy I work with, he is a contractor. He works for our employer and brings his own equipment with him. And he had the Latinos hang the flag up for him. He had them put it up on his own crane. And when I came back from lunch I saw the flag flying up there, and I went over to the other Latinos and I asked them, "Why did you put that flag up?" And they didn't know better. They didn't know what it meant. They just put it up there because the white guy told them to. And I said to them, "Don't you know that it's racist?" And they said, "No, we didn't know. Racist to whom?" And I said, "To the blacks." And so then I went over to the white contractor, and I asked him why he put that flag up. And he told me, "Because I don't like blacks. And some of those black guys working over there are messing up on stuff, so I decided to put up this flag so they'd know." And I thought about it for a while, it made me feel really bad, and then I looked at him and I said, "Well if you don't like the blacks very much, you probably don't like us Hispanics very much either, right?" And he laughed and looked back at me and said, "Nah, I like y'all just fine. You're really good workers." And then a black guy saw the flag and he came up to me, he was going on and on saying a lot of bad things to me, asking me why the hell we Latinos put that flag up. I explained to him that, "First of all, it wasn't me who put it up. And second, the other Latinos had no idea what the flag meant. They didn't know and they just did it because the white guy had told them to. They thought they were following directions like always." (Fieldnotes, Horacio, Hispanic Leadership Course, Module 4, Oct. 15, 2003)

After the class ended, Horacio told me that the black man eventually came to understand how the Hispanic workers had not been trying to actively discriminate against him. Horacio also said that this experience has given him a better understanding of how whites discriminate against African Americans by viewing them as the moral inferiors of Hispanic newcomers, whom whites "like" and view as sharing in whites' commitment to the value of "hard work." Together, the two examples illustrate how there is indeed some potential for Hispanic newcomers to identify closely with African Americans in the rural South. But they simultaneously emphasize how such identification often hinges on Hispanic newcomers' recognizing that whites actively discriminate against either blacks or Hispanics in clearly racial ways (Uhlaner 1991).[3] This recognition can produce black-Hispanic cooperation either by fostering an awareness among Hispanics that blacks harbor their greatest resentment toward whites, not Hispanic newcomers, or by fostering, as Juan reported in the beginning of Chapter 4, a shared sense of "what it is to be discriminated against." In rural Morrisville, Tennessee, for example, Hispanic newcomers' emergence as a chief target of racism by whites has engendered cooperation and sympathy, rather than conflict, between Hispanics and local African Americans (Smith 2003). And in urban Nashville, Winders (2009b) shows that Hispanic newcomers' sense of whites as distant, "courteously superficial," and even hostile has engendered a major identity cleavage between white "Americans" and all other "nonwhites," including immigrants, refugees, and African Americans.

The Challenge of Nonracial Discrimination
to the Minority Group View

In practice, however, recognizing racial discrimination is not so clear. In fact, the minority group view does not adequately capture the multiple dimensions along which Hispanic newcomers perceived discrimination and exclusion to operate in eastern North Carolina in the mid-2000s. In other words, it is significant that Horacio was the only Hispanic I encountered over the course of a full year who described such an explicit example of an attempt by white employers to divide and rule black and Hispanic workers. Allegations of such a strategy are frequently invoked by labor and political activists (including members of the Farmworkers Labor Organizing Committee and the North Carolina Coalition on Black and Brown Civic Participation in my field research) as well as academic scholars (see, for example, Alvarado and Jaret 2009; Jennings 1997; and Stuesse 2009), all of whom are deeply concerned about continuing racial discrimination and the structural constraints placed on American minority groups' prospects for upward mobility and political incorporation. Yet they were not common among my Hispanic respondents. In fact, many Hispanic respondents did indeed perceive that they are discriminated against, but they did not perceive such discrimination to be racial. Instead, they spoke about discrimination based on supposedly nonracial characteristics such as English language ability, class status, personal appearance, nativity, legal status, and so forth, and they frequently distinguished such discrimination from that based on race or skin color.

To illustrate, Neida is an immigrant from Michoacán, Mexico, who traveled for a long time throughout the United States on the agricultural circuit with her parents before settling down in North Carolina in 1988 and later naturalizing as a U.S. citizen. Neida could not recount any discrimination based on race or skin color, but she did draw a clear link between discrimination and personal appearance and class status:

Interviewer: Have you ever been discriminated against for being Hispanic or being an immigrant in this country?

Neida: Well, no. Look, right now, today, no. When I first got here to North Carolina, I did notice that [white] Americans looked at us in a pretty ugly way. But afterwards, a [white] American friend told me that what you have to do in order to not be discriminated against by Americans is when you go to apply for a job, always look presentable. When you go into an office—whatever office it is, maybe a clinic or a hospital or whatever, she told me—you should always look presentable, because Americans treat you according to how you look. Therefore, I had a very good experience from then on. Now if I go out with my children on the weekends, I try to have them be very clean. Well, more than anything, to go out nicely dressed so Americans don't say anything to me or my children!

Interestingly, Neida also reported learning how to avoid discrimination in the United States by dressing in a more "presentable" fashion through advice she received from a *white* female friend.

Other Hispanic respondents reported instances of discrimination linked primarily to their lack of English language ability or a poor English accent. One was Lidia, a legal permanent resident from Oaxaca, Mexico, who despite having moved up from her first job working in American agriculture to become an influential Hispanic community organizer and transnational political leader, reported once having been turned down as a volunteer for the Girl Scouts because of linguistic discrimination against people with foreign accents:

Lidia: Another discriminatory experience that I had was when I applied to the Girl Scouts as a volunteer. I feel that because I had a very strong accent back then, they never called me back. I filled out an application, and for the simple fact that my name was Latina and I had a strong accent, they didn't give me the opportunity to be a volunteer.

Likewise, Stephanie, a legal permanent resident who migrated illegally to California from Guanajuato, Mexico, in 1991 before settling down in North Carolina with her husband in 2001, also reported having experienced discrimination by Americans for not speaking English well, while she did not report any similar incident of discrimination due to race or skin color. In her words, she "feels a little bad" because natives have told her "that I speak English badly, that I don't know many things," and because one even told her "that I could confuse the kids" when she volunteers at her children's school.

Still other respondents reported instances of discrimination linked primarily to their foreign place of birth or foreign cultural practices. In this way, Alfonso, an unauthorized immigrant originally from Querétaro, Mexico, who lived all over the East Coast before settling down in Wilcox County, thought that discrimination negatively affects all people who are "not from here" irrespective of their race or skin color:

Interviewer: Have you ever been discriminated against for being Hispanic or being an immigrant in this country?
Alfonso: Yes.

Interviewer: How so?

Alfonso: For example, when you aren't from here, you don't have the same opportunities as the people from here, the Americans.

And finally, as illustrated by Eduardo, the unauthorized immigrant from Quetzaltenango, Guatemala, who described poor relations between black and Hispanic lineworkers in PPP in Chapter 4, discrimination based on foreign place of birth or cultural practices often includes many Hispanic newcomers' reports of being discriminated against for their unauthorized status, whether it is real or simply presumed:

Interviewer: Have you ever been discriminated against for being Hispanic or being an immigrant in this country?

Eduardo: Honestly, I think for being an immigrant.

Interviewer: How so? Can you give me an example?

Eduardo: Like if I go and I want to get my ID. They don't give me the right [to get a North Carolina ID] because I'm not legal. That's what I have felt. Not for being Hispanic, or for being anything else. Like if I am not legal, I can go to whatever office and they aren't going to pay any attention to me, because I don't have identification to present.

Interviewer: So you think it has more to do with being an immigrant, not with being Hispanic?

Eduardo: Yes.

For Alfonso, Eduardo, and many other Hispanic respondents, discrimination based on these characteristics associated with foreignness—especially discrimination based on lack of citizenship or legal status—trumps that based on race or skin color. And it is perhaps the most hurtful to them because it is legally and institutionally sanctioned by the U.S. government, which violates their moral expectation that Hispanics should be justly recognized for the positive contributions they are making to the United States through their hard work.

Such quotes are significant because they illustrate how Hispanic newcomers reported experiencing discrimination and exclusion not just from racial discrimination, wherein white natives can mark them as racially inferior along a *vertical skin color axis*. They also experienced discrimination and exclusion along other dimensions that, when viewed together, make up what Kim (1999) calls a *horizontal (non)citizenship axis* wherein both white and black natives can mark and ostracize them as undeserving civic and cultural outsiders.[4] This second horizontal axis is theoretically important because it serves to distinguish Hispanics' experiences of discrimination from those of African Americans, rather than ally-ing the two groups' experiences together, as is generally predicted by the minority group view. As B. E. Smith (2006) points out, it often generates tension between Hispanics and African Americans in the South because blacks' experiences are more strongly oriented around the vertical skin color axis, whereas Hispanic immigrants often consider their citizenship and immigration statuses to be "far more powerful determinants of their own unequal treatment":

> To African-American staff and activists in particular, the implication that their own U.S. citizenship represented a form of privilege was unpersuasive, even offensive, since racism was far more significant in their own experience and made them targets of discrimination despite the fact that—indeed, in a sense, because—they were blacks citizens of the United States. (243)

In fact, in many instances Hispanic respondents implicated their physical features or skin color as factors in how they experience discrimination only insofar as such traits serve to denote or signal civic and cultural "outsiderness" instead. Such is the case for Roberta, a 1.5 generation immigrant youth who accompanied her parents to North Carolina from Oaxaca, Mexico, in 1994. Roberta reported being discriminated against by her white American peers for her "ugly" appearance. But like the middle school students whom Nina described in the beginning of Chapter 4, who get teased by their native peers and told that they don't belong here and that it's not their country, Roberta ex-plained that whites rely on Hispanic students' physical features and skin colors primarily as a proxy for marking them as outsiders to the United States. "They see your color," she told me, "and they tell you that you're not from the United States. And they can tell you where you came from by the way your color is, and they always are like, 'Your color skin is so ugly.' They make fun of you."

Such is also the case for many Hispanic newcomers who reported being stopped by police officers or the highway patrol for "driving while Mexican" or "driving while Hispanic" (Armenta 2010). These respondents understood that law enforcement officials often identify them as "Hispanic" according to their physical appearances, yet they thought that this is primarily because their Hispanic features are associated with probable unauthorized immigrant status, which is something that ultimately serves to ostracize them along civic and cultural lines as undeserving "foreigners" instead (Bauer and Reynolds 2009; Weissman et al. 2009). As Jiménez (2008, 2010) argues, in the contemporary era of unprecedented Mexican immigration, race has become so tightly con-flated with nativity and citizenship that having dark skin, indigenous features, or a Spanish surname often serves the purpose of implying that Hispanics are foreign-born and likely also unauthorized, even if they are U.S.-born citizens. By this logic, Hispanic newcomers in eastern North Carolina are undergoing a complex process of racialization, yet it is one in which they perceived nonracial discrimination (particularly along the lines of noncitizenship) to be more important, with racial discrimination playing a compounding role.[5]

Greater Nonracial Discrimination by Blacks Than Whites

Interestingly, although Roberta reported being discriminated against by her white schoolmates, she also reported being discriminated against by her black schoolmates—but for things other than her skin color, such as her accent and foreign culture. Indeed, not only did the horizontal (non)citizenship axis frame Hispanic respondents' experiences of exclusion most strongly, but they often perceived blacks rather than whites to be its worst perpetrators. Such is the case for Merced and Octavio, a working-class unauthorized immigrant couple from Sinaloa, Mexico, who migrated to Bedford County in 1999 after their initial attempt to settle down with extended family on the West Coast didn't work out. Together they expressed great frustration with local blacks who "ignore them" when they attempt to communicate in English, whereas they noted that whites "try to help" them more:

Merced: Even though some blacks do understand you, they say they don't.

Octavio: Right. They say, "I don't understand what you are saying. What do you mean?" And if there is someone around who speaks a little Spanish, they'll say, "Wait a moment." But if there isn't, the bad thing is that they will just ignore you. They'll say, "I don't understand you."

Merced: Exactly! It's even happened to me! Sometimes I go up to our English teacher, and I'll ask him, "How do you say X thing?" And he says, "You say it like this." And then I say it back to him like he said it to me, and he tells me, "Yes, you've got it!" So I ask him, "How come some black people tell me they don't understand what I am saying to them?"

Octavio: Almost the majority of [white] gringos ask me to talk, and they will try to understand me. And they help me. I will say it, and they will try to understand and if there is a problem, they will correct it and say, "No, say it this way." However, there are other people who make fun of you. There is some difference [between whites and blacks] there.

Such is also the case for Raquel, a 1.5 generation unauthorized youth originally from Honduras, who dropped out of high school in Tennessee after the

10th grade. She recalled severe rejection by black schoolmates who ostracized her according to her "foreign" dress and personal appearance, compared to whites, who came to form her close circle of friends:

Raquel: I mean, it's kind of sad that even between blacks and Hispanics we've got that difference. Even in school. When I was in high school in Tennessee. There was a lot of violence in there, too. And most of it was coming from blacks, against Hispanics. I would say that most of my friends in there were white! [*laughs*] Because blacks were really . . . I mean, they don't really try to be nice at all! Most of the time it was just laughs and jokes about you. And, well, when I first got here, I didn't know how to dress. Because in Honduras, we just dressed normal! Shirts, any jeans. I mean, you didn't know about brands, you didn't know about what to match and all this. And they were always trying to make jokes. Always making jokes about my clothes! I was like, "Oh, my God." [*shakes her head in embarrassment*] There was a lot of pressure from them. Even when you rode the bus. On the school bus you'd feel like, "Oh, what now?" You'd just ride the bus and you'd have to fight for a seat. You'd just want to find somewhere to sit down. And ugh! It was hard. Because blacks were like, "No, no, no, you can't sit here." So whatever. They'd start cussing me out or whatever.

Like Merced, Octavio, and Raquel, other Hispanic respondents perceived that whites are more "open-minded" toward them and their foreign cultures than blacks, whom they perceived as "staying more separate" and attempting to exclude Hispanics more strongly. For instance, Laura, an immigrant from Chihuahua, Mexico, who migrated to eastern North Carolina in 2001 via Texas and New Mexico, thought that there is "more communication and common interests" between Hispanic newcomers and whites than between Hispanic newcomers and blacks. Perhaps this is because, she mused, "whites try to strike up more conversation with Hispanics" in order to get to know more about them and their backgrounds, while "blacks, well, not as much." Similarly, Stephanie, the legal permanent resident from Guanajuato, Mexico, quoted earlier, thought that "Hispanics and white Americans get along better" than Hispanics and blacks do "because the blacks put up a barrier, that you can't get across. Maybe because of their color. Because they feel like they are another race. And they just want to preserve their group."

Hispanic respondents' reliance on these kinds of cultural factors to portray black-Hispanic relations as more negative than white-Hispanic ones differs from relying on black-Hispanic competition for jobs or social space. And although social class may be positively related to cultural cosmopolitanism—in that people who have higher educational attainment and who are employed in higher-status occupations may not only display greater interest in foreign cultures but also be less threatened by immigrants' immediate presence[6]— Hispanic respondents did not make strong class distinctions when describing whites as "more open" than blacks. Rather, after acknowledging good and bad relations with members of both groups, they tended to describe blacks as more "closed off" and skeptical of Hispanic newcomers' cultures than whites are. For example, Dolores, an unauthorized immigrant from Puebla, Mexico, who migrated directly to Wilcox County in 1996, reported feeling more discriminated against by blacks than by whites, angrily recalling an incident when even a lower-middle-class African American coworker expressed disdain toward Hispanics' maintenance of their native language and cultural traditions. She understood that African Americans were forced by whites to relinquish many of their own traditions in the United States, but she thought that it is culturally insensitive of blacks to try to force Hispanic newcomers do the same:

Dolores: And there are also very nice black people, too. Nice black people. But like the black woman I was telling you about earlier told me, she said, "When we [our slave ancestors] arrived here, we didn't have any option. To speak our language or eat what we used to eat." But I said, "That's an issue of culture." That doesn't mean they should do that to us.

Together, these quotes demonstrate how many Hispanic newcomers— even some of the most socioeconomically disadvantaged Mexican and Central American labor migrants among them, many of whom are also unauthorized— often felt more excluded by blacks than by whites, rather than vice versa. In fact, Davíd, the immigrant from Medellín, Colombia, who reported in Chapter 4 that "the blacks don't like us, and it's worse than with the whites," also thought that the difference between Hispanics and African Americans in eastern North Carolina "will probably stay longer than the difference between Hispanics and white Americans" because "white Americans are more open-minded to those changes than black Americans." And even when Hispanics did not perceive whites as particularly open-minded, this did not mean they necessarily saw blacks as more so. For example, despite the fact that Silvia, the Puerto Rican American whom I introduced in the beginning of Chapter 1, thought that whites in eastern North Carolina and the American South are close-minded and racist, she reported getting "more hostility from African Americans than anyone else." Likewise, Eugenio, a 1.5 generation unauthorized youth from Oaxaca, Mexico, thought that although whites ostracize Hispanics as "dirty" and undeserving foreigners, blacks do so even more strongly. Here, Eugenio tapped into not only the acute threat of socioeconomic disenfranchisement that lower-class African Americans feel in the face of rising immigration (see Chapter 4) but also into their sense that they, like whites, are the kind of "real Americans" that Hispanics are not:

Eugenio: They always look at you and they say, "Well, you know, he doesn't speak English." Because I've been in restaurants and I've had black people sitting next to me, or white people. And they're just talking fast. They just keep on yapping, yapping, yapping. . . ." Look at that. He's dirty. And all these Hispanics come and steal our jobs." And this and that. Well, one time I turned around, I said, "Excuse me, what did you say? Because I couldn't hear you exactly. And I would like to hear what you said again." Those people just stood up and left. Because that's what I like doing. I like sitting down. I don't say a word, and I want to hear what people say about us. That's how I know what problems Hispanics have in this country. They'll sit there and, man, they'll just keep on talking trash about you.

Interviewer: This negative treatment, this talking trash—do you think Hispanics get it mostly from white Americans or black Americans?

Eugenio: They get it mostly from blacks.

Interviewer: And why?

Eugenio: Honestly, I don't know. Like one time, during Hurricane Floyd, all the lights went out. And the Salvation Army, or the soldiers would come over here to Bedford Mobile Home Park with dump trucks. And they would drop clothes off here, or water, or canned foods. In the center of the Mobile Home Park. And I overheard a conversation that a black lady had. She said, "You know, look at 'em. They come over here to our country, to our land, steal our jobs, steal our money. And now they even want to steal our needs [i.e., donated relief items]. Those needs are for us, the Americans." You know, I was just listening to that. They were saying this and that about us.

Racial Expectations vs. Encounters with Discrimination

Finally, Hispanic newcomers' perceptions of whites as more open-minded than blacks are exacerbated by the difference between their expectations about prejudice and discrimination versus their actual encounters with it on arrival in eastern North Carolina. On the one hand, many Hispanic respondents reported that despite having expected to encounter significant discrimination by whites, they have generally been surprised by how positively many (though not all) whites in eastern North Carolina treat them on an interpersonal level. Take, for example, this quote by Marta, the legal permanent resident from Hidalgo, Mexico, whom I introduced in the beginning of Chapter 2. On the basis of her knowledge of U.S. immigration policy and anti-immigrant vigilante activity on the U.S.-Mexico border, which she acquired primarily through watching television, as well as one very negative personal experience with a white man in Chicago, Marta thought that whites in the United States harbor a lot of anger toward Hispanics:

Marta: Whites have anger toward us Hispanics! There are many laws. More than anything, we Hispanics have problems with whites.

Interviewer: Like what?

Marta: Well, for example we see on the television that on the border there are a lot of illegal people that cross farms. And there are white people who mistreat them. Or we see in the news that the farmers, or the contractors, mistreat them. They hit them, they cheat them, they humiliate them. And with the blacks, not really. They don't get into problems with Hispanics like that. The majority of what you see in the news is with whites.

Interviewer: Why do you think this is?

Marta: Well, we think that whites think that we're coming to take away their jobs. They've said that. And once I was in a park in Chicago, with my children, and a little white girl came over to talk with my son. And her father grabbed her, and he took the girl away. And they left the park. So we learned how that man was racist. He didn't want his American girl hanging out with my Hispanic son. That was the first time that I saw that racism.

Continuing, Marta speculated that blacks probably do not discriminate against Hispanics as much as whites do because they see Hispanics struggling against racial discrimination just as they did in the past. However, couched within her description of common racial experiences between Hispanics and African Americans, Marta mentioned something important: she had not yet encountered "this type of discrimination" from whites in eastern North Carolina, where she reported that Hispanics and whites "talk normally" together:

Marta: So the problem is this. I have talked with the whites, but I haven't seen this type of discrimination here. We talk normally. But in the national news, in the reports, you realize that whites say that we come here to take away their things. Their jobs, their culture, their rights. That's what we've heard that they've said.

In fact, Marta then reported having received a lot of personal assistance from local white residents, in particular from a close white friend who was currently helping Marta and her husband finance the purchase of their own trailer, and also from a white stranger who once lent Marta a cell phone to use after a car accident. She also reported good interpersonal relations with both whites and African Americans at her children's schools and in her job in PPP, as well as having seen whites becoming closer friends with Hispanics outside the plant.

Marta's case, like those of several other respondents, is instructive. It demonstrates that even though Hispanic newcomers may have acknowledged racial discrimination from whites at a structural level, or reported negative interpersonal relations with whites elsewhere, many also reported positive interpersonal relationships with whites in eastern North Carolina, which has helped to improve their perception of white-Hispanic relations overall (see also Waters 1999).[7] By contrast, very few respondents expected to experience prejudice or discrimination from blacks. Many of those who were born abroad reported not knowing anything about African Americans at all before migrating to the United States,[8] while others reported knowing something about blacks' historical subordination in the United States, often mentioning slavery or the Civil Rights Movement. Thus, Hispanic respondents said that the expectations they have about blacks' relationship to prejudice and discrimination on their arrival in eastern North Carolina—if they have one at all—is that blacks will be treated poorly by whites, not that Hispanics will be treated poorly by blacks. In this context, the negative treatment that many reported coming from blacks has hardened their perception of black-Hispanic relations overall.

Such is the case for case for Ramona, Inés, and Mauro, three unauthorized immigrants originally from Oaxaca, Medellín, and Guatemala City, respectively. Ramona reported not knowing anything about racial groups in the United States before migrating to this country, and being surprised when she encountered blacks for the first time because she "had never gotten to know them" before. Importantly, one of the things that surprised her the most was how poorly blacks (but not whites) treated her: "In other states, the blacks are very bad. Like for example in Florida, they rob Hispanics. They go into their houses to steal their things." Similarly, one of the things that most surprised Inés in eastern North Carolina was encountering discrimination by blacks against Hispanic newcomers, not by whites against either blacks or Hispanics. "Here there is a lot of racism," she told me. "But it's actually more from the blacks than the whites. Because blacks are racist with Hispanics. You see that a lot in the schools. More than anywhere, in middle school. People have told me that they have seen cases of blacks beating up Hispanics." Finally, despite having heard about the KKK and anti-immigrant vigilante activity on the U.S.-Mexico border before migrating to the United States, Mauro reported being surprised to encounter interpersonal discrimination not from whites but rather from a black coworker who refused to return his smiles and greetings each morning at work. By contrast, "From what I have gotten to know of white Americans, they have always been very friendly. I have never felt any discrimination from them."

Intergroup Relations, Racial and Ethnic Identity, and the American Color Line

The preceding analysis demonstrates how citizenship creates lines along which Hispanic newcomers perceive blacks as well as whites to be acting as agents of discrimination against them. In so doing, it highlights how the contours of discrimination in the traditional South, historically employed to separate whites from blacks on the basis of racial differences in skin color, have now expanded to separate both whites and blacks from newcomers, drawing on differences more intimately related to citizenship and civic and cultural belonging than race or skin color alone. Simply put, Hispanic newcomers reported feeling most excluded from full incorporation into rural southern society not as racial subordinates by whites but rather as undeserving outsiders by blacks as well as whites.

This helps us understand why Hispanic newcomers' experiences with what they saw as prejudice and discrimination were not necessarily engendering strong affiliation or identification with African Americans in the mid-2000s, even though some Hispanic respondents also identified as nonwhites, acknowledged negative treatment by whites, and admired African Americans' struggles against white domination. In concert with the greater class-based competition that Hispanic newcomers perceived with blacks than whites (see Chapter 4) and also with Hispanic newcomers' predominantly nonblack racial and ethnic identifications (discussed below), it also helps us understand why many Hispanic newcomers have come to perceive that the boundaries separating themselves from whites, although existent, are somewhat more permeable than those separating either themselves from blacks or whites from blacks. In combination with immigrant newcomers' own antiblack stereotypes and whites' preferences for immigrants over African Americans, these perceptions of nonracial discrimination and horizontal exclusion by blacks carry important implications for how Hispanic newcomers are fitting into, and potentially challenging, the rural southern color line.

Models of the Changing American Color Line

Today, the historic American black-white racial binary is being challenged by rising immigration, and three models describe new configurations that may replace it. The first model—evident in the minority group or rainbow coalition of color view—predicts an emerging white-nonwhite color line where the central racial fault line divides the positions of whites from those of all other groups. Here, Asians and Hispanics/Latinos are predicted to become nonwhites owing to common experiences of colonialism, oppression, exploitation, and racialization, something that has arguably been furthered by inclusion of Asians and Hispanics in civil rights policies as "racial minorities," and in common language as "people of color" (Sears and Savalei 2006; Skrentny 2002, quoted in Lee and Bean 2007). Scholars and activists who see an emerging white-nonwhite divide point to persisting material gaps between whites and all other groups (including to the policies driving them), and to persisting feelings of racialization among Asians and Hispanics as well as blacks. According to this first model, we would expect Hispanic newcomers in the South to exhibit greater material, subjective, and behavioral distance from whites than from blacks, and such distance to stay stable or even increase over time. We may observe distinctions between Hispanics and blacks, but we would expect them to be less salient than those separating Hispanics from whites.

The second model also predicts an emerging binary color line, but one where the central racial fault line divides the positions of blacks (who in the American context have historically been defined as people with any African ancestry) from those of all other groups. Lee and Bean (2007) summarize how in the 1990s scholars began noticing the unique and enduring separation of blacks from all other groups at the same time that scholars were documenting how several formerly "nonwhite" European and Asian immigrant groups had actively distanced themselves from blackness and achieved upward socioeconomic mobility over time (Perlmann and Waldinger 1997; Yancey 2003). Here, Asians and Hispanics are predicted to become "nonblacks" who will likewise be able to achieve designation as whites or "honorary whites" with upward mobility, while African Americans will remain the sole "exception" who will not (Gans 1999; Sears and Savalei 2006).

Scholars who see an emerging black-nonblack divide point to growing material and behavioral gaps between blacks and all other groups, as well as to more quickly loosening feelings of racialization among Asians and Hispanics than blacks. For example, segregation in residential (Wilkes and Iceland 2004) and adolescent friendship (Quillian and Campbell 2003) patterns is higher among blacks and black Hispanics than among Asians and other Hispanics. White-Hispanic and white-Asian intermarriage rates are rising more rapidly than white-black ones (Lee and Bean 2007, 2010; Perlmann 2000; Qian and Lichter 2007; Rosenfeld 2002), and identity among multiracials with Hispanic and Asian heritage is more fluid and symbolic than that among multiracials with black heritage (Lee and Bean 2007, 2010). Continuing, in New York City it is specifically *blackness* that influences how nonwhite children of immigrants experience and respond to racial discrimination (Kasinitz et al. 2008). And in Los Angeles politics, blacks exhibit strong group-interested policy preferences and strong group consciousness, while among Hispanics these two indicators decline in strength among the U.S.-born and the more assimilated (Sears and Savalei 2006).

Some scholars argue that whiteness may even expand to include Asians and Hispanics as whites (Warren and Twine 1997), eventually reconstituting the white-black divide. However, it is important to note that the black-nonblack model does not require Asians or Hispanics to actually become whites, only that they be located meaningfully closer to whites than to blacks. So, according to this second model we would expect Hispanic newcomers in the South to exhibit greater material, subjective, and behavioral distance from blacks than from whites, and such distance to stay stable or even increase over time. We may observe distinctions between Hispanics and whites, but we would expect them to be less salient than those separating Hispanics and blacks, and certainly than those separating whites from blacks. We would also expect Hispanic newcomers to engage in distancing strategies from blacks, as they seek to gain upward mobility and greater acceptance by whites, and we would likewise expect whites to express preferences for Hispanics over blacks. Finally, we would expect to find central differences between the experiences of Hispanic newcomers who have African ancestry and those who do not.

The third model predicts an emerging triracial color line similar to those in Latin American countries that emphasize national unity and organize social hierarchies more in terms of class and skin color than racial ancestry (Bonilla-Silva 2002, 2004; Massey 2007). In this model, two central racial fault lines divide the positions of three broad groups, as whites allow some newcomers to become whites, create an intermediate racial group of "honorary whites" to buffer racial group conflict, and incorporate most new immigrants into a "collective black" stratum on the bottom. Here, even though some Hispanics are predicted to become accepted as whites or honorary whites, most Mexicans, Puerto Ricans, Dominicans, and Central Americans are predicted to become collective blacks because of their racialized incorporation as colonial subjects, refugees from wars, or illegal migrant workers (Bonilla-Silva 2002).

Scholars who see an emerging triracial divide point to growing material, subjective, and behavioral gaps both between and within contemporary racial groups, driven primarily by class and skin color. For instance, skin color influences the rates of intermarriage with whites among Asians and Latinos (Qian 2002), attitudes toward blacks among Puerto Ricans and Cubans (Forman, Goar, and Lewis 2002), and indicators of integration among Mexicans (Murguia and Saenz 2002). Class and skin color even influence identity choices among black-white multiracials, with a small group of middle-class and light-skinned ones constructing themselves as "culturally white" despite their African ancestry (Rockquemore and Arend 2002). Still, some of the evidence points to a black-nonblack divide. For instance, regardless of skin color Hispanics (especially Mexicans) resemble non-Hispanic whites more closely than they do non-Hispanic blacks in their racial attitudes toward blacks (Forman, Goar, and Lewis 2002), which suggests that many might not see themselves or think they are seen by others as collective blacks (Lee and Bean 2007, 2010). Likewise, "cultural whiteness" among black-white biracials is still the exception; most continue identifying as biracial or black, underscoring the enduring identity constraints on people with African ancestry (Rockquemore and Arend 2002). And even though increased socioeconomic gaps in the intermarriage rate with whites have emerged between more- and less-educated Asians and Hispanics over the past decade, intermarriage remains persistently low even among better-educated blacks (Qian and Lichter 2007). Finally, Murguia and Saenz (2002) point out that a three-tier racial system has always existed in the United States, and yet many groups residing in its middle tier have still been able to move up to its top tier over time, instead of remaining "secondary" and unequal to whites, as the triracial model predicts (Bonilla-Silva 2002).

Nonetheless, according to this third triracial model we would expect Hispanic newcomers in the South to exhibit varying degrees of material, subjective, and behavioral distance from whites and blacks depending on their class and skin color. We would expect those who are lightest-skinned and highest-class to exhibit greater distance from blacks than whites, yet still meaningful distance from whites. Vice versa, we would expect those who are darkest-skinned and lowest-class to exhibit greater distance from whites than blacks. Finally, we would expect to find variation in both anti-black distancing behavior among Hispanics, ranging from strongest among those regarded as whites to weakest among those regarded as collective blacks, and whites' preferences for Hispanics, ranging from strongest toward those regarded as whites to weakest toward those regarded as collective blacks.

Hispanic Newcomers' Racial and Ethnic Identifications

Hispanic newcomers' racial and ethnic identifications are suggestive, as are their patterns of intergroup relations, of how they might be fitting into and challenging the South's strong racial binary. In Bedford and Wilcox Counties, Hispanic respondents both self-identified (what is called "internal" or "assertive" identification in the literature) and reported being identified by southern natives (what is called "external" or "assigned" identification) most strongly as something other than whites or blacks—particularly as Hispanics, Latinos, or people of some "other race" (see Table 2). This includes respondents who were not asked how they identify but who nonetheless used the terms *Hispanic, hispano,* or *Latino* frequently in their interviews (25.0%). It also includes respondents who self-identified as part of this group secondarily, even when their primary identification was by national origin, such as Mexican or Peruvian (9.1%).

As illustrated by Ricardo and Noélia, an immigrant couple who migrated directly from Veracruz, Mexico, to Bedford County in 1996, foreign-born respon-

Table 2. Racial and ethnic self-identification of Hispanic respondents

Primary self-identification	N	Percentage
Hispanic or Latino	26	29.5
Question not asked (but respondent uses the terms *Hispanic, hispano,* or *Latino* throughout interview)	22	25.0
Question not asked or response not specified (or respondent did not understand the question)	12	13.6
National origin (6 Mexican, 1 Puerto Rican, 1 Argentine)	8	9.1
Hispanic or Latino (but respondent thought he/she was white before migration or is perceived as white by U.S. natives)	7	8.0
Mestizo, Spanish, or Indian	6	6.8
White or Caucasian (and/or does not think Hispanic/Latino is a race)	3	3.4
Other (American, "a string of things," "it doesn't matter")	3	3.4
Black	1	1.1
Total	88	100.0

Note: Questions asked to gauge respondents' racial and ethnic self-identification:
1. How do you define yourself in terms of race or ethnicity? Like when you receive any forms here or if people ask you, "What is your race or ethnicity?" how do you respond?
2. What do other people think you are? If people think you are Hispanic, do you ever do anything to tell them that you are [ETHNIC GROUP]?

dents in this group have generally picked up such terms up after migration, as available language to make sense of their new place as minorities in the South's racial hierarchy. This couple reported how in eastern North Carolina, Latin American–origin newcomers from a variety of countries get aggregated into a larger Hispanic or Spanish grouping that is sometimes reduced even more simply to "Mexican." In this grouping, they are portrayed as racially distinct from whites, blacks, and Asians (e.g., "Chinese") alike:

Interviewer: How do you define yourself in terms of race or ethnicity?
Ricardo: Well, in Mexico, we are Mexicans. And here, for everyone we are Hispanics. That's what they call people from Colombia, Paraguay, Uruguay, wherever . . . every one of them the same.
Noélia: It's the only thing that they have on forms for race or ethnicity.
Ricardo: "Hispanic."
Noélia: Hispanic, black, white, and sometimes they say "Chinese."
Ricardo: Or sometimes to play with us, and they say "Spanish" instead.

At the same time, other Hispanic respondents either self-identified or reported external identification by southern natives as whites. A few (approximately 3%) self-identified as whites, adamantly resisting both the Hispanic/ Latino and black labels even when natives see them as such. Others (approximately 8%) either self-identified ethnically as Hispanics/Latinos and racially as whites (as did Davíd, the immigrant from Medellín, Colombia, whom I introduced in Chapter 2) or thought that natives perceive them to be whites because of their light skin or hair colors (as did Isabel, the Hispanic ESL program coordinator in the Alexandria County school system quoted earlier):

Davíd: I consider myself white. I don't think Hispanic is a race. That just indicates where we come from.

Isabel: Until I open my mouth, people here think I'm American. Sometimes. And then when I open my mouth, many times they ask me if I'm German or Italian. But they don't think I'm Latin. Because I don't look like the stereotype of the Latin person.

Consistent with the triracial model, white racial identification emerged most strongly among light-skinned and more middle-class respondents from countries in South America and the Caribbean, while Hispanic and "other" racial identification emerged most strongly among dark-skinned and lower-class respondents from Mexico and Central America.[9]

By contrast, very few respondents identified or reported external identification by southern natives as blacks.[10] Only one self-identified as black (Carmen, a dark-skinned Hispanic American of Puerto Rican, Panamanian, and African American ancestry), and only two others reported ever being identified by natives as black, with both varying over time. The first was Lourdes, a Cuban American originally from Miami who migrated to Bedford County in 2001 in order to take a position as a Latino outreach coordinator in a local domestic violence nonprofit organization. Lourdes said that whereas she was identified as white in majority-white Minneapolis and later as black in a majority-black locale in Tennessee, she is now identified as Mexican (and even referred to by the generic name "María") in eastern North Carolina, because "there are so many Mexicans here."[11] The second was Lidia, the legal permanent resident from Oaxaca, Mexico, quoted earlier, who reported being discriminated against by whites and called black when she first migrated to North Carolina in 1980, especially by lower-class natives. But Lidia said that this is something that has changed since then, as immigration into the area has increased and natives have become more familiar with and willing to acknowledge Hispanics as a distinct group:[12]

Lidia: [I was discriminated against] the first few years when I came here. For example, at work. They always gave me the hardest jobs. And they called me names. They called me "black" and "X" thing.

Interviewer: Can you tell me a little more about when they would call you black at work?

Lidia: Yes. I feel like here in North Carolina, there is a segregation between whites and blacks. Here they only know those two races, white and black. And in that time, when only a few migrants were coming to this state, at first they considered us as part of the black category. That's how we were labeled. That's how they labeled us, to be like poor blacks. And that happened a lot, especially with ignorant people. I remember that I worked with a lot of people of low education, of low economic resources, very ignorant people.

Respondent: So it happened more with less educated people?

Lidia: Yes. I always felt like it was with ignorant people. People who didn't have any conception of culture or diversity. And that was the reason why people did that back then.

Therefore, respondents' strongest internal and external identification as Hispanic, Latino, or of some "other race" denotes an early pattern of incorporation that exhibits some collective social distance from both whiteness and black-ness, resisting full categorization into either of the traditional South's domi-nant binary racial categories. Yet respondents' stronger internal and external identification as "others" and whites than as blacks also denotes an early pattern of incorporation that exhibits greater collective social distance from blackness than whiteness. Class and skin color did influence respondents' racial identifi-cation, but they generally did so within a "nonblack" zone. Even dark-skinned, poor, and unauthorized Mexican and Central Americans tended neither to self-identify nor perceive external identification as black.

A New Mechanism Behind Racial Distancing

Several factors help explain these predominantly nonblack racial and ethnic identifications. First, the literature suggests that they are at least partially based on how race is organized in Latin America, where distancing from blackness is frequently encouraged. In contrast to how the legacy of the "one-drop rule" encourages many Americans to identify as blacker than their phenotypes might suggest, the legacy of white superiority encourages many Latin Americans to identify as whiter for the social rewards that doing so confers.[13] Upon migrat-ing to the United States, many Latin American immigrants therefore find that they are viewed as "darker" here, yet they continue to maintain their previous identification (Rodríguez 2000).

Second, my data show that antiblack stereotypes also play a role, as has been argued by various scholars of past European and Asian[14] and contemporary Hispanic, Asian, and West Indian immigration.[15] We saw this in Chapter 4 with Alicia, the legal permanent resident from Santiago, Chile, who described Afri-can Americans as "vulgar" and "fairly aggressive," and Anita, the unauthorized immigrant from Michoacán, Mexico, whose family described African Ameri-can men as "disrespectful" and "unrestrained." Two other examples go on to show how Hispanic respondents across a range of skin color, class status, and legal status expressed common antiblack stereotypes toward blacks in eastern North Carolina. One was Antonia, a legal permanent resident who migrated from Veracruz, Mexico, to Bedford County in 1994 and said:

> The blacks are louder, feistier. In my work I have seen that whites are like quiet-er. I think it's a question of education, or culture. I know a lot of black Ameri-cans who when they have a conversation with you, they talk loudly. When they call for you, they yell. You see what I mean? And whites are quieter, they say things more softly. That's the difference I see between blacks and whites.

Another was Nadia, a poor, dark-skinned, unauthorized immigrant who migrated from Mexico City to Wilcox County in 2000 and reported that "the blacks are sometimes pretty dirty. They don't do things right, or they don't want to work. They don't want to be responsible or work. They don't do what people tell them to. They drink a lot. [Their worst traits are that] they are very rude. They say ugly words."

Thus, as Nina argued at the outset of Chapter 4, many Hispanics in eastern North Carolina—including those whom the triracial model views as most likely to become collective blacks thanks to their dark skin color, low class status, or unauthorized legal status—learn to devalue blackness and make efforts to dissociate from it, since whiteness is privileged over blackness in both Latin America and the United States (Dzidzienyo and Oboler 2005). Regardless of whether such stereotypes ultimately originate abroad, after migration, or some combination of both, they all lead to Hispanic newcomers "avoiding" African Americans. Elena, a naturalized citizen from Michoacán, Mexico, whom we will meet again in Chapter 6, illustrated this directly:

Elena: Well, I don't have much [experience with blacks] . . . well, yes, I do. Because some robbed me in 1998 in Walton. So therefore I think that race is the laziest, the most shameful, in that sense. Right? They're the ones that steal from you. So that's why I stay away from them a little more. In Florida I ran away from them. I was scared of them because there they were really bad there. They stole a lot. And so that's why Hispanic people are scared of the black race. Yes, that is something that really scares me.

Even in instances where such antiblack distancing is less conscious, Jaime, a prominent bilingual and North Carolina–born Hispanic school employee in Wilcox County, still considered it strong enough to shape Hispanic newcomers' choice of residential location, both within new destinations such as North Carolina as well as traditional ones such as Florida:

Jaime: But is it that most of the Hispanics won't go to a place [in eastern North Carolina] that's predominantly black? Would it be that they think in their minds, "We're not going to settle there." My family is also in Florida and there's a lot of Haitians down there. They even call all blacks that, sometimes, racially ugly. They say, "That Haitian cut me off." And I'm going like, "How'd you know he was Haitian?"

Interviewer: And you think this is part of the issue here, too?

Jaime: Yeah, you know.

Third, my data show that whites' preference for Hispanic newcomers over African Americans plays an important role, just as scholars of past European and Asian immigration have pointed out. Those groups were not initially viewed as whites, but neither were they viewed as equal in place with blacks. Rather, scholars argue that they were viewed more like "almost blacks" or "in-betweens" whom whites preferred as cheap and docile labor and eventually afforded greater opportunity to move up into full or honorary whiteness (Loewen 1988; Roediger 2005; see also Rose 2007 on this for Native Americans). Indeed, in addition to perceiving that whites treat Hispanics better than blacks treat Hispanics, Hispanic respondents in eastern North Carolina perceived that whites treat Hispanics much better than whites treat blacks—a pattern I further confirmed in my ethnographic observations and interviews with key white and black natives.

To illustrate, Hispanics enjoyed clear preference over African Americans (and also sometimes whites) in low-wage workplaces.[16] All of the employers, managers, and supervisors I interviewed or spoke with informally claimed that they will hire "anyone who wants to do the work" (Maldonado 2009), but they generally saw Hispanic newcomers as having a better work ethic than African Americans (and also sometimes whites). Tobacco grower Danny extolled his Hispanic employees' work ethic: "They are good workers, and they are good people. And they will do manual labor—some work that the locals often feel they are above doing." Textile Mill co-employer Bob concurred, making an explicit comparison between more productive and reliable Hispanic immigrants and a lazier workforce "native to here":

Bob: I think [continuing to operate without Hispanics] would be difficult. Because again you've got a workforce out there now that is your Caucasian, your black, or whatever. That's native to here. That are not interested in doing work. I think they've come to rely on subsidies or giveaways from the government, and they don't feel they need to [work]. They're too good for this. And particularly that requirement of having to be here five days a week or six days, when we do work six days. I think that becomes too much for some people to handle. And money comes from other ways too easy anymore. It's not something that's earned, and it's a shame.

Other employers were even less forgiving in their evaluation of African Americans' work ethic. At least two reported not hiring blacks anymore "because they don't work out," and others openly chided African Americans for being lazy, wanting to collect welfare rather than work, and thinking that whites "owe them something for nothing."

Of course, this perceived difference in work ethic is often a misinterpretation of different groups' understandings of the relationship between work and citizenship, which come about largely for structural rather than cultural reasons (Gordon and Lenhardt 2008; B. E. Smith 2006, 2009; Stuesse 2009; Waters 1999). Nonetheless, these examples show how employers in eastern North Carolina often preferred to employ Hispanic newcomers over African Americans because they perceived them to be more loyal, pliant, and reliable, a finding that has been demonstrated elsewhere (Holzer 1996; Kirschenman and Neckerman 1991; Moss and Tilly 2001; Waldinger 1996; Waldinger and Lichter 2003) and that has now also become standard fare in studies of immigration into "new destinations" (Gordon and Lenhardt 2008). In North Carolina, for instance, Johnson-Webb (2003) finds that employers in the Research Triangle are "extremely critical of the attitudes and work orientations of black workers," aggressively recruiting Hispanic workers in part because they "are perceived to have a strong work ethic" (113–14), and Griffith (2005) documents a "readily admitted" preference for Mexican workers over African American among personnel managers in food processing plants across the state (66). In neighboring South Carolina, López-Sanders (2009) documents employers in a manufacturing plant ranking Hispanic over black employees, and unauthorized over legal Hispanic employees, because unauthorized immigrants are perceived to be the most hardworking and pliant yet least likely to report safety and labor violations (see also Maldonado 2009).

These preferences for Hispanic newcomers over African Americans further extend into residential and social relationships,[17] where they are visible not only to light-skinned and higher-class Hispanic respondents but also to dark-skinned and lower-class ones. For instance, Paco, a poor, dark-skinned, legal permanent resident crew leader from Jalisco, Mexico, who used to be unauthorized, saw a strong preference for Hispanic over African American workers among white growers in several states: "In my observation whites see Hispanics better than blacks. The people who are farmers, they want more people who are Hispanic to come to this country. For them it is better to have Hispanics than blacks." Paco also described whites in both Florida and North Carolina erecting a stronger residential boundary against blacks than Hispanics:

Paco: With the white people that I know, they like Hispanics here more than
    blacks. You see, over where I live [in Lake Placid, Florida] there are lots of
    [white] American people and only about four Hispanics there living with them.
    I have never had a problem with them, and they haven't had a problem with

me. They have never said anything to me, and me neither to them. Like, it's not an issue—everything is fine and there aren't any problems between us. But if a black person moves in there, the whites will start to sell their houses. Because they will become cheaper. So whites don't like the blacks. Why? I don't know.

In fact, Vera, the immigrant from Querétaro, Mexico, whom I introduced in the beginning of Chapter 1, recalled once having asked a white friend why it is that so few blacks live in a remote, rural part of eastern North Carolina, staying concentrated inside a nearby town instead. Vera laughed remembering how this white friend replied, "It's not [because of] us [whites]. It's that black people don't want to move here." She was still trying to understand whether whites "only want the Hispanics in these nice [rural] places or what," even going so far as to speculate that perhaps blacks might be afraid to move into them because of the high number of white resident "hunters."

The stronger boundary between whites and blacks than between whites and Hispanics even stretched into the realm of interpersonal relations. Immediately after describing how whites allow Hispanics but not blacks to live among them in the most remote of rural settings, Vera went on to recall "white American boys" who romantically pursued and then even married "a lot" of her female Mexican friends. Vice versa, she recalled how "my male Mexican friends—oh, they love white girls! Ooh, ooh—they go crazy! They even used to go out looking for them, and these white girls were looking for a Mexican man, too. Oh Lord, that was the fever of the 1990s!" By contrast, Vera remembered only one of her girlfriends ever getting married to an African American man. Likewise, over in Wilcox County, Armando, an immigrant who migrated directly from Monterrey, Mexico, in 1990 and later became a naturalized U.S. citizen through his father's white American wife, also illustrated how whites erect a stronger interpersonal boundary against blacks than against Hispanics:

Armando: I think whites feel like jeopardized. Because of the mixture. You know, whites dating Hispanics. I've heard it from several friends who are white that they would rather see their children go out with a Hispanic than with a black. Which in my eyes is advantageous. I mean, you're mixing, you know? Either way you're mixing cultures, you're mixing races.
Interviewer: Do you know of a lot of interracial dating around here?
Armando: Oh yes.
Interviewer: Mostly between whom?
Armando: Mostly between whites and Hispanics. It's very rare to see a black person married to a Hispanic.[18]

This crucial difference between how whites view blacks and how whites view Hispanic newcomers is nicely summed up by John, a bilingual white attorney in Bedford County. He distinguished between the strong and hostile *racial hatred* many whites in eastern North Carolina feel toward African Americans and what he called a more ambivalent *cultural xenophobia* they feel toward Hispanics, including Mexican immigrants, whom they know less well:

> John: And there is that [white] bias against the Mexicans here, too, but it's not the hostile "You oughta send all the niggers back to Africa." But it is a cultural, sort of xenophobic reaction. Like the district attorney down in the courthouse you talked to. When he learned what you were studying and he told you that, "The Hispanics are all OK. They just come in here, pay off their license/DUI tickets and go home." He is oblivious to the entire situation. And he's not even from a poor redneck heritage!

John's quote is important because it demonstrates how whites' visions of Hispanic newcomers in eastern North Carolina are still less negative and stable than their corresponding visions of African Americans, a finding that has also been demonstrated both at the national level and in other parts of the country (Bobo and Massagli 2001; Fox 2004; Taylor 1998). As Lamont (2000: 88–93) reasons, the central role that immigration has played throughout American history produces positive and ambivalent feelings as well as negative ones toward immigrant newcomers, whereas African Americans still serve as whites' true "other" in the American context.

This is certainly the case in the rural American South, where whites exhibited much greater ambivalence toward Hispanics (including unauthorized immigrants) in the mid-2000s than they did toward blacks (see also Rose 2007), frequently juxtaposing negative stereotypes of Hispanics with positive evaluations of their desire to work hard, better themselves, and support their families. One working-class white woman in Bedford County remarked that she would prefer to have Hispanics' "pretty" brown hair than blacks' "ugly" black hair, while another upper-class white man remarked that the Burger King "is just nicer now" with Hispanic employees, whereas blacks did not use to care enough to "keep it up." Even the few notable examples I documented of whites separating themselves from Hispanics in neighborhoods and schools— exemplified by the case of Michael in Alexandria County as well as a major redistricting attempt under way in 2004 in Wilcox County—could not rival the strong distaste whites exhibited toward living among or dating blacks. Likewise, McDermott (in progress) finds that the confused paternalism often exhibited by whites toward Hispanics in the Carolinas, Virginia, and Tennessee differs from the outright racial prejudice they exhibit toward blacks.

In sum, consistent with the past and contemporary literature on immigrants' racial incorporation, in the mid-2000s Hispanics' own antiblack stereotypes (which can be developed before or after migration) and whites' unique stigmatization of African Americans appeared to be facilitating Hispanic newcomers' incorporation into the rural southern racial hierarchy as nonblacks. Whiteness remains heavily privileged over blackness in both Latin America and in this binary region of the United States, giving Hispanic newcomers strong incentives to dissociate themselves from blacks and blackness in order to gain upward mobility. Whites' strong preference for immigrants over blacks further signals to Hispanic newcomers that the privileges of whiteness are ultimately more within their reach than that of blacks, and this has in turn given them even stronger incentives to distance themselves as they attempt to make a claim on full citizenship (Gordon and Lendhart 2008). Nonetheless, a third mechanism that is not featured in the past or contemporary literature—Hispanics' perception of discrimination and horizontal exclusion by blacks—also plays a role. It fosters feelings of confusion and sometimes even anger at what many Hispanic respondents perceived to be unfair and close-minded treatment, as when they reported being shunned by an "exclusive" African American community, taunted and beaten up by black youths in schools, or harassed by black adults as undeserving "outsiders" and told "to go back where they came from."

Of course, just why Hispanic newcomers perceived greater discrimination and exclusion from blacks than whites is still unclear. Opinion data show that lifelong southern blacks support less restrictive immigration policies and less exclusionary policies toward unauthorized immigrants than do lifelong southern whites (Griffin and McFarland 2007), and that within North Carolina blacks express somewhat more positive attitudes toward Hispanics than do whites— with the sole exception being in the realm of perceived economic impact (Miller 2010). In fact, McClain et al.'s data (2006) from Durham, North Carolina, show that blacks exhibit fewer negative stereotypes toward Hispanic immigrants than Hispanic immigrants exhibit toward them, which may be consistent with my observation that blacks in eastern North Carolina were not aware of how exclusively Hispanics perceived them to be acting. At the same time, opinion data also show that lifelong southern blacks espouse more particularistic ideas about what it takes to be American than do lifelong southern whites (Griffin and McFarland 2007), while additional surveys show that blacks exhibit greater concern about unauthorized immigrants than do whites, both in Virginia (Vallas and Zimmerman 2007) and in Durham (McClain 2006). So perhaps blacks in eastern North Carolina were simply unaware of how poorly they were treating Hispanics—particularly if the characteristics associated with noncitizenship, rather than aligning Hispanics and blacks as collective blacks at the bottom of the regional racial hierarchy, exacerbate feelings of competition instead. Or perhaps Hispanics' antiblack stereotypes or observations of whites' stigmatization of blacks were also flavoring their interpretation of white and black behavior, leading them to judge that of blacks as more harsh.

Regardless, Hispanic newcomers perceived negative treatment from blacks and described it as "unexpected," in contrast to perceiving more "surprisingly" pleasant interpersonal relations with whites, especially when they harbored initial expectations of encountering significant discrimination from whites rather than blacks, as Marta demonstrated. These perceptions of discrimination and horizontal exclusion by another minority group, much like those arising from economically induced competition, have in turn fostered resentment, stereotyping, and antiblack distancing among Hispanic newcomers (Kasinitz et al. 2008; Waters 1999), something perhaps most poignantly demonstrated by this excerpt taken from a Spanish-language newspaper circulated in North Carolina's central piedmont region:

> For María, Tuesday, July 24 was a normal day. In the afternoon when her husband got home from work they went to the Food Lion supermarket located on Blue Ridge Street near Interstate 440, to buy their groceries. While they were paying, they made conversation with the grocery bagger, also of Hispanic origin. The conversation took place in Spanish, which seemed to offend the African American cashier who was attending them, and she began to mistreat the Latinos verbally. "I left the store crying," said María. "Never in the five years that I have bought groceries at this supermarket have I been so offended. The cashier yelled at us to go back to Mexico. In addition to words, she gesticulated with her hands and kicked us out of the store," the angered Mexican immigrant told *La Conexión*. According to the Latinos, things didn't stop there. "My husband asked the cashier in English why she didn't like Spanish, but she simply said that it bothered her. We thought it was a joke. However, she kept on telling us to leave and go back to Mexico." The situation then became even more tense when the angered bagger told the cashier that if "they have to go back to Mexico, then you have to go back to Africa." The cashier became indignant at those words. (Jaramillo 2007; author's translation)

Summary

The rural American South has a well-earned reputation for racial and cultural intolerance. Even today, its "concentrations of poor, rural black southerners" constitute what sociologist and southern regional scholar John Shelton Reed calls a living "fossil" of the old South (1993: 7–8). Accordingly, it is within reason to expect that Hispanic newcomers might experience acute racial discrimination from rural white southerners, and moreover that such discrimination might give them strategic incentives to identify closely with African Americans. Indeed, my research confirms that in specific instances when Hispanic newcomers do perceive mistreatment by whites based on race or skin color, whether against African Americans or themselves, it can serve as a powerful tool for developing a sense of nonwhite identity or racial solidarity with African Americans. At the same time, I argue that in the mid-2000s the rural southern binary racial context was not fostering a rainbow coalition of color among Hispanic newcomers and African Americans, wherein common experiences of racial discrimination trump the two groups' internal distinctions. To the contrary, Hispanic newcomers—including many poor, dark-skinned, and unauthorized Mexican and Central American labor migrants—were neither self-identifying nor perceiving that they are treated as equal to "collective blacks" (Bonilla-Silva 2002, 2004) in everyday lived experience. Furthermore, not only did Hispanic newcomers report better interpersonal relations with whites than with blacks, but many also perceived greater discrimination from blacks than from whites.

However, I should be careful here to clarify that my data do *not* show that Hispanic newcomers' interactions with blacks in the rural South are always conflict-ridden, nor that those with whites are always smooth. Likewise, my data do not show that Hispanics have yet become "whites." Strong linguistic, cultural, and racial boundaries continue to separate Hispanic newcomers from whites, and as I discuss in the Conclusion a combination of both racial and nonracial discrimination from whites is indeed fundamentally harming Hispanic newcomers' wellbeing. Nonetheless, my data do reveal how perceptions of discrimination and exclusion on the part of blacks, in combination with other factors, have led many Hispanic newcomers to engage in antiblack distancing. They also reveal how such distancing might well contribute to development of a subjective black-nonblack color line, despite persisting gaps between the material positions of whites and Hispanic newcomers in the rural South. Taken together, my results suggest a classic pattern of racial assimilation, where Hispanic newcomers in eastern North Carolina seem to be joining a long line of American immigrant groups by quickly learning that one of the surest ways to demonstrate moral virtue and make a full claim on American citizenship is not just to be "not black," as Robert Smith (2006) writes, but also "anti-black" (24). They also suggest that it is still African ancestry—and not necessarily skin color, class status, or legal status—that continues to play the dominant role in determining where the most salient racial boundary in rural southern society lies.

Of course, I have painted a picture of Hispanic newcomers' racial incorporation during an early stage of immigration in the South, and appropriate caution is needed as we look to the future. Racialization processes depend on a multitude of factors, and intergroup relations stemming from them have been shown to vary across both place and time.[19] Thus, more research will be needed to determine how stable the patterns that I have uncovered in eastern North Carolina are, and how applicable they may be to places elsewhere in the South. It will be especially important to study this in places that have larger middle-class African American and Hispanic communities than do Bedford or Wilcox Counties, because poverty and lower-class status are central in fueling black-Hispanic tensions (Fabienke 2007; Mindiola, Niemann, and Rodríguez 2002). It will also be important to study this in places that have a smaller black population than either of these two counties do, because the boundaries separating whites from Mexican Americans have historically been least salient in places with large populations of other racial or ethnic groups (Telles and Ortiz 2008). Nonetheless, there are already some signs of similar patterns emerging in formerly binary locales both within and outside the South. In new destinations of the Carolinas, Virginia, and Tennessee, McDermott (in progress) and Rose (2007) argue that patterns of residential settlement, social relations, and institutional responsiveness indicate an assimilation of the Hispanic population toward whiteness and in opposition to blackness. And in small new destination cities in New York's Hudson Valley, Denton and Villarrubia (2007) find hostile black-Hispanic relations motivating Hispanic newcomers, who often live side by side with African Americans in very poor neighborhoods, to distance themselves from African Americans as soon as they can.

Other questions emerge as to how the patterns that I uncover in eastern North Carolina might develop over time and over generations, particularly as immigration continues and anti-immigrant sentiments sharpen, as they have since I conducted my research (see the Conclusion). On the one hand, we might imagine that such trends could lead first-generation Hispanic immigrants to perceive greater discrimination from whites, particularly if they also perceive blacks to begin exhibiting more solidarity and empathy rather than exclusion in the context of everyday interactions (see, for example, Jones 2010). On the other hand, we might also imagine that such trends could exacerbate tensions between first-generation Hispanic immigrants and blacks, increasing perceptions of economic and symbolic threat and the salience of noncitizenship more generally (see, for example, McDermott, in progress).

Looking even further beyond foreign-born Hispanic immigrants to focus on later generations of Hispanics born in the United States and the rural South will be even more telling. Even though evidence collected elsewhere suggests that second-generation children of Latin American immigrants do indeed come to view "race" and race relations differently than their first-generation parents do—generally exhibiting a stronger perception of discrimination by whites, a more favorable attitude toward blacks, and a stronger identity as a racialized minority—none of my 18 U.S.-born Hispanic respondents (with the exception of one who has African ancestry) identified as black, and few reported significantly better relations with blacks than did foreign-born respondents. Furthermore, the 1.5 generation Hispanic youths I interviewed expressed acute perceptions of discrimination from blacks, often in the context of negative experiences attending American middle and high schools. In these ways, I did not see the boundary separating blacks and Hispanics to be blurring into the second generation, or at least not yet. But further research will help flesh this out further, as well as pinpoint the specific role African ancestry will continue to play in the long-term racial incorporation of Hispanic newcomers and their descendants in the region over time.

A final area ripe for research will concern Hispanic newcomers' reactions to African Americans' efforts to include them in race-based "coalitions of color." Social scientist Barbara Ellen Smith (2006) offers a nuanced analysis of the promises and pitfalls of coalition-building practices in the traditional South, cautioning against natives' tendency to subsume new immigrants within preexisting southern social identities and political frameworks, such as race-based communities of color or class-based coalitions of workers. In her view this tendency is not wrong, but it still "avoids the particularity of Latino immigrants' status as *immigrants*, who challenge and potentially alter our regional sensibilities and strategies" (253; my emphasis).

On the basis of my research, I think such cautions are sage. Many Hispanic newcomers in eastern North Carolina resented the discrimination and exclusion they perceived from blacks in the mid-2000s; some were equally skeptical of early attempts being made by some African Americans to include them in black-brown coalitions. To be sure, some Hispanics did appreciate such efforts, especially when they were searching for ways to challenge racial discrimination from whites, or when they perceived that blacks are genuinely trying to get to know them better and to represent their interests within a common framework (Jones 2010). However, other Hispanic respondents perceived these efforts less positively. They wondered—some quietly, others vocally—if African Americans are simply trying to co-opt them into an existing African American agenda that will ultimately be resistant to substantive change, or if African Americans are simply reacting out of a selfish fear that the country's changing demographics will threaten their own status and power if Hispanics do not join them in a race-based coalition against whites.

In this respect, Hispanic newcomers in eastern North Carolina resembled Afro-Caribbeans in New York City, who often perceive that African Americans' appeals to common racial experiences are "half-hearted, begrudging, and lukewarm" (Rogers 2004: 296), and in my research a few of them were beginning to distance themselves from African American political appeals and agendas in response. Consequently, future research will do well to examine how and why such efforts are being extended by African Americans in the rural South, especially since 2005, as anti-immigrant sentiment sharpens. It will also do well to examine how Hispanic newcomers are interpreting and responding to them in return, not just at the elite level among political and community leaders but also on the ground among everyday workers and residents, where the tensions born out of strong economic competition remain most salient.

IV   Politics and Institutions

6 "We're Here to Serve Our Residents"

Service-Inspired Responsiveness to Hispanic Newcomers in Education and Health

ELENA FIRST MIGRATED from Michoacán, Mexico, to the United States when she was a teenager, in 1989. With only a sixth-grade education, she spent two years picking oranges in Florida. In 1991 she decided to come to Wilcox County instead, because she heard that "there were good jobs, that they paid you well, and that even if it rained or snowed or whatever happened, there was always work." After four years working in a poultry "killing plant," she began working as a waitress in a local restaurant and then moved on to Pork Production Farms, where her job involved monitoring the health of pregnant hogs and what she called their "little babies." Although by 2003 Elena was divorced from her husband, a fellow Mexican immigrant from the state of Guerrero whom she met in Wilcox County, she was also naturalized as a U.S. citizen in 2001 and made plans to stay in Wilcox County permanently, because she likes it there. She even bought two trailers, one single-wide in Walton that she rented out to bring in extra money and another double-wide[1] situated on a nice plot of farmland overlooking a worn rural highway, where she lived with her two playful U.S.-born children and met me for our interview one gray winter afternoon.

Elena was an ideal interview respondent for my research. She had "interfaced" with natives in a variety of local "mediating institutions" (Bump 2005; Lamphere 2005): in several workplaces (through her various jobs), in public schools (through her two children, who were enrolled in the third and first grades at predominantly African American Wright Elementary School), in social welfare services agencies (where she had received Medicaid a few years earlier), in the legal system (through several casual interactions with local law enforcement officers, not to mention through her divorce lawyer and her brother's lawyer, both of whom she has had to pay an interpreter just to communicate with), and in higher educational institutions and community politics (through her participation in the Hispanic Leadership Course offered by Wilcox County Community College in fall 2003; see the Appendix).

Because of Elena's substantial contact with mainstream Americans in all of these institutions, I was curious to know how she perceived their reactions to the dramatic growth of the local Hispanic population, and whether she considered such reactions to be more adaptive or more resistant across these spaces. Her responses were telling. On the one hand, Elena described elementary school teachers' reactions to her two children as not only positive but frequently proactive (see also Silver 2009). She recalled these teachers reaching out to her to discuss her daughter's academic difficulties and her son's behavioral issues, and also inviting her into the classroom to help her learn to work on the computer with her children:

Interviewer: And you said you have problems helping your children with their homework because you don't know English? Do you talk with their teachers or other parents about this?

Elena: Yes, I have gone to meetings with their teachers. They have invited me, or sometimes they tell me, "Look, your daughter is not reading well." They have called me to tell me that my son is being restless, but they also congratulate me when he is acting good, when he's being diligent. And their teachers have called me sometimes to tell me how to work with my children on the computer. We've even worked with them some on the computer. I have gone to some meetings, too. I do not go to all of them—it's not that I don't want to, but sometimes I forget and something else happens.

In fact, Elena went so far as to say that it was *teachers*, not Hispanic parents like herself, who were working the hardest to inculcate a positive vision of Mexican culture among youth:

Elena: The teachers want to show the children about Mexican culture, so they don't forget it, and they asked me if I could help them. Because the teachers have seen that many children have gone to Mexico and have come back speaking bad about Mexico. "Oh, I don't like Mexico. It's ugly." And the school is worried about that—that it's bad, that we parents don't teach them about our culture—and they want to teach our culture to the children. I like this school a lot because of that. Because I see them taking a lot of interest and supporting Hispanics. That makes me happy, so I said of course I would help.

By contrast, however, Elena evaluated her encounters with local social welfare workers and law enforcement officers in a decidedly gloomier light. In fact, the most discrimination she had felt in eastern North Carolina thus far came from social welfare workers, one of whom she once had to threaten to take to court just to get her Medicaid application approved:

Elena: I don't understand why I've had bad luck with Social Services. Once I went there to apply for Medicaid, and they told me that I was lying. They called me a liar! They thought that my husband was working, but he didn't have a job and he wasn't supporting me. And if you really know me, you know I cannot lie. Because I live straight. So I told them, "OK, if you know that he is working, bring the employer he works for to court, and he will say that he is not working." That got to the social worker. She didn't say anything to me, she just hung up on me and got mad. But in about two or three days, they gave me Medicaid. And so there I've also felt a little [discriminated against], or I guess let's call it bad luck.

Moreover, although Elena had met several "good" law enforcement officers who she said have made genuine attempts to help and protect her, most notably when she was once a victim of identity theft, she also described testy encounters with "bad" law enforcement officers who she felt discriminate against Hispanics, especially by engaging in racial profiling against those they assume do not have legal status and therefore a valid driver's license:

Elena: I've realized that if you are Hispanic, they pull you over and they say, "Driver's license." And they don't just stop you because you were driving bad. About a year ago I was driving home from a funeral at about 1:00 a.m. in the morning. And they had given me a soda there. When I came through Williamsburg I picked up my soda and I took a drink of it. There was a highway patrolman there, and I think he probably thought I was picking up a beer. Immediately he came out on the road, started following me, and waved me over. I was driving fine, at the speed limit, all OK. On the way out of Williamsburg, he came up really close to my car and turned on his lights. When he asked me for my license, I asked him back, "Why did you stop me?" He said, "Your license." And so I gave him my license. He said, "No beer?" I said, "No, no beer. Only soda." And I picked up the soda can and I showed it to him. He got closer to me to smell my breath, and then he said, "Oh, OK. I thought you were drinking and driving." And I said, "Right. But if I didn't have a driver's license, you would have given me a ticket." And he told me, "I'm sorry." And that really bothers me. They see a Hispanic, and they stop you. Why? Because they suspect your driver's license isn't valid. And many other people have told me that police stop them just for being Hispanic. So I would like people to know about it.

Interviewer: So you could say you have not had a very good relationship with police here?

Elena: No! Honestly. Although the police here in Wright are great. Like now they know me, and they say hello to me, and I say hello to them. They have never pulled me over to ask for my license. They have never pulled me over. And another time, some stranger came over here to my trailer and stopped his car in the driveway and was playing music and changing his tire. I called 911 and the police came immediately and talked with him to get him to leave. I think the man was Hispanic, and I also think he was the same one who had stolen my social security number earlier [and committed identity theft against me]. And I was alone, and I was scared, so I called the police. So for me, the police here are good in Wright. But the experiences that I've had with the police in Williamsburg, yes, those police are pretty bad.

. . .

What can Elena's responses tell us about patterns of institutional responsiveness to Hispanic newcomers in the rural South? She offered a ringing endorsement of the local public elementary schools, but she was skeptical that law enforcement agencies, and even more so social welfare services agencies, treat Hispanic newcomers as community residents who are equally worthy of the services and protection they provide to natives. Because many other respondents echoed her views, in this chapter and the next I highlight patterned variation in political and institutional responsiveness to Hispanic newcomers in eastern North Carolina—variation that emerged as largely similar in Bedford and Wilcox Counties despite the differences in the two counties' economic and demographic contexts.

Two main patterns are evident. First, despite rural resource disadvantages, how public bureaucrats in eastern North Carolina were responding to Hispanic newcomers demonstrated greater, not less, substantive responsiveness to their interests than how local and state politicians were. Second, reinforcing Elena's observations, those working in the most "service-oriented" bureaucracies, such as schools and nonregular medical services agencies, were acting most responsively, trailed by others working in bureaucracies that combine service with a stronger regulatory mission and role, such as social welfare services agencies, law enforcement agencies, and court systems.

My explanation for these patterns stresses the confluence of external government policies, which range from inclusive to exclusive across these institutional arenas, and bureaucrats' internal professional missions, which likewise range from service- to regulatory-oriented across them.[2] The most substantively responsive institutions, such as public elementary schools, are ones that combine inclusive government policies with strong service-oriented professional norms centering on a vision of Hispanic newcomers as equally worthy community residents, despite factors such as recent arrival or lack of legal status. By contrast, the least substantively responsive institutions, such as electoral politics and court systems, are ones that combine restrictive government policies with more regulatory-oriented professional norms centering on a vision of Hispanic newcomers as less equal community residents. Taken together, the patterns I present carry important implications for our understanding, first, of how Hispanic newcomers are achieving political incorporation in the rural South, and, second, of the relationship between electoral bodies and public bureaucracies in democratic societies.

Immigrant Political Incorporation in the Rural South

Despite contentious debate over immigration and its impacts on American society, surprisingly little is known about the processes through which immigrants, especially unauthorized ones, are being incorporated into (as opposed to excluded from) American society in locales that have few precedents or resources for responding to them. Rural new destinations suffer the most acute resource disadvantages in this regard (see Chapter 1). Not only are Hispanic newcomers who settle in rural new destinations relatively disadvantaged, but rural areas often have little institutional infrastructure with which to assist Hispanic newcomers and facilitate their economic mobility, much less their civic integration and political incorporation into "mainstream political debates, practices, and decision making" (Bloemraad 2006: 6–7). Ultimately, these contextual features of new rural destinations depress Hispanic newcomers' chances for group-level descriptive political representation, defined as representation of their own interests as political actors, because many newcomers are actively prohibited (if they are unauthorized) from naturalizing, voting, and participating in electoral politics, while others have fewer points of entry into electoral or non-electoral politics than they would in larger urban areas. In such situations, newcomers' incorporation depends more strongly, at least in the early stages of settlement, on an increase in substantive political representation, defined as representation of their interests by other political actors, namely elected officials.

However, in the mid-2000s I found little evidence of descriptive or substantive representation of Hispanic newcomers' interests and needs on the part of local and state politicians. For instance, even though Hispanic newcomers had gained some visibility in local bureaucratic positions, primarily as translators and interpreters,[3] no Hispanic occupied any formal political leadership position (such as local school board member, town council member, or county commissioner) in either county (see also Fraga et al. 2010). Regina, an African American Bedford County commissioner, illustrated this when she said, "I've worked with several people in nonprofit organizations who are working with the Spanish-speaking population and that kind of thing. But none who are actually in the political arena." Even more fundamentally, strict (and for unauthorized immigrants, indefinite) prohibition on participation in electoral politics by government policies on naturalization and voting left many Hispanic newcomers feeling irrelevant to politicians. According to Elisa, a naturalized citizen from Tamaulipas, Mexico, who worked as a Migrant Education Program recruiter and parent facilitator in the Bedford County public school system, "If they can't vote, they're not important at all."

This vision of Hispanic newcomers, especially unauthorized ones, as "non-clients" of the electoral political system was reinforced by Benjamin, a white Republican who represented part of Wilcox County in the state House of Representatives:

Interviewer: What kinds of things would you say that local political leaders and groups need to do to help Hispanics become more politically active or better represented?

Benjamin: Well, the main problem is this. If you can't vote, quite frankly politicians aren't going to pay a whole lot of attention to you. You're not going to help them get elected. It's the same with why they don't go to prison to court the prison vote—because they can't vote. So unless you're a citizen and you can vote, most politicians aren't going to side with you on the issues. They will probably represent the rest of the people in their district. I guess you could make a case that you represent them if they live in your district, but maybe they're here illegally. And if they are, well, do you really represent them? So there are some really big questions there that pop up with that, and that are going to have to be tackled. If you can't vote, now that's one problem. If you're not here legally, that's another.

Here, even though Benjamin recognized the serious "problem of representation and accountability" that is raised by people who live within the boundary of a liberal democracy but who can neither represent themselves through voting nor be well represented by elected politicians (Jones-Correa 2005a: 76–77), he demonstrated little incentive to reach out to them himself.[4]

In general, local and state politicians in eastern North Carolina lacked both contact with and substantive knowledge about Hispanic newcomers' needs, and generally they made only abstract calls encouraging Hispanics to get involved and contact their political leaders without highlighting a need to take concrete steps to contact Hispanics in turn. Mark, a white Democrat who represented Bedford County in the North Carolina Senate, even thought that unauthorized immigrants should return to their home country and reapply for legal entry:

Mark: I don't think that the Hispanic community wants to be a public burden. But I can see where 9/11, particularly for unauthorized . . . but I, you know, I just don't subscribe much to the fact that they cannot get documented if they want to.

Interviewer: You think they can?

Mark: Sure they can. I mean, now do they have to go back to Mexico and start all over again? Maybe. But I mean, if you want to do it, you can do it.

This statement angered several Hispanics I interviewed later, who lamented this politician's lack of understanding of their situation, as well as of the near impossibility of being able to qualify for a visa in their home country (see the Conclusion). It also showed how most politicians were not engaging in proactive efforts to reach out to Hispanic newcomers. If anything, they questioned their accountability to Hispanic newcomers' interests, especially to those who are unauthorized immigrants and whom they did not necessarily see as deserving political constituents.

Immigrant Bureaucratic Incorporation in the Rural South

Under such conditions of extremely low descriptive and substantive electoral representation, traditional political incorporation theories predict even less substantive responsiveness by local bureaucracies, such as schools, hospitals, and court systems. This is because traditional political incorporation theories, developed from the experiences of American racial and ethnic minority groups, especially African Americans, have specified that "the incorporation of new groups into city electoral politics generally will precede any improvements in the way that local bureaucrats treat members of those groups" (Lewis and Ramakrishnan 2007: 878).[5] In other words, as an outgrowth of political control over bureaucracy theories in political science—which argue that bureaucratic practices are correlated with, and highly responsive to, political control exerted by elected officials and electoral outcomes—traditional political incorporation theories predict that minority groups will be extended political rights and power in the electoral sphere before they are extended social ones in a lower bureaucratic sphere (Marshall 1964). By their logic, politicians "get bureaucrats to act in a way that they would not otherwise have done" (Meier and O'Toole 2006: 178).[6]

However, compared to elected politicians, bureaucrats in eastern North Carolina were responding more inclusively, rather than less so, to Hispanic newcomers, including unauthorized ones. In fact, the few local politicians who did express a desire to bring more Hispanics into local decision making—including the Wilcox County manager and several Wilcox County commissioners who joined the Hispanic Assistance Committee to learn more about their Hispanic neighbors; the Bedford County manager who expressed interest in bringing more Hispanics into county committee meetings; and Kendra, an African American human relations representative for the Archer Bluff city government who became an active member of *Latinos Unidos*—were seeking information from local bureaucrats, many of whom had greater knowledge about local Hispanics' needs through their professional activities.

To understand why this is so, I examine bureaucrats' responses to Hispanic newcomers in schools, social welfare, and medical services agencies in this chapter, and then I turn to corresponding responses in law enforcement and court systems in Chapter 7. All of these institutions are important because they are highly symbolic in the debate over the fiscal impacts of immigration,[7] and also because they are where Hispanic newcomers interact directly with public service workers, who, as "street-level bureaucrats," have substantial discretion to interpret, enact, and enforce government policies during execution of their work, even while remaining heavily influenced by rules and bureaucratic processes (Brehm and Gates 1999; Lipsky 1980: 3; Maynard-Moody and Musheno 2003; O'Leary 2006; Van der Leun 2003, 2006).

Inclusive Government Policies and Inclusive Professional Missions in an Exemplary Service Bureaucracy: Elementary Schools

Bureaucrats working in public elementary school systems in eastern North Carolina espoused a surprisingly favorable view of Hispanic youth (including unauthorized ones), envisioning them as automatically deserving clients even when politicians and bureaucrats in other institutions did not. Both counties' school systems had hired bilingual ESL program coordinators, assistants, and tutors (primarily in their newcomer-heavy schools), despite the substantial cost, and established policies to encourage Hispanic parents to become more active in their children's education. Such positive responses are not unique to eastern North Carolina. Scholars conducting research in other new destination states have also found schools responding to the increased presence of Hispanic/Latino immigrants "in a variety of ways, generally presenting fewer barriers" than other institutions (Dunn, Aragonés, and Shivers 2005: 172). The latter include local law enforcement agencies and state and local governments, many of whom enact more regulatory and exclusionary policies aiming to "exclude and penalize immigrants, especially unauthorized Latinos" (Odem 2008: 132).[8]

Part of public elementary schools' relatively positive response to Hispanic newcomers in eastern North Carolina is due to inclusive government policy, which has mandated their physical inclusion and also legitimated teachers and administrators' inclusive attitudes toward them. K–12 education is a federally mandated government service that extends to all youths, regardless of race or ethnicity, nativity, or legal status, in line with a 1982 Supreme Court decision (*Plyler v. Doe*) that ruled K–12 public schools could not use immigration legal status as a criterion for admission (Gonzales 2009; Johansen 2009; Konet 2007; Motomura 2008; Zota 2009c). Jenny, a white ESL teacher at Weakley Elementary School in Wilcox County,[9] explained that teachers and administrators had come to see all Hispanic newcomers as automatically deserving clients to be served on the basis of this policy, accepting them regardless of their possible unauthorized status:

Jenny: I would say 80 to 90% of the Hispanic students here are illegal. And probably 50% have false documents, although we're not trained here in the school to evaluate birth certificates. I do know that some of them share birth certificates, but we are obligated to take any birth certificate they give us.

Likewise, an elementary school principal interviewed by Kandel and Parrado (2006) in central North Carolina reported that she does not venture to speculate about her students' documentation status and considers it "irrelevant for her schooling purposes" (126). The situation mirrors that in emergency medical services, where Steven, a white Democrat who represented part of Bedford County in the state House of Representatives, explained how the Emergency Medical Treatment and Active Labor Act (EMTALA) mandates that health care providers in hospital emergency departments receiving federal funds stabilize all persons in an emergency situation (including labor and delivery[10]), regardless of their legal status or ability to pay:

Steven: If you go to the hospital in an emergency, you are immediately eligible for [emergency] Medicaid no matter whether you are a legal or illegal alien. [If you do not qualify for regular Medicaid] you will automatically get [emergency] Medicaid. In fact, some of these agencies' workers can't ask if they are legal or illegal. It's against the law.

Such inclusive government policies are so influential that they restrict space for counteracting discretion, which Maynard-Moody and Musheno (2003) define as "workers' adaptations of laws, rules, and procedures to the circumstances of cases" (10). Because automatic client status in American K–12 school and emergency medical services systems is federally mandated, bureaucrats have little ability to challenge students' eligibility for their services; as Jenny points out, they are "obligated" to enroll all Hispanic students, no questions asked. Furthermore, these inclusive government policies toward all immigrant youths also ensure that some serious responses to the increase in immigration are encouraged among local and state politicians who are called on in turn to increase annual funding to the public school and emergency health care systems accountable for receiving them. A case in point is Benjamin, the Republican state representative for Wilcox County whom we met in Chapter 4:

Benjamin: Immigration is something that we're going to have to seriously address, in terms of [emergency] Medicaid and school enrollment. We've had large school enrollment growth here. And we have to address that every year because in our Constitution[11] it says that you're guaranteed an education through the 12th grade. So you're probably going to deal with tuition increases.

Part of public elementary schools' relatively positive response to Hispanic newcomers in eastern North Carolina is also due to the professional *interests* of bureaucrats—an internal variable intrinsic to local bureaucracies that is distinct from professional *norms* but also influences how bureaucracies respond to demographic change (Jones-Correa 2008). This is because Hispanic population growth increases schools' fiscal resources; states often fund schools on the basis of average certified enrollment (Fennelly 2006; Kandel and Parrado 2006; Schoenholtz 2005). Teachers and administrators in both Bedford and Wilcox Counties reported that population growth has been beneficial in this respect, bringing in more money from federal and state funding sources that they can use to serve both native and newcomer students. However, Hispanic population growth is a mixed blessing in that it also requires additional staff and programs (Kandel and Parrado 2006). And so interests alone cannot account for the very strong and inclusive way in which educational bureaucrats were responding to Hispanic students, especially since these students' parents tended to have little education, low income, and limited English language ability, and to lack legal status, all of which elevated the costs of educating them relative to the benefits of receiving additional per-student funding. Indeed, Maynard-Moody and Musheno (2003) argue that self-interest cannot account for street-level bureaucratic behavior more generally, because bureaucrats often choose to make their jobs harder and even put themselves at risk to help clients they deem morally deserving.

A stronger factor has been, rather, a forceful client-serving ethic among these public bureaucrats. As members of large service bureaucracies dedicated to the concept of education as a public good, many displayed an orientation toward Hispanic newcomers that supported shared norms about promoting equity and opportunity for education. Nancy, an African American resource teacher/tutor in Weakley Elementary School, argued that Hispanic students "are our customers," to be served in accordance with a professional mission to educate all youths resident in the community.

Nancy: When I first started here, the Hispanic parents would not come to parent-teacher association meetings. And I told the other teachers, "We have to greet these parents when they come in. Because they're your customers!" [*laughs*] When you start looking at your kindergarten, and you look and they're at 75% Hispanic, and have to know what your customer is and understand what position you're in. And so that was one of the main efforts that we started doing when I first came here.

Thus, not only had inclusive government policy defined all Hispanic newcomers as automatically deserving clients of public elementary schools, but many teachers and administrators also extended their strong client-serving ethic to include them over time. In Nancy's words, this included "greeting their parents with dignity and respect," "smiling and saying the same" to them that they would to all parents, and actively encouraging them to come to PTA meetings and get more involved in their children's education.

That this response is partly due to a strong client-serving ethic as well as inclusive government policy was also illustrated by Randy, vice principal of Bedford Elementary School. In his view, public elementary schools are "ambassadors to the community" for Hispanic newcomers. When teachers and administrators do a good job incorporating Hispanic youths and their parents, they also fulfill public schools' broader public service mission of strengthening and uniting the whole community, not just newcomers themselves:

Randy: For all parents, their children are their most important asset. Their children belong to them, and parents want the best for them. And if the school is an organization that supports them and gives them everything that it possibly can, then it serves as an ambassador to the community. To also help the community foster the support and the welcoming that those people would need to successfully break into the community. If those parents are convinced and feel that we are supporting their children and them in their being here, and that they are welcome and that we are treating them fairly and justly, and we are loving them and giving them everything that we can, then that's a very positive thing. And it helps to know that the school is a big part of the community, and that it is a portion of the community that has brought them in.

Likewise, the influence of a strong client-serving ethic was noted by several parents of Hispanic schoolchildren. Like Elena, Stephanie, a legal permanent resident from Guanajuato, Mexico, who became a parent volunteer at Bedford Elementary School, recounted how the teachers she met have not only accepted Hispanic newcomers into their classrooms but also encouraged multicultural learning by drawing on their cultural contributions, such as Mexican *piñatas*. These are responses that go well beyond fulfilling simple bureaucratic tasks. Rather, they embody pluralist professional norms and missions in the contemporary American public school system, as well as North Carolina's implementation of an "aggressive and family-centered approach" to dealing with its rapidly growing limited English proficient (LEP) population (Kandel and Parrado 2006), one that is consistent with the state's strong historic commitment to public education (Key 1984).

In sum, public elementary schools' relatively positive response to Hispanic newcomers in eastern North Carolina reflects inclusive, federally mandated government policy that automatically defines all Hispanics as full clients of K–12 schools. Yet it also reflects the strong bureaucratic culture of public schools, which, as nearly pure service bureaucracies, employ bureaucrats who tend to come into frequent contact with newcomers, view and treat them as customers or clients, and therefore demonstrate significant responsiveness toward their interests (Brehm and Gates 1999). Of course, such institutional changes may happen slowly in rural new immigrant destinations. Jones-Correa (2005b) is careful to caution that bureaucratic change, even in the best of circumstances, may not happen instantaneously. Moreover, a lack of funding for innovative educational initiatives from state political leaders may dampen responsiveness at the local level (Bohon, MacPherson, and Atiles 2005; Fennelly 2006; Gouveia 2006; Jones-Correa 2008; McClain 2006), as may active or passive resistance to Hispanic students' status as automatic or deserving clients among some K–12 bureaucrats, especially in the initial stages of immigration (Bohon, MacPherson, and Atiles 2005; Gozdziak and Bump 2008; Wainer 2004).[12] Yet by and large, in eastern North Carolina's public elementary school systems institutional changes were happening "slowly but surely" (Grey and Woodrick 2005: 152), and they compared favorably to corresponding ones taking place in electoral politics and other local bureaucracies.

Mixed Government Policies and Inclusive Professional Missions in Higher Educational Institutions

In the mid-2000s, there was a large gap between Hispanic newcomers' level of incorporation into public elementary schools and higher educational institutions in eastern North Carolina. Less inclusive government policies in the latter arena explain much of the difference, weakening bureaucrats' requirements and abilities to respond to Hispanic newcomers' interests and needs.

To illustrate, in higher education variation in government policies regarding unauthorized immigrants' eligibility for admission and receipt of public financial aid produces inconsistent access across states and localities. Since 2001, 10 states have modified their policies to allow unauthorized students to attend public universities as "residents" under in-state tuition rates, usually if they can meet the residency criteria by having lived within a state for a certain length of time and graduated from one of its high schools.[13] By contrast, unauthorized immigrants in the other 40 states, including North Carolina, must pay higher tuition as out-of-state residents, if they are allowed to enroll at all. This blocks their access to higher education in a way that is not done at the K–12 level, because unauthorized immigrants tend to come from families with low average income and are also prohibited from receiving federal (and in most states also state) financial aid.[14] As a result, only between 5 and 10% of unauthorized immigrant youths nationwide currently go on to attend college (Gonzales 2007).

In North Carolina, until recently there was no strong, overarching government policy regulating admission of immigrant students, and thus educational bureaucrats had ample discretion to design and implement their own policies. In an internal memorandum passed through the state's community college system in December 2001, educational administrators barred unauthorized immigrants from enrolling in any degree-seeking program. Yet, after another internal memorandum was circulated throughout the system in October 2004, they began to allow each of the 58 member community colleges to establish its own policies. By April 2005, significant variation had emerged, demonstrating a pattern of increasing responsiveness to unauthorized immigrants' interests; almost one-third (N = 20) of community colleges still denied unauthorized students admission for any degree-seeking programs, but the other two-thirds (N = 35) had elected to admit them, with a third of the latter (N = 12) also drafting a written policy to this effect (NCSHP 2005).

Notably, it was not until after the outgoing president of the North Carolina community college system, Martin Lancaster, issued a new internal memorandum in November 2007 instructing all community colleges to accept unauthorized students that a prominent elected official joined in the mix. Outgoing governor Mike Easley issued a public directive in support of the November 2007 memorandum, mandating that unauthorized students be allowed to attend all community colleges starting in 2008, albeit still as out-of-state residents (Collins and Stancill 2008; Stancill 2007). The directive incited a public outcry throughout the state (Roberston 2007), and in response community college personnel requested that the state attorney general's office review it. In May 2008 the attorney general reversed the directive and, misinterpreting a federal statute to infer that higher education is a "public benefit" unavailable to unauthorized immigrants, advised community colleges to return to their pre-2004 practice of restricting all unauthorized students from access to degree-seeking programs.[15]

In September 2009, following continued controversy, the North Carolina Community College Board voted to change the policy yet again, this time moving back to the 2007 policy of allowing unauthorized students to enroll in degree-seeking programs in community colleges, though still as out-of-state residents, and this time provided they also meet two conditions: first, that they not displace an authorized state resident from a class or program, and second, that a GED be deemed not to qualify as an acceptable diploma for their enrollment (NCRCJI 2009). Because the September 2009 vote was still going through the rule-making process as of this writing (Collins 2009; Johnson 2010), I focus only on the 2007–08 period in the remainder of this analysis.

Both the 2007 directive and its 2008 reversal illustrate the power of electoral bodies to influence unauthorized immigrants' patterns of incorporation into bureaucracies. In 2007, government policy (coming down from the governor's office) forcefully confirmed and expanded their access to all of the state's community colleges, and employees of colleges that did not already accept unauthorized immigrants announced that they would immediately begin to "honor the system's directive," despite personal objections among some of them (Stancill 2007). Simultaneously, however, the policy discouraged higher educational institutions from responding to unauthorized immigrants' interests by continuing to categorize the latter as out-of-state residents—something that had long deterred many by subjecting them to tuition rates roughly five to six times higher than those of in-state residents.[16] Indeed, deterrence was projected to continue even as more community colleges came into compliance with the new policy:

> As a practical matter, high out-of-state tuition deters most from enrolling. With $10,000 a year in tuition, fees and books, Scott said, "you're not going to get many takers" (Stancill 2007).

In the other direction, in 2008 government policy (this time coming down from the attorney general's office) was reversed to restrict unauthorized immigrants' access to all degree-seeking programs in community colleges, despite the trend toward inclusiveness seen among educational bureaucrats in the five years prior. In response, the community college system announced that it would immediately cease admitting unauthorized immigrants to degree-seeking programs (Redden 2008), continuing a practice of "follow[ing] the rules set down for us" in setting admission policies (Collins and Stancill 2008).

In these ways, government policies restricting unauthorized immigrants from qualifying for in-state resident status, and then also from pursuing degree-seeking programs in community colleges, have forcefully defined the approximately 1,500 unauthorized youths who graduate from North Carolina's public high schools each year (Zota 2009c: 46) as "nonclients" of the state's higher educational institutions (Cuadros 2006; Silver 2009). In turn, this weakens higher educational bureaucrats' ability to respond as inclusively as their counterparts in K–12 schools have done. One unauthorized young adult, Yolanda, poignantly described going through this transition, which Silver (2009) calls "aging into exclusion." Yolanda remarked that even though some teachers and administrators may want to admit unauthorized immigrants into their colleges, as they did in her case in 2004, restrictive government policies are now strong enough to prevent them from doing so:

Yolanda: I worked really hard and I got my GPA up to the minimum requirements for college. And I was really excited about going to college. Until my senior year, when I found out that I really couldn't get in to go to college with any help, because of my [illegal] status. So pretty much my last half a year of high school was pretty sad. I mean, all my friends got to go to these schools, and I wanted to go to East Carolina University or UNC or all these big schools, you know? I had interviews with people and called people on the phone and talked to my counselor and all. But we just could not . . . I could not get any-body to let me in. But it's not their fault. They're just abiding by the govern-ment rule. And even now that rule is still there. I still know some people that have great potential, but they just can't do anything about it. Prayer helps. I remember I was 13 years old when I came here, and I was 18 when I was sup-posed to go to college. And I remember going to bed crying because I wanted to go to school so bad, and I couldn't. Because I worked so hard all those years. And then somebody to tell me, "I'm sorry, you can't come to school. You can't go to college." That was really hard, really hard on me.

Sadly, Yolanda received more support from her counselor and other edu-cational officials than did another unauthorized student, Moises, whom I met informally during my research in Bedford County. Moises and his parents had explored several potential options, with no success. Even with the best privately funded financial aid package he could qualify for—at a local private college,[17] since public colleges and universities could not offer him any financial assis-tance—his family could not afford the remaining $8,000 a year or more in tuition costs. One option, according to his parents, was to have Moises work part-time in college, yet as an unauthorized immigrant he is ineligible to par-ticipate in federal work-study programs. Another option was for them to try to work longer hours themselves, but they were pessimistic about this option. Moises's father was already being downsized at work, working fewer hours and having little success finding a second job, and even with Moises's mother al-ready working two jobs, they had managed to save only $2,000 despite tedious penny-pinching for almost a decade. Thus, in 2003–04 Moises was unable to find anyone who could help him successfully enroll in college. Unable to work legally, he was "waiting" in the hopes that government policy would change, as has been proposed in several rounds of renewed DREAM Act legislation.[18] In the meantime, he was looking into the option of attending a lower-quality but cheaper two-year community college, for which he is vastly overqualified. As Marisa, a Mexican American from Laredo, Texas, explained, for many un-authorized youths in positions like those of Yolanda and Moises, a high school diploma is no better than a "piece of toilet paper" since it does not ensure them access to legal employment or higher education.

Consequently, these youths' successful incorporation into higher educational institutions hinges very strongly on extremely service-oriented individuals working within or at the margins, including many who Zúñiga and Hernández-León (2005a) identify as potential "liaisons" between immigrants and community institutions, such as public educators and religious leaders (Bailey 2005; Bump 2005). Even before the November 2007 memorandum mandated that all immigrants be allowed to attend public universities and colleges, in a very few cases unauthorized students were able to attend ones that prohibited their enrollment, and also to receive financial assistance to do so. But this was only the case if one or more bureaucrats were willing to defy government policy and enroll or offer them financial aid *despite* their unauthorized status.[19] In this sense, these bureaucrats were engaging in what might be differentially termed "bending the rules" to fit the circumstance (Maynard-Moody and Musheno 2003), civil disobedience, "bureaucratic sabotage" (Brehm and Gates 1999), or even "guerrilla government" (O'Leary 2006) when their service-oriented ethical obligations sufficiently influenced their sense of what the "the right thing to do" for their clients or institutions was (Maynard-Moody and Musheno 2003).

To illustrate, according to Helga Mattei, then director of the North Carolina Community College System's (NCCCS) Hispanic/Latino Initiative, even before the October 2004 memorandum allowed individual community colleges to elect to admit unauthorized students, "a few community colleges in North Carolina weren't asking if students had authorized papers or not" but were still enrolling them (fieldnotes, Association of Mexicans in Wilcox County meeting, Jan. 19, 2004). Perhaps this occurred because some bureaucrats saw unauthorized immigrants as deserving clients in accordance with a professional mission that views education as fundamental to all members of the community, or perhaps even as a human right rather than one defined by national governments (Dunn, Aragonés, and Shivers 2005). Either way, it was likely a conscious decision on their part; it put them in clear violation of government policy at that time. As Mattei explained, "When authorities realize that students in the colleges are taking classes and getting credits for them, without papers, there can be problems."

As another example, Yolanda described how she was eventually admitted into a four-year university and awarded some financial aid despite her unauthorized status. Her entry was facilitated by a preacher (who, in contrast to restrictive government policy, viewed her as a deserving client) and an admissions officer (who, after some initial hesitation, also came to view her this way). Both of these actors saw some benefit in helping Yolanda attain a college education. Perhaps they envisioned the individual benefits that Yolanda would gain from attending college, as well as the broader public service mission that they believe higher educational institutions carry out for their respective communities. Evidence of both viewpoints is illustrated by Linda, a Venezuelan American who worked as the ESL coordinator and Spanish instructor at Alexandria County Community College. She argued that accepting unauthorized students helps individual students *and* individual community colleges; the latter "get paid and funded by the number of students we receive."[20] Linda also argued that it would improve the average educational and occupational levels and therefore the tax base of the whole community, not to mention help local community institutions fill needed personnel gaps with well-trained local (rather than imported) bilingual personnel:

Linda: It's in the benefit of the whole county to educate unauthorized students, regardless of where they are from. Education is really the key for everything. For better incomes, for better states and counties and cities, for better taxation! You know, you can't tax on low income. And not only that—it's disturbing when you need to send more people to school to respond to the increasing need for bilingual professionals. Hospitals continue to bring in immigrant doctors and nurses, and schools continue to bring in immigrant teachers from abroad. Because we don't have enough of them here. But see, we *do* have these people here already. We just don't allow them to educate themselves and fill that gap.

Evidence of both viewpoints is illustrated in the opposite direction by Santos, a legal permanent resident who used to be unauthorized and who argued that continuing to deny a college education to unauthorized youths hurts not only them but also total community wellbeing, when they are forced to choose a "worse" path for lack of better opportunity:

Santos: I went to school with some really smart kids. And I hate to see their potential wasted when they could be helping the Latino community. And we Latinos are still seen like as the lowest kind of people. I mean, there's still racism and prejudice, and we are probably all still seen as ignorant people. So by denying education to these kids, you're just going to make it worse. Because that means less money for Latinos. That means less education. And that would be the worst type of life. There would more of a chance that they would become gang members or criminals and such.

Similarly, evidence for both viewpoints is illustrated by several Bedford community college personnel during a heated legislative battle over extending in-state resident status to illegal immigrants in 2005 (see Stancill 2005). They argued that accepting unauthorized immigrants demonstrates a strong commitment not only to individual students but also to the normative concept of public education, and by extension, total community wellbeing:

> One staff member put it succinctly, saying that a community college exists to serve its residents; in his opinion, regardless of legal immigrant status, if a person is a Bedford County resident, he or she should be eligible for student status in this community college, including in-county tuition. Other supportive comments pointed out North Carolina's historic commitment to public education, particularly public higher education;[21] also the obvious value to a community of developing an educated, income-producing population, regardless of legal status. Whatever frustration there may be among the local populace concerning illegal immigrants, these educators seemed to regard their mission to teach as something separate, beyond any national debate. (postfieldwork notes, April 2005)

Finally, although the state's community college system decided to comply immediately with the attorney general's restrictive 2008 directive prohibiting unauthorized youths from accessing degree programs, the state's public university system has resisted to date, stating that it will not change its policy to be more exclusionary until it receives "further clarification of federal law" (Collins and Stancill 2008). Beneath this request for clarification lies a strong professional orientation to the needs of potential immigrant clients, including a view of the larger mission of public higher educational institutions as best "serving the state during a changing economy" and a desire to avoid creating "another permanent underclass" (Collins 2007b).

My research shows that bureaucrats in the state's community college system share this inclusive professional orientation despite the restrictive 2008 directive preventing them from acting directly on it. At a regional conference on Hispanic/Latino integration in June 2008, three county community college directors voiced their strong disapproval of the directive, vowing to "press forward to change it" and highlighting their will to "remain committed to the mission of democratization of higher education," to "increase access to education," to "help a whole community by helping one person," to "facilitate upward mobility and skill training," and "to do more to serve residents of eastern North Carolina in the future" (postfieldwork notes, June 2008). They even speculated that the state-level community college system director may have gone along with the directive not out of agreement with it but rather based on a desire to protect the system's remaining unauthorized students who are enrolled in non-degree-seeking programs—such as GED classes, ESL classes, and classes for high school credit (Collins and Stancill 2008)—from an even harsher attack. Their collective lamentation of the directive stems directly from recognition that community colleges serve as a crucial "bridging mechanism" connecting unauthorized youths to greater economic and social opportunity (Kasinitz et al. 2008; Portes and Fernández-Kelly 2008; Rumbaut 2008; Zhou et al. 2008).

Together, these examples illustrate how government policies fundamentally structure both the degree and the pace of higher educational bureaucrats' responses to Hispanic newcomers, particularly unauthorized ones. Lacking the same strong incentives encouraging responsiveness that inclusive government policy mandates in K–12 schools, higher educational institutions have responded more slowly to demographic shifts in their client base. Still, some bureaucrats working within these institutions envision Hispanic newcomers, including unauthorized ones, as worthy clients to be served in accordance with a strong service-oriented professional mission. And during tense moments when restrictive government policies have collided with their sense of the right thing to do, they have interpreted, bent, and sometimes even broken those policies in order to rationalize their judgments and facilitate newcomers' incorporation.

It is within this theoretically important space that public service bureaucrats have often employed their service-inspired discretion to encourage immigrant incorporation. In one notable example of it working against restrictive government policies, an educational bureaucrat even went so far as help Agustín, an adult unauthorized immigrant who migrated from south-central Mexico to eastern North Carolina in the mid-1990s, to get hired as a Spanish teacher in a local elementary school. His lack of legal status prevented him from enrolling in a local community college to get his teacher's certification, and therefore from staying on in his job for more than one year, but Agustín thought that the majority of his coworkers at that school cared more about the "contribution" he was making to their larger educational mission (in terms of "teaching Spanish" and "promoting diversity") than about the restrictive government policy that officially prevented him from working there. Continuing, another educational bureaucrat, whom Agustín described as a "compassionate white lady," then did him a "big favor" and got him hired in a second job teaching Spanish to adults in a nearby community college. Even though an African American coworker from the personnel department there took to him poorly after just two months, initiating a review of his immigration and social security records that ultimately led to his termination, Agustín thought that her reaction was "unique" among higher educational administrators there:

Agustín: You see, a friend of mine she used to say, "Man, you've got a professional background. You've got a good education. Go to school—teach Spanish. It can pay you good. Your educational background is good enough that they're gonna accept you." I said, "OK." Finally she convinced me. I even found some good people who helped me translate all my papers. In their county [elementary] schools. They accepted me, and I worked for their county school system for one year teaching Spanish. They accepted my experience from Mexico, and instead of paying me $20,000 a year, they paid me $24,000 a year! And it was really good. [And] at that time, they tolerated me. They probably suspected that I was undocumented. They probably knew, but they tolerated everything. Because they saw the advantage that my skills and my culture brought, and they saw the value of me sharing my language with the students. Instead of just seeing the value of my legal status. So they valued what I was giving them more than my legal status. But the black lady in that community college's personnel department, as soon she realized that I was Hispanic she started to review all my papers immediately. To call the INS, to call Social Security, to call everybody to see if my papers was OK. So she found out everything about me, and after two months there, they called me in and said, "Agustín, you can't continue teaching here. You have to get straight your papers with INS, and then come back."

Interviewer: So it comes down to one lady?

Agustín: Yes. And she told me straight out. She said, "I called everybody, and I found out about you." I said, "OK. Thank you very much."

Agustín's experience once again demonstrates the power of electoral bodies to influence unauthorized immigrants' patterns of incorporation into bureaucracies. Even though many elementary and higher educational bureaucrats saw him as a valuable coworker who could contribute to their pluralist educational mission, restrictive government policy effectively prevented him from becoming fully incorporated into either system. Moreover, his friends and liaisons were unable to help him stay on in either position, although they tried repeatedly. In 2003 Agustín worked as a supervisor in a food services company and longed for the days when he earned more money, worked better hours, received better benefits, and was "treated with dignity" by local natives.

Mixed Government Policies and Mixed Professional Missions
in Social Welfare and Medical Services Bureaucracies

In the mid-2000s, a large gap also existed between Hispanic newcomers' level of incorporation into public elementary schools and various social welfare and non-emergency medical services agencies in eastern North Carolina. As was the case with higher educational institutions, less inclusive government policies in many of the latter arenas explain much of the difference, weakening bureaucrats' requirements and abilities to respond to Hispanic newcomers' interests and needs.

For example, a variety of government policies prohibit or discourage institutional responsiveness in social welfare and non-emergency medical services agencies by requiring U.S. citizenship, a social security number, or proof of at least five years of legal residency to be defined as worthy clients. The Personal Responsibility and Work Opportunity Reconciliation Act of 1996 (PRWORA) made it more difficult even for legal noncitizens coming to the United States after August 22, 1996, to gain access to welfare benefits and explicitly restricted them from receiving other benefits, including Temporary Assistance for Needy Families (TANF), food stamps, Medicaid, Supplemental Security Income (SSI), and other health and social service programs.[22] More than 40% of legal immigrants have now entered the country since this cutoff date (Ku and Papademetriou 2007), and moreover, unauthorized immigrants, who were already denied virtually all federal assistance by a range of federal restrictions enacted during the mid-1970s (Fox 2009), continue to be barred from public health insurance for non-emergencies, with very few exceptions.[23]

In 2003–04, these restrictive government policies severely dampened responsiveness in many social welfare and medical services bureaucracies, compared to that in K–12 schools. According to Silvia, a bilingual pre-K parent educator in Bedford County who used to work at the Department of Social Services, "Schools have to take you whether you're legal or not." Particularly in social welfare agencies, and reinforcing Elena's observations, Silvia illustrated how more restrictive government policies have also amplified some bureaucrats' regulatory roles—something I discuss in further detail in Chapter 7—and legitimated their vision of Hispanic newcomers as undeserving clients to be regulated instead of deserving ones to be served:

Interviewer: Do you think schools do a better job incorporating Hispanics?
Silvia: Oh, yeah. I think so.
Interviewer: How come?

Silvia: I think because they have no choice. [*laughs*] Number one, the schools have to take you whether you're legal or not. In Social Services, they don't. Of course, if you have legal papers to be here—or if your child is born here and is considered American, even if you're not legal—Social Services have to assist you. I went today to Social Services with someone, and she's not here legally but her child qualified because he was born in this country. So they couldn't do nothing. They may not like it, but it's that they have to. I wasn't too thrilled with the way people treated Hispanics at Social Services. Every time one, a Hispanic, walked in, it was like the rolling of the eyes. In my opinion, I guess they do not cater to Hispanics and their needs. Because let's say you are accepted for food stamps. You need to go to a class and also get your card and a PIN number and whatever. Well, the classes are only offered on Fridays. But now they have a Hispanic girl who works at Social Services translating, but only on Thursdays. So I have called them and said, "Well, if so-and-so is there on Thursdays, why won't you just let the Hispanics come in to take the class on Thursdays, too? Because when you tell them to come in on Fridays at 2:00 p.m., the translator's not there. And so they're not going to understand the business, so what's the sense of them even coming in?" They still haven't changed it. It's been a year. They don't care.

Yet a strong client-serving professional mission among other bureaucrats working in such agencies has also produced creative efforts to respond to newcomers' needs. Many were taking place in what Dunn, Aragonés, and Shivers (2005) call "nonregular" charitable and safety-net health care institutions onto whom the costs of uncompensated care largely fall (Ku and Papademetriou 2007), as opposed to local departments of social services, hospitals, ambulance services, and "regular" medical clinics. Research in other new immigrant destinations also suggests that the latter have been relatively slow to respond to Hispanic population growth (Bailey 2005; Bump 2005; Dunn, Aragonés, and Shivers 2005; Porter 2006), placing the brunt of the burden onto the former institutions, particularly safety-net clinics that offer walk-in non-emergency care, are obligated to provide health care to anyone in need, or have "a more friendly and sympathetic staff." Even in metropolitan Charlotte, reactions to Hispanic newcomers among social welfare and regular medical service providers are described as "unwelcoming at best" and culturally intolerant and condescending at worst (Smith and Furuseth 2006b).

To illustrate this difference in eastern North Carolina, consider Ana Luz, a legal permanent resident from Oaxaca, Mexico, who migrated directly to Bedford County in 1995. She reported severe problems accessing services at the local Bedford County hospital because they had not yet hired an onsite translator/interpreter. This barrier was corroborated by Nina, a naturalized citizen from Cali, Colombia, who worked as the director of Hispanic/Latino programs at Bedford County Community College and who used to work in the Bedford County health department, and before that, teaching Spanish and ESL courses in Bedford Middle School. When asked to give examples of local institutions that have responded best and worst to the growth of the Hispanic population, Nina identified the county Department of Social Services and the local Bedford County hospital as the worst:

Nina: The bad example—I would say I have struggled a lot with the Department of Social Services. For a long time they didn't have a bilingual translator/interpreter down there, even though they knew that they needed to and that they had a Hispanic population that was growing. For a long time they never hired anyone to help these people when they came in. And the same situation exists with the hospital. They've made some efforts. They have a phone line in Spanish now, where you can call in and talk in Spanish. But I've tried to make them aware that while phone lines are great and while they're better than nothing, sometimes Hispanics feel more comfortable talking with someone face to face when they're sick and they have a problem. Migrants will trust someone more face to face than on the phone. They want the personal contact—someone there in front of them to tell their problem to. But I think the hospital might have done the phone line thing because it was cheaper than hiring a person.

By contrast, Nina thought that the Bedford County health department had done a better job, adding bilingual personnel to strengthen its relationships with Hispanic clients:

Nina: The positive example—I believe it's the health department. They have really improved their services since I worked there. Now they have a bilingual nurse and two more interpreters, in addition to me. The health department director at the time was trying very hard to make changes and put them in place, and that was very nice.

Likewise, Ana Luz reported that medical personnel at the local Bedford community clinic had hired a translator to assist with routine vaccinations, resulting in a more receptive context for local Hispanics who would rather go there:

Interviewer: Would you like to speak English better?
Ana Luz: Yes, I would.

Interviewer: How come?

Ana Luz: Because when you go the hospital here with your children when they are sick, there isn't anyone there who speaks Spanish.

Interviewer: They don't have a translator over there?

Ana Luz: No, not in the hospital. They have one in the Bedford clinic where you go for vaccinations and stuff, but there isn't anyone there at the hospital.

Even Bedford County tobacco grower Danny said that his farm's Mexican migrant workers did not frequent social welfare agencies or regular medical clinics in the area. Though he thought this was primarily because they do not need such agencies—he considered them hard workers who do not "live off" public services—he also thought this was partly due to many regular area medical institutions not offering Hispanics affordable non-emergency medical care. Consequently, he reported that the farmworkers tended to frequent smaller, nonregular medical institutions that make explicit attempts to offer a less hostile, impersonal, and bureaucratic context of reception (see also Easterbrook and Fisher 2006):

> If anything, they use medical services. There is a new program over at Acorn Health Clinic[24] that is cheap and easy to use. They go there every now and then, and it's more comfortable for the migrants to use. They don't get charged $150 for pills, for example, and they don't have to fill out all kinds of insurance forms. It's not as good care, but it's much easier for them to use and to afford. (fieldnotes, Danny, July 10, 2003)

In Wilcox County, Christopher, former vice president of Poultry Processing Plant, saw similar institutional variation emerging. He described positive responses by some local institutions, especially elementary schools and several medical agencies, including a new mobile dental unit and Worthington Medical (a nonprofit medical center located at one end of the county that had indeed put significant resources into hiring bilingual personnel and strengthening its relationships with Hispanics):

Christopher: Wilcox County has worked very hard at delivering . . . let's call it the appropriate education to the foreign national, if you will. They come in, they survey quite a bit. They are trying to find out what they need to do to reach Latinos. They are very much aware of what some of the conflicts are. Like that older children have to stay home from school and babysit their younger siblings, and now you have two kids out of school. Or a family that doesn't value education, because they have made it their whole life without any, so a kid goes to school just enough to get a job here and then go out to make money. The [public elementary] school system has worked very hard to reach these kids, make sure they have resources for them, and then have English courses for their parents in the evening. Wilcox County Partnership for Children has worked very hard to provide child care for these families. And various parts of the county health system have worked together fairly well. They have that mobile dental clinic, and Worthington Medical, which is a nonprofit medical center that delivers health care in the Worthington area. For the most part, all those were driven by the needs of the community, which is in large part made up of Latinos.

These instances of increased outreach support Dunn, Aragonés, and Shivers's finding (2005) in new immigrant destinations across the Delmarva peninsula that "a number of local organizations and advocates, often religious-affiliated, are finding creative ways to secure at least some of the medical care needed by Mexican and other Latino immigrants, including the undocumented" (169; see also the collected essays in Anrig and Wang 2006; Gozdziak and Bump 2008). Dunn and colleagues believe that these measures indicate growing willingness among local residents and organizations to provide at least some meaningful health care assistance to Hispanic newcomers, despite (1) restrictive government policies categorizing them as nonclients ineligible for most non-emergency medical services and benefits, (2) the fact that "much more medical care access and cultural awareness on the part of medical institutions are needed" (170), and (3) less proactive responses by many state politicians (Fennelly 2006; Gouveia 2006). Particularly illustrative are some of the creative outreach measures Acorn Health Clinic employees were undertaking to respond to migrant farmworkers' medical needs, because farmworkers are often fearful of approaching them:

> We also do some screening in the field. The outreach program coordinators spend a lot of time going out to the individual camps. And that's good, but it takes a lot of time and there are so many camps. So depending on time and resources, we also try to do some programs. We brainstorm on ideas, like once we went to a laundromat on a Sunday morning to try and reach people "where they are." We did some education and information promotion programs: HIV/AIDS prevention, STD prevention and information, diabetes information, because those are the issues that we see running rampant in the community. (fieldnotes, Hispanic Assistance Council meeting, Dec. 3, 2003)

Likewise, during my field research Carolina Family Health Centers (not a pseudonym) was conducting needs assessments in order to finalize plans to build a new health clinic in the Bedford/Broward area of Bedford County. As a federally qualified health center (FQHC), this clinic would serve primarily low-income persons—regardless of legal status and including "migrants"[25]—who either have commercial or Medicaid insurance coverage or can qualify for its services according to a sliding income scale and local residency requirements (fieldnotes, Hispanic Assistance Council meeting, Dec. 3, 2003). Providers there were hoping that the new clinic could be a Bedford County equivalent of the Acorn Health Clinic in Alexandria County and the Carson clinic in neighboring Carson County, offering "better" (i.e., more accessible and more affordable) medical services than do most private health providers and reducing the distance Bedford County residents currently have to travel to access such services, which are operating "at full capacity."

Importantly, as in higher educational institutions, the bureaucrats and their liaisons promoting such creative outreach efforts often cited a public service mission of improving the wellbeing of their larger communities, not just of newcomers themselves. William, an employee of a nonregular public health institution near Wilcox County, reported that he and his coworkers were not yet willing to risk violating government policy to hire unauthorized immigrants as employees. However, he reported that they *were* willing to bend, and sometimes break, government policy to serve unauthorized Hispanic clients by accommodating their need for using two names (i.e., their real names and their false names under which they are often employed; Cuadros 2006: 122; Grey 2006). Without such accommodation, William and his coworkers worried that unauthorized immigrants would have trouble leaving work to access needed health services, endangering their institution's professional mission to improve community health:

> At the agency, we have clients from local workplaces. And their problem is that they could get in trouble at their job if they use their real name here at the agency when they're using a different name at work. Like if they're not able to provide a note to their employers proving that they were here when they were missing work. So in our agency, some of the workers actually take both names of the person. [Interviewer: *They do?*] We will take clients and put their real name and all their records under their real name, and then put "aka, also known as . . ." and then their working name. So that we can give them a note with the name that they use at work on it [so that their employers will excuse

their absence]. And immigrants are scared to tell both of their names. But the ones I know I tell to not be scared. That they should do it because people have actually lost their jobs when they don't. (fieldnotes, Nov. 18, 2003)

Of course, not all medical services providers were willing to put themselves at risk by violating government policy this way, as Victoria, an immigrant from Veracruz, Mexico, illustrated in a separate case:

Victoria: A friend of mine just lost her baby. But she was working under another false name. And so the doctor wouldn't let me put down her false name based on the papers that she gave him. And so my friend told me, "They're going to fire me at work. Because I don't have papers, and how am I going to prove my absence from work?"

Yet as Victoria continued explaining, the fact that some providers and other liaisons were willing to do so demonstrates just how powerful a service-oriented professional mission can be in facilitating bureaucratic responsiveness before its electoral counterpart takes place:

Victoria: I told this to one of my friend's middle bosses at work. I said, "Look, my friend has this situation, and you know that we are illegal and that we don't have papers." And that boss said, "Hold on. Let me see if there is anything that I can do to help." And he helped us with the forms, he gave us advice. And so my friend went to another doctor and was having her consultation. And the doctor asked what her false name was, and he did put that name down on the paper and said that there wouldn't be any problem. Because my friend was sick, and she was vomiting. So that doctor brought the paper with her false name to where we worked. He brought it to her middle boss, who helped us from there. *But not everyone* [will do this]. *There are people who don't do this. It's personal, it's something about that doctor, and something about that middle boss* [my emphasis].

In fact, in Alamance County (not a pseudonym), in the central piedmont region of the state, county officials recently ordered a sheriff's investigation of the health department when they heard that some bureaucrats there were accepting unauthorized immigrants' false names in order to give them care. The department's medical director and one of its nurse practitioners were subsequently suspended for two weeks,[26] an unauthorized immigrant whose medical records showed that she had received prenatal care there two years prior was ordered deported with her family, and a fight broke out over medical privacy rights and the appropriate role that health providers should be playing in assisting unauthorized immigrants in accessing medical care. The president of the North Carolina Medical Society joined in the debate by emphasizing the confidentiality of medical records as a "central tenet" of health care providers' code of ethics, and the importance of serving unauthorized immigrants in improving total community health (Callaway 2008), but Alamance County commissioners passed a resolution attempting to prohibit the health department from offering non-emergency services to all unauthorized immigrants (Collins 2008c). Such service-inspired efforts to incorporate immigrants into social welfare and medical services bureaucracies, like those in higher education, may still appear exceptional in the face of restrictive government policies. But they are instructive when they depart from the responses of elected officials so starkly.

Summary

Despite rural resource disadvantages, in the mid-2000s public bureaucrats in eastern North Carolina were responding to Hispanic newcomers in ways that demonstrated greater, not less, substantive responsiveness to their interests and needs than were local and state politicians. Not only did they demonstrate more knowledge about Hispanic newcomers, but they had also implemented more programs and initiatives to assist them. Furthermore, natives working in the most service-oriented bureaucracies, such as schools and nonregular medical services agencies, were acting most responsively, trailed by others working in bureaucracies that combine service with a stronger regulatory mission and role, such as social welfare services agencies.

I have begun to explain these patterns by focusing on the dual roles of external government policies and bureaucrats' internal professional missions. Bureaucrats' professional missions were indeed playing an independent role in determining responses to Hispanic newcomers, one analytically distinct from the role played by electoral pressures (Jones-Correa 2008; Van der Leun 2003, 2006), but it is important to note that external government policies remained influential in structuring these patterns in at least two ways. First, government policies defined the basic institutional rules of the game in which bureaucrats could (or could not) translate their professional orientation toward Hispanic newcomers into concrete action. Second, as I explore further in the next chapter, where I extend my analysis into law enforcement and court systems, inclusive government policies enhanced bureaucrats' service role, while restrictive ones enhanced their regulatory role, which in turn influenced how bureaucrats conceptualized their professional responsibilities toward Hispanic newcomers. Thus, even when bureaucrats tended to see themselves as "advocates on a mission" rather than as simple implementers of policy (Moody and Musheno 2003), and even though some bureaucrats were indeed willing to employ administrative discretion to facilitate Hispanic newcomers' incorporation, restrictive government policies increased the likelihood that bureaucrats fell in line unwillingly, especially when the risks of violation were high.

As other scholars have pointed out, these results demonstrate the enduring significance of government policies in immigrant newcomers' lives—particularly through the government-defined categories that are used to determine newcomers' positions vis-à-vis American law, their identity as either full or limited participants in American society, and their entitlement to (as opposed to restriction from) various resources and benefits.[27] In so doing, these results reinforce the call for more proactive immigrant integration policies—to encourage Hispanic newcomers' economic, social, and political incorporation through inclusive government policies and not simply through creative local-level efforts by public service bureaucrats and other "liaison" individuals who are attempting to do the job, case-by-case, in their absence (Gozdziak and Martin 2005).

7 "If I Didn't Trust You Before, I Don't Even Want to See You Now"

Regulatory Ambivalence in Law Enforcement and the Courts

IN THIS CHAPTER, I extend my analysis from Chapter 6 into law enforcement and court systems, to further examine how the confluence of external government policies and bureaucrats' internal professional missions helps to explain patterned differences in institutional responsiveness to Hispanic newcomers in eastern North Carolina. Law enforcement officers and court officials work in street-level bureaucracies well known for combining service with a strong regulatory mission (Lipsky 1980; Van der Leun 2003). Indeed, as in the case of social welfare agencies, the mixture of service and regulatory mission resulted in slower and less inclusive responses to Hispanic newcomers by law enforcement and court systems compared to those taking place in more purely service-oriented institutions. Furthermore, the direct and indirect roles that restrictive government policies play in retarding immigrant incorporation processes are especially visible in legal bureaucracies.

Immigrant Bureaucratic Incorporation in the Rural South

Mixed Government Policies and Mixed Professional Missions in Legal Institutions

In the mid-2000s, there was a large gap between Hispanic newcomers' level of incorporation into public elementary schools and law enforcement and court systems in eastern North Carolina. Once again, as in the case of higher educational institutions and social welfare and medical services agencies (see Chapter 6), less inclusive government policies in the latter arenas explain much of the difference because they weaken bureaucrats' requirements and abilities to respond to Hispanic newcomers' interests and needs.

To illustrate, in law enforcement agencies, government policy prohibits non-citizens (who can often communicate with coethnic newcomers) from working as officers. In courtrooms, newcomers are sometimes, but not always, entitled to a state-funded interpreter free of charge, depending on whether the case is being tried in civil or criminal court (NCAOC 2005), and the Legal Aid Bureau, a principal legal resource for low-income people, is prohibited from taking unauthorized immigrants as clients (Dunn, Aragonés, and Shivers 2005). In DMV offices, Hispanic newcomers are sometimes, but not always, eligible to obtain a driver's license, and as I discuss further, government policy in this arena has become more restrictive over time.

Yet law enforcement agencies and court systems also suffer from the same contradictions in professional goals and missions as other bureaucracies that combine a service with a strong regulatory role, such as social welfare agencies (Armenta 2010; Brehm and Gates 1999; Derthick 1979; Jones-Correa 2005b; Van der Leun 2003). For instance, whereas law enforcement officers have a service mission to prevent crime and protect all individuals who fall under their jurisdiction, they also have a regulatory mission to investigate crimes and enforce rules. Similarly, whereas court personnel have a service mission to give equal and quality protection to all individuals who appear before them, they also have a regulatory mission to deliver even-handed judgment against all individuals accused or convicted of a crime. Indeed, Maynard-Moody and Musheno (2003) point out that although teachers, social service workers, and police officers all share the core (and sometimes competing) features of street-level bureaucratic work, legal bureaucrats occupy the most regulatory space because they are uniquely "authorized to employ the state's coercive power" (39–40). In eastern North Carolina, legal bureaucrats' service mission competes with their regulatory one, creating strong internal contradictions within what Zezima (2007) terms the "core mission" of law and ultimately dampening their responsiveness toward Hispanic newcomers' interests and needs.

Wilcox County's white sheriff, Gregory, nicely illustrated these competing missions in law enforcement. Despite taking two years of Spanish in college, he did not speak or understand it very well in 2004. However, he wished he did because "it would certainly be beneficial," he felt, for law enforcement officers like himself to be able to communicate better with the Hispanic "clients" they increasingly encounter in their daily routine.[1] He also noted that having Spanish-speaking officers not only improves the level of protection law enforcement officers can provide to innocent Hispanic members of the community but also helps them do their job of catching Hispanics who have committed crimes. Thus, even though he did not oversee any Hispanic sheriff deputies in 2003–04, which he reported was primarily due to government policy prohibiting noncitizens from working as officers, Gregory supported the idea of recruiting more Hispanic sheriff deputies to help his agency reach out to Hispanics in the community and fulfill its multiple professional roles:

Interviewer: Do you speak any Spanish?

Gregory: No, ma'am. I wish I did. From a law enforcement perspective, it would certainly be beneficial to know more. Hispanics are a large part of our population now, and they are routinely victims of crimes. They're also suspects of crimes. They use the court facilities just like other citizens do. So I would venture to say there's not a law enforcement officer in the county who doesn't deal with them on a regular basis. At times our experiences trying to communicate with them have been very frustrating, and the biggest barrier obviously would be the language barrier. When you're called to a scene and a Hispanic is a victim of a crime, and they're distraught and they need immediate help, and you can't communicate with them, that causes great frustration on behalf of both parties, I guess. I would love to be able to recruit some Hispanic employees.

Interviewer: Do you have any?

Gregory: No, we do not. I've had two apply since I've been here. One was offered a higher-paying position in a larger town. The other was not a naturalized citizen. He would have made a very good employee, but here in North Carolina, by training standards laws, they have to be a citizen here to be sworn into that position. Although I think ideally the officers should mimic the general population of the county. Because it would be very helpful to have someone of a Hispanic background going into these situations where the people are primarily Hispanic. It's common sense. Until then we have been offered help from several of the Hispanic leaders in our county who have volunteered with translations. Like if we have a certain issue, people have been willing to volunteer to come with us [into the community to translate]. That's been helpful but it's still not the same as having support full-time.

Bedford County's African American sheriff, Adam, seconded the interaction of the strong service and regulatory missions embedded in local "community policing" policies and norms (Gozdziak and Bump 2008; Lewis and Ramakrishnan 2007; MCC 2006; Tramonte 2009) when he remarked, "We play a big role in Hispanic life. And the more capable we are at communicating with Hispanics, the better off we are and then also the better service that they will get."

Court personnel illustrated similar competing missions. Ashley (a pseud-onym), the state-level director of the foreign-language interpreter certifica-tion program run by North Carolina's Administrative Office of the Courts (NCAOC 2005), noted that having appropriately trained and certified inter-preters[2] not only improves the quality of service court personnel can provide to their non-English-speaking clients—thereby fulfilling a professional service mission of ensuring that immigrants' "access to justice is not impeded"[3]—but also helps them do their job of making even-handed judgments, thereby ful-filling a regulatory mission as well. Additionally, Ashley noted that having ap-propriately trained and certified interpreters fulfills the professional interests of court personnel by ensuring that all court procedures are followed properly, which protects decisions from being subject to appeal and reversal.[4] Together, Ashley thought that these mutually reinforcing benefits explain why a "surpris-ing" number of judges, magistrates, clerks, and attorneys throughout North Carolina have been actively seeking out her help to improve translation and interpretation services in their courtroom, despite some "bad apples":

Ashley: Our court officials repeatedly ask me for Spanish classes. They repeatedly
    beg me for certified interpreters. And the response in North Carolina has been
    so great to my program and my presentations that I have been asked to speak in
    other states to their judges. So what would seem to be a difficult crowd has re-
    ally been quite a good crowd. They are concerned that access to justice is being
    impeded. In some counties they have even prosecuted interpreters for practic-
    ing law without a license. In some counties they've banned interpreters who are
    no good from their courtroom. In some rural counties they have tried to put up
    signs in Spanish, and they've tried to have some of their local forms translated.
    I've even had people from mountain counties call me and want me to read the
    marriage ceremony over the speakerphone, in Spanish. I mean, just really mov-
    ing experiences where court officials have just really gone out of their way to
    make sure that the Hispanic folks they are dealing with are getting a fair shake.

However, in both institutions the regulatory mission of enforcement ul-timately competed against that of customer service, weakening the capacity of legal bureaucrats to respond to Hispanic newcomers in a way that reflects their interests and needs. Instead of citing positive or neutral relations with law enforcement officials within a service-oriented context of protection, most Hispanic respondents cited poor relations within a regulatory-oriented con-text of enforcement. For instance, Guillermo, an unauthorized immigrant who migrated directly from San Pedro Sula, Honduras, to Bedford County in 2000 to join his father and uncles who were working there, explained that Hispanics and American police officers "get along bad in general. There are a lot of Hispanics who have contact with police for driving drunk. And others for not having a license, which is the biggest problem I think."

The predominance of this regulatory-oriented mission over its service-oriented counterpart is of special concern in Hispanic respondents' reports of being unjustly targeted (if not discriminated against) for what they call "driving while Mexican" or "driving while Hispanic" (Armenta 2010). Reinforcing Elena's concerns from Chapter 6, Antonia, a legal permanent resident who migrated directly to Bedford County from Veracruz, Mexico, in 1994, reported that a friend of hers was stopped by a local police officer in a fairly clear-cut case of racial profiling:

Antonia: Once a friend of mine was driving on a private back road back there. Supposedly she had done something wrong driving, and a policeman stopped her and asked her for her driver's license. So she showed it to him. Then he asked her for her social security number. You see, around here the police are really bad. Like then, they also started asking her questions that didn't have anything to do with the situation. Like if she was married, where she comes from, what was she doing here—things like that, which have nothing to do with the driving situation. Why does it matter to him whether she is married or single? That shouldn't have happened.

Likewise, Lidia, a legal permanent resident from Oaxaca, Mexico, who was then director of housing at Poultry Processing Plant and also a prominent local, state, and transnational political leader, thought that many Hispanics in eastern North Carolina have had negative experiences being unjustly targeted and regulated by local law enforcement officers:

Lidia: Law enforcement has generalized all of us in the same category. They think that none of us have driver's licenses! [*laughs*] And that we all have false immigration documents, that we live a "double life" or have a "double identity," and that we are all from Mexico. So in general Latinos who come into contact with law enforcement find out about mistreatment and the conception that they have about us. I'll share a personal experience that I had with you. When I first bought my car, I was working at PPP. It was brand new, and I was out driving it around 11:30 p.m. or midnight. And two police officers followed me, one in front of me and another behind me. And they stopped me. And you know how when a policeman stops you, the first thing he usually does is ask you for your driver's license, right? And then your registration? Well, this policeman told me to write my name down on a piece of paper. And I told him, "No. If you want to see my license, I will give it to you. But I will not write my name down." And after they checked out my license, I asked the policeman why they pulled me over, what my infraction was. "No, it's nothing, ma'am," they said. "It's just that your car looks new and we thought it was similar to a stolen car." So I told them, "Mr. Officers, when you pull someone over the first thing you should do is ask them for their driver's license and then for their registration." "Yes, ma'am," they said. "We were looking to see if you were the correct person or not." You know what I said then? "Well, you know what, sir? I know your boss. And tomorrow morning I am going to his office and I am going to tell him about what just happened." They immediately apologized. "No, no, no—we're sorry. Please forgive us, please forgive us," they told me. You see, in that moment, they generalized against Hispanics unfairly, thinking that my new car had been stolen.

Interviewer: Would you say that most Hispanics have similar experiences?

Lidia: I think so. I think the majority are telling similar stories.

In these ways, a strong regulatory mission has produced significant distrust toward American law enforcement officers among Hispanics like Elena, Guillermo, Antonia, and Lidia, who felt skeptical that the officers treat Hispanic newcomers as community residents equally worthy of the services and protection they provide to natives. Unauthorized immigrant respondents were the most skeptical and fearful, and they went to great lengths to evade detection by law enforcement officials (Chavez 1998; Coutin 2000), who they felt "hunt" and discriminate against Hispanics who drive or go out in public (Córdova Plaza 2009; Jones-Correa and Fennelly 2009; Preston 2008b; Sabogal 2005).

In court systems, several respondents also reported insufficient and slow responsiveness to the growth of the Hispanic population. Soledad, an unauthorized immigrant who migrated from San Marcos, Guatemala, directly to Bedford County in 1998, pointed out that there was no certified interpreter for Hispanics in the Bedford County courtroom in 2004. In her view, this harmed both court personnel, by slowing down their daily operations, and non-English-speaking individuals who came before the court, who she worried might be found guilty instead of innocent, or guilty of a more serious crime than they committed, when court personnel cannot gain accurate information about their cases:

Soledad: It's very important for the courts to have qualified interpreters. It's incredibly important because sometimes the person in court is not 100% bilingual. And if you are not totally sure that someone has said it right, you could go to jail!

In more heavily Hispanic Wilcox County, Karen, the executive director of federal programs in the Wilcox County Public Schools, reported that court personnel's response to the growing need for interpretation has also been slow. In fact, she reported that it has been so slow as to be negatively affecting Hispanic youths, who she saw being encouraged by "dismissive" court personnel to skip school in order to interpret for their parents:[5]

Karen: One problem which we still see some, even though we're not seeing as much of now as we did in the beginning, is that you've got parents who can't speak English and so they keep their kids home a lot to go with them to court to translate. So we have problems with kids staying out of school too much. And this is just a personal thing, but the court is not very supportive of us. They're like, "Don't take them back to school. They're not going to school anyway." Sometimes I think the court system needs a course on culture. I think they need to support us more.

Other respondents who did acknowledge some degree of service mission among local court personnel nevertheless thought that they, like law enforcement officers, focused disproportionately on enforcing and regulating Hispanic newcomers' behavior at the expense of establishing good relations with and serving them. For example, Octavio is an unauthorized immigrant who migrated from Sinaloa, Mexico, to Texas in 1999, and then later to Bedford County in 2000, where his brother was working. Octavio reported that unfriendly and unhelpful court personnel have not taken adequate steps to offer quality interpreting services to Hispanics in Bedford County, which in turn has made Hispanics feel unworthy and unattended when they go into court:

Octavio: You always feel like a small rat in court. You arrive in there, and you have no idea what is going on. You don't understand anything, you are just standing there like a small rat that doesn't understand anything. They are saying all these things to you, but you don't understand anything. Like they tell Hispanics, "Blah blah blah blah blah blah . . ." I tell you, who knows what that means? They need somebody in there, who can interpret for you. And there isn't one. You have to bring your own, like a friend, or you have to pay for one.

Interviewer: And they don't have an interpreter there for you?

Octavio: No. Unfortunately there isn't. You have to bring your own, like a friend, or you have to pay for one.

Interviewer: So what does that feel like?

Octavio: Well, we are in a state where when it is a more serious issue, they pay
for you to have a lawyer, right? But what if that lawyer doesn't speak Spanish?
How is that going to help them understand you? If you don't speak English
and your lawyer doesn't speak Spanish? I would say that I think that's what
this small town lacks. Policemen or some other people who are able to speak
both languages, English and Spanish. Because I have not seen any policemen
here who speak Spanish. Well, some speak a few words, but they don't speak
enough of it to be able to understand us. That's a problem.

Because I personally witnessed several incidents where court personnel
treated Hispanics poorly—such as when they assumed a common regulatory
role in trying to "catch" Hispanics who they thought were trying to "trick" them
into showing leniency by pretending not to speak or understand English—I
consider respondents' descriptions of such incidents to be valid.[6] As in law enforcement, they reduced Hispanic newcomers' feelings of trust and incorporation into local court systems by making them feel more regulated than served.
Consequently, the inclusive efforts that bureaucrats such as Ashley were making
were simultaneously being hindered, producing weaker forms of incorporation
than those evident in schools.

In fact, during a module of the Hispanic Leadership Course in Wilcox
County, I witnessed an episode that poignantly demonstrates the symbolic
regulatory and exclusionary role of law enforcement officers and court officials
in Hispanic newcomers' lives in eastern North Carolina in the mid-2000s. Lidia
started the meeting off by passing out a bilingual flyer advertising the services
of the Self Help Credit Union, a group that specializes in providing financial
services, information, and loans to low-income and minority groups. Lidia encouraged members of the course to attend an informational meeting that Self
Help was scheduling for the following evening at the local health department
in the county seat of Wilcox. Members of the course, many of whom lived in
surrounding towns and areas and were not familiar with driving around Wilcox proper, asked Lidia to tell them where the health department was located.
For the next 10 minutes, Lidia and two other students tried to give out driving
directions, naming several prominent buildings near the county health department (including the public library) that might serve as common landmarks
for members to find, but with little success. Only when they asked if members
knew where the county courthouse was did they receiving a resounding reply;
everyone in the room responded quickly with an overwhelming yet apprehen-
sive chorus of "Yes!" After a short pause, and realizing what had just happened,

course members looked around the room at each other and started laughing sheepishly. They all had known where the county courthouse was located, but not where the county library and health department were. Moreover, they had all recognized that a collective fear of American legal authorities accounted for the difference (fieldnotes, Oct. 22, 2003).

The Impact of Government Policy Changes
on Legal Bureaucrats' Professional Missions

Two recent sets of restrictive government policy changes are notable for having retarded responsiveness to Hispanic newcomers' interests and needs in legal bureaucracies even further, by defining more Hispanics as automatic nonclients of the local legal system and requiring legal bureaucrats to abide more strongly by the regulatory mission than the service mission of their job as they come into compliance with the policy changes. The first set of changes has restricted many Hispanic newcomers' eligibility for obtaining a North Carolina state driver's license, while the second set of changes has made Hispanic newcomers more vulnerable to everyday surveillance through what scholars call the "cross-deputization" of state and local law enforcement officers as federal immigration agents. Together, both sets of changes have made many Hispanic newcomers in eastern North Carolina even more distrustful of local legal bureaucrats than they already were. In fact, several respondents saw these trends as evidence that state and local legal institutions are "regressing" from more positive practices that previously attempted to incorporate Hispanic newcomers, especially unauthorized ones, as worthy clients. Some were equally miffed to see such regression occurring alongside then president George W. Bush's calls for a more open and inclusive federal immigration policy in early 2004, including proposals for a temporary guest worker program and potential amnesty for long-term unauthorized immigrants.

To illustrate how the first set of policy changes has dampened incorporation patterns, consider that until February 2, 2004, North Carolina was widely considered to be one of the most open states in terms of immigrants' ability to obtain a driver's license. Before 1997, there was no legal prohibition in the state for issuing a driver's license to an applicant who failed to provide a social security number (SSN; Denning 2009). As of March 2005, North Carolina was still one of only 12 states that did not have a lawful permanent residency requirement[7] and one of only six states that accepted the individual tax identification number (ITIN, a number issued by the Internal Revenue Service for tax collection purposes) as an alternative to an SSN[8] for an applicant wishing to obtain a state driver's license, a practice it had begun in 2001 (Denning 2009; NILC

2009a). In an interview conducted in September 2003, Ricardo, an immigrant who migrated directly from Veracruz, Mexico, to Bedford County in 1996, illustrated how Hispanic newcomers were grateful for North Carolina's pre-2004 policies in this regard:

Ricardo: There are lots of states where Hispanics can't drive with licenses. And that's a privilege that the whole community here does have. I think it is very important, because it allows us to move back and forth to our jobs without any problems. It's different than other states that are very hard on that.

However, on February 2, 2004, a statewide policy change went into effect, restricting the documents that would be accepted thereafter for obtaining a state driver's license. Among the documents no longer accepted as proof of identity after this date were the Mexican national identification card (known in Spanish as the *matrícula consular*) and any birth certificate issued outside the United States, Puerto Rico, and Canada (Collins 2008e; Easterbrook 2004a, 2004b; McClain 2006; Smith and Furuseth 2006b). From late December 2003, when the policy change was publicly announced, through the spring of 2004, confusion abounded in the state's Hispanic community as to which documents would continue be accepted for a new or renewed driver's license,[9] and private attorneys struggled to figure out how the policy changes would affect those immigrant clients with special circumstances (fieldnotes, spring 2004). Opponents angrily decried the changes as anti-immigrant,[10] while supporters of the change cited national security concerns. People caught in the middle, like Mark, a white Democrat who represented part of Bedford County in the state Senate, generally supported a liberal state driver's license policy but felt ambivalent in light of national security rhetoric after the September 11 terrorist attacks and the restrictive winds of change coming down from the federal government:

Mark: I think that the state DMV commissioner has a real challenge. He's got the restrictive directive from Washington as far as the Department of Homeland Security [DHS] is concerned. He's also got the need that there are a lot of people in the Hispanic community who are driving in North Carolina right now, and that we need to have them licensed properly and aware of what the rules and laws of the road are. The head of the N.C. Driver's License division is a very considerate man who will do the best he can to try to accommodate the Hispanic community. But I think he has restrictions.

Then, on August 27, 2006, further restrictive state legislation in the form of North Carolina Senate Bill 602 (the Technical Corrections Act) went into effect, eliminating an applicant's ability to present an individual tax identification number (ITIN) as an alternative to a social security number when applying for a North Carolina driver's license (Denning 2009). To prove in-state residence, Hispanic applicants now face the challenge of presenting at least two forms of identification approved by the North Carolina Division of Motor Vehicles Commissioner when applying for a driver's license, where neither the *matrícula consular* nor a birth certificate issued by a Latin American country other than Puerto Rico will be approved. To prove their lawful presence in the state, they also face the additional challenge of presenting a valid SSN or a valid visa issued by a U.S. government agency, since the ITIN will no longer be accepted.

Obviously, these two sets of driver's license policy changes have affected unauthorized immigrants most harshly, just as they have in other states that enacted similar measures; according to Denning (2009) "the upshot is that unauthorized immigrants may no longer obtain a North Carolina driver's license . . . learner's permit, or identification card" (2). However, according to immigrant advocates, they have also affected many legal immigrants—for example, those whose foreign birth certificate no longer qualifies for acceptance as a valid form of identification. In the fall of 2006, confusion once again abounded in the state's Hispanic community as to which documents would continue be accepted for a new or renewed driver's license, and Hispanic residents poured into community meetings requesting clarification about the policy changes and seeking assistance from coethnic leaders about how obtain original and renewed licenses in the future:

> [A Mexican immigrant] stood near the back of the room and listened to the presenter. He has a driver's license, but worries about renewal. "I can drive now, but what will happen when I need to renew?" he asked. He does not want to break the law of his adopted homeland, doesn't want to get in trouble. He needs to get around, however. (*Bedford Newspaper*, Nov. 26, 2006; also *Evergreen Times*, Oct. 8, 2006; and Collins 2008e)

These driver's license policy changes have also retarded several legal bureaucrats' efforts to respond to Hispanic newcomers' interests and needs, precisely by amplifying their regulatory professional role as they come into compliance with the policy changes. In 2004, a number of Hispanic respondents (including employees of local legal bureaucracies) argued that the first restrictive policy change was exacerbating existing tensions and distrust between Hispanic newcomers and local law enforcement officers and court officials, making it even harder for legal bureaucrats to build trusting relationships with Hispanic clients and therefore do their jobs optimally.[11] Felipe, a 1.5 generation youth from Oaxaca, Mexico, illustrated the point:

Felipe: It's really going to hurt a lot of Latinos, because a lot of us commute to work. I mean, I used to have an hour and a half commute to get to work! And I know a lot of other people do too. So honestly, I think people are still going to drive, but it'll just make them drive now without a license. And also there will be a better chance that somebody that has no clue what a stick shift is, or they don't know what cruise control is, and they just get in a car and get in a wreck. And there will be a better chance that they will hurt themselves or hurt somebody else. I mean, honestly I think it's just a dumb law. It'll make everybody hate each other, too. *I mean, like if Latinos didn't trust the police before . . . like if I didn't trust you before, I don't even want to see you now!* [my emphasis]

Other respondents concurred that using government policy to restrict Hispanic newcomers' eligibility to obtain a state driver's license harms not only newcomers themselves, by (in the words of one Hispanic advocate) "inviting them to break the law" (*Bedford Newspaper*, Nov. 26, 2004), but also local law enforcement officers, by decreasing Hispanic newcomers' willingness to communicate and cooperate with them; court personnel, by increasing caseloads in local traffic courts; and the general public, by increasing the costs associated with driving infractions caused by unlicensed and uninsured drivers, primarily through higher insurance premiums that get passed on to other insured drivers (Collins 2008e; NILC 2008b).

To illustrate how the second set of policy changes has also dampened incorporation patterns by amplifying legal bureaucrats' regulatory role over their service role, consider that many state and local law enforcement officers have been cross-deputized as federal immigration agents since the early 2000s, within a larger federal context that has stressed "vertical integration" of immigration enforcement (Newton and Adams 2009). In 1996 the Illegal Immigration Reform and Immigrant Responsibility Act (IIRIRA) added Section 287(g) to the Immigration and Nationality Act. This section authorized U.S. Immigration and Customs Enforcement (ICE) to enter into memoranda of agreement with state and local law enforcement agencies to train selected state and local officers to perform certain functions of immigration officers, at their own cost and under the supervision of federal ICE officers. Functions include searching selected federal databases and conducting interviews to assist in identifying those individuals who are in the country illegally. Under memoranda of agreement, state and local law enforcement officers have direct access to ICE databases and can act in the stead of ICE agencies by processing aliens for removal, which goes beyond their previous ability to communicate indirectly with ICE regarding the immigration status of individuals, or to otherwise cooperate indirectly with ICE in identification and removal of aliens not lawfully present in the United States.[12]

The 287(g) program is just one of 14 covered by the umbrella of ICE's Agreements of Cooperation in Communities to Enhance Safety and Security (Rodríguez, Chishti, Capps, and St. John 2010), and its stated goal is to help remove those unauthorized immigrants convicted of "violent crimes, human smuggling, gang/organized crime activity, sexual-related offenses, narcotics smuggling, and money laundering"—in other words, to target "the most violent and dangerous criminals" who pose the "greatest threat to society" and are the "first priority for removal" (Weissman et al. 2009: 25–26). Overall, there was little interest in cross-deputization between 1996 and 2001, but it rose after the September 11 terrorist attacks. The first 287(g) agreement was signed by the state of Florida in 2002, and by February 2009, 67 state and local agencies in 23 states, including 951 individual officers, were participating in this program, with 42 additional requests by state and local agencies to join still pending. In fiscal year 2008, approximately 43,000 illegal aliens were arrested under the program (Fitzgerald 2011; U.S. GAO 2009a, 2009b).

By October 2009, seven North Carolina county sheriff departments had entered into cross-deputization programs,[13] as had the Durham city police department, whose Hispanic chief reported holding "a perspective on immigration [that] balances the need to protect the public from dangerous illegal immigrants with the imperative to gain the trust and cooperation of all city residents, including undocumented aliens" (Schwade 2008). Together, they had identified more than 15,000 people in the state as being suspected illegal aliens since 2006, referring them to ICE for a decision on deportation (Caldwell 2009). In fact, the only state with more agencies officially entered into 287(g) memoranda of agreement by this date was Virginia (Collins 2008g; Nguyen and Gill 2010; Verdaguer 2008; Weissman et al. 2009).

Moreover, the increase in 287(g) cross-deputization has come on the heels of North Carolina House of Representatives Bill 2692—which in 2006 approved establishment of a state immigration court to speed up deportation of unauthorized immigrants and pressured the U.S. Congress to make impaired driving a deportable offense (Lacy and Odem 2009; McClain 2006)—but also North Carolina Gen Stat. §162-62—which in 2007 began requiring *all* North Carolina county and local jails to verify the immigration status of persons in their facilities detained on felony or impaired driving charges (Caldwell 2009; Markham 2009; Weissman et al. 2009). Finally, it has been further encouraged by national-level immigration law enforcement acts in 2003, 2005, and 2006,[14] including the CLEAR Act of 2003 during the time of my research.

According to several respondents, the cross-deputization being encouraged by the CLEAR Act of 2003 was exacerbating existing tensions and distrust between Hispanic newcomers and local law enforcement officers and court officials in the mid-2000s, even though it had not yet been officially implemented in either county. For instance, Carmen, a bilingual Hispanic assistant district attorney in Wilcox County, reported that prior to 2004 court officials already had trouble convincing Hispanics to report crimes to law enforcement officials or comply with court officials—something that was especially worrisome to her in cases of domestic abuse, when unauthorized immigrant women fear being deported or separated from their children if they seek legal assistance. In 2004, she was concerned that passage of the CLEAR Act of 2003 was making these barriers against reaching out to Hispanic abuse victims even worse, by increasing victim's incentive not to cooperate with court personnel lest authorities make unwanted inquiries into their legal status. Likewise, in the realm of law enforcement, Marco, an island-born Puerto Rican schoolteacher who was instrumental in promoting improved relations between Hispanics and law enforcement officers in Bedford County, was hoping that the CLEAR Act of 2003 would not pass precisely because many of the local law enforcement officers he knew were against it, out of fear that it would reverse important gains recently made in developing trust with Hispanics in the community:

Marco: They do not want the border control's job of immigration enforcement and are mad that they are now being asked to do so. They are saying, "Screw you, INS. We have spent a lot of resources and time to win the trust of immigrants in these areas, and we're not going to turn around now and mess that up."

Indeed, although support for cross-deputization in North Carolina comes primarily from sheriffs and county commissioners, who are elected officials (Gill et al. 2009; Nguyen and Gill 2010), nationwide non-elected local police officers seem to share with their counterparts in Bedford County a much less enthusiastic response.[15]

Moreover, as was the case with ever more restrictive state driver's license policies, the mere threat of potential cross-deputization even in counties where it had not yet been officially implemented was exacerbating many Hispanic respondents' fears of state and local legal authorities, particularly local police officers and the highway patrol (Armenta 2010; Donato 2009; Gill et al. 2009; Jones-Correa and Fennelly 2009; Nguyen and Gill 2010). Pilar, an unauthorized immigrant who migrated from Lima, Peru, directly to Bedford County in 2002, poignantly demonstrated how she was already doing everything she could to avoid contact with local law enforcement officers in 2004, who she feared would try to deport her from the country simply for being unauthorized:

Interviewer: You said earlier that for you, any policeman is the INS.

Pilar: Yes, I have that idea. I know it's not like that, but I am very careful of that. I prefer . . .

Interviewer: You try to stay away from them as much as possible?

Pilar: Yes, I protect myself. Exactly. I've never had any experience with a policeman. And I prefer it that way, to stay away from the police.

Interviewer: Why is it that you feel like all policemen are immigration officials? What gives you that feeling?

Pilar: Because I know I don't have documents. I know that even though I know one day the government might offer me an amnesty—and I am hopeful about that—but right now I'm not legal.

Passage of the CLEAR Act of 2003 and other subsequent national-level immigration law enforcement acts have reinforced this association that Pilar and other unauthorized immigrants make among state and local law enforcement officers, court officials, and federal immigration agents. In turn, this association has diminished their willingness to approach and communicate with local law enforcement officers and court officials in any way, even in instances where they are victims of a serious crime (Nguyen and Gill 2010; Tramonte 2009; Weissman et al. 2009).

Carmen, Marco, and Pilar's concerns parallel those of prominent legal and immigrant advocacy groups, government agencies, and even law enforcement associations, in North Carolina and beyond.[16] On the one hand, such groups worry that cross-deputization has not been appropriately envisioned, supervised, or funded by federal immigration officials, which raises the potential for inappropriate intimidation of immigrants by law enforcement officers as well as the financial costs of enforcement assumed by host communities. On the other hand, they worry that cross-deputized state and local law enforcement officials disproportionately seek out unauthorized immigrants who have committed only minor violations (such as driving with an open container) rather than serious felonies, thereby fostering the incidence of racial profiling and discrimination against all Hispanic newcomers (Donato 2009; Gouveia 2006),[17] decreasing trust between Hispanic newcomers and law enforcement officers, and undermining community policing objectives and overall community safety and trust.[18]

Indeed, despite arguments from advocates of the 287(g) program, such as Caldwell (2009), that it "works to make communities safer" (4), there is mounting evidence within North Carolina that by promoting law enforcement officers' regulatory mission over their service mission, cross-deputization has begun to negatively affect the very "noncriminal" unauthorized immigrants, as well as other Hispanic newcomers, that the program reports espousing a service mission to protect. In 2008, deportation proceedings in Mecklenburg County (where Charlotte is located) had begun against 4,333 illegal immigrants, "even though approximately 90 percent of these 'tough, hardened criminals' were snared by misdemeanor arrests" (Schwade 2008). Likewise, in 2007 only 64 of the 434 people who were processed for deportation in Alamance County, in the central piedmont region of the state, were charged with felonies, while 302 were arrested on traffic violations (Collins 2008c; Gill et al. 2009). In May 2008, 83% of the immigrants arrested by 287(g) officers in Gaston County, also in the central piedmont region of the state, were charged with traffic violations (Weissman et al. 2009). And overall, in a study of five counties using the program (Alamance, Cabarrus, Gaston, Mecklenburg, and Wake), 86.7% of all booked individuals were charged with misdemeanors—mostly traffic violations and DWIs, which Nguyen and Gill (2010) argue are partially the result of a lack of driver's education and training thanks to the inability of unauthorized immigrants to apply for and receive state driver's licenses—compared to just 13.3% with felonies.

These varied data have led Weissman et al. (2009) to conclude that Section 287(g) in North Carolina is "utilized not as a tool to aid law enforcement, but instead as a localized immigration weapon and tool for intimidation and isolation of foreign nationals and Hispanic residents and citizens.... The arrest data appear to indicate that Mecklenburg and Alamance counties are typical in the targeting of Hispanics for traffic offenses for the purposes of a deportation policy" (28–29). Moreover, such a conclusion is supported by reports from the U.S. Government Accountability Office and the Migration Policy Institute, both of which confirm that the 287(g) program has come to target "low-hanging fruit" instead of the most dangerous criminals (GAO 2009b; Rodríguez et al. 2010). Going still further, the conclusion is also supported not only by national FBI and Census data—which show that 287(g) agreements have expanded in places where the rate of Latino population growth is higher even though the property and violent crime indices are *lower* than national averages (Shahani and Greene 2009)[19]—but also by North Carolina violent and property crime data, which show no evidence that either rising immigration or Hispanic population growth is associated with a higher crime rate (Nguyen and Gill 2010). Even staunch advocates of the 287(g) program have had to admit that people convicted of less serious crimes get deported under the program. According to Caldwell (2009), a full 31% of the charges made against all inmates in 2008 in North Carolina involved violations of motor vehicle law, another 24% involved driving while impaired, and still another unreported percentage of what he categorizes as "serious criminal violation" in fact involve "trespass" (16)—in other words, unlawful presence in the country, which is actually considered to be a civil rather than criminal offense under current federal immigration law (Brettell and Nibbs 2010; Gill et al. 2009).

Ever more restrictive government policies in the two arenas of driver's licenses and cross-deputization have thereby visibly discouraged incorporation of Hispanic newcomers, especially of unauthorized immigrants. They have defined new rules that directly prohibit service-oriented responsiveness to Hispanic newcomers' interests and needs; they have also prioritized legal bureaucrats' regulatory mission over their service mission. As perhaps the most direct evidence of the latter, in January 2007 the North Carolina Sheriffs' Association (the nonprofit agency responsible for administering funds for cross-deputization in North Carolina) illustrated an enhanced regulatory mission in a resolution it sent to state and federal legislators, where it called for more resources to cross-deputize local and state law enforcement officers with the goal of collectively deporting all illegal immigrants from the state.

Of course, some legal bureaucrats in law enforcement agencies, court systems, and DMV offices still exhibit a service-oriented mission regarding Hispanic newcomers, as Marco and Carmen illustrated earlier in this chapter (see also Armenta 2010; and Winn 2007), and as proliferation of local policies of "noncompliance" with federal immigration enforcement efforts throughout the country attests (Newton and Adams 2009). In 2003–04, these bureaucrats were arguing vocally against the two sets of restrictive policy changes and working creatively to promote responsiveness within the bounds of existing policies as best they could. This was perhaps most evident in their attempts to disseminate information and "teach" their coworkers how to respond more positively to a growing population of Hispanics, in accordance with a broader public service mission of promoting community safety. For example, Joaquin, a bilingual attorney in Union County, was working to spread the argument that a driver's license is primarily meant to confirm that drivers who are on the road are certified, know the rules of the road, and will be responsible for any accidents they cause. He even argued that using it as a tool to validate or invalidate a person's immigration status is inconsistent with international law:

Joaquin: There clearly has been a targeting of immigrants [in these driver's license policies]. As for the documentation that's being accepted, I think it's simply a lack of knowledge of how international laws interrelate. When people want to accept documents and they're not certain as to whether or not they are valid documents, there has been a procedure for validating international documents for 100 years! The way you validate an international document is you have the document sent to the American consul in the country where the document was generated. And have them certify it, by the American consul. Once that document that has been certified by the American consulate it can be presented and accepted in the United States. At that point we can extend international law and treatment to that document. And that's how you do that. Like with a birth certificate, if you don't know if it's valid or not. That's been the procedure forever. So I guess that the question with North Carolina not accepting foreign birth certificates now is, "What is the state most interested in: ensuring that knowledgeable and safe driving occurs on our roads, or enforcing immigration laws, or both?" What are they trying to promote? See, if it's enforcing immigration laws, then this newly passed legislation will assist them.

Similarly, Ashley and Lenora (the sole bilingual court interpreter in Wilcox and Union Counties) were working to spread the argument that restrictive driver's license policies only decrease community safety, as unauthorized immigrants are forced to pay more money to obtain a fake driver's license on the black market, producing a situation where North Carolina residents will be less safe on the roads, assume greater risk for identity theft, and bear a greater fiscal burden for uninsured and unlicensed immigrant motorists (Collins 2008e; NILC 2008b). And following a conference in nearby Beaufort County (not a pseudonym), which was held in October 2008 to oppose several pieces of blatantly anti-immigrant legislation recently passed by its board of county commissioners (Allegood 2007; Collins 2008b; Parsons 2007; Voss 2007), the sheriff of another neighboring county recounted to me his "extreme frustration" at the "anti-immigrant" statements he had been hearing from his fellow North Carolina sheriffs in their internal state-level meetings, further detailing his unsuccessful attempts to change their views (postfieldwork notes, October 2008).

Nonetheless, in contrast to higher educational and nonregular medical institutions, where I uncovered a few notable cases of bureaucrats defying government policies in order to serve Hispanic clients in accordance with a strong service-oriented mission, very few of these legal bureaucrats seemed able (or willing) to do so; the only instance of policy violation among DMV bureaucrats I observed came secondhand and was unconfirmed.[20] In short, service-inspired defiance of government policies in any institution entails considerable effort and risk, even for the clients deemed most morally worthy. In law enforcement and court systems, it may carry even greater risk, not the least of which is symbolic for bureaucrats who have devoted their professional career to upholding existing laws and who are influenced by a strong regulatory mission as well as a service one. Thus, even legal bureaucrats who were driven by a strong service-oriented mission were finding it extremely difficult and risky to battle restrictive trends in government policies in 2003–04, which have only continued apace. As of 2008, 42 states had passed DMV laws similar to the one North Carolina passed in 2006, and passage of the federal REAL ID Act of 2005 (whose full implementation was required in all 50 states by the extension date of December 2009) has institutionalized the two requirements of presenting a social security number and proving one's lawful immigrant presence throughout the country.[21] And by February 2009, at least 20 new North Carolina law enforcement agencies had also requested to cross-deputize (Weissman et al. 2009).

Perhaps even more important, by 2009, 13 counties in North Carolina[22] were among 116 jurisdictions in 16 U.S. states that had begun participating in voluntary pilot programs for a new ICE Secure Communities plan, which is intended to take advantage of the "full interoperability" of the federal government's biometric identification systems to identify and remove "criminal illegal aliens." Projected to be made available to all of the nation's 1,200 state and federal prisons and 3,100 local jails by the end of 2013 (Rodríguez et al. 2010), under this plan state and local law enforcement officers can check *all* detainees' fingerprints, and thereby their immigration status and prior immigration violations, against FBI and DHS records as part of routine booking processes (Markham 2009). As Gill et al. (2009) note, the Secure Communities plan is important because it represents the most thorough devolution to date of responsibility for federal immigration enforcement, including civil immigration violations, to the local level. Unfortunately for many Hispanic newcomers, even though the plan's stated goal is to target the most dangerous criminal aliens, under it any unauthorized immigrant can be deported for any suspected crime once he or she has been brought into custody. And perhaps to no one's surprise, based on the record of the 287(g) program, arrest data from Secure Communities' first year of operation show that about half of all people deported through it have been charged with minor offenses, not felonies (quoted in Nguyen and Gill 2010: 43).

Summary

The characteristics of Hispanic newcomers in the rural new destinations combine with severe resource disadvantages to depress their chances for group-level political incorporation. Traditional political incorporation theories, envisioning politician "principals" wielding substantial control over their bureaucratic "agents," predict even less substantive bureaucratic responsiveness. Indeed, an enormous body of historical research documents African Americans in the Jim Crow South and Mexican Americans in the Southwest suffering from various forms of bureaucratic disenfranchisement, in line with their communities' generally conservative cultural mores.[23] Such disenfranchisement was a major reason leaders of those racial and ethnic minority groups targeted federal electoral politics and courts during the Civil Rights Movement, in the hopes of effecting responsiveness that could be enforced, from the top down, onto resistant state and local politicians, and by extension their bureaucratic arms.

However, compared to elected politicians, bureaucrats in eastern North Carolina were responding more inclusively, not less, to Hispanic newcomers, even unauthorized ones. This suggests that a new pattern of bureaucratic rather than traditional political incorporation—one where Hispanic newcomers are extended social rights in bureaucracies *before* they are extended political ones (Guiraudon 2000; Jones-Correa 2008; Lewis and Ramakrishnan 2007; Marrow 2009a)—is under way in the rural South, despite severe resource and financial constraints that tend to encourage exclusive treatment of clients (Jones-Correa 2008; Lipsky 1980; Meier and O'Toole 2006). Indeed, professional missions played an independent role in determining institutional responses to newcomers across the public bureaucracies I examined, a role analytically distinct from that played by electoral pressures. Many bureaucrats spoke about their response to Hispanic newcomers in normative ways, highly reflective of their professional orientation to promote equity and community wellbeing, not just of government policies. And it was workers in the most service-oriented helping professions who were most likely to ignore, stretch, bend, and if need be break restrictive government policies to provide more than routine service to newcomer clients they deemed worthy.

Nevertheless, over these two chapters I have also shown how external government policies remained influential in structuring incorporation patterns, by exerting both direct control over bureaucrats' behaviors and what might be better termed indirect "influence" (Meier and O'Toole 2006) over bureaucrats' conceptions of their professional role. This suggests that bureaucratic incorporation is not yet occurring independently but still in interaction with traditional political incorporation. Put differently, some of the inclusive government policies that were encouraging inclusive bureaucratic responses in eastern North Carolina in the mid-2000s—such as *Plyler v. Doe* in K–12 schools, EMTALA in emergency medical services agencies, required use of certified interpreters and translators in various public bureaucracies, and even the United States' *jus soli* citizenship policy, which automatically grants citizenship to all persons born within U.S. territory—are products of past efforts by racial and ethnic minority groups and their coalition partners to achieve substantive electoral responsiveness. Likewise, some of the service-oriented professional norms that were encouraging inclusive bureaucratic responses—such as ideals of pluralism and diversity in schools and the ideal of community policing in law enforcement—have also grown out of past electoral political pressures (Lewis and Ramakrishnan 2007).

Notably, these patterns challenge the dominant view in theories of bureaucracy that direct bureaucratic responsiveness to clients is "dangerous" to democratic governance, because politicians are given oversight over bureaucrats precisely in order to ensure that the latter do not deviate from the will of their governing publics. Some scholars have identified a positive and redistributive role for bureaucratic discretion, but most continue to view it as negative and worry about its potentially unequalizing effects (Brehm and Gates 1999; Keiser and Soss 1998; Lipsky 1980). To be sure, street-level bureaucrats can resist the inclusive efforts of politicians and government policies, as when a school administrator in Leadville, Colorado, wrongly told immigrant parents that they could not volunteer in their children's school without proof of legal status (Nelson and Hiemstra 2008); when DMV bureaucrats in New York defied former governor Eliot Spitzer's proposal to allow unauthorized immigrants to obtain a driver's license (Hakim 2007); when county hospital providers in Morristown, Tennessee, stopped filing citizenship paperwork for babies born to unauthorized immigrants (Winders 2008b); when the circuit clerk in Scott County, Mississippi, began requiring proof of legal presence from applicants seeking a marriage license (Weise 2008); and when staff at food stamp offices and health care agencies erroneously told their clients that they are required to report any applicant who is an unauthorized immigrant to the authorities (Cacari Stone 2004; Hagan et al. 2003; Porter 2006). But the most service-oriented bureaucrats in my research instead represent discretion working in the opposite direction (Van der Leun 2003, 2006).

This forces us to critically reengage one of the central questions in the literature on democracy, citizenship, and immigration: Are immigrants (especially unauthorized ones) part of the "public" to which elected officials and, ultimately, bureaucrats are held accountable? If some bureaucrats are answering this question in the affirmative before either elected officials or other non-immigrant members of the public, then it is time to reconsider their roles as active and independent facilitators of responsive democratic functioning as well as of immigrant incorporation. Nevertheless, creative local-level efforts by bureaucrats and other liaison individuals to incorporate Hispanic newcomers into public service bureaucracies are still an imperfect substitute for strong, inclusive government policies. The latter, as demonstrated by the exemplary case of public elementary schools, encourage incorporation not only directly but also indirectly by enhancing bureaucrats' service over their regulatory role and influencing how they conceptualize their professional responsibilities toward newcomers.

Conclusion

Promises and Pitfalls in the Rural American South

IN 2000, Eduardo left his hometown in the department[1] of Quetzaltenango, Guatemala, because his earnings in agriculture there were no longer enough to support himself. With the assistance of a professional smuggler, he headed north across the Mexico-Guatemala border and then across the U.S.-Mexico border after that. Once in the United States, he met up with another man who specialized in transporting immigrants to "places where there is work." For a more modest fee ($600 "for gasoline"), this man drove Eduardo directly to Wilcox County, eastern North Carolina, where Eduardo spent the next two years harvesting tobacco, cotton, and cucumbers. He then settled into the poultry processing industry because it offered him better-paying, cleaner, and more permanent work. In 2003, Eduardo was informally married and living together [*juntado* in Spanish] with a woman he knew back in Guatemala but did not start dating until they re-encountered one another in Wilcox County. I caught up with Eduardo after I attended a Guatemalan Catholic church service with another one of my acquaintances, Gloria, on a sunny fall Sunday morning. Eduardo proudly introduced me to his new U.S.-born son, who was one year old, before joining me for an interview at a picnic table outside the church, which was situated on a rural side road near Poultry Processing Plant.

Although Eduardo offered many deep insights into the Hispanic newcomer experience in rural North Carolina, none were more powerful than those he offered regarding lack of legal status. After we finished our interview, he admitted that he hadn't known what the interview was going to be about at first, and that he had even been anxious about it. But once the interview got going, he told me, he really started to enjoy it and decided to open up about his experiences as an unauthorized immigrant because he considers them very important for natives to know more about. "We need people who are like you," he told me, people who will "work a lot" to tell Americans about the problems Hispanics are facing and prepare them "so that they can help us."

Like many other unauthorized respondents, Eduardo explained that he likes the United States and the atmosphere of being here. In Guatemala, he reported, there is no future for low-skilled people like himself to find decent-paying jobs and try to work themselves up the ladder to build stable lives, and so his "dream is to be here in the United States" forever. Eduardo explained how the opportunity for legalization would not only solve a plethora of practical struggles that he faces every day, which range from not being able to present a valid social security number to employers or DMV bureaucrats "for identi-fication purposes" to having to always be ready "to run if Immigration comes tomorrow." It would also, in his words, serve the more symbolic purpose of giving him the "rights to work legally, to report my taxes, and to be legal in front of the law" without having to lie—three things he associates with the "very big" promise of freedom inherent in American identity. In this sense, Eduardo poignantly captured many unauthorized respondents' desires to become legal and law-abiding members of their new American communities, and also their ambivalence about having to migrate and work illegally in order to fulfill their moral duty to support their family:

Eduardo: I want to be a good citizen here. I want to follow the rules and the laws of this country. I love this country. It has opened its doors to me and given me opportunities that I didn't have in Guatemala. Here I can raise a family, I can buy a car, I can work and make money for my work and try to fulfill my dreams. I wake up every morning and I ask forgiveness from God for having to do what I do in order to live my life. I don't like doing it, and I wish there were another way. It's very hard. That's why I say it would be better to make people legal. Because we want to follow the rules, but we have to live our lives and support our families and children, too.

· · ·

In this book, I have moved the focus of American immigrant incorporation research out from major immigrant gateways and into the new destination region where questions of immigrant incorporation and exclusion are most intriguing: the rural and small-town American South. I have argued that shift-ing our focus to new destinations of the rural American South alters how we must think about at least three main things in relation to contemporary immigration: assimilation, race relations, and political and institutional responsiveness to immigrants. Compared to what would be the case in many major immigrant gateways, the rural South makes a difference to Hispanic newcomers' experiences and opportunities for incorporation and assimilation in America by *weakening the economic barriers* separating these newcomers from local mainstream American natives, by *strengthening the cultural and racial barriers* separating these newcomers from local mainstream American natives, and by *depressing these newcomers' opportunities for achieving political incorporation through descriptive representation,* at least during the early stages of settlement. In this chapter, I summarize the main theoretical and substantive contributions of my research, discuss its major policy implications, and speculate on the negative impact of troubling changes that have occurred in the rural South since I conducted my fieldwork in 2003–04, changes that now threaten to reverse many of the encouraging outcomes I have documented in this book.

Theoretical Contributions to the Literature

My main theoretical contribution is that *context matters* to immigrant incorporation processes, not only across places in the United States but also across receiving institutional spheres and policy levels. In the literature, context tends to be broadly conceptualized or ambiguously operationalized in ways that make it difficult to understand how processes of immigrant inclusion and exclusion might play out at the micro level in new immigrant destinations. As noted in the Introduction, sociologist Alejandro Portes and his associates have come closest to theorizing and operationalizing how the structural and cultural features of the specific receiving contexts that immigrants enter in the United States come to affect their experiences and opportunities, *above and beyond* the role played by immigrants' own individual characteristics or motivations. In their model, the most relevant dimensions of context of reception that structure the mobility paths of immigrants and their descendants are the policies of the receiving government, the conditions of the receiving labor market, the characteristics of newcomers' own receiving ethnic communities, and the reactions of receiving non-ethnic communities.

All of these dimensions emerged as highly significant to immigrant incorporation processes in rural eastern North Carolina in the mid-2000s. However, they did so in several distinct and overlapping ways, which I have attempted to capture and demonstrate throughout this book. First, context mattered in a vertical spatial and institutional or political sense (see the vertical axis in Figure 1). That is, in eastern North Carolina Hispanic newcomers were affected

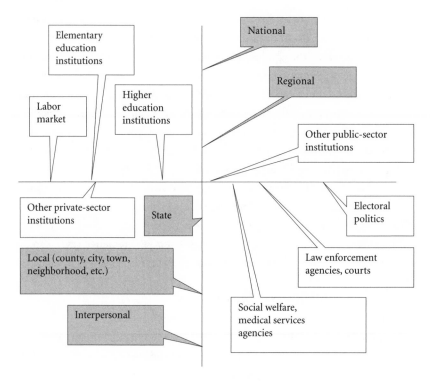

Figure 1. Multiple dimensions of contexts of reception

by a national American context, intermediate regional and state contexts, intermediate subregional and substate contexts, more proximate local town or rural area contexts, and then more proximate interpersonal contexts as well. In this vertical spatial and institutional or political understanding of contexts of reception, newcomers could experience all of the contextual dimensions of Portes's contexts-of-reception model distinctly—yet also simultaneously—at every level.

To illustrate, the policies of the receiving government might have been relatively restrictive at the national level, yet more inclusive or neutral at the regional, state, subregional or substate, or local level, while they could even be subverted or ignored at the interpersonal level. Vice versa, the policies of the receiving government might have been inclusive or undefined at the national level, yet more restrictive at lower levels of analysis. Such vertical differentiation could also emerge in other dimensions of the model from Portes and colleagues. For instance, regarding the conditions of the receiving labor market and the reactions of receiving non-ethnic communities, I uncovered evidence of some supervisors and managers at PPP in Wilcox County not only hiring unauthorized workers but also actively encouraging them to get more education and move up in the plant on an interpersonal level, despite both restrictive government policies against hiring unauthorized immigrants coming down from the national level and a stronger level of anti-immigrant sentiment among Wilcox County residents outside the plant compared to inside (see Chapters 2 and 3). Similarly, I uncovered evidence of several bureaucrats in educational and nonregular medical services agencies in eastern North Carolina bending and sometimes even breaking what they considered to be overly restrictive government policies coming down from both the national and state levels, in their efforts to reach out to and incorporate Hispanic newcomers "more practically" at the local and interpersonal levels (see Chapters 6 and 7). On the other hand, I also found evidence of bureaucrats in a variety of institutions in eastern North Carolina beginning to align their responses to Hispanic newcomers with national- and state-level policies, many of which are becoming more restrictive over time (see Chapters 6 and 7). In effect, this means that in the highly federalized political geography of the United States, where there are "multiple layers of governance" (Odem 2008: 122; the collected essays in Anrig and Wang 2006; Price and Singer 2008), Hispanic newcomers could experience the various dimensions of Portes and colleagues' contexts-of-reception model at several distinct spatial and institutional or political levels, complicating any singular notion of what context meant for their experiences in the rural South on the ground. Sometimes what they experienced across these levels seemed to work in concert (i.e., as generally restrictive or as generally inclusive), while at other times it was subject to competing cross-pressures.

Second, context mattered in a horizontal spatial and institutional sense. In eastern North Carolina, how Hispanic newcomers were incorporated or excluded from rural southern life was strongly affected by the particular structures, actors, and goals and missions that made up the specific institutional spaces in which they were embedded (see the horizontal axis in Figure 1). In this book, I have examined such incorporation processes in the formal labor market, elementary educational institutions, higher educational institutions, social welfare and medical services agencies, law enforcement agencies, court systems, and last but not least electoral and non-electoral politics. Other institutional arenas with their own contextual features also exist, and they are both private (e.g., formal and informal markets, law firms, churches, newspapers, nonprofit organizations, and so forth) and public (e.g., libraries, zoning offices, and so forth). As with its vertical counterpart, in this horizontal spatial and institutional understanding of contexts of reception, newcomers could experience each contextual dimension of Portes and colleagues' contexts-of-reception model distinctly—yet also simultaneously—in all the institutional spheres.

To illustrate, the policies of the receiving government, particularly toward unauthorized immigrants, emerged as relatively restrictive in the formal labor market, social welfare services agencies, and the electoral political arena, yet they were often more inclusive or neutral in such institutions as schools, universities, and some medical services agencies (see Chapters 6 and 7). Such horizontal differentiation could also emerge in other dimensions of this model. For instance, regarding the reactions of receiving non-ethnic communities, I uncovered evidence of natives reacting more positively and inclusively to Hispanic newcomers in some institutional arenas than in others, not only because of the influence of various government policies across them but also to the influence of various professional norms and missions held by bureaucrats working in each one (see Chapters 6 and 7). Similarly, I uncovered evidence of natives reacting more positively and inclusively to Hispanic newcomers in some workplaces than others, which is due to differing understandings of labor market dynamics and necessities. Again, in effect this complicated any singular notion of what context meant for Hispanic newcomers' experiences in the rural South on the ground. As was the case with respect to its vertical counterpart, what Hispanic newcomers experienced across these institutional arenas sometimes seemed to work in concert but at other times seemed to work in opposition.

Finally, context mattered in a larger sense, differing across several types of broad receiving contexts, around four of which I have organized the sections of this book: geographic, economic, racial and demographic, and political and cultural (see Figure 1; for other broad receiving contexts, such as religious ones, see also Levitt et al. 2008). Consequently, I documented Hispanic newcomers in Bedford County having broadly different experiences than their counterparts in Wilcox County, located just a few hours' drive away—on the back roads, of course. Not only has Bedford County's local economy been undergoing long-term decline (receiving economic context) but it also has a very large population of historically disadvantaged African Americans (receiving racial and demographic contexts). These two factors have in turn affected how Hispanic newcomers are differentially received by natives in the two counties. Specifically, I documented more newcomers in Wilcox County achieving some short-distance upward mobility in the low-wage yet large and expanding food processing industry, compared to their counterparts in Bedford County, who were facing a more difficult upward climb in the low-wage and declining agricultural and routine manufacturing and textiles industries (see Chapters 2 and 3). Similarly, I documented variation in African Americans' reactions to Hispanic newcomers across the two counties as well as between the broad economic and political arenas (see Chapter 4).

Indeed, the economic, racial and demographic, and political and cultural contexts characterizing Bedford and Wilcox Counties often criss-crossed the vertical and horizontal axes identified in Figure 1. Therefore, context matters greatly to immigrant incorporation processes in eastern North Carolina, across these two contrasting counties, across the various receiving institutional spheres I have examined, and also across policy levels. Yet in reality this context of reception is impressively complex, multidimensional, and even "schizophrenic" (Chavez 2007), involving "simultaneous processes of inclusion and exclusion" that are deserving of continued empirical investigation and theoretical understanding.

Substantive Contributions to the Literature

My main substantive contribution is that the rural southern immigrant experience is more positive than we might have expected it to be, given the rural South's historic reputation as an economically depressed and racially intolerant region of the country. First, many Hispanic newcomers, especially lower-status ones, considered their lives in rural America and their relationships with its mainstream natives to be positive (or at least neutral) rather than negative. For them, life in the rural South is safe, slow-paced, and friendly compared to life in major metropolitan gateways. Such characterizations would not surprise many of the residents of eastern North Carolina's small towns and rural areas, who take neighborliness and good manners as serious points of pride.

Second, many Hispanic newcomers employed in the low-wage food processing industry seemed to be on their way to carving out a living and setting the stage for their children's future upward incorporation into a distinct sort of rural working class (to which a relatively large proportion of rural mainstream natives also belong). These jobs do not pay well by American standards, but they were providing many Hispanic newcomers in eastern North Carolina with access to relatively secure opportunities to participate in the labor force. As noted by Eduardo, the unauthorized immigrant quoted at the beginning of this chapter, this gives them the basic yet crucial chance to make money in return for their work and try to fulfill their dreams. Moreover, it does so in places where the cost of living is dramatically lower than in many metropolitan areas, and also where a good number of natives both understand and value this sort of working-class enterprise, as illustrated by Jesús, the Mexican husband of one of my interview respondents:

Jesús: I came to North Carolina because a friend recommended it to me. He told me that there was work here, and that's the main reason. I came for work. Hispanics in this country, we are mostly here to work. But also my friend said that the rent here was lower, and it was easier to pay rent and get along here than in California.

Interviewer: Do you like North Carolina? Or like, what are the biggest differences you see between North Carolina and California?

Jesús: Yeah, it's very, very different here! [*laughs*] But I love it. I love the peacefulness of it all here. I grew up in San Jose, near San Francisco, although today San Jose is even bigger than San Francisco. And there is so much gangs, drugs, and people not working out there. I didn't like it. You know, a big difference I see is that here in North Carolina—in Bedford, in this area—everybody works. I mean *everybody*. That includes Hispanics, blacks, Americans, Asians, even old people. They all work. In the big cities you don't see that. There are lots of people there who, well, they blame everything on the immigrants, right? But meanwhile lots of people just don't work. They want the government to support them instead. When I first came here, I worked for a year at [a local textile mill], and they had me on a shift that started at 3:00 a.m. And you know what? Everybody there showed up. All the blacks and Americans, too. That wouldn't never happen in California! I would be the only person showing up at 3:00 a.m., it would be just me. And here, everybody works. It is impressive.

Third, many Hispanic newcomers appeared to be on their way to achieving incorporation into mainstream rural southern society as nonblacks, on the more privileged as opposed to disadvantaged side of an emerging black-nonblack color line. Many analysts have feared for the fate of Hispanic newcomers in a region well known for its intolerant white population, but Hispanic newcomers in eastern North Carolina reported coming into contact with as many whites who are kind and friendly as they reported coming into contact with whites who are not. Although their struggle to be treated fairly and accepted into rural southern life by what Mexican respondent Alvaro described as "the 50% of whites who really don't accept the Hispanic community" continues, the fact that many respondents felt that another 50% of whites *do* support their quest for incorporation and upward mobility—and moreover, that this proportion is notably higher than its corresponding figure among African Americans—is significant.

Finally, many Hispanic newcomers described encounters with natives who, by virtue of their strategic position in several service-oriented mediating institutions, support newcomers' quest for incorporation and upward mobility. Among them were teachers and educational administrators, medical services providers, certified court interpreters, attorneys working in private practice, domestic violence outreach workers, law enforcement officers (especially those explicitly put in charge of building better community relations with newcomers; Jones-Correa 2005b), and a range of "liaison" actors, particularly religious leaders, heads of nonprofit organizations, and community organizers (Zúñiga and Hernández-León 2005a). Restrictive government policies do prohibit many of these natives from reaching out to fully incorporate Hispanic newcomers, especially unauthorized ones, but in many cases a strong service-oriented mission within the context of a profession or institution still pushes in this direction.

Together with an American legal framework that protects newcomers and guarantees an array of rights to all persons regardless of their place of birth, citizenship, legal status, or local place of destination within the United States (Gozdziak and Bump 2008; Gozdziak and Martin 2005; Kerwin 2007; Luna and Ansley 2009), all of these things lent support to a cautiously optimistic view of immigrants' opportunities for incorporation and upward mobility in new destinations across the rural South from the vantage point of the mid-2000s, despite clear tradeoffs and drawbacks. An expanding and flexible labor market across this region has generally facilitated newcomers' incorporation by making employment relatively easy to find (Gozdziak and Martin 2005; Johnson and Kasarda 2009).[2] Moreover, the profound institutional changes occurring within the American culture and its workplaces since the Civil Rights Movement (Alba and Nee 2003) have expanded the opportunities for Hispanic newcomers to achieve some short-distance upward mobility within parts of this labor market in important ways. Such changes reach deep into the rural South, where even a notoriously bad workplace such as PPP instituted several changes that have had the effect of encouraging upward mobility among Hispanic newcomers—including active recruitment and promotion of minority workers through the two supervisor training programs, active racial and ethnic integration of departments in the plant, and a zero-tolerance policy against discrimination within the workplace (see Chapter 2; and Marrow 2006).[3]

Outside the labor market, immigrant incorporation in the rural South, as elsewhere, is aided by other government laws and policies—namely birthright (*jus soli*) citizenship, which is granted automatically to all children who are born on U.S. territory (Gozdziak and Bump 2008; Gozdziak and Martin

2005). As emerging studies are beginning to point out (see Kasinitz et al. 2008), birthright citizenship is a crucial element of the relatively good track record in the United States of incorporating the children of contemporary immigrants, especially compared to those in several countries in Western Europe, where second- and third-generation children of immigrants face far worse realities of marginalization and disenfranchisement. Other inclusive government policies and basic constitutional protections—including those guaranteeing all persons the right to a K–12 education and to emergency medical stabilization, regardless of legal status (see Chapters 6 and 7; and Kerwin 2007)—are also working to encourage immigrant incorporation in several key institutional arenas in the rural South, as they are elsewhere in the country.

This is the positive side of immigration in the contemporary rural and small-town South that I uncovered during my research in 2003–04. It is what was granting many Hispanic newcomers, even unauthorized ones, the option to redefine their quest for the American dream in response not just to the harsh economic realities that have pulled and pushed them to new destinations (see the Introduction) but also to their own personal tastes and preferences. This is well illustrated by Alicia, an immigrant from Santiago, Chile, who migrated directly to Bedford County in 2000:

Interviewer: What other places have you visited here in the United States?
Alicia: Miami, South Carolina, and New York.
Interviewer: Do you notice any differences among them, versus here?
Alicia: [*laughs*] Oh, well I come from a big city. Very big! Parts of Chile are undeveloped, but we have technology there. And I think that New York is a very big city, too, but it's very stressful. To me, Miami is better than New York. However, it's also a big city. North Carolina is the country of the United States!
Interviewer: That's funny. And why do you say that?
Alicia: It seems very pretty to me. But it also seems to me that we're a little behind in technology! [*laughs*] But I love the peace. It's the difference in people's American dreams. I never had the typical American dream. I had the dream of looking for a calm place. And that's what I have here.
Interviewer: So you would say you've adapted to it here?
Alicia: Yes, I have adapted and I like it.

On a practical level, such findings challenge the stereotypical and single-minded ways in which outsiders often view residents of both southern and rural areas. Common conceptions that living in the South or in a rural area is categorically worse and more inhospitable than living in other regions or in more "advanced" metropolitan areas abound, in academe and in much of upper-middle-class popular opinion. But to many Hispanic newcomers—not to mention many natives—who are living in this subregion of the rural South, the general quality of life and the specific interactions between coworkers and neighbors have taken on positive features that distanced onlookers might never imagine.

At a more theoretical level, such findings illustrate how many small town and rural areas appeared to be offering newcomers a strategic hole of opportunity within which to establish themselves and make a go at moving up and achieving the American dream over time, precisely when similar opportunity has begun to stagnate, become saturated, or even decline in the traditional immigrant gateways. This may be most significant for lower-status Hispanic newcomers, who have been documented as facing the most hostile contexts of reception in those places (Gans 1992; Portes and Rumbaut 2001; Portes and Zhou 1993; Zhou 1999). For instance, in eastern North Carolina, lower-status (and often unauthorized) Hispanic newcomers perceived greater non-economic benefits from living in rural areas in eastern North Carolina than did their higher-status counterparts (see Chapter 1). Contrast this to metropolitan Charlotte, where H. A. Smith (2008) notes that depression is on the rise among Hispanic women who are originally from rural places in Latin America. Confronted with a "loud, busy, car-dependent and sprawling city," she writes, "they can become quickly overwhelmed and isolated" (255–56). Also contrast this to Miami, where scholars find that lower-status Mexican, Guatemalan, Peruvian, and Haitian newcomers face frequent disparagement from higher-status immigrants and coethnics, who look down upon them along class, racial, and legal status lines (Aranda, Chang, and Sabogal 2009).

For lower-status Hispanic newcomers such as these, rural new destinations may offer a strategic hole, as I say, within which to garner access to a changing low-wage labor market and a more affordable housing market. They may also offer a place within which to develop positive (or at least neutral) relationships with other working- and lower-middle-class coworkers and neighbors. This has certainly been the case for Jesús, quoted earlier, in comparison to his previous experience in San Jose, California, and for many unauthorized youths interviewed by Silver (2009) who have developed strong bonds of trust with many of their native teachers, counselors, coaches, lawyers, and religious leaders in the context of safer rural areas and small towns. Of course, as I demonstrate in this book, the racial and cultural distance between Hispanic newcomers and natives in the rural South is often quite large, and reducing it will indeed take time and serious effort (see Chapters 4 and 5). But because the economic distance between them is often smaller than in many urban areas, newcomers can begin carving out a stable living and setting the stage for their children's future upward incorporation into a distinctively rural and working-class economic mainstream (see Chapters 2 and 3).

This latter point lends support to some of the current research reconceptualizing processes of assimilation and incorporation among pre- and post-1965 immigrants. In much of popular opinion and in some academic opinion as well, assimilation is held up as one single, successful, middle-class, and non-ethnic endpoint, at which the old immigrants arrived and at which the new immigrants are commonly expected to arrive very quickly. Even in the most sophisticated critiques and revisions of classic assimilation theory, new immigrants' options for incorporation still alternate generally between two successful, middle-class routes—one non-ethnic, the other ethnic—and one unsuccessful and downwardly mobile "underclass" route.[4] Yet several scholars now point out that some of the originally lower-status European immigrant groups (namely the Irish, Italians, Poles, and Hungarians) followed a more intermediate, bumpier, and longer-term path into the American middle class, one that worked its way into and progressively up through the American working class over time and generations. According to these scholars, even though some sectors of new and lower-status immigrant groups, particularly Mexicans and Central Americans, may indeed be at risk of permanent downward mobility and assimilation, other sectors among them appear to be following in the footsteps of their old counterparts, into and perhaps one day up through the gates of the American working class (see, for example, Alba and Nee 2003; Perlmann and Waldinger 1997; Waldinger and Feliciano 2004; and Waldinger, Lim, and Cort 2007). Hispanic newcomers' positions within this working class may sometimes be mistaken for actual or potential downward mobility, but they may instead represent early stages of longer-term and incremental upward mobility.

For most Hispanic newcomers in eastern North Carolina, assimilation will certainly not mean rapid incorporation into the rural southern economic mainstream, at least not if that mainstream is defined in traditionally middle-class terms, as it has been in much of the past and contemporary literature (Alba and Nee 2003). Most of the jobs relocating to or expanding in these areas—the jobs most of the newcomers have been following—are low-wage ones in the agricultural, manufacturing, food processing, construction, and services industries (see the Introduction). And because of the vast changes in the American economy since the early twentieth century, future upward mobility and assimilation into the American middle class may take much longer for them to achieve than it did for many European immigrant groups who came at that earlier time. Nonetheless, mere access to a job is a crucial first step toward moving up into the lower working class. I find that, even at relatively low wages, the expanding food processing industry—a major pull factor attracting immigrants to rural areas across the American South and Midwest—was offering many Hispanic newcomers limited yet much-needed economic stability, and in some cases additional avenues for short-distance upward mobility (see Chapters 2 and 3).

Yet despite this generally positive picture, there was an ominously negative side to the rural southern immigrant experience in the mid-2000s as well. Many factors conditioned it, but the most important one was lack of citizenship and legal status, which seriously marked and threatened many Hispanic newcomers' prospects for successful incorporation and upward mobility at all of the vertical levels and in all of the horizontal institutional arenas I analyzed. In a variety of workplaces, including in the rural southern food processing industry, lack of legal status made whatever progress many Hispanic newcomers might have been enjoying subject to immediate repeal at any time. This challenged their prospects not only for achieving upward mobility in the future but also for maintaining limited economic stability in the present (see Chapters 2 and 3). In this way, as the most worrisome feature of the *national-level* negative context of reception toward Latin American immigrants at the turn of the twenty-first century (albeit one that has filtered down to many state and local levels in the contemporary rural South), lack of legal status has left many Hispanic newcomers extremely vulnerable, threatening at every moment their possibility of obtaining a basic measure of economic incorporation, namely, mere participation in the labor force. Lack of legal status also presents the greatest barrier to many unauthorized foreign-born 1.5 generation youths' prospects for long-term upward mobility in the rural South, since their access to higher education and American employment is formally restricted by the state. In fact, as one of the first states to officially attempt to bar unauthorized youths from enrolling in degree-seeking programs in its community colleges entirely,[5] and as one of the 40 states that still deny them eligibility for in-state tuition and state financial aid even after having reversed this major policy attempt in 2009, North Carolina and several of its southern neighbors have chosen to actively endorse and exacerbate, rather than alleviate, the major barriers and obstacles that unauthorized young people already face, despite there being no federal law that bars their admission to state institutions of higher education (see Chapter 6; Silver 2009; and Zota 2009c).

Outside the workplace, lack of citizenship and legal status marred Hispanic newcomers' relationships with many mainstream Americans. Even in the rural South, where one might expect the racial dimensions of discrimination and exclusion to affect Hispanic newcomers most negatively, I found that (non) citizenship was actually the more central axis along which many Hispanic newcomers reported experiencing discrimination and cultural exclusion on an interpersonal level (see Chapter 5). This axis even affected some Hispanic newcomers who were U.S. citizens or documented immigrants; they were also often presumed by both white and black insiders to be undeserving outsiders. In this way, lack of citizenship and legal status—both real and presumed—has made many Hispanic newcomers socially and culturally as well as economically vulnerable, which threatens at every moment their possibility of being seen and treated by their neighbors as equally deserving human beings (Massey 2007). These findings suggest a dire need to revisit classic and modern conceptualizations of nativism alongside racism in the future literature on prejudice and discrimination in the traditional South (Higham 1955; Lacy and Odem 2009).

Going further, I found that lack of citizenship or legal status has excluded many Hispanic newcomers from inclusion in the formal body politic and also circumscribed and threatened their successful incorporation into a variety of social and legal institutions in the rural South. Increasingly restrictive government policies enacted at the national, state, and local levels play an extremely powerful role in this respect, denying many Hispanic newcomers access to services and equal treatment in such institutions, and further denying many natives the ability to serve and incorporate them at the local and interpersonal levels despite inclusive beliefs and missions (see Chapters 6 and 7).

What do Hispanic newcomers who lack citizenship or legal status do in these precarious situations? My research showed that they simply did their best, often finding creative ways to, in Eduardo's words, "live our lives and support our families and children, too" even though "it is very hard" and takes a great toll on their physical and mental health. Like Eduardo, they often paid lots of money to obtain "hot papers"—taking on all the risks entailed by doing so (see Chapters 2 and 3)—and felt guilty and reluctant but bereft of another choice. Or they might have tried to "do the right thing" and search for employment without using false papers. This was often difficult because many employers would not hire them, as was the case for Mauro, the unemployed Guatemalan immigrant I described in Chapter 3 who had no job prospects on the line during my entire field research period. Other times it was easier if employers did not ask them to show any papers, although my respondents who went this route still reported living in fear of being terminated from their job and thrust into poverty at any moment. Most important, just as Van der Leun (2003) describes with unauthorized immigrants living in the Netherlands, all went to great lengths to draw a line between what they viewed as noncriminal acts of migrating and working with false documents in order to make a living and feed their family, in contrast to other more serious crimes. Indeed, they often viewed their engagement in the former as a way to prevent their need to engage in the latter, in an ongoing attempt to assert their identity as law-abiding members of their new communities, to whom they wished to do no harm.

These newcomers also worked creatively to find a way to move forward (*adelantarse* in Spanish). Before North Carolina's government policies became more restrictive, unauthorized immigrants obtained state identification cards, SSNs, and driver's licenses in addition to ITINs,[6] and those who were able to obtain them used them whenever they could to open bank accounts, rent trailers or apartments, purchase homes and cars, and open their own businesses (Hernández-León 2008). They sent their children to American public schools and sought out information from friends and trusted community members as to which higher educational institutions might be willing enroll their children and offer them financial aid. They paid sales and consumption taxes on all the goods they purchased, real estate taxes on the trailers and homes they purchased (or taxes that accrue indirectly through their rent), and federal and state income taxes when they worked in the formal labor market[7]—and respondents who worked informally reported a desire to work legally and pay their taxes instead. They worked creatively to fashion an affordable living situation, taking on roommates and boarders even when they preferred not to (Atiles and Bohon 2003; Bohon 2006, 2008). And they sought out affordable and available forms of health care (see Chapter 6), developed their own medical remedies (Cuadros 2006: 120–23; Hagan et al. 2003; Heyman, Núñez, and Talavera 2009; Portes, Fernández-Kelly, and Light, forthcoming), acquired medicines from their home country or on the black market (Gouveia 2006; Ku and Papademetriou 2007), or simply went without[8]—as did many respondents who were not offered medical benefits through their workplace, as well some who were offered them but chose not to use them for fear of having someone discover they were not working legally under their real name.

Like Eduardo, many of these newcomers and their families "suffered" under the weight of accumulated physical and psychological stresses (Córdova Plaza 2009). They developed complex coping mechanisms for warding off negative labels and stereotypes as bad or undeserving outsiders, turning to God, their coethnic communities, and sometimes even a few trusted natives in order to locate meaning and positive self-definition. They stayed away from people they associated with immigration officials and the American legal system as much as possible—often including the very law enforcement officers, court officials, domestic violence outreach workers, and private attorneys who struggle to convey to newcomers that they exist "to help" and not to harm them—circumscribing their movements so as to minimize any contact or potential chance of deportation (Collins 2007a; Hernández-León 2008; Lacy 2007; Preston 2007, 2008b). With workplace enforcement gaining steam in several key industries since the mid-2000s, they also increasingly feared being discovered at work and separated from their family members, many of whom are young children and U.S. citizens (Capps, Castañeda, Chaudry, and Santos 2007; Collins 2007a; Hegeman 2007; Preston 2007). Finally, many went without seeing their family back home for an indefinite period of time, now that crossing the border to go back home entails great difficulty in coming back. Some even endured very painful physical and emotional separation from family members (Córdova Plaza 2009), as when an unauthorized immigrant child of one of my respondents was taken into custody by immigration authorities and deported back to his home country without her.[9]

In these ways and others, many Hispanic newcomers were living out their lives in eastern North Carolina hoping for the best as they continually crossed and navigated the borders between economic, social, cultural, legal, and political "existence" and "nonexistence" (Coutin 2000; Menjívar 2006a, 2006b, 2008). In my research, even though many factors conditioned their prospects for incorporation and upward mobility—chief among them being the rural South's two historic demons of race and class—lack of citizenship and legal status complicated, and often superseded, all of them in important ways (Silver 2009; B. E. Smith 2006). It placed many Hispanic newcomers in this region—like their counterparts elsewhere in the country—in a precarious position where they were made constantly subject to actual or potential policing and disenfranchisement as undeserving outsiders who do not belong (Bauer and Reynolds 2009; Cantu 1995; Chavez 2007).

Troubling Policy Implications and Developments Since 2003–04

Unfortunately, this has only become more strongly the case since I conducted my field research in 2003–04. Various scholars now describe a shift from the more welcoming, hospitable, or at least benignly ambivalent context of reception that

greeted Hispanic newcomers in the traditional South in the 1980s and 1990s—
especially in the region's rural areas—to a more openly hostile and negative one
after 2005.[10] In many ways, then, 2003–04 represented a defining and theoretically significant moment to analyze the immigrant experience in the rural South.
On the one hand, 2000 U.S. Census data documenting the geographic dispersion of immigrants outside of traditional gateways were just beginning to attract
widespread media and scholarly attention; Hispanic newcomers in many areas
of the rural South were gaining in critical mass as the initial stages of immigration (1980s to mid-1990s) were giving way to intermediate ones (late 1990s to
mid-2000s),[11] and then president George W. Bush was just beginning to reinstate
his pre-September 11 call for a more inclusive federal immigration policy in early
2004, including proposals for a temporary guest worker program and potential
amnesty for long-term unauthorized immigrants. On the other hand, 2003–04
largely preceded escalation of restrictive state- and local-level policy making toward unauthorized immigrants, growth in cross-deputization of state and local
law enforcement officers as federal immigration agents, and emotional polarization of the national debate regarding unauthorized immigration. All picked
up speed in 2005 and would continue through passage of the REAL ID Act (see
Chapter 7) and (U.S.) HR 4437 in 2005,[12] the immigrants' rights marches of 2006,
the 2006 midterm elections, the 2008 presidential election, and most recently
Arizona's damning passage of the extremely restrictive Senate Bill 1070 in 2010.[13]

Indeed, anti-immigrant sentiment has become more pervasive in eastern
North Carolina since 2003–04, just as it has in other parts of the state (McClain
2006) as well as in many other new destinations throughout the country. Even
journalistic coverage of immigration became much more visible and polarized
in the region after 2005. Many natives in eastern North Carolina distance themselves from the blatantly racist and nativist rhetoric of official anti-immigration
groups, but private and public discussion of Hispanics and immigration has
grown noticeably more negative in recent years—to such a degree that one
white resident of Bedford County recently remarked to me that "the things I
now hear being said about Hispanics, you didn't even use to hear being said
about blacks" (postfieldwork notes, June 2008). In April 2008, I was even privy
to a private conversation involving another white resident, who suggested that
the easiest way to "deal" with rising numbers of Hispanic newcomers might be
to "line them up" in one of eastern North Carolina's ubiquitous agricultural
fields "and let the deer hunters take care of 'em." Of course, this sentiment is by
far not characteristic of all rural southern whites; in fact, it has even generated
its own pro-immigration countermovement among them, especially within

some church congregations. Yet it does illustrate a rising tendency among natives in the rural South, as elsewhere, to view Hispanic newcomers as "less than human" by virtue of a racialized association with unauthorized legal status (Lee and Fiske 2006; Massey 2007). To illustrate, McDermott (in progress) finds that attitudes among southeastern natives toward Hispanic newcomers have crystallized for the worse since the 2006 immigrants' rights marches and the 2008–10 economic recession; she reports that natives increasingly racialize them as threatening Hispanics and illegals, whereas attitudes prior to 2006 were more "confused" and "paternalistic." Public opinion data collected in late 2008 also show an overall pattern of negativity in the attitudes of North Carolinian natives toward immigrant newcomers, one Miller (2010) describes as only slightly more positive among blacks than among whites.

Adding fuel to the fire, restrictive government policies against hiring and harboring unauthorized immigrants, against receipt of many public services and benefits by unauthorized immigrants, against public use of the Spanish language, and toward cross-deputization of state and local law enforcement officers as federal immigration agents have also been proposed in several eastern North Carolina counties (see Chapters 6 and 7; Luebke 2011; Nguyen 2007; Nguyen and Gill 2010; and Zota 2009a), just as they have been in many other new destination states and localities.[14] Restrictive state-level bills proposed during North Carolina's 2009 legislative session alone[15] included:

- Senate Bill 337, NC Illegal Immigration Reform Act, an omnibus act that would (1) require city and county governments to use federal verification systems to verify work authorization info on all new employees; (2) require those contracting and subcontracting with public agencies to take part in federal programs to verify that new employees are in the country legally; (3) permit enforcement of private employers' hiring of "unauthorized aliens" through a complaint process by which a citizen could anonymously report the alleged violation; (4) make it an unfair trade practice to discharge a lawfully authorized employee while knowingly employing an unauthorized worker; (5) require the state or any local governments to verify any applicant for state, local, or federal public benefits; (6) require the attorney general to enter into an agreement with federal Homeland Security for enforcement of federal immigration laws by law enforcement officers designated by the state; (7) prohibit any city or county from limiting enforcement of state immigration laws; (8) require registration by nonattorneys providing assistance to immigrants in completing government paperwork (with the exception of certain nonprofits recognized by the Board of Immigration Appeals); (9) prevent employers, when calculating their state income taxes, from taking a tax deduction for wages paid to unauthorized workers; (10) make it more difficult for an unauthorized immigrant arrested for a violent felony, drug offense, or gang offense to obtain pretrial release; (11) make it a felony for someone to transport an unauthorized person "knowingly or in reckless disregard of the fact" that the person is not authorized, if it is with the "intent to further that person's unlawful entry into the US or avoid apprehension or detection by . . . authorities" (with a similar provision applying to "conceal[ing], harbor[ing], or shelter[ing] from detection" an unauthorized immigrant, with exceptions for soup kitchens, domestic violence shelters, churches, and health care providers); (12) make it a felony to use someone else's identity to obtain employment; and (13) prohibit unauthorized students from being admitted to either the community college system or the UNC system

- Senate Bill 398, Security and Immigration Compliance, an act that contains several of the items from the aforementioned Senate Bill 337

- Senate Bill 32, Employers Must Use Federal E-Verify Program, an act that would require many North Carolina employers to use a federal database program to verify the legal status of employees

- House Bill 344, Employers Must Use Federal E-Verify Program, an act similar to the aforementioned Senate Bill 32

- Senate Bill 237, Voting Materials in English, an act that would restrict voter registration forms and ballots to the English language except as required by federal law

- House Bill 437, Modify Requirements for School Admission, an act that would require parents enrolling a child for the first time in a school to present a birth certificate and record of immunization, and to state that the child is a citizen or to state the child's immigration status, for purposes of "fiscal analysis only"

- House Bill 294, No Postsecondary Education/Illegal Aliens, an act that would prohibit illegal aliens from attending North Carolina Community Colleges and Universities

- Senate Bill 155, Community Colleges Can't Admit Illegal Aliens, an act similar to the aforementioned House Bill 294

- House Bill 84, No Bail for Certain Illegal Aliens, an act that would deny bail to unauthorized immigrants who are charged with specified crimes (including sex offenses, violent felonies, driving offenses, drug offenses, and gang offenses) or with other crimes for which federal Immigration and Customs Enforcement would begin deportation proceedings

- House Bill 922, North Carolina Illegal Immigration Prevention, an act that would establish the North Carolina Illegal Immigration Prevention Act to provide for comprehensive regulation of persons in this state who are not lawfully present in the United States

- Senate Bill 290, No Federal Stimulus Money for Illegal Aliens, an act that would prohibit use of these funds except as required by federal law or where necessary to ensure receipt of the funds (http://www.welcome theimmigrant.org/legislative-updates/, last accessed Mar. 3, 2010)

Perhaps most important, unauthorized immigrants have lost the limited yet crucial access to driver's licenses and degree-seeking programs in community colleges that they had when I conducted my field research in 2003–04. These are two things that the few incorporative bills proposed in the same legislative session hoped to target:

- Senate Bill 464, Prevent Racial Profiling, an act that would amend the law requiring collection of traffic law enforcement statistics in order to prevent racial profiling

- House Bill 362, Access to Higher Education, an act that would prevent the North Carolina community college system from "soliciting information regarding the immigration status of prospective students," thus allowing unauthorized students the opportunity to access higher education (albeit at an out-of-state tuition rate)

- Senate Bill 848, Ensure College Access/High School Graduates, an act that would ensure that graduates of North Carolina high schools have access to higher education (http://www.welcometheimmigrant.org/legis lative-updates/, last accessed Mar. 3, 2010)

Consequently, many Hispanic newcomers' access to jobs in eastern North Carolina, even low-wage ones, has become much more precarious since I conducted my field research, and this has placed them under a more immediate threat of poverty, debt, detention, and deportation, even independent of the devastating impacts of the 2008–10 economic recession (Massey 2007; Massey and Sánchez 2010). Similar to what has happened elsewhere in the country where recent increases in interior enforcement against employers' hiring of unauthorized immigrants have taken place,[16] many Hispanic newcomers' lives are seriously circumscribed in eastern North Carolina, driven both inside and underground as most choose to dig in rather than leave the country (Preston 2007). In fact, drawing on in-depth interviews conducted with community officials and elected leaders, focus groups with Hispanic residents, and a randomized household survey of 409 Hispanic residents in two rural counties in the central piedmont section of North Carolina, Jones-Correa and Fennelly (2009) show that the rising threat of interior enforcement since 2005—which includes ICE workplace raids, ICE fugitive operations (e.g., those carried out in "home raids," often in immigrant-heavy trailer parks), and routine law enforcement policing (especially against unlicensed drivers)—has had deleterious effects on Hispanic newcomers' participation in public and civic life. Hispanics who are worried about deportation, who are unauthorized immigrants, or who have children are significantly less likely than others to leave their home after hearing about specific immigration raids. The larger "penumbra" threat of being targeted by law enforcement officials while driving or going to work also creates a huge sense of anxiety among Hispanics there, not only making them feel less comfortable but also depressing their engagement in schools and religious organizations even in the absence of specific raids.

In turn, many Hispanic newcomers' efforts to establish a secure foothold in their community have been problematized by the rising economic insecurity and fear produced by this lethal combination of rising anti-immigrant sentiment, interior enforcement, and restrictive government policy making. Zúñiga and Hernández-León (2009) point out that in Dalton, Georgia, since Georgia Senate Bill 529 (the Georgia Security and Immigration Compliance Act) was passed in spring 2006, some Hispanic newcomers have been choosing to postpone large and long-term expenditures, such as purchasing a home, in anticipation of potential dislocation. Many of those in eastern North Carolina are also being prevented from making other long-term investments, such as purchasing a car, starting up a new business, pursuing an educational degree, and most important, sending their children on to college.

Four Broad Sets of Policy Recommendations

This is the clearest starting point for a discussion of the major policy implications that emerge from my research findings, which need to be strongly emphasized to politicians and policymakers who continue to operate on unsophisticated opinions and assumptions about the dynamics of international labor migration, producing nothing but disastrous results in practice. Put simply, beefed-up border security, workplace raids, and restrictions on immigrants' access to social welfare and medical services have *not* succeeded in their goals of radically deterring and reducing the size of the unauthorized immigrant population.[17] Rather, their most immediate effects are, whether intentionally or not, to strengthen and officially endorse multiple barriers to upward mobility and successful incorporation among Hispanic newcomers, especially those who are unauthorized immigrants and who have, ironically, decided in increasing numbers to stay here thanks to our very efforts to try to keep them out (Cornelius and Lewis 2007; Massey, Durand, and Malone 2002). This in turn has had the effect of obstructing a growing number of Hispanic newcomers' access to the labor market, family supports, and social welfare and medical services, and of promoting physical and emotional suffering among them—both directly for unauthorized immigrants and indirectly via spillover effects onto other members of their families, including their children, nearly three-quarters of whom are now U.S. born (Massey 2007; Massey and Sánchez 2010; Passel and Cohn 2009).

With increasing restrictions on access to jobs, higher education, health care, and political participation, Hispanic newcomers and their children in the rural South now face far more serious prospects for marginalization and disenfranchisement as well as slimmer prospects for moving up than I documented during my field research in 2003–04. Moreover, as several respondents repeatedly noted to me during my research, many of the effects of this large-scale disenfranchisement will eventually diffuse out into local American communities, where natives will also be forced to pick up the pieces of destruction when Hispanic newcomers and their families become too weakened by restrictive government policies to do so themselves. Indeed, many of these "collateral damage" effects are already beginning to be felt, especially in places where state and local law enforcement officers are actively engaging in cross-deputization as federal immigration agents (Donato 2009). This is illustrated by Wilcox County sheriff Gregory, according to whom cross-deputization will only exacerbate the existing level of distrust and suspicion among Hispanic communities and impede law enforcement officers' ability to solve crime and provide community protection:

Gregory:　In cases where we go out to investigate the situation, and they are illegal, Hispanics immediately believe that maybe we have to deport 'em. And so there is that hesitancy to talk to law enforcement about any issue. To draw any attention to themselves. A lot of times it can keep us from being able to solve a case or improve the situation. (See Chapter 7.)

Let's pause to assess the numerical tally of the unauthorized immigrant population here, to consider the scope of what we are discussing. In 2009, the unauthorized population was estimated to comprise approximately 11 million people (Hoefer, Rytina, and Baker 2009, 2010), of whom about 13% were youths under the age of 18. Moreover, nearly half of unauthorized immigrant households consisted of a couple with children, and almost three-quarters of those children were U.S. citizens (Passel and Cohn 2009). Now let's consider another numerical tally: the number of unauthorized immigrants living in this country in 2010 was higher than the number of African Americans who lived under Jim Crow segregation in the American South in 1954 (Suro 2007). On the one hand, the sheer size of this population means that it is simply not economically feasible to attempt to remove all unauthorized immigrants from the country, nor to ask them to return to their home country and put in an application for legal return.[18] The amount of money that would need to be spent to perform such a mass repatriation is enormous, and it would come on top of what is already being spent on border security, which several prominent migration scholars have criticized as ineffective and wasteful (Massey, Durand, and Malone 2002). Furthermore, such a strategy would not do anything to eliminate the central push and pull factors associated with economic development that initiate labor migration in the first place, or the other factors that work to sustain them over time (see the Introduction).

On both civic and moral grounds, removing the entire unauthorized immigrant population from the country becomes even more problematic, harkening back to earlier discussions of removing the entire African American population—which was also desired for its profitable labor while being despised for its social presence—from the country and relocating it back to Africa. Arguing that all unauthorized immigrants are "illegal beings" and permanently removable on simple legal or policy grounds fails to rectify this central dilemma in any satisfactory way. Moreover, new efforts such as Arizona's Proposition 200 (passed in 2004), HB 2008 (passed in 2009), and SB 1070 (passed in 2010), which not only attempt to deputize human services agents and hold them accountable for reporting unauthorized immigrants to federal authorities but also forbid American natives from "aiding" unauthorized immigrants in various ways (Chishti and Bergeron 2010), speak less to any abstract rule of law than they do to legally endorsed yet ethically questionable efforts carried out by dominant members of the state to repress subordinate members throughout American history (Lovato 2008). One such effort was the Fugitive Slave Act of 1850, which effectively endorsed repression of African Americans by criminalizing the act of harboring or aiding a slave who escaped from the South to a free state in the North, and by requiring police to arrest accused runaway slaves and assist in returning them to their alleged owners (Alvarado and Jaret 2009).

Thus, when existing law or policy becomes a *de facto* weapon for defining a given subpopulation as the "other" and subordinating it accordingly[19]—as with today's full-scale condemnation of unauthorized immigrants as "criminals" and "violators" of the American "rule of law" throughout the country (Brettell and Nibbs 2010; Chavez 2008)—it is far better to make adjustments to the law or policy than to continue reinforcing it at a debilitating cost (Massey 2007). Fortunately, public opinion polls show that most Americans consistently reject the punitive measures and harsh rhetoric that rely only on enforcement to control illegal immigration, instead favoring a more pragmatic approach. In 2007, 85% of Americans disagreed that deporting all unauthorized immigrants from the country is "a realistic and achievable goal"; 76% also considered that requiring unauthorized immigrants to return to their home country to apply for legal entry is equally unrealistic; and a full 63% even favored legalization. As Suro (2009) concludes, the evidence from public opinion surveys "clearly contradicts" the widespread misconception, frequently touted by anti-immigrant media and politicians, that a large percentage of the American public oppose legalization.

Therefore, at the most basic of levels U.S. government policy *must* acknowledge that unauthorized and other noncitizen immigrants are living within its territorial boundaries, and then make several real attempts to give them critical opportunities to achieve economic stability and upward mobility. To demand that these newcomers suddenly "assimilate" while denying them key opportunities to do so is not only ineffective but also hypocritical; immigrant incorporation is a two-way street that requires effort among both newcomers and the members of host societies who receive them (Fix 2007; Massey and Sánchez 2010; Penninx 2003; Portes and Rumbaut 2006).

Such real attempts should begin, most importantly, with greater *access to legal status*. One element of this must be an *earned legalization program*, or amnesty, that will in turn impart greater security and political voice to adult unauthorized immigrants, coupled with an immediate and wholesale legalization program for all migrants who came to the United States as youths and who have good moral standing and no criminal record (IPC 2009). As Massey and Sánchez (2010) write, "Whatever one's beliefs about the morality of an amnesty for people who knowingly broke the law, *this is the only politically viable and practical option*" (248; my emphasis) for dealing with the current population of 11 million unauthorized immigrants who have put down roots and are not likely to return to their home country, unless we want to continue down our present path toward turning them into a permanent underclass (Ansley

2009; Massey 2007). And the best time to pass an earned legalization program is now, since the numbers of new incoming unauthorized immigrants have dropped to almost zero and, consequently, the border is currently "under control" (Giovagnoli 2010; Massey 2011; Massey and Sánchez 2010).

Laudably, President Barack Obama has made comprehensive immigration reform a central tenet of his first-term agenda. However, as of this writing, the prospects for passing more than piecemeal reform are tenuous at best (Packer 2010). Moreover, even if an earned legalization program is eventually approved, various barriers to its effective and thorough implementation will undoubtedly arise. That is, requiring adult unauthorized immigrants to show proof of an uninterrupted history of employment, receipt of income, payment of income taxes, or residence in order to qualify for legalization is likely to constitute a *de facto* barrier for many who apply. The most likely to be disenfranchised in this way will be unauthorized immigrant women; they are more heavily concentrated in the informal economy (particularly domestic service) and therefore more likely than their male counterparts to lack proof of an uninterrupted history of employment, receipt of income, and payment of income taxes.[20] Yet formal employment restrictions have also restricted many unauthorized immigrant men to low-paid jobs in the informal economy, and as a result many of them will have trouble piecing together proof of such a history, too.

Additionally, the formal employment restrictions that have forced many unauthorized immigrants into purchasing hot papers (i.e., other people's social security numbers; see Chapter 3) are also likely to constitute a de facto barrier for many immigrants who apply for legalization. In my research, unauthorized respondents felt caught between a rock and a hard place with respect to using a false SSN at work. On the one hand, they felt they had no other choice but to use it if they wanted to be allowed to work, and they could not afford to be unemployed. On the other hand, they were scared that developing a work history using a false name or SSN would hurt their chances for future legalization if an amnesty is eventually passed. And so they were caught in a struggle between wanting to stop using their fake name and SSN but not being able to—unless they were working in the informal economy, in which case they still knew that the disadvantage of not paying income taxes would probably cancel out the benefit of working under their real name if an amnesty is eventually passed. Therefore, effective and thorough implementation of any future legalization program will need to reduce not only the bureaucratic barriers associated with the difficulty of presenting proof of an uninterrupted history of employment, receipt of income, or payment of income taxes but also those associated with working in the informal economy or having been working under a false name and social security number. Moreover, it will need to reduce the bureaucratic barriers associated with the difficulty of presenting proof of an uninterrupted history of residence, because many unauthorized immigrants have to live with multiple family members, friends, and even roommates and boarders in order to pool their meager incomes.

Increases in the opportunity to migrate legally to the United States must be a second element of providing greater access to legal status to Hispanic new-comers. Today, each migrant-sending country is allotted only 25,600 legal visas per year, to cover both nonfamily immigrants (such as those categorized in the employment preference categories) and all "nonimmediate" family immigrants. Even Mexico receives this same allotment, despite the fact that it shares a spe-cial geographic and economic relationship and over a century of international migration with the United States (Massey, Durand, and Malone 2002). Thus unauthorized immigrants, especially those from Mexico, argue that "there is no line to stand in" to receive legal visas in their home countries. Even if someone has a family member who has already become a U.S. citizen or legal permanent resident, and who can therefore apply for other family members to receive legal visas outside the annual allotment, the bureaucratic backlog for persons born in Mexico currently ranges between 5 and 17 years' processing time—and it is a backlog larger than for applicants coming from any other country. In May 2010, the backlog was so extensive that even unmarried Mexican-born sons and daughters of U.S. citizens—who fall in the first and, ironically, highest-priority immigration family preference category—were finally receiving visas based on applications they had filed back in October 1992![21] Mexican-born spouses and children of legal permanent residents—who fall in the second and, ironi-cally, most "quickly" processed immigration family preference category—were finally receiving visas based on applications they had filed back in June 2005 (Travel.State.Gov 2010).[22] Obviously, the number of legal visas must be raised, especially for Mexico and Canada, the most integral trading partners of the United States, in order to fit the new contours of the North American regional and global economies.

The number of temporary guest worker slots should also be raised, in order to afford future immigrants greater opportunities to migrate temporar-ily to the United States (Massey, Durand, and Malone 2002; Massey and Sán-chez 2010). At the same time, however, there are major flaws in the temporary H-2A and H-2B guest worker system as it is currently structured (Donato, Stainback, and Bankston 2005; Griffith 2005, 2006; Smith-Nonini 2005, 2009;

Thompson and Hill 2005). Not only does it tie immigrant guest workers to a single employer, but it is also dominated by complex layers of labor brokers; altogether this serves to exacerbate power differentials and abuse and exploitation of immigrant guest workers both in transit and in the workplace. Going further, it denies immigrant guest workers access to many benefits and services of the American safety net to which other American workers are entitled (e.g., social security, unemployment, and medical care), and it even places them in a more socially and spatially isolated situation than is the case for unauthorized immigrants (Donato, Stainback, and Bankston 2005; Griffith 2005). Therefore, future expansion in the number of temporary guest workers, which has now already surpassed the level imported during the *bracero* program era (Massey 2011), must give guest workers greater control and power over their labor in order to avoid becoming a system of de facto indentured servitude.

Second, real attempts to promote unauthorized immigrants' economic stability and upward mobility should include *expanded access to the labor market.* As the driving force behind unauthorized labor migrants' reasons for migration and subsequent socioeconomic incorporation, without employment availability and relative job security many Hispanic newcomers' prospects for attaining even limited economic stability are bleak. Once basic access to the labor market is offered and ensured, issues of job quality and upward mobility can then be addressed (see Beeler and Murray 2007), but the latter are clearly secondary to the former (see Chapters 2 and 3). More generally, it serves no one's interest to take a selective, highly motivated, and generally patriotic group of labor migrants[23] and restrict their access to the labor market wholesale, forcing them and their families into joblessness and poverty. Of course, opportunities for employment and upward mobility will clearly need to be made available to native workers as well, and this is a central dilemma facing the American economy in a larger sense, especially after the 2008–10 economic recession. Nonetheless, categorically restricting unauthorized immigrants' access to the labor market does little to alleviate the dilemma, and it further ignores (as does most public sentiment about immigrants) the real and extremely complicated dynamics that produce and sustain international labor migration.[24]

Third, real attempts to encourage unauthorized immigrants' economic stability and upward mobility should include *expanded access to affordable higher education.* In an era in which a college degree has become a prerequisite for significant economic advancement, restricting unauthorized immigrant youths' access to affordable higher education—especially in community colleges, which serve as a crucial bridging mechanism connecting unauthorized youths to greater economic and social opportunity (Kasinitz et al. 2008; Portes and Fernández-Kelly 2008; Rumbaut 2008; Zhou et al. 2008)—does not only officially endorse subordination of this significant subpopulation of American society (Ansley 2009). It also prevents these young people from realizing their aspirations, from continuing on their parents' upward path into and hopefully up out of the American working class, and from gaining the educational and financial wherewithal to lend future economic assistance to their immigrant parents, other members of their family, and their local community. Again, it serves no one's interest to take the children of a selective, highly motivated, and generally patriotic group of unauthorized labor migrants and restrict their access to higher education, the labor market, and socioeconomic advancement more generally. As several of my respondents argued, doing this only increases their frustration, sending them the signal that other "worse routes" may be more lucrative. Also, they argue, it hurts American communities in the long run, when these youths have less ability to give back.

Fourth, real attempts to promote unauthorized immigrants' economic stability and upward mobility should include *expanded access to affordable health care*. Many American natives continue to believe in the myth that unauthorized immigrants are getting something for nothing vis-à-vis public benefits and services. But the literature conclusively shows that labor migrants follow job opportunities, not public benefits and services, and furthermore they use such benefits and services at *lower* rates than do natives (Fix 2007; Goldman, Smith, and Sood 2006; Kaushal 2005; Ku and Papademetriou 2007). This is especially the case for unauthorized immigrants, who have been formally blocked from accessing most public benefits by restrictive government policies since the mid-1970s (Fox 2009). In fact, rather than overusing or abusing health care, evidence shows that unauthorized immigrants actually have severely depressed access to and utilization of preventive care, chronic care, and specialty services in the United States, and, moreover, a "uniquely" large fraction of them have no formal contact with the American health care system at all.[25] That many unauthorized immigrant women rely on limited emergency Medicaid coverage when giving birth—the most prominent public allegation of abuse made against them today—belies the paucity of preventive (including prenatal) health care available to them outside of limited medical emergencies (Gozdziak and Bump 2008). As several medical services personnel argued emphatically during my research, categorically restricting and denying non-emergency health care to all unauthorized (and also to many legal) immigrants has deleterious effects not only on their individual health and general wellbeing but also on that of their family members (many of whom are U.S. citizens) and on the American communities where they live.

Thinking broadly, granting and ensuring access to these four things—legal status (in both permanent and temporary forms), the labor market, higher education, and health care—would significantly improve the situations and prospects of many Hispanic newcomers and their families in eastern North Carolina and elsewhere today, even without the addition of higher-level benefits, services, and political rights, which I personally advocate but acknowledge may have to come as next steps in the discussion. Moreover, my research findings suggest that access to these things will need to be facilitated via more inclusive integration policies, and not simply through creative local-level efforts by public service bureaucrats and other liaison individuals who are attempting to do the job in their absence (Gozdziak and Martin 2005). The current laissez-faire approach to immigrant integration and citizenship in the United States, which places the onus and costs of immigrant integration on immigrants, private institutions, and local governments (Bada et al. 2010; Bloemraad 2006; Gozdziak and Bump 2008), should be supplemented with federal policies and financing in order to produce more efficient and desirable results. At the very least, it is critical to develop new methods of transferring the surplus money that unauthorized immigrants contribute to federal government coffers (Bean and Stevens 2003; Fix 2007; Porter 2005; Schumacher-Matos 2010; Smith and Edmonston 1997) down to state and local governments and institutions that are, in practice, responsible for carrying out the job of receiving and integrating newcomers (Brettell and Nibbs 2010).

Finally, even though some degree of border enforcement is a necessity in all modern nation-states, we must recognize that the border security system we are currently operating under—whether in its dimension of attempting to construct a new Great Wall of China along the U.S.-Mexico border, its dimension of raiding workplaces that employ unauthorized immigrants in arbitrary fashion, or its dimension of detaining, deporting, and criminalizing thousands of individual immigrants for the simple "crime" of trying to work and support themselves and their families—is working in obvious competition with larger economic development processes, both in this country and abroad. Adapting to the changes brought about by these processes in ways that can produce the greatest long-term benefits to newcomers as well as to natives is a much more pressing need than continuing to focus on restricting the movement of certain people across international borders while further facilitating the corresponding movement of capital (Massey, Durand, and Malone 2002). Our current (latter) policy is not only failing to achieve its goals, owing to its inherent problems and contradictions, but also making citizenship and legal status more salient axes of social stratification within our borders (Aranda, Chang, and Sabogal 2009; Gleeson 2008; Massey 2007; Massey and Sánchez 2010; Menjívar 2008). Today, the early signs of this great "wakeup call," in the words of my island-born Puerto Rican respondent Enrique, are showing up in traditional immigrant gateways such as New York and California and deep in the heartland as well:

Enrique: I mean, the segregation that we had in the past was based on color, but now we're gonna have [it] based on immigration status. This is our wakeup call.

Indeed, although existing research convincingly demonstrates that racial inequality will continue to be one of the central features of American society in the near future, this wakeup call resonates ominously with my research findings in eastern North Carolina. Exclusion based on lack of citizenship and legal status was already emerging as a fundamental axis structuring the economic, social, and political fortunes of Hispanic newcomers living in the small communities dotting this region in 2003–04, and it has only grown stronger since then (Massey 2007). Having been intentionally produced by American immigration law and border enforcement policies over the course of the twentieth century[26] and exacerbated by recent heightening of interior enforcement (Hincapié 2009; Massey and Sánchez 2010; Terrazas 2008), this exclusion must be dismantled and reconfigured as soon as possible. This is imperative, if downward mobility among Hispanic newcomers is to be avoided, intergroup relations and community trust improved, responsive American democratic politics rejuvenated, and development of a new system of legally sanctioned and socially institutionalized "Juan Crow" inequality (Lovato 2008) prevented.

Response to Criticisms

Finally, for the purpose of forthright discussion, let me summarize my main research findings in a way that some readers might be tempted to use to misinterpret them: in 2003–04, rural southerners were reacting positively toward Hispanic newcomers; low-wage jobs (including those in food processing) were providing wonderful opportunities for Hispanic newcomers; limited economic stability was sufficient for Hispanic newcomers even when they could not move up over time; African Americans were to blame for pervasive black-Hispanic tensions; and the school systems in rural eastern North Carolina were doing extremely well at incorporating and responding to the needs of their Hispanic newcomer populations. Moreover, as a white middle-class native, I can interpret the Hispanic newcomer experience as relatively unproblematic in each of these ways, and then return to the comforts and privilege of elite universities—or of my parents' middle-class home in a nice neighborhood in a small town in eastern North Carolina—and avoid all of its negative consequences.

To interpret my findings in such a way would be both misguided and overly simplistic. Hispanic newcomers in eastern North Carolina noted several features of life in the rural South that were clearly negative. Among them were a relative lack of cosmopolitanism and familiarity with diversity among rural southerners; serious rural resource disadvantages that contributed to social and political isolation in their communities (see Chapter 1); and several forms of negative reaction from whites (e.g., nativism, racism, paternalism, etc.) as well as from blacks (see Chapters 4 and 5). Moreover, those employed in PPP noted several problems with the quality of their jobs, and some saw better opportunities to move up outside rather than inside the industry (see Chapter 2). Both whites and many Hispanic newcomers alike espoused negative attitudes toward African Americans, which structured and contributed to black-Hispanic tensions (see Chapter 5). And finally, the local elementary educational systems in Bedford and Wilcox Counties were still plagued by a host of problems in 2003–04. Among them were what one of my respondents called "total lack of understanding" of Hispanic newcomers' diverse cultures and educational needs; inadequate resources to attend to those needs even when they were acknowledged; relegation of all "Hispanic issues" to the one or two key Hispanic teachers or administrators hired in particular schools; negative stereotypes of Hispanic newcomers as uninterested in education, or in learning English, or in assimilating more generally; insufficiently integrated educational opportunities for both immigrant parents and youths; and more often than not, a lack of support for Hispanic newcomers and their student children among natives within their larger communities (see also Bohon, MacPherson, and Atiles 2005; McClain 2006; and Wainer 2004).

Nonetheless, despite the myriad problems, much of how Hispanic newcomers experienced their jobs, interpersonal relations, and opportunities in eastern North Carolina was positive rather than negative, and furthermore, many workplaces and elementary school systems were indeed doing better than other local institutions at responding to the needs and interests of their Hispanic employees and clients.[27] Given the predominantly negative ways in which the rural South and its residents are portrayed in the academic literature and in much of upper-middle-class public opinion, this was the finding that surprised me most as a researcher and advocate for disadvantaged immigrant newcomers, and the one that I have therefore expended the most effort to understand and explain throughout this book. I have stayed as close as possible to the data that I collected from my respondents, both Hispanic and non-Hispanic, to do so. As such, the experiences of these newcomers exemplify the complexity of the rural southern immigrant experience and also challenge a variety of interpretations and judgments of that experience, especially those based on ideological conviction rather than empirical data.

Let me illustrate three examples of this point here. First, arguing that Hispanic newcomers "like" their low-wage poultry processing jobs may draw the ire of groups on the left end of the political spectrum. It may also erroneously suggest to groups on the right end of the political spectrum that no improvements or regulations are needed to improve workers' lot in low-wage American workplaces, and that these workers will remain satisfied working in them over time. Further, arguing that Hispanic newcomers see some notable opportunities for upward mobility in the low-wage food processing industry may draw the ire of groups on the left end of the political spectrum, particularly those who want these low-wage workplaces to offer more solid rungs connecting the low and high ends of the occupational ladder. It may also erroneously suggest to groups on the right end of the political spectrum that Hispanic newcomers have ample opportunity to move up into the working class and then the middle class over time, and that if they do not it is their own fault rather than that of the increasingly unequal American economic structure and restrictions drawn around (non)citizenship and legal status.

The reality of most Hispanic newcomers' experience in eastern North Carolina in the mid-2000s lay not with any one of these perspectives, but somewhere in the middle of them. Hispanic newcomers in eastern North Carolina did not consider low-wage food processing jobs to be good in any intrinsic sense, and they would have gladly welcomed the chance to obtain better-paying, more secure, or less strenuous jobs—and therefore to move more rapidly toward upward assimilation into the American middle class. In the meantime, however, they did indeed consider their food processing jobs to be better than the economic opportunities available to many of them in their home country, as well as better than the very limited economic opportunities available to them in other American economic sectors. Moreover, the opportunities they saw for upward mobility in the food processing industry were primarily short-distance rather than long-distance, and they were viewed most positively when compared with worse opportunities elsewhere. Thus, Hispanic newcomers' experience in the rural southern food processing industry was complex. On the one hand, it did cry out for major improvements, yet at the same time it embodied achievements that often go underappreciated or unnoticed. Furthermore, the greatest problem many Hispanic newcomers had in relation to American workplaces regarded first-level access and not second-level mobility, and so my argument that Hispanic newcomers appreciated employment availability and relative job security even when they were not moving up does not pit left against right. Rather, it simply underscores how questions of survival were taking precedence over questions of mobility for many Hispanic newcomers in eastern North Carolina in the mid-2000s, and how the former must first be ensured for the latter to be attained.

Second, arguing that Hispanic newcomers felt they are more discriminated against by blacks than by whites—and that blacks' role in excluding them as outsiders to rural southern communities is as important as the role of whites— may draw the ire of African Americans, many of whom feel they are losing out to entrenched white prejudice as well as to the growing number of low-skilled Hispanic newcomers. It may also suggest to whites that they are not as prejudiced as blacks—perhaps giving whites the erroneous impression that blacks and other minorities should "stop complaining" about racial discrimination. Further arguing that Hispanic newcomers perceived greater discrimination along a horizontal (non)citizenship axis than a vertical race or skin color one may draw the ire of African Americans, whose experiences have been shaped profoundly by both historic and contemporary forms of racial discrimination, as well as that of black-Hispanic coalition builders, who often make explicit attempts to magnify similarities in the forms of discrimination that African Americans and Hispanics experience. It may also erroneously suggest to whites that racial discrimination is no longer important in the United States, even though the existing literature shows that it is, especially for people with African ancestry and phenotypes (see Chapter 5).

Again, the reality of most Hispanic newcomers' experience in eastern North Carolina lay not with any one of these perspectives, but somewhere in the middle. Whites' negative attitudes about and behavior toward blacks have very clearly structured the class-based rural southern racial hierarchy into which Hispanic newcomers are now entering. Furthermore, whites' deeply entrenched and stigmatizing views of African Americans have created strong material and emotional incentives for Hispanic newcomers to distance themselves from African Americans in order to distinguish themselves in a more positive light (see Chapter 5). Yet micro-level interactions between Hispanic newcomers and white and black natives in eastern North Carolina, as elsewhere, often take place without any broader understanding of this macro-level structure (Stuesse 2009). As such, when Hispanic newcomers reported walking down the street and seeing some whites smiling at them versus more blacks "ignoring" them, when Hispanic newcomers reported that blacks derided them more often than whites did as undeserving outsiders who should "go back where they came from" and stop "taking our jobs," and when Hispanic youths reported being beaten up and made fun of in middle and high schools by blacks more so than whites, the macro-level structure of white-on-black domination faded from view while the micro-level structure of black-on-Hispanic domination moved in to replace it.

I have argued that this bodes poorly for African Americans' position in the American racial hierarchy in the long run. The fact that it may be determined primarily by the structure and history of white-on-black domination did not reduce feelings among many Hispanic newcomers on the ground in eastern North Carolina that it is primarily blacks who do not like them, do not want them in "their" country, and will not go to the same lengths to assist them in their endeavors as will whites. Consequently, black-Hispanic tensions in a variety of arenas, both inside and outside the workplace, are an important feature of contemporary rural southern life that needs serious attention in the future—from whites, blacks, and Hispanic newcomers alike. Fortunately, I did also uncover evidence of several Hispanic newcomers reporting positive interpersonal relations with African Americans, especially in the context of the workplace, and it was usually these newcomers who reported being most willing to work toward common goals in tandem with African Americans in the future (Marrow 2006). Thus, improving micro-level interactions between blacks and Hispanic newcomers on the ground may go a long way toward supporting higher-level black-Hispanic coalition-building efforts, which have been expanding throughout the South in recent years, particularly at the elite level among political organizers and community leaders (see Chapter 4). With anti-immigrant sentiment on the rise among whites, it may also offer Hispanic newcomers new ways to contextualize and understand the prejudice and discrimination that they endure.

Third, my argument that Americans' attempts to get tough on unauthorized immigration are doing great harm to many Hispanic newcomers' chances for short- and long-term stability and mobility is solid. This may draw a mixture of support and ire from different groups of people who oppose unauthorized immigration on either ideological or simple legal and policy grounds. It will draw support from them because they are not interested in promoting unauthorized immigrants' chances for stability and mobility in the first place.

Yet it will also draw ire, because they will refuse to acknowledge any responsibility for the adverse consequences they are helping to generate, further claiming that such consequences are justifiable according to existing law and policy. Unfortunately, this position places more emphasis on ideologically based convictions about maintaining one's own power or restricting the movement of certain people across international borders than it does on the increasing body of data demonstrating the adverse human consequences of our nation's current enforcement-oriented stance on unauthorized immigration, which are difficult to support from any perspective. American law and policy have served to subordinate large swaths of people before, and allowing them to continue to do so calls their authority into question, rather than demonstrating patriotism.

Finally, the fact that I am a white middle-class native may draw the charge that I can interpret the Hispanic newcomer experience as relatively unproblematic and avoid all of its negative consequences. It should be clear in this Conclusion, if not throughout the entire book, that the Hispanic newcomer experience in eastern North Carolina is far from unproblematic. Yet the difficulties that exist within this experience—and that I have argued revolve primarily around lack of citizenship and legal status—should not prevent us from acknowledging the accomplishments that have been made, and the possibilities that exist for the future. Figuring out what those accomplishments and possibilities are allows us to focus our energies more precisely on the problems that remain, thereby contributing to better-informed public policy in the long run. Relying on the data given to me directly by my respondents convinces me that there are several things helping to make Hispanic newcomers' experience in eastern North Carolina positive, and they should be preserved as we move forward. On the other hand, it also convinces me that there are several pressing problems in need of immediate attention. Basic access to legal status, the labor market, higher education, and health care needs to be granted and ensured for all persons living in this country. Restricting such access does not eliminate the unauthorized immigrant population; rather, it creates a host of serious problems that are being borne primarily by Hispanic newcomers and their families, but that are also filtering out into local communities across the country.

To the extent that these problems are left unaddressed, dire predictions about the potential downward mobility and permanent disenfranchisement of the descendants of certain segments of new immigrant groups—namely, lower-status and unauthorized ones from Mexico and Central America—may indeed come to pass. And they may come to pass not because of some alleged unwillingness of members of these immigrant groups to speak English or assimilate, but rather because of the policies that we as American natives are intentionally designing to prevent them from doing so, particularly after 2005 (Massey and Sánchez 2010). However, if these problems can be addressed in a more fruitful and enlightened way, my research findings suggest that there were both opportunities and grounds for optimism in rural southern "new immigrant destinations" in 2003–04, and that these could be made to work to the benefit of Hispanic newcomers and natives alike.

Reference Matter

Appendix:
Terminology and Methodology

Notes on Terminology

Metropolitan Status

Although there are technical distinctions between *metropolitan* and *urban* as well as between *nonmetropolitan* and *rural* (Brown and Swanson 2003: 3–4; Kandel and Cromartie 2004), I use these two sets of terms interchangeably in this book. Also, because I am concerned with the immigrant experience as it is playing out in comparison between rural areas and small towns (together) and central cities and suburbs (together), my use of "metropolitan" and "urban" does not differentiate between the central cities and suburbs within them.

Immigrants

Foreign-born people of many cultures and backgrounds are settling in the traditional South today (Hill and Beaver 1998; Reimers 2005; Smith and Furuseth 2006a; Winders 2009a). In North Carolina, Japanese and Asian Indian immigrant professionals have settled in the Raleigh-Durham-Chapel Hill "Research Triangle" metropolitan area (Kurotani 2005; Subramanian 2005), and in the 2000 U.S. Census the seven most commonly spoken foreign languages in the state were Spanish, French, German, Chinese, Vietnamese, Korean, and Arabic.

However, not all foreign-born persons in the traditional South are "immigrants." They also include tourists, businesspeople, exchange visitors, contract workers, and other officially designated "nonimmigrants" who are in the region temporarily. In official parlance, these temporary migrants are distinct from immigrants, who come for permanent settlement and are deemed "legal permanent residents" (Ngai 2004: xiv). Moreover, the foreign-born population also includes "political refugees" and "asylees" whose experiences differ from those of labor and professional immigrants (Portes and

Rumbaut 2006; Winders 2009a). In North Carolina, refugees and asylees have settled mostly in the central piedmont region of the state (Bailey 2005; Gozdziak and Bump 2008; Smith and Furuseth 2006b).

As distinct groups, I do not consider temporary tourists and businesspeople or refugees and asylees in this book. However, I do consider temporary "nonimmigrants" (especially those working on H-2A and H-2B visas[1]) and unauthorized immigrants. I do so because of the growth of temporary contract worker programs and unauthorized immigration at the turn of the twenty-first century (Massey, 2001; Portes and Rumbaut 2006), especially in rural areas of the South with strong agricultural bases.[2] Therefore, I commonly use the term "newcomers" instead of immigrants in this book to denote my inclusion of these groups whom the U.S. government does not recognize as legal immigrants.

Also, rather than focusing on all newcomers, I concentrate specifically on Hispanic ones. By *Hispanic* I mean of Latin American ancestry regardless of nationality, place of birth, or racial self-identification, in accordance with the U.S. Census's official definition of *Hispanics/Latinos*: all "persons of Mexican, Puerto Rican, Cuban, Central or South American, or other Spanish culture or origin, regardless of race" and regardless of whether they are born in the United States or abroad. I do so because the majority of nonwhite and nonblack newcomers who have arrived in the traditional South since the 1980s are Hispanics/Latinos,[3] and the great preponderance of them are foreign-born, primarily in Mexico.[4] Thus, even though not all newcomers to the region are Hispanics, by focusing on Hispanics I capture the experiences of the largest group in the region.

Unauthorized Immigrants

There is significant debate over what the appropriate terminology for this group of people is: *unauthorized immigrants, illegal immigrants, undocumented immigrants, illegals, illegal aliens,* and so forth. In the context of this book, all of these terms refer to people who are residing in the United States but who are not U.S. citizens, have not been admitted for permanent residence, and are not in a set of specific authorized temporary statuses permitting longer-term residence and work—regardless of whether they initially entered the country unlawfully ("entered without inspection") or lawfully using visas they later overstayed ("visa overstayers"; Bean and Lowell 2007; Passel 2005). I rely primarily on the term *unauthorized* in this book because it best captures the position of Hispanic newcomers in my field research as people who do not have *valid* U.S. immigration documents (*no tienen papeles* in Spanish). Nonetheless, even though unauthorized Hispanic newcomers forcefully resisted being deemed "illegal people" by natives, distinguishing between what they saw as the "noncriminal" act of migrating to work to feed their families and other more serious "crimes" (Van der Leun 2003), they did acknowledge that their presence in the United States is not yet officially authorized by the government and therefore is illegal in this more limited sense (*ilegal* in Spanish). Thus, for all intents and purposes I use the terms *unauthorized* and *illegal* interchangeably in this book, but I rely more prominently on the former and I recognize that both terms are heavily loaded in the wider political debate.

Hispanics

There is ongoing debate over usage of the terms *Hispanic* and *Latino* to describe various subpopulations of people in the United States who have ancestral ties to Latin America. In Chapters 4 and 5, I pay special attention to how Hispanic respondents understood, defined, accepted, or resisted these terms as racial and ethnic self-identification, as well as to how they thought rural southern natives see them. Still, I employ the term *Hispanic* in this book for two reasons.

First, it is a convenient way to capture the experiences of both foreign- and U.S.-born individuals who fit the U.S. Census's official definition of *Hispanics/Latinos*. More important, it reflects how the terms *Hispanic* and *Latino* were used in eastern North Carolina in the mid-2000s—interchangeably and in reference to both foreign- and U.S.-born individuals, many of the latter internal migrants from other parts of the United States[5]—while maintaining consistency by only using one term. To illustrate, I encountered both terms in various organizational settings during the course of my research, including settings characterized primarily by natives seeking to address the needs of newcomers and in others composed of newcomers themselves. In all of these settings, *Hispanic* and *Latino* were used equally to denote anyone with Latin American ancestry regardless of national or ethnic origin (e.g., Mexican, Cuban, Guatemalan, Ecuadorian, Argentine, Maya, or Mixteco) or place of birth (e.g., New York, Texas, North Carolina, Puerto Rico, or abroad). Furthermore, most newcomer respondents did define themselves either primarily or secondarily as "Hispanics" or "Latinos," and even among those who resisted the terms as racial self-identifiers, there was an acknowledgment that they are frequently labeled as such by natives, plus an understanding of their connection to the group that the terms are intended to describe (Chapters 4 and 5).

Thus, even though I recognize that the term *Hispanic* is controversial, especially in other parts of the country, it acknowledges the dominant racializing discourse operating both in major public institutions and on the ground in eastern North Carolina in the mid-2000s. To be sure, both *Hispanic* and *Latino* are primarily *imposed on* incoming newcomers of Latin American ancestry in eastern North Carolina, but in response they are creating an ethnic minority by arbitrarily defining a group despite its members' internal differences (Itzigsohn 2004).

Blacks

In this book, I employ the terms *black* and *African American* interchangeably. In the mid-2000s local discourse in eastern North Carolina followed the common institutional practice of separating Hispanics from non-Hispanic blacks, despite the U.S. Census's acknowledgment that these groups are not mutually exclusive (Patterson 2001). Furthermore, even though African immigrants and refugees (Bailey 2005) and Afro-Mexicans (Jones 2010; Vaughn 2005; Vaughn and Vinson 2007) are now prevalent in the central piedmont region of the state, there were few foreign-born blacks in eastern North Carolina in the mid-2000s, and the terms *black* and *African American* still referred largely to a cohesive group of individuals who share a collective history of slavery and racial subordination in the United States.

Whites

I also employ the term *white* in this book, noting that "Anglo" and "Chicano" (see Calafell 2003) are not common terms in the traditional South. As with "black" and "African American," local discourse in eastern North Carolina tended to follow the common institutional practice of separating Hispanics from non-Hispanic whites, despite the U.S. Census's acknowledgment that these groups are not mutually exclusive. In Chapters 4 and 5, I discuss several cases of Hispanic respondents who either self-identified or appeared as white to rural southern natives. However, when most people used the term *white* in this region, their reference was almost always to native-born, non-Hispanic whites. Thus, although it is possible that the identification of some Hispanic newcomers as white may engender a reformulation of the boundaries around whiteness in eastern North Carolina in the future (see Chapter 5), in the mid-2000s this had not happened yet.

America and Americans

Finally, as Jiménez (2010) notes, the term *American* can be used to refer to North, Central, and South America alike, and the use of this term to refer to the United States alone is indicative of the hegemonic relationship between the United States and other nations in the western hemisphere (303). However, I employ the terms *United States* and *America* interchangeably in this book, alongside the term *Americans* to refer to its longer-established residents, because, as Jiménez also notes, no other widely recognized and parsimonious terms exist to refer to them.

Notes on Research Methods

Locating Interview Respondents

I located interview respondents by combining theoretical and snowball sampling designs across four institutional arenas in each county: workplaces, elementary school systems, law enforcement and court systems, and politics. Paying special attention to the views of Hispanic newcomers, I first employed a theoretical sampling design to generate categories of respondents in each of these arenas, based on the probability that they might have unique and theoretically informative experiences regarding important issues I wanted to examine. For example, I chose different types of people in each of the three workplaces where I conducted interviews to highlight issues of occupational (im)mobility and intergroup relations in the workplace. This included lower-status Hispanic labor immigrants with little formal education and English-speaking ability, as well as upwardly mobile immigrant and U.S.-born Hispanics, whose perspectives were important for shedding light on how some Hispanics *are* succeeding (Saenz and Torres 2003). My methodology was similar in each of the other arenas, so that the 129 respondents would ultimately include:

- In workplaces: lower-status Hispanic workers and upwardly mobile Hispanic line managers and supervisors, plus some non-Hispanic employers and line managers, supervisors, and administrative personnel
- In elementary school systems: Hispanic school officials, former students, or parents of Hispanic children in school, plus some non-Hispanic school officials familiar with educational issues affecting the local Hispanic population
- In law enforcement and court systems: Hispanic clients or personnel in local law enforcement or court systems, plus some non-Hispanic legal personnel familiar with legal issues affecting the local Hispanic community
- In politics: established or emerging Hispanic political leaders, plus some non-Hispanic political leaders in local and state politics (including the county manager, two county commissioners, and two state-level political representatives from each county)

Some respondents fit into more than one arena, as when Hispanic community leaders were also employed in educational or social welfare institutions, or when Hispanic workers had children in educational institutions or had come into contact with social welfare, medical, or legal institutions. Therefore the bulk of my data pertain to the four arenas listed above, but I also collected data on Hispanic newcomers' experiences with higher educational institutions and social welfare and medical services agencies.

To locate these interview subjects, I drew on existing social networks to contact the employers of the three workplace settings that I wanted to study—a tobacco farm and a textile mill in Bedford County and a large poultry processing plant in Wilcox County—as well as several local politicians and service providers who I thought or had heard would be familiar with each county's Hispanic population. Through these initial contacts, I met various Hispanic "key informants" who in turn helped me locate other Hispanic respondents who would fit into my theoretical sampling categories through an informal snowball sampling design. Interviews ranged from 30 minutes to three hours (most lasted for one and one-half to two hours), and respondents were asked a battery of questions regarding their migration history and employment and adaptation experiences (if they were Hispanics) and experiences with the local Hispanic community (if they were non-Hispanic employers, school or legal personnel, or political leaders).

Ethnographic Research

I supplemented the interviews with several forms of ethnographic research:

- Making observations around my key workplace settings
- Accompanying key Hispanic respondents throughout their workday
- Attending local school board meetings, parent-teacher association meetings at elementary schools, and traffic courts
- Reviewing county commissioner meeting agendas and state and local newspaper archives
- Attending meetings of the one emergent Hispanic association in each county as of May 2004 (*Latinos Unidos* in Bedford and Alexandria Counties and the Association of Mexicans in Wilcox County)
- Attending meetings of groups formed by native politicians and service providers to assess their Hispanic populations' needs (such as the Hispanic Assistance Council in Bedford and Alexandria Counties, the Hispanic Assistance Committee in Wilcox County, and other groups such as local Agricultural Extension Services, Partnerships for Children, and so forth)
- Enrolling in a Hispanic Leadership Course offered by Wilcox County Community College in fall 2003[6]
- Investigating local connections to Hispanic political groups and initiatives at the state level (such as the Latino Community Development Corporation and the North Carolina Coalition for Black and Brown Civic Participation in Durham, and the Association of Mexicans in North Carolina, El Pueblo, Inc., and the Governor's Office for Hispanic/Latino Affairs in Raleigh)[7]
- Speaking informally with newcomer and native residents throughout the year

Entrée and Identity in the Research Process

As in all research projects, the characteristics of the researcher influence both collection and analysis of the data. In addition to choosing Bedford and Wilcox Counties as my field research sites for the theoretical and comparative reasons highlighted in the Introduction, I also chose them for practical reasons. Because I grew up in eastern North Carolina and my family is still located there, several factors enhanced the quality of my research: knowledge of the geographical layout and history of this subregion of the state; knowledge of how social relations and customs function in this subregion (including the dialects and accents among local social groups); easy access to housing, a telephone, a car, state and local newspapers, and the Internet while living at home with my parents for the year; and despite having lived outside of North Carolina since high school, a set of social networks that helped me not only to gain entrée into all three of the workplaces where I conducted interviews but also to contact various state and local politicians and service providers with a greater degree of "local legitimacy" than an outsider can. (I used social connections to gain initial entrée into all three workplaces. That most Hispanic respondents expressed both negative and positive views about their working conditions helps to limit concern about such connections producing methodological bias in my results.)

During my research, I found that local legitimacy was extremely important in establishing rapport with rural white southerners, many of whom were skeptical of my past Ivy League affiliations and current northeastern residence. Both of these factors give off impressions of wealth, privilege, and liberal-minded politics in eastern North Carolina, inhibiting establishment of good rapport with many rural white natives, especially those who are more conservative or feel they are the type of "average folks" whom urbanites, even those from nearby southern cities, look down on. In fact, rural white southerners tend to be skeptical of anyone parachuting in to conduct research on them from a university setting, even one that is local and public, such as the University of North Carolina at Chapel Hill. Therefore, I found that a shared white racial identity was not sufficient to establish rapport with them, because of the many other differences between us. So it was always very important to stress my insider status as someone who was also born and raised in eastern North Carolina, with family roots tracing back deep into the region. As my father likes to put it, I can speak with a local southern accent, which helped me to "grease wheels," and I also know how to "speak Rotarian," a quality that, when employed appropriately, helped me establish a better connection with white native respondents, as well as with the various other rural white southerners I spoke to informally over the course of the year.

To illustrate, whites (especially lower-middle-class and working-class ones) repeatedly asked me where I was from with a skeptical eye. However, once they learned more about me, they became more relaxed and forthcoming in their interactions with me, even conceding initial skepticism about the goals and purpose of my project. On hearing my questions about Hispanic newcomers or race relations, they often felt the questions were meant to judge them as bad or racist individuals. Thus, I went to great lengths to reassure them that my purpose was to explore broad patterns in race relations in the region—as opposed to simply characterizing all white individuals as racists—and that this would include uncovering stories of good as well as bad interactions between whites and other racial and ethnic groups. In almost every interview I conducted, I noticed that these extra efforts, as well as my local roots, made them less suspicious of me and more willing to talk frankly about their feelings. In some cases, they were all too frank, to the point where I doubted they would have expressed the same negative feelings about African Americans or Hispanic newcomers with as much intensity to someone who did not share their regional, ethnic, or (Protestant) religious background.

On the other hand, I found that local legitimacy was less important in establishing rapport with rural southern blacks. Although I have the disadvantage of not being African American and therefore of not having as strong a cultural link with black native respondents as I did with white native respondents in the project, I do not think that this difference significantly affected the quality of the information I received in my interviews with blacks, for two reasons. The weaker of the two is that although we belong to separate racial groups, we still share some common local history and experience, including that of being natives of this subregion of North Carolina. The stronger of the two is that asking them questions about race relations and exposing my past Ivy League affiliations and current northeastern residence frequently made them more—rather than less—relaxed and eager to talk to me. I can only suspect that this is because they began to see me as someone interested in issues of racial inequality, attuned to empathizing with their history and experience rather than reacting defensively against it. Indeed, on only one occasion did I perceive my being white as a significant barrier to my relationship with African Americans, and they were not official interview respondents in the project but rather state-level black-Hispanic coalition organizers who made it clear that, as a white woman, I was not welcome in their meetings. Although the experience was deeply troubling to me, I have tried to treat it as a data point in my research—as an important example of how white-black relations in the rural American South continue to be marred by a historical animosity that does not yet characterize white-Hispanic relations there to the same degree.

Finally, I found that local legitimacy was not important at all in establishing rapport with Hispanic respondents. This is not surprising since most of my Hispanic respondents were not born and raised in eastern North Carolina, and so they did not share the same excitement about such "local" linkages as did white or black native respondents.[8] Instead, I relied on my ability to speak Spanish and my knowledge about their countries of origin to establish rapport and legitimacy with them. Here, of course, it is important to note that eastern North Carolina is a very different context from Los Angeles, New York City, or the U.S.-Mexico border. As many Hispanics repeatedly told me over the course of my fieldwork, very few natives in the region speak more than the basic Spanish they learned in high school—which is generally not enough to communicate with—and still fewer know anything substantive about Latin America. Consequently, although I will never be a full "insider" among Hispanic newcomers in eastern North Carolina, my ability to speak Spanish and my previous experiences living and traveling in various Latin American countries[9] helped me stand out to them in a way that facilitated dialogue and countered our other differences in nationality, race, and class status. In fact, I am still referred to as "the white girl who speaks Spanish [*la bolilla que habla español* in Spanish]" by a good friend's family in Bedford County,[10] and in Wilcox County I was invited to join both the Association of Mexicans in North Carolina (AMEXCAN)—of which I am still an adjunct member—and the Hispanic Leadership Course offered in fall 2003 at Wilcox County Community College.

Furthermore, many foreign-born respondents openly told me that they were unauthorized immigrants or working with false names in the United States, which suggests that they were comfortable with me to at least a certain degree. And during their interviews, many Hispanic newcomers treated me as a sort of interlocutor between themselves and local natives, asking me to help "tell their stories" to natives who might not otherwise understand why they are here, how they want to work and create a better life for themselves and their children, how they do not want to do Americans any harm, how they want to learn English, and how those of them who are unauthorized want to become technically "legal" and law-abiding members of their new communities. In these ways, I was often surprised by how much—rather than how little—they were willing to confide in me once I had gained their initial trust (see also Griffith 2005).

In sum, even though my nationality, race, class status, gender, and other characteristics have no doubt influenced and affected the data I collected and the analyses that I present in this book, I do not think that they have seriously compromised the quality or significance of my research findings. One's identity is never fixed; the line between insider and outsider is always fluid because various situations can activate elements of one's identity in different ways (Merton 1972). I share both commonalities and differences with all groups of interview subjects in this project: Latin American immigrants, U.S.-born Hispanics, and both white and black "key native informants." Depending on the situation, I learned to negotiate these commonalities and differences in such a way that all respondents might feel more comfortable sharing their thoughts and experiences with me. Indeed, my efforts to establish forms of fictive kinship with different respondents in order to facilitate rapport involved what Lee (2002) calls "constant negotiation—pushing certain statuses into the foreground while keeping other facts tucked away" (207). Ultimately, I agree with my colleague Tomás Jiménez that what makes an ethnographic researcher successful is polite curiosity and willingness to listen. I hope these two criteria have not only made my research more successful but also helped me overcome any shortcomings produced by the influence of my identity.

I also hope that future research conducted by researchers of other national, racial and ethnic, and class backgrounds can help to fill in any holes in my work. For instance, I suspect that if an African American or Hispanic researcher were to replicate my in-depth interviews and ethnographic fieldwork in eastern North Carolina, he or she might uncover more negative depictions of white employers or middle-class white residents, or more negative depictions of white-Hispanic compared to black-Hispanic relations (see, for example, Jones 2010). It would indeed be important to reconcile such findings with those I present. On the other hand, an African American or Hispanic researcher also might not uncover the same degree of black-Hispanic tension, which though uncomfortable to discuss is nevertheless important to address. Finally, I want to make it clear that both my Hispanic and African American respondents *did* voice negative views about whites to me. Usually they prefaced them with leading phrases intended to disassociate me as a white individual from whites as a group, such as, "Don't take this the wrong way, but whites . . ." or "I don't mean this toward you, but whites. . . ." When this happened, I responded by laughing and telling them to continue on without worrying about my taking any personal offense. In this way, I believe I have appropriately taken my nonwhite respondents' negative views about whites into careful consideration in my analyses.

Protecting Research Subjects

In addition to changing the names of all locations in eastern North Carolina and concealing the identities of the three workplaces where I conducted my field research, I have gone to great lengths to protect the identities of individual interview subjects in my project. All names of interview respondents presented in this book are pseudonyms, and I have altered their identifying information (such as their sex, state or country of birth, year of arrival in the United States, migration trajectory, occupation and department of work, etc.) during multiple phases of de-identification. In accordance with a National Institutes of Health (NIH) Certificate of Confidentiality that I received in June 2003, which protects against compelled disclosure of any personally identifiable information from the project, I have also altered all identifying information regarding illegal activity, as well as the identities of the many natives and newcomers I met informally during my ethnographic research.

In this way, I always maintain "plausible deniability"—the ability to plausibly deny any claim that a particular respondent in my research corresponds to a specific individual in real life. Admittedly, I do remember who several political leaders, community figures, and "key contacts" in the project were, yet through multiple phases of de-identification even I have forgotten the real names of most other interview respondents. So, even if the identity of an individual respondent seems familiar to readers, I have probably changed enough information about the respondent that any move to sanction him or her runs a serious risk of sanctioning someone I did not actually interview or speak with. This is especially important to clarify for unauthorized immigrants, whom I have taken special care to protect, even if other individuals are more recognizable to the residents of these communities.

It is equally important to note that respondents risked no physical harm by participating in this project. Depending on their individual circumstances, they may have risked some social or psychological harm in thinking about the kinds of sensitive questions I asked them (especially concerning racial identity, race relations, group hierarchies, and stereotypes and prejudices). However, before I conducted my interviews I always made sure to clarify that respondents' participation was voluntary, that I was interested in their relations with other people in terms of broad patterns rather than as specific individual behaviors, that my goal was to hear and understand their viewpoints and opinions rather than to pass judgment on them as individuals, and that I would never use their real names in any written publication. Doing this helped minimize their risk of social or psychological harm through participating in my project.

However, some respondents may still have risked serious legal harm if they were unauthorized immigrants. By participating in my project and having their voices and opinions publicized, negative action against them may occur by outside parties unbeknownst to me.[11] To help protect against this kind of harm, I made it clear to all interview subjects that I could not promise full confidentiality in the case of any extreme circumstances, so that they could decline the interview if they were fearful of legal sanction. Fewer than five foreign-born immigrants turned down my request for an interview; only a few other native-born Americans did so. Additionally, I made it clear to all immigrant subjects that they should withhold any information regarding their legal status if they were concerned about legal sanction. Surely some did, and I will never know who or how many they were. Many unauthorized respondents, however, were surprisingly forthcoming about their lack of legal status. Repeatedly, they expressed to me how important being unauthorized was in their lives, how much they wanted Americans to know about the struggles they face as *migrantes sin papeles* in the United States today, and how much they wanted to become legal and law-abiding members of their new communities. Having gone to these lengths to protect their identity, I therefore engage lack of status as a central issue in their lives.

Notes

Introduction

A small portion of this chapter was adapted from "Race and the New Southern Migration, 1986 to the present," in Mark Overmyer-Velázquez, ed., *Beyond* La Frontera: *The History of Mexico-U.S. Migration.* © 2011 Oxford University Press Reprinted with the permission of Oxford University Press, Inc., www.oup.com.

1. The "lowland" or "lowcountry" South has a strong legacy of plantation agriculture and a relatively large number of African Americans, two characteristics that distinguish it from the "highland," "upcountry," "hill," "mountain," or "Appalachian" South. Such distinctions are *subregional* ones used within the South and are not equivalent to the rural-urban distinction more familiar to natives of other American regions. There are both rural and urban areas within the lowland and highland South (Reed 1986, 1993; Zarrugh 2008).

2. For other descriptions of the black belt, see Delpar (2008); McDaniel and Casanova (2003); Reed (1993); and RSS (2006a, 2006b). For more detailed descriptions of eastern North Carolina, see Griffith (1993, 1995a, 1995b, 2005); Key (1984); Torres, Popke, and Hapke (2006); and Torres et al. (2003).

3. Here, I define the traditional South as the 11 former confederate states minus Florida and Texas, which have greater experience with "Hispanics/Latinos" (Bankston 2007; Borjas 2004; Mohl 2003; Saenz 2000). "Hispanics/Latinos" are an official American ethnic group that the U.S. Census defines as all "persons of Mexican, Puerto Rican, Cuban, Central or South American, or other Spanish culture or origin, regardless of race" and regardless of whether they are born in the United States or abroad. See the Appendix for more detail.

4. Whereas the proportion of the total non-Southern population that was foreign-born in 1860 was 14%, the corresponding figure in the South was only 5%. In 1910, following mass immigration from Europe and Asia, these figures widened to nearly

15% and 2% respectively (Reimers 2005; see also Berthoff 1951), and even as late as 1950 only 1.6% of the South's population was foreign-born, compared to 6.9% nationally and 13.4% in the immigrant-heavy Northeast (Eckes 2005). Figures in the "traditional South" were even lower. In 1910 only 0.3% of North Carolina's population was "foreign-born white," and Alabama, Georgia, Mississippi, North Carolina, and South Carolina together contained less than 1% of the country's total foreign-born population (Delpar 2008; Hartch 2008; Schmid 2003). As late as 1950, all of the traditional southern states still exhibited less than 1% foreign-born (Eckes 2005).

5. Because of rising immigration, by 2000 approximately two thirds of Hispanics/Latinos were either first- or second-generation immigrants (Schmidley 2001: 24, table 9-1).

6. For good reviews of these trends, see Bohn (2009); Bump, Lowell, and Pettersen (2005); Fischer and Tienda (2006); Fry (2008); Lichter and Johnson (2009); Marrow (2005); Massey (2008b); Massey, Durand, and Malone (2002); Singer (2004, 2008); Singer, Hardwick, and Brettell (2008b); Suro and Singer (2002); Suro and Tafoya (2004); Vásquez, Seales, and Marquardt (2008); and Zúñiga and Hernández-León (2005b).

On immigrants moving into new central city and suburban locations, especially within the American South, see Alba et al. (1999); Bada et al. (2010); Bohon, Massengale, and Jordan (2009); Brettell and Nibbs (2010); Card and Lewis (2007); Ciscel, Smith, and Mendoza (2005); Cornfield (2009); Donato and Bankston (2008); Donato, Bankston, and Robinson (2001); Donato, Stainback, and Bankston (2005); Engstrom (2001); Fussell (2009); Greenbaum (1998); Guthrie-Shimizu (2005); Hagan, Lowe, and Quingla (2009); Hernández-León (2008); Hernández-Léon and Zúñiga (2000, 2003, 2005); Jensen et al. (2006); Johnson, Johnson-Webb, and Farrell (1999); Johnson and Kasarda (2009); Johnson-Webb (2003); the collected essays in Jones (2008); Jones-Correa (2008); Kandel and Parrado (2006); Kasarda and Johnson (2006); Kurotani (2005); Lattanzi Shutika (2005, 2008); Levitt et al. (2008); Lippard (2008); Logan (2001); McClain (2006, in progress); McClain et al. (2006, 2007); McDermott (in progress); Morando (2009); Odem (2004, 2009); Reimers (2005); Rich and Miranda (2005); the collected essays in Singer, Hardwick, and Brettell (2008b); B. E. Smith (2006, 2009); B. E. Smith, Mendoza, and Ciscel (2005); H. E. Smith and Furuseth (2006b); R. C. Smith (2005, 2006); Solórzano (2005); Stamps and Bohon (2006); Subramanian (2005); Wainer (2004); Walcott and Murphy (2006); Weeks, Weeks, and Weeks (2007); Winders (2005, 2008a, 2009a, 2009b); and Zúñiga and Hernández-León (2001, 2009).

On immigrants moving into new small towns and rural areas, especially within the American South, see Allegro (in progress); Atiles and Bohon (2003); Bailey (2005); Barcus (2006); Broadway (2000, 2007); Bump (2005); Cady Hallett (in progress); Cantu (1995); Cravey (1997); Cuadros (2006); Dale, Andreatta, and Freeman (2001); Donato et al. (2007, 2008); Drever (2006, 2009); Dunn, Aragonés, and Shivers (2005); Elliott and Ionescu (2003); Emery, Ginger, and Chamberlain (2006); Erwin (2003); Fennelly (2005, 2008); Fennelly and Leitner (2002); D. Fink (1998); L. Fink (2003); Furuseth and Smith

(2006); Gouveia, Carranza, and Cogua (2005); Gouveia and Saenz (2000); Gouveia and Stull (1997); Gozdziak and Bump (2004); Grey (1999); Grey and Woodrick (2005); Griffith (1993, 2005, 2006, 2008); Griffith et al. (1995, 2001); Guthey (2001); Hansen (2005); Hiemstra (2008); Jones-Correa and Fennelly (2009); Kandel and Cromartie (2004); Kandel and Parrado (2004, 2006); Lichter and Johnson (2006); McConnell and Miraftab (2009); McDaniel and Casanova (2003); McDermott (in progress); Millard and Chapa (2004); Mohl (2002, 2003, 2009); Nelson and Hiemstra (2008); Rose (2007); Saenz (2000); Saenz et al. (2003); Saenz and Torres (2003); Schoenholtz (2005); Smith-Nonini (2005); Striffler (2005a, 2005b, 2009); Studstill and Nieto-Studstill (2001); Stuesse (2009); Stull and Broadway (2004, 2008); the collected essays in Stull, Broadway, and Griffith (1995); Torres, Popke, and Hapke (2006); Torres et al. (2003); and Zarrugh (2008).

7. "Illegal" or "unauthorized" immigrants are a group of people who are residing in the United States but who are not U.S. citizens, have not been admitted for permanent residence, and are not in a set of specific authorized temporary statuses permitting longer-term residence and work—regardless of whether they initially entered the country unlawfully ("entered without inspection") or lawfully using visas they later overstayed ("visa overstayers"; Bean and Lowell 2007; Passel 2005). See the Appendix for more detail on how I use these terms throughout this book.

8. See Hoefer, Rytina, and Baker (2010); Massey (2011); Massey and Sánchez (2010); Passel (2006); and Passel and Cohn (2008, 2009).

9. Massey, Durand, and Malone (2002) show that the rise in unauthorized immigration is the result of increasingly restrictive American immigration policies toward Latin Americans over the past half century, which function in direct opposition to growing economic interdependence among the United States, Canada, and Mexico since the 1980s. In December 1964, the United States eliminated the *bracero* program, which was begun in 1942 and, over the course of its operation, accepted an average of 450,000 lawful Mexican temporary agricultural contract workers per year. In 1968, the United States also began enforcing a 170,000-person ceiling on legal immigration from the Western hemisphere for the first time. Together, these two policies reduced Latin American immigrants' available legal routes of entry as either temporary contract workers or legal immigrants, and new arrivals would increasingly have to enter as unauthorized immigrants, despite increasing economic interdependence stimulated by North American trade agreements such as GATT and NAFTA. These changes affected Mexicans most strongly, especially after 1976, when an amendment further established a numerical limit of only 20,000 annual visas for legal immigrants per sending country (Massey et al. 2002: 43; for further information on how increasingly restrictive American immigration policies have created the expanding unauthorized immigrant population, see also Cornelius and Lewis 2007; De Genova 2005; Durand, Telles, and Flashman 2006; Ngai 2004; and Telles and Ortiz 2008).

10. In North Carolina, an estimated 45% of the Hispanic population, and fully 76% of foreign-born Hispanics arriving between 1994 and 2004, were unauthorized

immigrants in 2005 (Johnson and Kasarda 2009; Kasarda and Johnson 2006; Miller 2010; Weeks, Weeks, and Weeks 2007).

11. For concise overviews, see Hirschman and Massey (2008); the collected essays in the first half of Massey (2008b); McConnell (2008); Odem and Lacy (2009); Vásquez, Seales, and Marquardt (2008); and Zúñiga and Hernández-León (2005a).

12. Within North Carolina, see Cravey (2003); Fink (2003); Griffith (1993, 1995a, 1995b, 2005); Johnson-Webb (2003); and Smith-Nonini (2005, 2009).

13. In 2000 U.S. Census data, only 15.6% of the traditional South's foreign-born population and 22.7% of its Hispanic population resided in nonmetropolitan areas. Moreover, only 2.8% and 2.7% of the traditional South's nonmetropolitan areas were foreign-born and Hispanic, respectively, compared to 6.7% and 4.1% of the region's metropolitan areas, respectively (Ruggles et al. 2004, weighted data, author's analysis). The disproportionate concentration of the foreign-born population in southern metropolitan areas is even greater in the "high-growth" states of Georgia, Virginia, and North Carolina compared to slow-growth ones in the "Deep South Triad" of Mississippi, Alabama, and Louisiana (Elliott and Ionescu 2003).

14. On the children of immigrants, see Bean, Brown, Leach, and Bachmeier (2008); Kasinitz, Mollenkopf, and Waters (2002, 2004); Kasinitz, Mollenkopf, Waters, and Holdaway (2008); Portes and Fernández-Kelly (2008); Portes and Rumbaut (2001); Rumbaut (2008); Rumbaut and Portes (2001); Telles and Ortiz (2008); and Zhou, Lee, Vallejo, and Tafoya-Estrada (2008). On political incorporation, see de la Garza, Falcón, Garcia, and Garcia (1992) and Lien, Conway, and Wong (2004). For notable exceptions, see Bada et al. (2010); Bullock and Hood (2006); Ellis and Goodwin-White (2006); Fraga et al. (2010); Gouveia and Powell (2007); Ramakrishnan (2005); Zhou and Bankston (1998); and the 2006 Latino National Survey and the 2008 National Asian American Survey, both of which included respondents in several new destination states.

15. See, for example, Bada et al. (2010); Brettell (2008); Donato and Bankston (2008); Donato et al. (2005); Fennelly (2008); Gleeson (2008); Gouveia et al. (2005); Griffith (2008); Jones-Correa (2005b, 2008); Jones-Correa and Fennelly (2009); Kandel and Parrado (2006); Levitt et al. (2008); McClain (in progress); McDermott (in progress); Nelson and Hiemstra (2008); Odem (2008); Okamoto and Ebert (2010); Perreira (in progress); Price and Singer (2008); B. E. Smith (2006, 2009); Van Hook, Brown, and Bean (2006); and Winders (2008a).

16. The one exception could be contracted seasonal farmworkers, who were often isolated on farms and had little interaction with other residents. However, even the Hispanic agricultural workers I interviewed had some contact with whites and blacks within their workplaces. For an opposing view arguing that Hispanic newcomers are isolated in rural new destinations, see Nelson and Hiemstra (2008). They argue that Hispanic newcomers and natives inhabit different residential as well as temporal spaces in the small town of Leadville, Oregon, with the two groups frequenting stores, agencies, churches, and public spaces at distinct times.

17. Consider, for example, that in the 2000 U.S. Census only 13.2% of native-born Americans age 25 and older who were living in nonmetropolitan areas of the traditional South held a bachelor's degree. This compares unfavorably to their counterparts living in traditional metropolitan gateways (as examples, 31.5% in Los Angeles–Long Beach, 32.9% in New York–northeastern New Jersey, and 39.4% in San Francisco–Oakland–Vallejo) and also in new metropolitan destinations (for example, 32.0% in Atlanta, 33.6% in Minneapolis–St. Paul, and 43.3% in Washington, DC/Virginia/Maryland; Ruggles et al. 2004, author's analysis, weighted data).

18. Obviously, racism, xenophobia, and outright rejection exist at one end of the spectrum of how natives greet newcomers in new destinations, with several sources documenting intense anti-immigrant and racially tinged actions directed at Hispanic newcomers by whites, including members of white or European supremacy groups (Bauer and Reynolds 2009; Cuadros 2006; Griffith 1993: 167–72; Hincapié 2009; Holthouse 2009; Lacy and Odem 2009; Mohl 2002, 2003, 2009; B. E. Smith 2006; Zúñiga and Hernández-León 2009). However, antiracism, egalitarianism, human rights, and sympathy for newcomers' plights inform responses at the other end of the spectrum, often emerging in direct response (see, for example, Fennelly 2006; Striffler 2009; Striffler and Weise 2008; and Zarrugh 2008). For the many interpretations that stress ambivalence and variation in response to newcomers across the South, see Alvarado and Jaret (2009); Armenta (2010); Bump (2005); Cornelius (2002); Cuadros (2006); Delpar (2008); Erwin (2003); Fennelly (2006, 2008); Fennelly and Orfield (2008); Fraga et al. (2010); Gouveia (2006); Grey (2006); Grey and Woodrick (2005); Griffith (2008); Hirschman and Massey (2008); Lattanzi Shutika (2008); McClain (in progress); McConnell and Miraftab (2009); McDermott (in progress); Neal and Bohon (2003); Nelson and Hiemstra (2008); Price and Singer (2008); Rich and Miranda (2005); Rose (2007); Schoenholtz (2005); Singer (2008); Solórzano (2005); Striffler and Weise (2008); Wainer (2004); Winders (2008b, 2009b); and Zúñiga and Hernández-León (2005a, 2009).

19. Griffin and McFarland (2007) find that lifelong southerners advance more restrictive immigration policies, evaluate immigrants more negatively, and espouse more particularistic and exclusive ideas of what it takes to be American than do lifelong nonsoutherners or southern "transplants/exiles," and their results hold among both white and black southerners.

20. To illustrate, by 2007 I documented only eight nongovernmental and community organizations devoted explicitly to servicing the immigrant, Hispanic, or farmworker communities in my fieldsite region of eastern North Carolina. By contrast, Cordero-Guzmán, Martin, Quiroz-Becerra, and Theodore (2008) locate 173 organizations serving large proportions of foreign-born clients in Chicago and another 381 in New York City in 2005, while de Graauw (2008) locates 300 migrant-serving nonprofit organizations in San Francisco in 2006–07. Religious institutions are also an important space for Hispanic newcomers to come together in various parts of the South

(Bada et al. 2010; Griffith 2008; Odem 2004, 2009; Zarrugh 2008), although they too are fewer in number in rural areas than in larger southern cities.

21. In 2006, North Carolina and Georgia had the lowest percentages of Hispanics eligible to vote of all U.S. states, at 20 and 21, respectively (Taylor and Fry 2007). These figures are strongly linked to both states' high proportion of recent unauthorized arrivals.

22. On the sociolegal production of unauthorized status in the United States, see Cornelius (2009); Cornelius and Lewis (2009); De Genova (2005); Hincapié (2009); Massey, Durand, and Malone (2002); and Ngai (2004). On increasing enforcement of it, see Hincapié (2009); Massey and Sánchez (2010); and Terrazas (2008). One example is the steady rate of border apprehensions (hovering between 800,000 and 1.2 million per year) since the 1980s, and a second is the rise of deportations from approximately 25,000 per year in 1980 to 359,000 per year in 2008. As Massey and Sánchez (2010) write, "This level has never been seen before in U.S. history. . . . In a very real way, then, the United States increasingly looks like a police state to immigrants, whatever their documentation. Under current conditions, it is as if the militarized border program of 1953 and 1954 (Operation Wetback) has been made permanent and the mass deportation campaigns of 1929 to 1934 have been institutionalized at three times their earlier size" (78).

Chapter 1

1. Vera even applied for a job at the worksite I call Poultry Processing Plant (a pseudonym) in Wilcox County in the late 1990s, where she was told that she qualified for an "easy" position thanks to her education and English language skills (see Chapter 3). However, she was turned off by seeing "all those chickens hanging around," employees working "so hard, they was working like crazies," and a female worker crying in the nurse's office over her fingers, which were "messed up from the work."

2. Although some components of traditional southern culture (such as ethnocentrism and religious fundamentalism) have declined, other aspects (political attitudes, some aspects of religious behavior, attitudes toward violence) persist even after southerners' individual characteristics, including rurality, are controlled for (Reed 1986, 1993).

3. See Chapter 7 for an overview of recent policy changes restricting immigrants' ability to obtain a North Carolina driver's license.

4. Alvarado and Jaret (2009); Barcus (2006); Bauer and Reynolds (2009); Bohon, Macpherson, and Atiles (2005); Cuadros (2006); Drever (2006); Dunn, Aragonés, and Shivers (2005); Erwin (2003); Fraga et al. (2010); Gouveia (2006); Gouveia, Carranza, and Cogua (2005); Hiemstra (2008); Kandel and Parrado (2006); Millard and Chapa (2004); Stuesse (2009); Stull and Broadway (2004); Torres, Popke, and Hapke (2006); Winders (2008b).

5. See Falk and Lobao (2003); Jensen, McLaughlin, and Slack (2003); and Mc-

Granahan (2003) on this point, within broader discussions of the dilemmas of rural economic development.

6. Torres, Popke, and Hapke (2006). See also Allegro (2008); Bohon (2008); Cantu (1995); Drever (2006); Fennelly (2005); Hernández-León and Zúñiga (2000, 2003); Kelley and Chavez (2004); Lacy (2007, 2009); Leach (2004); Nelson and Hiemstra (2008); Schoenholtz (2005); and Striffler (2009).

7. Atiles and Bohon (2003); Bohon (2008); Mantero (2008: 223); Nelson and Hiemstra (2008). Other research shows that residential patterns in several new immigrant destinations are not characterized by "ghettoization." In fact, it argues that less strict zoning laws in some southern and rural areas may instead lead to patterns of deconcentration and dispersion (Barcus 2006; Drever 2006; McConnell and Miraftab 2009; Schoenholtz 2005; Winders 2008b, 2009b), at least in the initial stages of immigration, as may the extremely tight housing market in food processing boomtowns (Stull and Broadway 2004: 110–11).

8. Many newcomers in rural new destinations come from rural areas and small villages abroad, and so they have a lot of experience working in agriculture yet little education, English-speaking ability, or experience participating in politics (Griffith 1993, 2006; Griffith et al. 1995; Kandel and Cromartie 2004; Kandel and Parrado 2006; McDonnell 2008; Torres, Popke, and Hapke 2006; Torres et al. 2003). In my research, these respondents tended to fit a pattern of *rural-to-rural international migration* (e.g., from rural Mexico to rural North Carolina, perhaps passing through other states on the agricultural circuit along the way).

9. These respondents tended to fit two general patterns: (1) *urban-to-rural international migration* (e.g., from Bogotá or Mexico City to rural North Carolina, perhaps passing through a large U.S. city along the way), and (2) *urban-to-rural domestic migration* (e.g., from New York City or Houston to rural North Carolina).

Chapter 2

1. North Carolina is a "right-to-work" state, meaning that it prohibits the requirement of joining a union as a condition of employment (Cornfield 2009).

2. This uniform helps protect employees against temperatures varying from below freezing to more than 100 degrees across different departments in the plant, and against occupational injuries that frequently result from workers' use of heavy equipment.

3. As Drever (2009) and Papademetriou and Ray (2004, quoted in Gouveia 2006: 175) note, lower home prices and cost of living in new destinations offer Hispanic newcomers greater opportunity to save money and enter into home ownership than is possible in many traditional immigrant gateways, such as New York, Chicago, and Los Angeles.

4. Card and Lewis (2007); Fischer and Tienda (2006); Kochhar (2003, 2006, 2008a, 2008b); Pew Hispanic Center (2007a); Singer (2004); the collected essays in Singer, Hardwick, and Brettell (2008b); B. E. Smith (2006, 2009); and Vásquez, Seales, and

Marquardt (2008). On these industries and immigration to the South, see Atiles and Bohon (2003); Bailey (2005); Barcus (2006); Brettell (2008); Ciscel, Smith, and Mendoza (2003); Dunn, Aragonés, and Shivers (2005); Fussell (2009); Guthrie-Shimizu (2005); Hagan, Lowe, and Quingla (2009); Johnson and Kasarda (2009); Johnson, Johnson-Webb, and Farrell (1999); Johnson-Webb (2003); Kasarda and Johnson (2006); Kochhar, Suro, and Tafoya (2005); Kurotani (2005); Lacy (2007); Lippard (2008); Mohl (2002, 2003, 2009); Odem (2008, 2009); Odem and Lacy (2009); Parrado and Kandel (2008); Reimers (2005); Rich and Miranda (2005); B. E. Smith (1998); Smith, Mendoza, and Ciscel (2005); H. A. Smith (2008); Smith and Furuseth (2006b, 2008); Subramanian (2005); Weeks, Weeks, and Weeks (2007); and Winders (2005, 2008a, 2009a).

5. Bankston (2007); Donato et al. (2007, 2008); Durand, Massey, and Capoferro (2005); Fraga et al. (2010); Kandel and Cromartie (2004); Krissman (2000); Parrado and Kandel (2008); Stull and Broadway (2004); the collected essays in Stull, Broadway, and Griffith (1995). On agriculture and immigration to the South, see Atiles and Bohon (2003); Bailey (2005); Barcus (2006); Bump (2005); Dale, Andreatta, and Freeman (2001); Emery, Ginger, and Chamberlain (2006); Erwin (2003); Gozdziak and Bump (2004); Griffith (2005, 2006); Griffith et al. (1995); Griffith et al. (2001); McDaniel and Casanova (2003); Rich and Miranda (2005); Smith-Nonini (2005); Studstill and Neito-Studstill (2001); Thompson and Hill (2005); Torres, Popke, and Hapke (2006); Torres et al. (2003); Turnbull (2008); and Zarrugh (2008).

6. On agribusiness and food processing and immigration to the South, see Atiles and Bohon (2003); Bump (2005); Cravey (1997); Cuadros (2006); Drever (2006, 2009); Erwin (2003); Fink (2003); Gozdziak and Bump (2004); Griffith (1993, 1995a, 1995b, 2005, 2006); Guthey (2001); Kandel and Parrado (2004); Parrado and Kandel (2008); Schoenholtz (2005); Striffler (2005a, 2005b, 2009); Stuesse (2009); and Zarrugh (2008).

7. On manufacturing and textiles and immigration to the South, see Atiles and Bohon (2003); Donato and Bankston (2008); Donato, Bankston, and Robinson (2001); Donato, Stainback, and Bankston (2005); Engstrom (2001); Hernández-León (2008); Hernández-León and Zúñiga (2000, 2003, 2005); Kasarda and Johnson (2006); Kochhar, Suro, and Tafoya (2005); López-Sanders (2009); Morando (2009); Willis (2005); and Zúñiga and Hernández-León (2001, 2009).

8. Broadway (2000); Fennelly and Leitner (2002); Fink (1998, 2003); Hall (1995); Striffler (2005a, 2005b, 2009); Stull (1994); Stull and Broadway (2004).

9. Alexander (2008); Bauer and Reynolds (2009); Cuadros (2006); Gouveia and Stull (1997); Griffith (1995a); Hall, Alexander, and Ordoñez (2008); Schlosser (2001); Striffler (2005a); Stull and Broadway (2004).

10. On labor control mechanisms in the poultry processing industry, see Fink (1998) and Griffith (1993, 1995a, 1995b, 2005, 2006).

11. Griffith (1995a) writes of Further Processing: "These sections produce a range of more or less desirable and hazardous tasks. Most common are those that require a

single cut or set of cuts on one portion of a bird all day long, creating conditions for re-petitive motion injuries. Less hazardous positions include those that involved testing products for internal temperature during or after cooking, mixing vats of marinade, or staffing the pricing or labeling machines" (135; Striffler 2005a).

12. Calculated from her reported (posttax) $286 weekly earnings, assuming that Liliana worked 40 hours per week (receiving no overtime but also not having to work reduced hours during any week of the year).

13. Calculated at a pretax reported wage of $8.00 per hour, assuming that Nadia worked 40 hours per week (receiving no overtime but also not having to work reduced hours during any week of the year), for 52 weeks in a year.

14. *Federal Register*, Vol. 71, No. 15, Jan. 24, 2006, pp. 3848–49, http://www.gpoaccess .gov/fr/index.html.

15. Poultry Processing Limited (PPL) is a pseudonym for another poultry process-ing plant in Wilcox County. It is not affiliated with PPP.

16. Stull and Broadway (2004) document a typical range of hourly wages for American meat and poultry workers in the late 1990s as falling between $6.80 and $11.20, translating into gross annual salaries between $14,144 and $23,296. Although the authors concur that such wages are among the highest in rural areas where these food processing plants are located, they also point out that they remain below the level required for a family of four's participation in one or more federal assistance pro-grams—meaning, they do not provide workers a living wage sufficient to feed, clothe, and shelter their families (74–75).

17. In 2003–04 PPP offered several insurance plans for workers to opt into: health and medical, dental, life, and (for salaried employees only) vision and 401(k) retire-ment plans. It also offered seniority-ranked paid vacation leave (one week for one to five years, two weeks for six to 10 years, and three weeks for longer), the option to live in company-subsidized trailers, and an educational reimbursement program. Of course, respondents debated whether the company's temporary housing policy was good or bad. And since workers did have to contribute a percentage of their paychecks to enroll in its health and medical plan, many Hispanic lineworkers elected not to do so, considering it to be too expensive and preferring to collect their full weekly earn-ings instead, especially if they were working illegally and feared trying to access bene-fits using a false name or social security number.

18. The implication of Joseph's statement is that most of the Hispanic immigrants were less well off in their sending country compared to the Asian contract workers, and that because they have already had to do this kind of hard work before they are "used to it" by the time they arrive at PPP and do not expect much better. However, see Donato, Stainback, and Bankston (2005) for a discussion of this view of Latin Ameri-can immigrants as "misinterpreted."

19. Drever (2009); Griffith (1995a, 2005); Smith-Nonini (2005); Striffler (2009); Striffler and Weise (2008); Zarrugh (2008).

20. Broadway (1994); Fennelly (2005); Fink (1998); Gouveia and Stull (1997); Griffith (1993, 2005, 2006); Striffler (2005a); Striffler and Weise (2008); Stull and Broadway (2004).

21. Since the 1960s, wages of food processing workers have declined even compared to those of workers in other manufacturing sectors (Bjerklie 1995; Drabenstott, Henry, and Mitchell 1999; Stull and Broadway 2004), from approximately $21.75 per hour in 1980 to $12.03 per hour in 2007 (expressed in 2009 dollars; Kammer 2009).

22. Outside the workplace, Hispanic population growth has also created ethnic queues in which bilingual, native-born, well-educated, and otherwise well-established Hispanics have moved up into "intermediary" leadership and other types of "brokering" positions to assist the newcomer and native communities in communicating with one another (Erwin 2003; Schoenholtz 2005; Striffler 2009; Williamson 2009).

23. PPP's official policy in 2003–04 was that it does not hire unauthorized immigrants, but in practice its policy was to put the burden of proof of legal immigrant status on immigrant workers themselves. In other words, as long as immigrants gave the company sufficient documentation of legal immigrant status, the requirement of not "knowingly" hiring unauthorized immigrants could be satisfied. This policy has been representative of most workplaces that hire immigrant workers in the United States since the passage of the Immigration Reform and Control Act of 1986, or IRCA (Massey, Durand, and Malone 2002: 118–26); its employer sanctions clause is widely recognized to have led to proliferation of labor subcontracting and brokering practices, rising vulnerability among unauthorized immigrant workers, and expansion of the black market for fraudulent documents, but *not* to reduction in unauthorized migration (Hincapié 2009; Massey, Durand, and Malone 2002; Massey and Sánchez 2010; Smith-Nonini 2009; Striffler 2009).

24. Even some of the clerical personnel I interviewed earned around $24,960 per year, calculated at a pretax reported wage of $12 per hour, assuming they worked 40 hours per week (receiving no overtime but also not having to work reduced hours during any week of the year), for 52 weeks in a year. Still, if this amount were doubled by two earners in a household, it would approximate the $44,000 per year income that Millard and Chapa (2004) argue helps Hispanic newcomers in light manufacturing build "lower-middle-class suburban communities" in the rural Midwest (see Chapter 3).

25. As former PPP vice president Christopher openly stated, "We don't want to be another Siler City. Two years ago things there were in a very bad state" (fieldnotes, PPP, July 2003).

26. But see Zarrugh (2008) for an alternative account of Hispanic newcomers moving into self-employment in Harrisonburg, Virginia, owing to barriers to their upward mobility within the food processing industry.

Chapter 3

1. As is the case in Kentucky, Nebraska, and Tennessee (Gouveia 2006; Rich and Miranda 2005; Winders 2005, 2008, 2009b), in North Carolina Cubans and most South American immigrant groups have stronger socioeconomic profiles than do Mexicans and most Central American immigrant groups. This translates into internal social and political divisions, too, since most leadership positions are occupied by members of the more privileged groups despite Mexicans making up the large majority of the state's Hispanic population. Among foreign-born immigrants age 25 and older in North Carolina, 2000 U.S. Census data show that at least 70% of Guatemalans, Hondurans, Mexicans, and Salvadorans had less than a high school education, compared to fewer than 15% of Argentines, Bolivians, Brazilians, Chileans, Cubans, Panamanians, Paraguayans, Peruvians, Uruguayans, and Venezuelans. (Other Latin American immigrant groups fell somewhere in between.) Roughly similarly, whereas Argentines, Bolivians, Cubans, Panamanians, Peruvians, Puerto Ricans, and Venezuelans age 25 to 64 and in the labor force all earned wage or salary income of $20,000 or greater, Chileans, Colombians, Costa Ricans, Ecuadorians, Guatemalans, Hondurans, Mexicans, and Salvadorans all earned $15,000 or less. (Again, other Latin American immigrant groups fell somewhere in between; Ruggles et al. 2004, weighted data, author's analysis.) On the internal stratification of Hispanics/Latinos in urban Charlotte and rural western North Carolina by national origin, year of arrival, legal status, class status, skin color, and race or ethnicity, see also Rose (2007); H. A. Smith (2008); and Smith and Furuseth (2006b).

2. This finding is descriptive, not evaluative. That is, I describe how respondents interpreted their own opportunities for mobility in PPP rather than making value judgments as to whether their interpretations are causally accurate or not. A wide body of research argues that workers have low aspirations because they have limited opportunities for upward mobility, not vice versa (Kanter 1977).

3. Maldonado (2009) criticizes similar ways in which agricultural employers in rural Washington use a static notion of "culture" to explain both racial and gender hierarchies in their workplace.

4. This could happen when outside governmental parties notify plant personnel that a worker's immigration documentation is not valid. It could also happen when an unauthorized worker feels comfortable enough with an administrative or supervisory employee to openly admit to being unauthorized, in which case the administrative or supervisory employee would be obligated to pass along that information to the plant employer, who would then be obligated to terminate the worker.

5. Obviously, this opportunity for short-distance mobility has decreased as Immigration and Customs Enforcement (ICE) agents step up workplace "interior enforcement" against employers' hiring of unauthorized immigrants, particularly those working in large workplaces in select industries such as food processing.

6. Many businesses in the service sector pay low wages and only offer part-time employment (Gouveia and Stull 1997; White 2004). Indeed, Crowley, Lichter, and Qian (2006) find that Mexican immigrants employed in construction and nondurable manufacturing (including food processing) have lower odds of being in poverty than do their counterparts working in agriculture or low-level services.

7. Rural areas have accounted for roughly half of all job losses in the South since 1979 (Cobb 2005).

8. Interestingly, Schoenholtz (2005) also uncovers an increasing stabilization of turnover in food processing plants in rural Arkansas, yet he attributes it to the influence of financial classes offered to workers there by local bank officials. The purpose of these classes was to increase "hope" among immigrant workers who were deemed not to be aware of opportunities for betterment, and bank officials brought food processing officials on board by telling them that the classes would help encourage permanent settlement and also reduce turnover (218–19; see also Bump and Gozdziak 2008).

9. Hernández-León (2010) also reports that many Hispanics who were employed in carpet manufacturing in Dalton, Georgia, have moved into poultry processing in North and South Carolina, and also Canada, in response to the carpet industry's contraction following the 2008–10 economic recession.

10. Perhaps a difference attributable to rural versus urban location, these manufacturing plants offered Hispanic newcomers much less opportunity for upward mobility than the oil tools and technology industry in Houston. There, skilled and semiskilled blue-collar industrial workers from Monterrey, Mexico, have been able to create a niche working in high-skilled, well-paid, and nonseasonal posts such as machinist, precision welder, industrial maintenance mechanic, and oil pipe repairman (Hernández-León 2004, 2008).

11. On the distinctions among labor force participation, wage level, and job quality as measures of economic incorporation, see Waldinger (2001) and Waldinger, Lim, and Cort (2007).

12. Between 2000 and 2006, Bedford County continued to lose population at a faster rate (−3.0%) than it did between 1990 and 2000 (−1.9%). By contrast, Wilcox County continued to gain population (7.6%), although at a slower rate than between 1990 and 2000 (21.4%; http://www.fedstats.gov, last accessed Jan. 8, 2009).

13. The unemployment rate in Wilcox County declined by one percentage point between 1999 and 2001, while those in both North Carolina and Bedford County remained constant. Likewise, the percentage of persons living in poverty in Wilcox County declined by two percentage points between 1999 and 2003, while that in North Carolina rose by one percentage point, and that in Bedford County remained constant (http://www.fedstats.gov).

14. These figures compare unfavorably with 13.2% across the entire rural "traditional" South, 22.5% in North Carolina, 24.4% in the United States as a whole, and, as

documented in the Introduction, higher percentages in many metropolitan gateways, including those in the South (http://www.fedstats.gov, last accessed Jan. 8, 2009).

15. By 2006, the unemployment rate in Wilcox County remained notably lower (5.2%) than its counterpart in Bedford County (8.1%), as did the poverty rate in Wilcox County (17.9%) compared to its counterpart in Bedford County (21.5%; http://www.fedstats.gov, last accessed Jan. 8, 2009). Even before the onset of the 2008–10 recession, a community activist also reported that the unemployment rate in Bedford County had risen above 11%, signaling continued economic difficulty (postfieldwork notes, October 2008).

16. To illustrate, approximately 50 unauthorized Hispanic workers were fired for presenting false information when federal immigration officials carried out a raid on the nearby Smithfield Foods pork processing plant in Tarheel in November 2006, and an additional 21 workers were arrested and primed for deportation by federal immigration officials on "administrative immigration charges" during a raid on the same plant on January 24, 2007 (Collins 2007a). In the intervening months, another 300 workers or so had to leave the Tarheel plant after being informed that their personal information did not match up with the Social Security Administration's records (Associated Press 2007; Gartner 2007a, 2007b). A Smithfield company spokesman illustrated how these workers' prospects for economic stability and upward mobility can be dashed in a moment's notice by workplace raids, remarking that "some of these people had been here seven, eight, or nine years" (Gartner 2007b).

17. These local industries were notorious for not requiring proof of legal status or a social security number, or for being less stringent about checking the documents that applicants do provide, during the time of my research.

18. Unauthorized immigrants frequently lose a portion of their salary to subcontractors and other labor brokers who arrange for their employment (Drever 2006; Griffith 2005; Massey 2007; Massey, Durand, and Malone 2002).

19. Since I conducted my research in 2003–04, a rising number of government workplace raids have increased fear and uncertainty among Hispanics in eastern North Carolina, as they have done elsewhere (Alexander and Ordóñez 2008; Jackson 2008; Lopez and Minushkin 2008; Ordóñez 2008; Ordóñez and Alexander 2008; Ordóñez and Henderson 2008; Pew Hispanic Center 2007b; Preston 2007, 2008a, 2008b, 2008c; Zota 2009b). Still, despite the recent uptick in workplace interior enforcement efforts, the chances of an employer being investigated, much less fined, for hiring unauthorized immigrants remain small, as do the chances of an unauthorized immigrant being caught in a workplace raid (Brownell 2005; Fitzgerald 2011; Zota 2009b).

20. According to the March 2008 American Community Survey, there were approximately 1.5 million unauthorized immigrant youth under the age of 18 in the United States. They made up approximately 13% of the total unauthorized immigrant population, and approximately 27% of the total population of children of unauthorized immigrant families, in that year (Passel and Cohn 2009).

21. Even the most optimistic voices in the literature caution that unauthorized youths, most of whom are Mexicans and Central Americans, face a difficult road toward upward mobility over time, even if only into the ranks of the working class (Alba and Nee 2003: 275; Bailey 2005; Bean and Stevens 2003: 111–12; Drever 2006; Gouveia and Powell 2007; Kandel and Parrado 2006; Kasinitz and Holdaway 2008). Others foresee a very bleak future and serious potential for downward mobility, not just stagnation or lateral mobility (Abrego 2006; DeParle 2009; Portes 2007; Portes and Rumbaut 2006).

Chapter 4

Much of this chapter contains material that is a substantially revised version of "Hispanic Immigration, Black Population Size, and Intergroup Relations in the Rural and Small-Town U.S. South" (Marrow 2008, reprinted with permission). Other portions of Chapters 4 and 5 originally appeared in Marrow (2009b) and in Marrow (2011b), reprinted with the permission of Oxford University Press, www.oup.com).

1. In 2009, the price for smuggler services at the U.S.-Mexico border averaged around $2,750, up from approximately $1,250 in the late 1990s (Hanson 2009; MMP 2009).

2. On the "repeated trials model," see Espenshade (1990) and Massey, Durand, and Malone (2002: 45).

3. On how U.S. policies of border militarization have increased the number of migrant injuries and deaths along the border, see Eschbach et al. (1999) and Massey, Durand, and Malone (2002).

4. Bada and Cárdenas (2009); Bobo and Johnson (2000); Bobo and Massagli (2001); Camarillo (2004); Cummings and Lambert (1997); Diamond (1998); the collected essays in Dzidzienyo and Oboler (2005); Fraga et al. (2010); Gay (2006); Jennings (1997); Jones-Correa (2009); Kaufmann (2003); Mantero (2008); Mindiola, Niemann, and Rodríguez (2002); Morawska (2001); Oliver and Wong (2003); Rodríguez (1999).

5. Cravey (1997); Gordon and Lenhardt (2008); Griffith (1993, 2005); LeDuff (2000); Mantero (2008); McClain (2006, in progress); McClain et al. (2006, 2007); Mohl (2002, 2003, 2009); Odem (2008); Price and Singer (2008); Rich and Miranda (2005); H. A. Smith (2008); Smith and Furuseth (2006b); Striffler and Weise (2008); Stuesse (2009); Swarns (2006a, 2006b); Torres, Popke, and Hapke (2006); Wainer (2004); Weeks, Weeks, and Weeks (2007); Weise (2008); Winders (2008b, 2009b). Most accounts of black-Hispanic conflict in the South, as elsewhere in the country, also acknowledge black-Hispanic cooperation. Nonetheless, it is clear that tensions have emerged in many places, and moreover that efforts to promote cooperation are often motivated by a desire to avoid leaving such tensions unaddressed. For instance, Turnbull (2008) describes how the 2006 Beyond Soul and Salsa forums in Winston-Salem, North Carolina, were designed to address conflict between the city's African American and Hispanic residents by helping to "dispel stereotypes, identify common concerns, and examine barriers to cooperation" (621–22). In addition, even though there have been

improvements in elite-level black-Hispanic coalition building since the mid-2000s (Alvarado and Jaret 2009; Bohon 2008; Gordon and Lenhardt 2008; Schmid 2003), barriers to alliance still exist among black and Hispanic workers, who perceive themselves in greater competition (Alvarado and Jaret 2009; Gordon and Lenhardt 2008; Mohl 2009; Stuesse 2009; Weise 2008). Lacy (2008b) and McDermott (in progress) even argue that tensions among working-class black and Hispanic southerners have been increasing since the early 2000s, owing to rising perceptions of job competition.

6. In 2000 U.S. Census data, the economic profile of Hispanics living in nonmetropolitan areas of the traditional South was closer to that of non-Hispanic African Americans than either non-Hispanic whites or non-Hispanic Asian Americans. For instance, 60.9% of Hispanics age 25 and older had less than a high school education, compared to 41.1% of African Americans but only 23.8% of Asian Americans and 26.3% of whites. Similarly, Hispanics age 25 to 64 and in the labor force earned a median wage and salary income of $15,000, compared to $17,000 among African Americans but $19,000 among Asian Americans and $23,000 among whites. Roughly the same hierarchy appears in nonmetropolitan North Carolina, where in 2000, 64.4% of Hispanics age 25 and older had less than a high school education, compared to 37.0% of African Americans age 25 and older but only 26.2% of Asian Americans and 23.0% of whites. Hispanics age 25 to 64 and in the labor force in North Carolina earned a median wage and salary income of $14,600, compared to $18,200 among Asian Americans, $18,500 among African Americans, and $24,000 among whites (Ruggles et al. 2004, weighted data, author's analysis).

7. Supporting such a labor market competition perspective, a survey conducted in June 2007 in Virginia finds that African Americans there are more "cautious" and "fearful" of unauthorized immigrants than are whites, as are all lower-class Virginians compared to their higher-class counterparts. African Americans in the survey agreed more strongly than whites that unauthorized immigration takes jobs away from American workers, lowers the wages and salaries of American workers, hurts American customs and way of life, and increases the danger of terrorism (Vallas and Zimmerman 2007).

8. Data from the 2000 U.S. Census on educational level, labor force participation, unemployment rate, occupational distribution, and median wage and salary income (not shown here) confirm that the economic profile of African Americans living in the nonmetropolitan traditional South is considerably weaker than that of their white counterparts. Indeed, whereas whites in Bedford and Wilcox Counties are internally divided along class lines, belonging either to the middle class or to the poor and working classes, overall blacks' socioeconomic position there is much weaker, with most still belonging to the poor and working classes in the mid-2000s and only a handful belonging to the lower middle class. As one white resident from Bedford County noted, "It is sad, but you know, really, I could count [local middle-class blacks] on my hands. And I know who all of them are" (postfieldwork notes, Nov. 26, 2004). This

situation reflects the rural South's lack of an established black middle class, as opposed to some larger metropolitan areas in the region such as Durham or Atlanta, which have large black lower-middle and upper-middle classes (McClain et al. 2006, 2007; Odem 2008). For a discussion of internal class divisions among whites in the "highland" southern cities of Dalton, Georgia, and Greenville, South Carolina, see Hernández-León and Zúñiga (2005) and McDermott (in progress); for a discussion of it among whites and blacks in the "lowland" southern region of the Mississippi Delta, see Duncan (1999) and Loewen (1988).

9. On individual-level economic competition between low-skilled immigrants and natives, especially African Americans and Hispanic immigrants, see Borjas (1998), Butcher (1998), and Hamermesh and Bean (1998). On group-level economic competition between low-skilled immigrants and natives, see, for example, Burns and Gimpel (2000) and Citrin, Green, Muste, and Wong (1997).

10. The scholarly literature is mixed on the question of whether immigrants replace or displace native workers. On the one hand, immigrants' economic impact on natives at the national level has been shown to be minimal; if anything, immigrants lower the wages of *other immigrants* (Bean and Stevens 2003: 222; Friedberg and Hunt 1999; Hamermesh and Bean 1998; Hanson 2009; Raphael and Ronconi 2007; Shierholz 2010; Smith and Edmonston 1997). On the other hand, various studies in large cities document immigrants displacing low-skilled native workers, mostly because employers prefer to hire immigrants over natives (Waldinger 1996, 1999; Waters 1999). Still, even they are contradicted by other research showing that immigrants do not just take natives' low-skilled jobs but also help to push natives upward in the occupational stratification system (Cornelius 1998; Rosenfeld and Tienda 1999; Tienda and Stier 1998).

11. In metropolitan new immigrant destinations, the growth in Mexican immigration has been shown to have no discernible negative impact on low-skilled natives' wages (Card and Lewis 2007). In North Carolina, there is no satisfactory evidence regarding whether Hispanic immigrants replace or displace native workers (Skaggs, Tomaskovic-Devey, and Leiter 2000), but as I report in Chapter 5, existing research does show strong employer preferences for Hispanic over African American, and sometimes also white, native workers (Griffith 2005; Johnson-Webb 2003).

12. The fact that Hispanic students' test scores are higher than those of black students in several schools in both counties has generated intense debate. Some educational officials pointed out that only some Hispanic students are exhibiting rapid achievement, while others deserve continued attention because they are continuing to suffer academically and socially. Furthermore, both school- and county-level educational officials fiercely debated potential structural and cultural explanations for the emerging gap. Dominant structural explanations for Hispanics' rapid educational success included positive immigrant selectivity and increased attention to Hispanic students on the part of school personnel, while dominant cultural ones included dif-

fering expectations for student achievement between black and Hispanic parents. Perspectives that mixed both structural and cultural explanations included differing definitions of poverty and differing modal family structures between black and Hispanic parents, which educational officials in turn argued shape parental resources and expectations for children's achievement in school.

13. On the sociological group position model of intergroup relations, which emphasizes not only groups' objective conditions of economic deprivation or political disempowerment but also their subjective beliefs and representations toward their own group and others, see Bobo and Hutchings (1996), Bobo and Johnson (2000), Bobo and Tuan (2006), and Morawska (2001).

14. There are few reliable survey data on Hispanics' partisan attachments in the traditional South, primarily due to small sample sizes and the fact that most states do not track their voter registration and turnout data directly by Hispanic ethnicity (Bullock and Hood 2006; personal communications with political scientists Luís Fraga and Louis DeSipio, August 2005). Indeed, the North Carolina State Board of Elections began including a "Hispanic/Latino" ethnic category only in 2003, and registering voters are still not required to identify themselves as Hispanic/Latino. Hence, anyone who registered to vote before 2003 did not have the option to identify as Hispanic/Latino and would have had to actively reregister after 2003 as well as voluntarily identify as Hispanic/Latino to be counted as such. For these reasons, there is undoubtedly a large undercount of registered Hispanic voters in the state. Still, of the few Hispanics who were registered to vote in Bedford (N = 10) and Wilcox (N = 60) Counties in 2003–04—county Board of Election officials told me there was "certainly an undercount" (fieldnotes, Feb. 24, 2004)—most were more closely affiliated with the Democratic (50–70%) than the Republican party (23–30%), albeit less closely than African Americans were. The independent 2006 Latino National Survey also finds that Latino registered voters in several traditional southern states identify more strongly as Democrats and Independents than as Republicans, although by lesser margins than do Latino registered voters in nonsouthern states.

15. It was also a principal goal of several other initiatives and groups that I did not observe directly during my own field research. These include the North Carolina African American/Latino Alliance, a subsidiary of Black Workers for Justice, a state-level African American labor organization; as well as the Hispanic Outreach Project, an initiative formed by the Carolina Alliance for Fair Employment, another state-level and formerly African American labor organization (Gordon and Lenhardt 2008: 1161). Even more black-Hispanic coalition-building efforts have emerged at the state level since the time of my research, including a Black/Brown Unity conference held in the central piedmont city of Greensboro in October 2008, sponsored by the Beloved Community Center (Alvarado and Jaret 2009).

16. In both counties, there are more examples of black-Hispanic cooperation in social service and nonprofit agencies than in the electoral political arena (see Chap-

ter 6), where newly appointed Hispanic bureaucrats and service providers come into contact with African American coworkers and often become good acquaintances. In Archer Bluff, Hispanic respondents spoke positively of an African American mayoral candidate who had expressed interest in the local Hispanic community, while Kendra, an African American human relations representative for the Archer Bluff city government, was an active member and supporter of *Latinos Unidos*, an emerging Hispanic professional association. Still, in 2003–04 nothing in Bedford or nearby Alexandria County could rival the Hispanic Leadership Course in Wilcox County as an example of an explicit attempt to build a black-Hispanic coalition in the realm of civic and political leadership development.

17. Interestingly, after my field research was completed, I learned that Bedford County manager Clarence had invited Nina, as an emerging local Hispanic educational and political leader, to head up planning for the county's 2005 Martin Luther King Jr. Day festivities (*Bedford Newspaper* [a pseudonym], Dec. 22, 2004).

Chapter 5

Much of this chapter originally appeared as "Intergroup Relations: Reconceptualizing Discrimination and Hierarchy" (Marrow 2011a, used with permission of the publisher). Other portions of Chapters 4 and 5 originally appeared in Marrow (2009b) and in Marrow (2011b, reprinted with the permission of Oxford University Press, Inc., www .oup.com).

1. On white (and some black) flight out of Hispanic-heavy schools in Siler City, North Carolina, see also Cuadros (2006: 37–42).

2. Notably, Isabel and Esperanza were miffed that few of their African American coworkers were willing to extend this show of support in public.

3. By contrast, Kaufmann (2003) finds no empirical support for the role of perceived discrimination in increasing Hispanics/Latinos' affinity for developing political coalitions with African Americans.

4. On the historical and contemporary "racial triangulation" of Native, Asian, and Hispanic Americans as outsiders to the American nation-state, in contrast to the inclusion of African Americans as "insiders," albeit ones subordinate in racial status to whites, see De Genova (2006); Kim (1999); and Telles and Ortiz (2008). Of course, other scholarship takes a different angle, arguing that race has so fundamentally influenced ideas of American citizenship that African Americans should also be considered "domestic foreigners" or "alien citizens" who have not yet been granted the full economic, social, and political rights of American citizenship despite having been granted the formal legal rights of citizenship (Cohen 2007; Shklar 1991). For new research showing how immigration complicates lines of nativity and citizenship as well as race in the South, see Gordon and Lenhardt (2008) and Winders (2009).

5. For an overview of how Mexican Americans have historically been racialized along multiple lines of nonwhite race or skin color, low class status, and illegality, see

De Genova (2005); Massey, Durand, and Malone (2002); Ngai (2004); and Telles and Ortiz (2008).

6. See Haubert and Fussell (2006) on the role that cosmopolitanism, as opposed to group threat and labor market position, plays in Americans' views of immigrants. My data suggest that some whites in eastern North Carolina are indeed reaching out to Hispanics with a sense of open-mindedness toward their languages and cultures, but other whites are reaching out to them initially out of self-interest (as employers often do) or a rural or small-town sense of good manners and hospitality. This latter might be more appropriately termed "parochial" or local rather than cosmopolitan, but it is still significant that Hispanic respondents felt it more frequently in their relations with whites than with blacks.

7. See also Torres, Popke, and Hapke (2006) for a discussion of why Hispanics have more positive experiences with white growers in eastern North Carolina than in Florida, where farms are larger and more corporate and impersonal.

8. Stuesse (2009) finds little understanding of African Americans' history of racial oppression and economic exclusion among Hispanic poultry processing lineworkers in rural Mississippi.

9. The former also identify more strongly as whites in 2000 U.S. Census data than the latter, at both the national and North Carolina state levels (Ruggles et al. 2004; weighted data, author's analysis).

10. In the 2000 U.S. Census, members of all Latin American immigrant groups in North Carolina identified more strongly as whites and "other race" than as blacks, and the only two groups with high black racial identification (Panamanians at 19.0% and Dominicans at 10.5%) make up a small portion of North Carolina's Hispanic population (Ruggles et al. 2004; weighted data, author's analysis). However, it is important to concede that most Hispanics in North Carolina (and in most of the traditional South) are Mexicans, and many others are Central and South Americans (Kochhar, Suro, and Tafoya 2005: 14). Except in certain locales, these countries have weaker "African roots" than do the Spanish-speaking countries of the Caribbean or Brazil (Falcón 1988; Forman, Goar, and Lewis 2002; Vaughn 2005), and consequently their members frame their identity in relation to blackness less strongly (Itzigsohn 2004). Indeed, even though there is variation in my Hispanic respondents' skin color, ranging from very light to very dark, most dark-skinned respondents come from these countries with a relatively weak history of African presence and thus have mixed indigenous rather than mixed African ancestry.

11. Lourdes's experience demonstrates how race is what sociologists call "situational" for many Hispanics. That is, racial identification can vary with the local context, not just within Latin America (see Rodríguez 2000) but also within the United States (see Telles and Ortiz 2008). It can even vary with local context *within* the traditional South, as Lourdes's comparison of Tennessee and eastern North Carolina demonstrates.

12. See McDermott (in progress) for a description of white and black natives' "con-fused" conceptions of Hispanic newcomer racial identities in the Southeast prior to the 2006 nationwide immigrant rights marches. Among the terms she heard natives de-scribing them were Greek, Indian, Chinese, white, and black, with Hispanic (and not Latino) being used only by the most educated natives. Since the 2006 nationwide im-migration rallies and the onset of the 2008–10 economic recession, she finds that natives increasingly employ racialized terms such as Hispanic, Mexican, and even "illegal."

13. Bailey (2001); Jones-Correa (1998); Nobles (2000); Oboler (1995); Wade (1997). This is one of the three basic ways in which conceptions of race in Latin America differ from those in the United States. Another is that characteristics other than ancestry—such as skin color, hair color, physical features, and even socioeconomic characteris-tics—are more commonly used to determine racial identity in Latin America than they are in the United States (Rodríguez 2000; Wagley 1965). The third is that subtle distinctions between black and white are more commonly recognized in Latin Amer-ican countries than in the United States, leading scholars to speak generally of a ra-cial "continuum" in Latin America as opposed to racial "polarization" in the United States. Such polarization has contributed to a cohesive sense of racial identity and "linked fate" among African Americans in the United States (Dawson 1994), which is largely lacking in Latin America, although some Afro-Latin Americans have been working to develop one in recent years (Nobles 2000; Telles 2004).

14. Brodkin (1998); Ignatiev (1995); Jacobson (1998); Loewen (1988); Perlmann and Waldinger (1997); Roediger (1991, 2005).

15. Fraga et al. (2010); Gordon and Lenhardt (2008); Kim (2004); McClain et al. (2006); Mindiola, Niemann, and Rodríguez (2002); Stuesse (2009); Telles and Ortiz (2008); Waters (1999).

16. See Cady Hallett (in progress) for an illuminating account of how Hispanic newcomers in Danville, Arkansas, learn to assert their deservingness to upper-class whites and employers by differentiating themselves from unworthy "rednecks" and "white trash." In her account, their self-assertion as good workers facilitates their in-corporation and access to social networks and resources in that community, yet it also disciplines them into a singular identity as workers who will not complain or make use of public benefits.

17. McDermott (in progress) also finds that Hispanic immigrants in the Caroli-nas, Virginia, and Tennessee are much more likely to live in predominantly white than black neighborhoods, to marry white than black spouses, and even to be buried from white than black funeral homes.

18. I documented several types of intimate interracial encounters in my research, including dating, marriage, prostitution, and general romantic interest (see also Hernández-León and Zúñiga 2005). But those involving whites and Hispanic newcom-ers were by far more prevalent than ones involving blacks and Hispanic newcomers. Interestingly, my field research concurs with the findings of Rose (2007), who reports

that interracial encounters between native and immigrants in western North Carolina take place largely along class lines (e.g., working-class Mexican men with working-class white and Native American women, versus middle-class South American immigrants with middle-class white professionals).

19. Almaguer (1994); Foley (1997); García (1991); Montejano (1987); Ngai (2004); Telles and Ortiz (2008).

Chapter 6

Much of Chapter 6 originally appeared as "Immigrant Bureaucratic Incorporation: The Dual Roles of Professional Missions and Government Policies" (Marrow 2009a) and has been revised and expanded to fit this book.

1. Many Hispanic newcomers in eastern North Carolina, especially migrant farmworkers, did endure crowded, inadequate, and unhealthy living conditions in manufactured homes, colloquially known as "trailers" (Atiles and Bohon 2003; Bauer and Reynolds 2009; Cuadros 2006; Lacy 2007; Nelson and Hiemstra 2008). However, trailers vary greatly in ownership and condition, and other Hispanic newcomers lived in better-kept or larger double-wide ones. Elena's example confirms the need to view trailers not just as a mark of disadvantage but also as a potential asset for lower-income families (Skillern and Wolfram 2005), including Hispanic newcomers.

2. All bureaucracies are complex organizations that exhibit both service- and regulatory-oriented functions and employ bureaucrats across a range of internal offices and roles (Brehm and Gates 1999; Gonzales and Gleeson 2009), but they nonetheless occupy different aggregate positions along a continuum running from pure service to pure regulatory ideal types (Marrow 2009a).

3. Hispanics have been increasingly employed, particularly as interpreters and translators, in county- and municipal-level bureaucracies in both counties, in county health departments, community colleges, town clinics, and nonprofit agencies such as the local Partnerships for Children.

4. For two classic discussions of the incentives political parties have to incorporate immigrants, see Dahl (1961) and Wolfinger (1972). For more recent critiques of this scholarship and discussion of how political parties lack incentives to incorporate contemporary immigrants, see Andersen and Cohen (2007); de la Garza, Menchaca, and DeSipio (1994); DeSipio (2001); Erie (1988); Gerstle and Mollenkopf (2001); Jones-Correa (1998, 2005a); Shefter (1994); Sterne (2001); and Wong (2006).

5. See also Browning, Marshall, and Tabb (1984); Dahl (1961); Jones-Correa (2008); and Meier, Juenke, Wrinkle, and Polinard (2005).

6. Other perspectives stemming from principal-agent theories in a variety of disciplines and overhead democracy theories in public administration have critiqued this top-down vision of political control over bureaucratic behavior. In situations of goal conflict between politician "principals" and their bureaucratic "agents," they

argue that bureaucrats' technical expertise and autonomy, as well as internal values, often limit politicians' power (Brehm and Gates 1999; Keiser and Soss 1998; Maynard-Moody and Musheno 2003; O'Leary 2006; Waterman and Meier 1998; Wilson 1989). In fact, Meier and O'Toole (2006) argue that what may sometimes look like political control over bureaucracies may in fact be autonomous bureaucratic action within a context of "goal consensus" between politicians and bureaucrats.

7. Natives frequently direct concerns that immigrants, especially unauthorized ones, "abuse the system" and constitute a net fiscal burden, especially in the domains of education, social welfare, health, and criminal justice (within North Carolina, see Collins 2008h; Cuadros 2006; Easterbrook and Fisher 2006; Hartsoe 2007; Johnson and Kasarda 2009; Kasarda and Johnson 2006; Maguire 2006; Mayo 2007; McClain 2006; Parsons 2007; Rives 2006; Smith and Furuseth 2006b; Turnbull 2008; Voss 2007; and Weeks, Weeks, and Weeks 2007). However, it is important to note that there is a large "spatial mismatch" between immigration's negative fiscal impact at many state and local levels and its positive fiscal impact at the federal level (Bean and Stevens 2003; Fix 2007; Smith and Edmonston 1997), which such concerns typically overlook.

8. See also Bohon (2008); Bump (2005); Gouveia, Carranza, and Cogua (2005); Grey and Woodrick (2005); Jones-Correa (2005b); Lacy and Odem (2009); Price and Singer (2008); and Zúñiga and Hernández-León (2009).

9. In 2002–03 Weakley Elementary School's Hispanic student population had grown from single digits to more than 40% in less than 10 years. Like many other schools in new immigrant destinations (Bailey 2005; Bump 2005; Schoenholtz 2005; Solórzano 2005; Wainer 2004), it was struggling with various consequences of rapid population growth, including overcrowding, provision of ESL instruction, and inter-group tensions between new immigrants and U.S. natives.

10. Emergencies are defined as including labor and delivery (although not prenatal care) for pregnant women and "treatment after the sudden onset of a medical condition manifesting itself by acute symptoms of sufficient severity, including severe pain, such that the absence of immediate medical attention could reasonably be expected to result in: (a) placing the patient's health in serious jeopardy; (b) serious impairment to bodily function; or (c) serious dysfunction of any bodily organ or part" (DuBard and Massing 2007: 1086).

11. Benjamin incorrectly attributes this legal obligation to the U.S. Constitution rather than to a 1982 Supreme Court decision (*Plyler v. Doe*).

12. In Wilcox County, respondents reported instances of Hispanic youths being "ignored" by teachers who could not communicate with them in Spanish and relegated them to the back of their classroom, in the mid-1980s to early 1990s. In Bedford County, respondents reported instances of African American teachers mistreating Hispanic youths in the mid-2000s. However, respondents also reported improvement in educational bureaucrats' responses to Hispanic youths over time and as immigration has continued to increase, even while there are still barriers to overcome.

13. Kaushal (2008); Konet (2007); Newton and Adams (2009); NILC (2009a); Solór-zano (2005); Zota (2009c). Since 2001, these states include Texas, California, Utah, Washington, New York, Illinois, Kansas, New Mexico, Nebraska, and also Minnesota (which, in 2007, eliminated its nonresident tuition rate in a number of public colleges, thereby allowing anyone to qualify for flat-rate tuition). Notably, in 2007 the Okla-homa Taxpayer and Citizen Protection Act ended in-state tuition benefit and state fi-nancial assistance for unauthorized immigrants, originally passed in 2003 (Batalova and Fix 2006; Gonzales 2009; Zota 2009c).

14. Abrego (2006); the collected essays in Anrig and Wang (2006); Bailey (2005); Batalova and Fix (2006); Cuadros (2006); Fitzgerald (2011); Gonzales (2009); Gozdziak and Bump (2008); Kaushal (2008); Konet (2007); NCSHP (2004); Seif (2004); Wainer (2004); Yablon-Zug and Holley-Walker (2009); Zota (2009c).

15. Collins and Stancill (2008); Cuadros (2008); Linnartz (2008); Redden (2008); Yablon-Zug and Holley-Walker (2009); Zota (2009c).

16. In November 2007, only 112 of an estimated 297,000 degree-seeking students in the state's community college system, and only 27 of an estimated 200,000 students in the state's university system, were unauthorized immigrants (Collins and Stancill 2008; Yablon-Zug and Holley-Walker 2009). In 2007, North Carolina in-state tuition rates ranged from $1,500 to $3,700, compared with $10,000 to $20,000 for out-of-state students (Collins 2007b).

17. All youths can enroll in private higher educational institutions and receive pri-vately funded financial aid to do so, regardless of legal status.

18. Batalova and Fix (2006) estimate that if the DREAM Act had been signed into law in 2006, approximately 360,000 unauthorized high school youth graduates age 18 to 24 would have been eligible for conditional legal status nationwide, and an addi-tional 715,000 unauthorized youths age 5 to 17 would have become eligible for con-ditional and then permanent legal status sometime in the future (see also Gonzales 2009; Konet 2007; Motomura 2008; NILC 2009b; Silver 2009; and Zota 2009c).

19. In Arkansas, Georgia, and North Carolina, Wainer (2004) also documents many people "working behind the scenes" to get unauthorized Hispanics "admitted on an individual basis," despite "unclear" admission and tuition practices, although he speculates that this individual practice may end with increased governmental over-sight (30). Sociologist Leisy Abrego also reports that this kind of bureaucratic dis-cretion occurs in traditional immigrant gateways, where unauthorized students and their college counselors become familiar with specific people in higher educational institutions, especially local community colleges, who know how to bend the rules to get them admitted, sometimes also providing them with financial aid (personal communication, Leisy Abrego, January 2007). In a recent visit to Bedford County, a middle-class white woman told me that she was "working on" trying to get an unau-thorized immigrant student accepted into the local community college.

20. Community colleges in North Carolina receive reimbursement from the state

if they can prove sustained participation of at least 10 students in class (Bailey 2005). See also Yablon-Zug and Holley-Walker (2009), who cite Stephen Scott, president of the North Carolina Association of Community Colleges, as saying that North Carolina "would actually make about $2,000 per illegal or undocumented student" (112).

21. See Key (1984) for a brief description of North Carolina's early commitment to public education, which was unique among southern states. The University of North Carolina at Chapel Hill was the nation's second chartered public institution of higher education (in 1789) and the first to open its doors to students (in 1795). The North Carolina community college system is also the third largest in the country today, enrolling more than 800,000 students in degree programs and continuing education classes across 58 campuses (Stancill 2007).

22. Bean and Stevens (2003: 66–67); Fremstad and Cox (2004); Gouveia, Carranza, and Cogua (2005); Hagan, Rodriguez, Capps, and Nika (2003); Newton and Adams (2009); Quill, Aday, Hacker, and Reagan (1999).

23. Although all unauthorized immigrants qualify for in-kind disaster relief, attorney general–specified services, and select public health and nutrition measures (including immunizations, WIC, and testing and treatment for communicable diseases; Fremstad and Cox 2004), they can qualify for only a limited form of Medicaid called "emergency Medicaid" (which covers only labor and delivery and other designated "emergencies") if they fall into certain categories such as for low-income children or pregnant women. Moreover, even though unauthorized immigrants can qualify for non-emergency coverage in a handful of states that use either federal SCHIP funds or their own state funds to offer it to all low-income pregnant women or children regardless of legal status (Fremstad and Cox 2004; Goldman, Smith, and Sood 2005, 2006; Quill et al. 1999), new destination states have been least responsive in this regard (Cunningham, Banker, Artiga, and Tolbert 2006; Derose, Escarce, and Lurie 2007; DuBard and Massing 2007; Staiti, Hurley, and Katz 2006; Zúñiga, Castañeda, and Averbach 2006).

24. Acorn Health Clinic is a federally qualified health center (FQHC) located in neighboring Alexandria County that also serves residents of Bedford County. During my research, I met various people who were working hard to encourage migrants to make use of it, providing them with transportation when they were fearful of using other regular area medical institutions. One was Elisa, a Migrant Education Program recruiter and parent facilitator in Bedford County public schools. Elisa could only offer "official" (i.e., reimbursable) transportation to migrant children who were enrolled in the MEP program, or to their parents, but she also volunteered her own uncompensated time and money to transport other immigrants not affiliated with the program.

25. Here, migrants are defined the same way as they are within the public educational system's MEP, as "migrant farmworkers who have, within the last 36 months, moved across school district boundaries in order to obtain temporary or seasonal employment in agriculture or fishing" (Gelatt and Fix 2007: 65).

26. Ultimately they were not fired, because they were able to justify their actions in terms of "helping the community" (personal communication with Michael Jones-Correa, Oct. 16, 2009). The probe by the State Bureau of Investigation requested by the Alamance County sheriff's department cleared them of wrongdoing, finding that they were "forced to follow conflicting directions from state and federal officials regarding the release of information about illegal immigrants" and had committed no crime (quoted in Gill, Nguyen, Parker, and Weissman 2009: 16).

27. Coutin (2000); Gouveia (2006); Hernández-León (2008); Menjívar (2006a, 2006b, 2008); Portes and Rumbaut (2006: 91–102); Silver (2009).

Chapter 7

Much of Chapter 7 originally appeared as "Immigrant Bureaucratic Incorporation: The Dual Roles of Professional Missions and Government Policies" (Marrow 2009a) and has been revised and expanded to fit this book.

1. On creative efforts by law enforcement officers and court officials elsewhere in the South to learn Spanish and respond more inclusively to Hispanic newcomers, see Armenta (2010); Gozdziak and Bump (2008); Hartch (2008); Price and Singer (2008); and Weise (2008).

2. Examples of the use of uncertified interpreters in my research included cases where they double-bill their clients or demand other unauthorized payments for services rendered, fail to interpret exactly what is being said in the tone in which it is being said by their clients, and inappropriately offer legal counsel to their clients. Interpreters are also not lawfully authorized to engage in any kind of legal advocacy discussion with their clients outside of directly interpreting or translating conversations between them and court personnel.

3. The concern that North Carolina courts have not been servicing their non-English-speaking clients as well as they could be (i.e., not giving them the same protection and treatment before the law) is what prompted creation of the foreign-language interpreter certification program run by North Carolina's Administrative Office of the Courts in the early 2000s. This program has certified court interpreters in a variety of foreign languages and translated and made available several brochures, pocket cards, and official court forms in Spanish. The program's website even explicitly identifies a professional mission of customer service, stating that the North Carolina judicial branch "must continue to find ways to make the courts more accessible and understandable to those who speak other languages" (http://www.nccourts.org/Citizens/CPrograms/Foreign/Default.asp, last accessed Dec. 8, 2006).

4. Here, Ashley pointed to the "horrible" visibility of specific cases appealed or overturned when a lack of qualified interpreting services raised serious questions about whether or not there was sufficient evidence to convict a non-English-speaking individual of a crime.

5. Interestingly, Karen contrasted this poor response from local court personnel with very good responses from the Wilcox County sheriff's department and PPP. This illustrates how variation in responsiveness to demographic change can exist both within and across different bureaucracies, not just between service and regulatory ones (Gonzales and Gleeson 2009).

6. See Coutin (2000) on the "rites of domination" that take place between legal personnel and the subjects whom they "discipline" during immigration proceedings. My research documented significant rites of domination, subjugation, and disciplining of Hispanic newcomers taking place in local court systems in eastern North Carolina.

7. By January 2007, the number of states that did not have a lawful permanent residency requirement had fallen to eight (Hawaii, Maine, Maryland, Michigan, New Mexico, Oregon, Utah, and Washington) and by April 2009 to just four (Hawaii, New Mexico, Utah, and Washington; NILC 2009c).

8. In April 2009, all five other states (Illinois, Kentucky, New Mexico, Utah, and West Virginia) still accepted the ITIN (NILC 2009c).

9. This confusion was acknowledged explicitly by the director of the North Carolina Driver License Section in a January 2004 email memorandum. Additionally, between December 2003 and February 2004, I saw notices that DMV offices both would and would not accept the ITIN instead of an SSN as a valid form of identification to obtain a state driver's license. Finally, Lidia reported that various flip-flopping went on during this time period as to whether Puerto Rican and Canadian birth certificates would be accepted as valid forms of identification to obtain a state driver's license, although there was never any question that the Mexican *matrícula consular* would not be.

10. John, a bilingual white American lawyer in Bedford County, sarcastically described the new policy changes as part of a larger nativist and racist sentiment displayed by Americans against Mexicans: "[It's] a disaster. It only promotes insuranceless drivers. And it's a mere ploy to 'get back' at the 'damn Mexicans' who can't understand the cosmopolite, sophisticated members of the American bureaucracy who hate the Mexicans because they give the Mexicans orders, can't communicate their personal importance to the Mexicans, and think that the ignorant Mexican bastards who don't know that 'God speaks English' cause them to have to work extra. Take that in any way that suits your convenience."

11. Bailey (2005); Bump (2005); Grey (2006); Lacy and Odem (2009); Schoenholtz (2005); Smith and Furuseth (2006b); Solórzano (2005); Verdaguer (2008).

12. There are three general 287(g) models. The most common is the "jail model" or "correction model," which allows correctional officers working in state prisons or local jails to screen individuals arrested or convicted of a crime by accessing federal databases to ascertain a person's immigration status. The second, "task force" or "field," model allows law enforcement officers to use federal databases to screen the immigration status of individuals arrested for a minor crime or violation such as a traffic of-

fense during the course of their daily operations outside of prisons and jails. Finally, some agencies have been approved to operate both models concurrently in the "joint model" (Chishti and Bergeron 2009; Donato 2009; Rodríguez et al. 2010; U.S. GAO 2009a). In practice, the line between the three models is often blurry, and there is some evidence that under North Carolina's jail models individuals have been arrested under circumstances where they otherwise would not have been, merely for the purpose of having their immigration status checked by 287(g)-deputized corrections officers (Weissman et al. 2009).

13. These included the sheriff's departments in Alamance, Cabarrus, Cumberland, Gaston, Henderson, Mecklenburg, and Wake Counties (Caldwell 2009; Collins 2008a; Gill et al. 2009; Weissman et al. 2009). By February 2010, Guilford County had entered into a new 287(g) agreement but not yet implemented it, and Cumberland County did not renew its memorandum of agreement as of October 2009 (Nguyen and Gill 2010).

14. The Summary of Clear Law Enforcement for Criminal Alien Removal Act of 2003 (CLEAR) HR 2671, known as the CLEAR Act of 2003 (NILC 2003), has had profound effects on local law enforcement systems throughout the country. It was followed by the Summary of Clear Law Enforcement for Criminal Alien Removal Act of 2005 (CLEAR) HR 3137 (NILC 2005), and later by the Immigration Law Enforcement Act of 2006 (HR 6095), which was passed by the U.S. House of Representatives on September 21, 2006, to affirm "the inherent authority of state and local law enforcement to assist in the enforcement of immigration laws, to provide for effective prosecution of alien smugglers, and to reform immigration litigation procedures" (http://www.congress.org/congressorg/issues/votes/?votenum=468&chamber=H&congress=1092, last accessed Mar. 21, 2007).

15. Grey (2006) also notes that most police chiefs in Iowa do not want to enforce immigration law, and that even those who "may be philosophically inclined to do so" do not necessarily want to use up precious resources or personnel in such an effort (55). A similar situation exists in Nebraska and Minnesota, where some state legislators have even been "surprised" by opposition from law enforcement agencies to enforcing immigration law (Fennelly 2006; Gouveia 2006).

16. Chishti and Bergeron (2009); Lindsay and Singer (2002); MCC (2006); McKinley (2006); NILC (2004a, 2004b, 2008a); Shahani and Green (2009); Tramonte (2009); U.S. GAO (2009a, 2009b); Weissman et al. (2009).

17. On racial profiling within ICE's Criminal Alien Program, see Gardner and Kohli (2009).

18. Within North Carolina, see Alvarado and Jaret (2009); Associated Press (2008); Collins (2008a, 2008b, 2008c, 2008h); Gill et al. (2009); Nguyen and Gill (2010); Perez (2008); Staff Reports (2008); and Walker (2008).

19. Criticism of the use of 287(g) agreements to target ordinary immigration-status violators rather than immigrants with felony convictions has grown so strong

in recent years that ICE has been pressured to issue new rules regarding the program's implementation (Rodríguez et al. 2010). Similar pressure has also been targeted at its workplace enforcement and National Fugitive Operations Program interior enforcement efforts, in light of recent evidence that they target noncriminal "low-hanging fruit" and "collaterals" instead of the most violent offenders (Bernstein 2009; Chishti and Bergeron 2009; Lopez and Light 2009; Mendelson, Strom, and Wishnie 2009; Tramonte 2009). Even in the Netherlands, Van der Leun (2003) shows that police officers pursue easy targets over serious criminal offenders, who are harder to deport.

20. In January 2004, Lidia reported that DMV bureaucrats were resisting the proposed February 2004 driver's license changes somewhere in the central piedmont region of the state: "Maybe it was in Carrboro, but I can't remember where it was they've stood up to this. They have said they will accept the *matrícula consular*. So it can be done."

21. Collins (2008e); Denning (2009); Fitzgerald (2011); Hincapié (2009); Motomura (2008); Newton and Adams (2009); NILC (2008b); Odem (2008).

22. These were Buncombe, Cabarrus, Catawba, Cumberland, Duplin, Durham, Gaston, Harnett, Henderson, New Hanover, Orange, Robeson, and Wake Counties (Markham 2009).

23. Although local relief officials and social welfare advocates exhibited a strong service orientation toward European and Canadian immigrants in the early twentieth century, they exhibited a strong regulatory one toward Mexican Americans, especially in the Southwest, where they were also not strongly opposed by local politicians (Fox 2007; Ngai 2004).

Conclusion

1. Departments in Guatemala are roughly equivalent to states in the United States.

2. Lacy and Odem (2009) document a contraction in economic opportunity in the traditional South after 2005. This is certainly the case, but economic opportunity has also contracted elsewhere in the United States during the same time period, and immigration into the traditional South, as those authors point out, continues.

3. PPP may be an outlier among food processing plants in terms of its positive reaction to Hispanic newcomers, especially compared to other plants affiliated with large national chains. Still, it can serve as a model for good practices in this respect.

4. On "segmented assimilation," see Portes and Rumbaut (2001); Portes and Zhou (1993); and Zhou (1999).

5. In 2008, South Carolina became the first state to ban all unauthorized immigrants from attending any of its public institutions of higher education; Alabama, following North Carolina's lead, introduced legislation to ban unauthorized immigrants from enrolling in degree-seeking programs in its public community colleges; Georgia enacted laws to prevent unauthorized immigrants from receiving state scholarships and loans; Virginia extended its existing policy of not admitting unauthorized immi-

grants to any of its public institutions of higher education to further deny in-state tu-ition to their American citizen children; and Arkansas began requiring all students to present social security numbers and proof of residency to register (Yablon-Zug and Holley-Walker 2009; Zota 2009c).

6. ITINs are the only one of these that unauthorized immigrants are still able to obtain in North Carolina.

7. Bernstein (2007); Capps and Fix (2005); Drever (2009); Johnson and Kasarda (2009); Kasarda and Johnson (2006); Lacy and Odem (2009); Maguire (2007). In North Carolina in 2005, Johnson and Kasarda (2009) and Kasarda and Johnson (2006) esti-mate that Hispanics as a group contributed an estimated $756 billion in income taxes, property taxes, direct sales taxes, indirect business taxes, and indirect personal taxes, on top of enhancing the state's economic output and the cost competitiveness of key industries (specifically agriculture and construction).

8. One example was of migrant farmworkers who suffered from "green tobacco" disease (*tabaco verde* in Spanish) from working with pesticides and other chemicals that seeped into their bloodstream (Cuadros 2006: 85). I met several of them over the course of my research who reported simply having to "wait through it," exper-imenting with various home remedies (such as "drinking milk") because they did not have transportation, money, or insurance coverage to access appropriate medical treatment. Moreover, even for those who could access treatment, illiteracy, language barriers, and lack of translation and interpreting services often inhibited them from understanding their diagnoses. To illustrate, one female immigrant handed Elisa and me a 40-plus-page diagnosis of a severe medical problem she had received from the Bedford hospital on a recent visit to the emergency room, written entirely in English, when we went to visit her trailer one afternoon. The diagnosis was so technical as to be virtually impossible for either Elisa or me to translate adequately into Spanish, and it was painfully clear that this woman did not understand even the most basic steps it had instructed her to take in order to get better (e.g., drink lots of fluids, take med-icine, not work until she felt better, return to see the doctor, and so forth; fieldnotes, Sept. 16, 2003).

9. My respondent reported that it took several years for her child to be allowed to return to the United States to be reunited with her, and in the meantime she ex-perienced several bouts of medical depression. This example is significant because it illustrates how even an extreme form of current immigration policy—deporting a child—does not always encourage an unauthorized immigrant to return home.

10. Bohon (2006); Lacy (2007, 2008a); Lacy and Odem (2009); Lippard and Galla-gher (2011); Mantero (2008); McClain (2006); Mohl (2009); Odem (2008); Singer (2008); Singer, Hardwick, and Brettell (2008a); Smith and Furuseth (2006b); Torres, Popke, and Hapke (2006); Winders (2008b); Zúñiga and Hernández-León (2009).

11. By the early 2000s, seasonal agricultural migration had begun transforming into permanent settlement in various rural southern communities, while secondary

internal migration from traditional immigrant gateways had begun giving way to direct international migration.

12. Popularly known as the Sensenbrenner-King Bill, the Border Protection, Antiterrorism, and Illegal Immigration Control Act of 2005 (HR 4437) was a harsh, Republican-sponsored bill that proposed to make "unlawful presence" in the United States a felony, further criminalize employers and anyone else who harbored or assisted unauthorized immigrants, and build a double fence along the entire U.S.-Mexico border. Although it passed in the U.S. House of Representatives on December 2005, it never went through the U.S. Senate and thus never became law. Still, its passage in the House prompted a mass mobilization of immigrants in spring 2006 (Portes and Rumbaut 2006: 152, 347–48), since it would have rendered 12 million people instantly subject to incarceration had it been passed, representing the largest potential expansion of the prison industrial complex in history (Massey 2007: 156; also Hincapié 2009).

13. Arizona's controversial Support Our Law Enforcement and Safe Neighborhoods Act (SB 1070) criminalized anyone (including family members, but making select exceptions for child-protection workers and emergency medical assistants) who transports or harbors unauthorized immigrants; gave residents of Arizona the authority to bring lawsuits against municipalities and law enforcement agencies that limit or restrict the enforcement of immigration law; required state and local law enforcement officers to question the immigration status of anyone they stop for possible violations of any state or local law or ordinance if an officer has a "reasonable suspicion" that an individual is unauthorized; made it a state (and not just federal) crime for noncitizens to fail to carry proof of their immigration status; and gave state and local law enforcement officers the authority to arrest and detain individuals who cannot provide proof of their legal status in the United States, in order to request verification of detainees' legal status from the federal government. As of this writing, the law was scheduled to take effect in late July 2010, although several lawsuits challenging it had been filed in federal court (Chishti and Bergeron 2010).

14. See the collected essays in Anrig and Wang (2006); Bailey and Emerson (2010); Brettell and Nibbs (2010); Hincapié (2009); Hopkins (2010); Lacy (2008a); Lacy and Odem (2009); Luna and Ansley (2009); Motomura (2008); MPI and NYU (2007); Newton and Adams (2009); Rodríguez (2008); Singer (2008); Singer, Hartwick, and Brettell (2008a); Varsanyi (2008); Wells (2004); and Yale-Loehr and Chiappari (2007).

15. By April 2010, no restrictive laws had yet been introduced in North Carolina, but the state's 2010 legislative season did not start until May (Bailey and Emerson 2010).

16. Research shows that increasing policies of immigration enforcement and surveillance have produced feelings of suspicion, harassment, humiliation, detachment, and nonbelonging among recent immigrants in Florida (Vaquera and Aranda 2009), as well as in Oklahoma, where they have made many Hispanics so uncomfortable that

they have either migrated to surrounding states or become discouraged from going out in public (Allegro, in progress).

17. As noted in the Introduction, the inflow of unauthorized immigrants leveled off after 2005, and especially after 2007. Still, the stock of unauthorized immigrants residing in the United States has remained relatively stable since 2005, at roughly 11 million (Hoefer, Rytina, and Baker 2009, 2010; Massey and Sánchez 2010; Passel and Cohn 2008, 2009), since relatively few unauthorized immigrants have returned to their home country out of fear of potentially having to cross back through a heavily militarized border (Cornelius 2009; Cornelius and Lewis 2007; Papademetriou and Terrazas 2009). Moreover, since migration scholars consider the contraction of the American economy to be the driving factor behind the reduced inflow of unauthorized immigrants, they note that inflows of new unauthorized immigrants will likely rise again as the American economy improves (Massey and Sánchez 2010).

18. Several respondents noted sarcastically that natives are "insane" to think that unauthorized immigrants would uproot themselves from their jobs, families, and other obligations in the United States to return to their home countries and "wait and see" if they might be allowed to come back.

19. As Penninx (2003) notes, "Migrants are newcomers, who are often regarded as the classic 'other' who does not belong. Such constructions of the 'other' may be based on legal grounds, physical appearance or race, (perceived) cultural and religious differences, class characteristics, or on any combination of these elements. Such constructions have been used politically, e.g., by the anti-immigrant movement, and express themselves in discriminatory practices, deteriorating inter-ethnic relations, and weakening of social cohesion in communities, cities, and states."

20. On similar disenfranchisement that took place during implementation of the Immigration Reform and Control Act in 1986, see Hagan (1994).

21. For Latin Americans from other sending countries, the corresponding original application month was September 2004.

22. For Latin Americans from other sending countries, the corresponding original application month was December 2006.

23. Natives often charge Hispanics, especially Mexicans, with being loyal to their home country and therefore unpatriotic and disloyal to the United States (Huntington 2004). Such conceptions are painfully misguided, as Mexican Americans are shown in survey data to endorse core American values such as individualism and patriotism as much as, and sometimes more than, Anglo Americans (de la Garza, Falcón, and García 1996). In my research, Hispanic newcomers—such as Eduardo, whose comments open this chapter—expressed open appreciation for the United States as a country offering them greater economic opportunity, safety, and freedom than they were able to find in their home country (regardless of other positive ways in which they continued to relate to their home country). Several who were enrolled in the Hispanic Leadership Course in Wilcox County in fall 2003 also expressed open

appreciation for U.S. civic ideals and the political structure, which they hoped to learn more about and even use one day in their efforts to help "change things" in Latin America.

24. One of the main arguments for restricting unauthorized immigrants' access to the labor market is that doing so would open up to natives the jobs they currently occupy, especially to those who are members of domestic racial minority groups. Whether this is actually the case on the ground is an extremely complicated question, and it depends on whether natives are in fact willing to perform those jobs, the degree to which employers are willing to raise wages and the quality of those jobs (if natives are willing to take them only under certain conditions), the degree to which employers hold flexible or unchanging stereotypes about different groups of workers, and the range of qualifications among and other employment opportunities facing natives, among other factors. In my research, all natives (including African Americans) expressed unwillingness to perform labor-intensive agricultural work in eastern North Carolina. By contrast, some groups of natives expressed more willingness to perform food processing work, and even more expressed willingness to perform routine manufacturing or textiles, construction, and services work—although sometimes only under certain conditions. In the declining routine manufacturing and textiles industry, employers reported being unable to raise wages and the overall quality of jobs because of extreme foreign competition, whereas their counterparts in food processing, construction, and services had somewhat more leeway. In all of these industries, however, negative stereotypes about groups of workers (especially African Americans, but sometimes also whites) often worked to the detriment of natives, and several employers of low-wage service companies that have recently relocated to the region expressed surprise over the "unemployability" of many of their native applicants (postfieldwork notes, May 2007). As such, both the educational qualifications of natives—which reflect the efficacy of eastern North Carolina's public educational systems as much as the abilities of individual natives—and employers' willingness to hire them will need to be considered before removal of unauthorized immigrants can result in perfect native-for-immigrant substitution in the labor market.

25. Berk, Schur, Chavez, and Frankel (2000); Goldman, Smith, and Sood (2005, 2006); Heyman, Núñez, and Talavera (2009); Marshall, Urrutia-Rojas, Mas, and Coggin (2005); Ortega et al. (2007); Portes, Fernández-Kelly, and Light (forthcoming); Portes, Light, and Fernández-Kelly (2009); Schur, Berk, Good, and Gardner (1999); Staiti, Hurley, and Katz (2006).

26. Cornelius (2009); Cornelius and Lewis (2007); De Genova (2005); Hincapié (2009); Massey, Durand, and Malone (2002); Ngai (2004).

27. In fact, Perreira, Fuligni, and Potochnick (2010) find that positive treatment by peers and encouragement by teachers in North Carolina's schools are helping to counterbalance Latino students' experiences of discrimination, and keep their academic motivation high.

Appendix

1. The H-2A visa program allows growers to import temporary foreign workers to work in agriculture when the U.S. Department of Labor determines that a domestic labor shortage exists (Griffith 2005, 2006; Griffith et al. 1995). By contrast, the H-2B visa program allows employers to import temporary foreign workers to work in *nonagricultural* sectors, such as food processing or forestry, in similar situations (Griffith 1995a).

2. The number of temporary Mexican guest workers entering the United States reached 361,000 in 2008, a level last seen in 1959, at the height of the infamous *bracero* guest worker program (Massey 2011; Massey and Sánchez 2010). Furthermore, at the end of the 1990s, North Carolina was importing a full 40% of Mexican H-2A agricultural guest workers—more than any other state in the country (Smith-Nonini 2005, 2009).

3. Ansley and Shefner (2009); Furuseth and Smith (2006); Greenbaum (1998); Kochhar, Suro, and Tafoya (2005); Lippard and Gallagher (2011); McClain (2006); Odem and Lacy (2009); Saenz, Donato, Gouveia, and Torres (2003); Vásquez, Seales, and Marquardt (2008).

4. Studies show that although the traditional South's Hispanic population increase was initiated by native-born Hispanics and foreign-born "secondary migrants" coming from traditional gateway states in the late 1980s and early 1990s, it gradually shifted to include more direct migrants from Mexico by the late 1990s (Leach 2004; Leach and Bean 2008; Marrow 2011b).

5. As Bohon (2008) describes in Georgia, most Hispanics in North Carolina share a newcomer identity. In 2005, four-fifths were born outside the state—either abroad (58.6%) or in another U.S. jurisdiction (20.7%)—while only one-fifth were born in the state (Johnson and Kasarda 2009; Kasarda and Johnson 2006).

6. In 2002, the Wilcox County Center for Leadership Development (a pseudonym) used external grant money to expand an eight-week leadership training course originally designed to promote underrepresented African American leadership in the county to the newer Hispanic community in Spanish. The course ran through 2004, and then through 2005 in modified form.

7. I do not use pseudonyms for these state-level organizations; they were not primary subjects of my research.

8. Jaime was the notable exception. Born in Wilcox County, he could trace parts of his family tree all over eastern North Carolina, including some rural areas near Tarboro that my own ancestors are from.

9. I have studied abroad in Brazil, Ecuador, Mexico, and Spain, taught Spanish and English in Belize, and traveled in Argentina, Costa Rica, Guatemala, Peru, Puerto Rico, and Uruguay.

10. *Bolillo/a* and *moyo/a* are derogatory terms used by many Hispanic newcomers in eastern North Carolina to refer to "whites" and "blacks," respectively (the more

literal meaning of *bolillo/a* is "bread," "cookie," or "cracker"). However, according to one of my respondents, a bilingual ESL teacher, *bolillo/a* is now used so commonly that it has lost some of its sting. In this instance, it is being used without any intention to sting.

11. Employers at all three of the workplaces where I conducted interviews reported having previously been targeted by either what was then the Immigration and Naturalization Service (INS) or the Social Security Administration (SSA) for hiring unauthorized immigrants. Therefore, I do not consider my research in and of itself to constitute a significant threat to my unauthorized immigrant respondents' economic positions. Their workplaces, like many others today, have already come under increased government scrutiny, independent of my research.

References

Abrego, Leisy Janet. 2006. "'I Can't Go to College Because I Don't Have Papers': Incorporation Patterns of Latino Undocumented Youth." *Latino Studies* 4(3): 212–31.

Alba, Richard D., and Nancy Denton. 2004. "Old and New Landscapes of Diversity: The Residential Patterns of Immigrant Minorities." In *Not Just Black and White: Historical and Contemporary Perspectives on Immigration, Race, and Ethnicity in the United States*, edited by Nancy Foner and George M. Frederickson, pp. 237–61. New York: Russell Sage.

Alba, Richard D., John R. Logan, Brian J. Stults, Gilbert Marzan, and Wenquan Zhang. 1999. "Immigrant Groups in the Suburbs: A Reexamination of Suburbanization and Spatial Assimilation." *American Sociological Review* 64(3): 446–60.

Alba, Richard D., and Victor Nee. 2003. *Remaking the American Mainstream: Assimilation and Contemporary Immigration.* Cambridge, MA: Harvard University Press.

Albrecht, Don E. 2006. "Nonmetro/Metro Migration: Economic and Noneconomic Outcomes." *Southern Rural Sociology* 21(1): 1–24.

Alexander, Ames. 2008. "Labor Law Fails to Help Workers: Under N.C. Program Aimed at Preventing Retaliatory Firings, 1 Percent Are Rehired." *Charlotte Observer* (September 14).

Alexander, Ames, and Franco Ordoñez. 2008. "More Than 300 Arrested in S.C. Raid at Poultry Plant: Largest Immigration Operation in Carolinas Is Part of Ongoing Federal Probe of Employment Practices at House of Raeford." *Charlotte Observer* (October 8).

Allegood, Jerry. 2007. "Not in English? Not in Our County, Beaufort Says." *News and Observer* (Raleigh, NC; February 19).

Allegro, Linda. 2008. "Oklahoma." In *Latino America: A State-by-State Encyclopedia*, edited by Mark Overmyer-Velásquez, pp. 657–66. Westport, CT: Greenwood Press.

———. In progress. "Border Control in the U.S. Heartland: A Tenuous Attempt at Employer Sanctions in a Right-to-Work State." In *Latino Migrations to the U.S. Heart-*

land: Redrawing Boundaries, Forging Communities, and Shaping Geographies, edited by Linda Allegro and Andrew Wood. Durham, NC: Duke University Press.

Almaguer, Tomás. 1994. *Racial Fault Lines: The Historical Origins of White Supremacy in California.* Berkeley: University of California Press.

Alvarado, Joel, and Charles Jaret. 2009. "Building Black-Brown Coalitions in the Southeast." Atlanta, GA: Southern Regional Council.

Andersen, Kristi, and Elizabeth F. Cohen. 2005. "Political Institutions and Incorporation of Immigrants." In *The Politics of Democratic Inclusion*, edited by Rodney E. Hero and Christina Wolbrecht, pp. 186–205. Philadelphia: Temple University Press.

Anrig, Greg, and Tova Andrea Wang, eds. 2006. *Immigration's New Frontiers: Experiences from the Emerging Gateway States.* New York: Century Foundation Press.

Ansley, Fran. 2009. "Conclusion: Toward a Just and Humane Immigration Policy." In *Global Connections & Local Receptions: New Latino Immigration to the Southeastern United States*, edited by Fran Ansley and Jon Shefner, pp. 319–50. Knoxville: University of Tennessee Press.

Ansley, Fran, and Jon Shefner, eds. 2009. *Global Connections & Local Receptions: New Latino Immigration to the Southeastern United States.* Knoxville: University of Tennessee Press.

Aranda, Elizabeth, Rosa E. Chang, and Elena Sabogal. 2009. "Racializing Miami: Immigrant Latinos and Colorblind Racism in the Global City." In *How the United States Racializes Latinos: White Hegemony and Its Consequences*, edited by José A. Cobas, Jorge Duany, and Joe R. Feagin, pp. 149–65. Boulder, CO: Paradigm.

Armenta, Amada. 2010. "Policing Immigrants: The Local Dilemmas of Immigration Law Enforcement." Paper presented at the Annual Meeting of the American Sociological Association, Atlanta, GA (August 14–17).

Associated Press. 2007. "21 Pork Plant Workers Charged with Immigration Violations." *News and Observer* (Raleigh, NC; January 25).

———. 2008. "ACLU Probes NC Sheriff Who Said Hispanics 'Trashy.'" *News and Observer* (Raleigh, NC; September 9).

Atiles, Jorge H., and Stephanie A. Bohon. 2003. "*Camas Calientes*: Housing Adjustments and Barriers to Social and Economic Adaptation Among Georgia's Rural Latinos." *Southern Rural Sociology* 19(1): 97–122.

Bada, Xóchitl, and Gilberto Cárdenas. 2009. "Blacks, Latinos, and the Immigration Debate: Conflict and Cooperation in Two Global Cities." In *How the United States Racializes Latinos: White Hegemony and Its Consequences*, edited by J. A. Cobas, J. Duany, and J. R. Feagin, pp. 166–82. Boulder, CO: Paradigm.

Bada, Xóchitl, Jonathan Fox, Robert Donnelly, and Andrew Selee. 2010. "Context Matters: Latino Immigrant Civic Engagement in Nine U.S. Cities." Washington, DC: Woodrow Wilson International Center for Scholars.

Bailey, Benjamin. 2001. "Dominican-American Ethnic/Racial Identities and United States Social Categories." *International Migration Review* 35(3): 677–708.

Bailey, Jennifer, and Bill Emerson. 2010. "2010 Immigration-Related Bills and Resolutions in the States (January–March 2010)." Washington, DC: Immigrant Policy Project, National Conference of State Legislatures (NCSL; April 27).

Bailey, Raleigh. 2005. "New Immigrant Communities in the North Carolina Piedmont Triad: Integration Issues and Challenges." In *Beyond the Gateway: Immigrants in a Changing America*, edited by Elzbieta M. Gozdziak and Susan F. Martin, pp. 57–86. Lanham, MD: Lexington Books.

Bankston, Carl L. 2003. "Immigrants in the New South: An Introduction." *Sociological Spectrum* 23(2): 123–28.

———. 2007. "New People in the New South: An Overview of Southern Immigration." *Southern Cultures* 13(4): 24–44.

Barcus, Holly R. 2006. "New Destinations for Hispanic Migrants: An Analysis of Rural Kentucky." In *Latinos in the South: Transformations of Place*, edited by Heather A. Smith and Owen J. Furuseth, pp. 89–110. Aldershot, UK: Ashgate Press.

Barreto, Matt A., and Gabriel R. Sanchez. 2009. "Black-Brown Relations in the New South: Results from the Latino National Survey." Paper presented at the National Conference on Latino Politics, Power, and Policy, Brown University, Providence, RI (October 24).

Batalova, Jeanne, and Michael Fix. 2006. "New Estimates of Unauthorized Youth Eligible for Legal Status Under the DREAM Act." Immigration Backgrounder. Washington, DC: Migration Policy Institute (October).

Batalova, Jeanne, and Michael Fix, with Peter A. Creticos. 2008. "Uneven Progress: The Employment Pathways of Skilled Immigrants in the United States." Washington, DC: Migration Policy Institute and Institute for Work and the Economy (October).

Bauer, Mary, and Sarah Reynolds. 2009. "Under Siege: Life for Low-Income Latinos in the South." Montgomery, AL: Southern Poverty Law Center (April).

Bean, Frank D., Susan K. Brown, Mark A. Leach, and James Dean Bachmeier. 2008. "Parental Pathways: How Legalization and Citizenship Among Mexican Immigrants Relates to Their Children's Economic Wellbeing." Paper presented at the Annual Meeting of the American Sociological Association, Boston (September 1–4).

Bean, Frank D., Susan K. Brown, and Rubén G. Rumbaut. 2006. "Mexican Immigrant Political and Economic Incorporation." *PS: Political Science and Politics* 4(2): 309–13.

Bean, Frank D., and B. Lindsay Lowell. 2007. "Unauthorized Migration." In *The New Americans: A Guide to Immigration Since 1965*, edited by Mary C. Waters and Reed Ueda with Helen B. Marrow, pp. 70–82. Cambridge, MA: Harvard University Press.

Bean, Frank D., and Gillian Stevens. 2003. *America's Newcomers and the Dynamics of Diversity*. New York: Russell Sage.

Beeler, Amy, and Julie Murray. 2007. "Improving Immigrant Workers' Economic Prospects: A Review of the Literature." In *Securing the Future: US Immigrant Integration Policy—A Reader*, pp. 107–24. Washington, DC: Migration Policy Institute.

Berk, Marc L., Claudia L. Schur, Leo R. Chavez, and Martin Frankel. 2000. "Health Care Use Among Undocumented Latino Immigrants." *Health Affairs* 19(4): 51–64.

Bernhardt, Annette, Ruth Milkman, Nick Theodore, Douglas Heckathorn, Mirabai Auer, James De Filippis, Ana Luz Gonzalez, Victor Narro, Diana Polson Perelshteyn, and Michael Spiller. 2009. "Broken Laws, Unprotected Workers: Violations of Employment and Labor Laws in America's Cities." New York: National Employment Law Project.

Bernstein, Nina. 2007. "Tax Returns Rise for Immigrants in U.S. Illegally." *New York Times* (April 16).

———. 2009. "Target of Immigrant Raids Shifted." *New York Times* (February 4).

Berthoff, Rowland T. 1951. "Southern Attitudes Toward Immigration, 1865–1914." *Journal of Southern History* 17(3): 328–60.

Bjerklie, Steve. 1995. "On the Horns of a Dilemma: The U.S. Meat and Poultry Industry." In *Any Way You Cut It: Meat Processing and Small Town America*, edited by Donald D. Stull, Michael J. Broadway, and David Griffith, pp. 41–60. Lawrence: University Press of Kansas.

Bobo, Lawrence D., and Vincent L. Hutchings. 1996. "Perceptions of Racial Group Competition: Extending Blumer's Theory of Group Position to the Multi-Racial Social Context." *American Sociological Review* 61 (6): 951–72.

Bobo, Lawrence D., and Devon Johnson. 2000. "Racial Attitudes in a Prismatic Metropolis: Mapping Identity, Stereotypes, Competition, and Views on Affirmative Action." In *Prismatic Metropolis: Inequality in Los Angeles*, edited by Lawrence D. Bobo, Melvin L. Oliver, James H. Johnson, and Abel Valenzuela, pp. 81–163. New York: Russell Sage.

Bobo, Lawrence D., and Michael P. Massagli. 2001. "Stereotyping and Urban Inequality." In *Urban Inequality: Evidence from Four Cities*, edited by Alice O'Connor, Chris Tilly, and Lawrence D. Bobo, pp. 89–162. New York: Russell Sage.

Bobo, Lawrence D., and Mia Tuan. 2006. *Prejudice in Politics: Group Position, Public Opinion, and the Wisconsin Treaty Rights Dispute*. Cambridge, MA: Harvard University Press.

Bloemraad, Irene. 2006. *Becoming a Citizen: Incorporating Immigrants and Refugees in the United States and Canada*. Berkeley: University of California Press.

Bohn, Sarah. 2009. "New Patterns of Immigrant Settlement in California." San Francisco: Public Policy Institute of California (July).

Bohon, Stephanie A. 2006. "Georgia's Response to New Immigration." In *Immigration's New Frontiers: Experiences from the Emerging Gateway States*, edited by Greg Anrig and Tova Andrea Wang, pp. 67–100. New York: Century Foundation Press.

———. 2008. "Georgia." In *Latino America: A State-by-State Encyclopedia*, edited by Mark Overmyer-Velásquez, pp. 197–214. Westport, CT: Greenwood Press.

Bohon, Stephanie A., Heather Macpherson, and Jorge H. Atiles. 2005. "Educational Barriers for New Latinos in Georgia." *Journal of Latinos and Education* 4(1): 43–58.

Bohon, Stephanie A., Laum Gerard Massengale, and Audrey Jordan. 2009. "Mexican Self-Employment in Old and New Places." In *Global Connections & Local Receptions: New Latino Immigration to the Southeastern United States*, edited by Fran Ansley and Jon Shefner, pp. 197–222. Knoxville: University of Tennessee Press.

Bonilla-Silva, Eduardo. 2002. "We Are All Americans! The Latin Americanization of Racial Stratification in the USA." *Race & Society* 5: 3–16.

———. 2004. "From Bi-Racial to Tri-Racial: Towards a New System of Racial Stratification in the USA." *Ethnic and Racial Studies* 27(6): 931–50.

Borjas, George J. 1998. "Do Blacks Gain or Lose from Immigration?" In *Help or Hindrance? The Economic Implications of Immigration for African Americans*, edited by Daniel S. Hamermesh and Frank D. Bean, pp. 51–74. New York: Russell Sage.

———. 2004. "The Rise of Low-Skill Immigration in the South." *Insights on Southern Poverty* 2(2): 1–6.

Brehm, John, and Scott Gates. 1999. *Working, Shirking, and Sabotage: Bureaucratic Response to a Democratic Public*. Ann Arbor: University of Michigan Press.

Brettell, Caroline B. 2008. "'Big D': Incorporating New Immigrants in a Sunbelt Suburban Metropolis." In *Twenty-First Century Gateways: Immigrant Integration in Suburban America*, edited by Audrey Singer, Susan W. Hardwick, and Caroline B. Brettell, pp. 53–86. Washington, DC: Brookings Institution Press.

Brettell, Caroline B, and Faith G. Nibbs. 2010. "Immigrant Suburban Settlement and the 'Threat' to Middle Class Status and Identity: The Case of Farmers Branch, Texas." *International Migration* (online first, DOI: 10.1111/j.1468-2435.2010.00611.x).

Brewer, Cynthia A., and Trudy A. Suchan. 2001. "Mapping Census 2000: The Geography of U.S. Diversity." Census 2000 Special Reports (CENSR/01-1). Washington, DC: U.S. Department of Commerce, Economics and Statistics Administration, U.S. Census Bureau (June). http://www.census.gov/population/www/cen2000/atlas/pdf/censr01-1.pdf (last accessed December 17, 2009).

Broadway, Michael J. 1994. "Beef Stew: Cattle, Immigrants, and Established Residents in a Kansas Beefpacking Town." In *Newcomers in the Workplace: Immigrants and the Restructuring of the U.S. Economy*, edited by Louise Lamphere, Alex Stepick, and Guillermo Grenier, pp. 25–43. Philadelphia: Temple University Press.

———. 2000. "Planning for Change in Small Towns or Trying to Avoid the Slaughterhouse Blues." *Journal of Rural Studies* 16: 37–46.

———. 2007. "Meatpacking and the Transformation of Rural Communities: A Comparison of Brooks, Alberta and Garden City, Kansas." *Rural Sociology* 72(4): 560–82.

Brodkin, Karen. 1998. *How Jews Became White Folks and What That Says About Race in America*. New Brunswick, NJ: Rutgers University Press.

Brown, David L., and Louis E. Swanson, eds. 2003. *Challenges for Rural America in the Twenty-First Century*. University Park: Pennsylvania State University Press.

Brownell, Peter. 2005. "The Declining Enforcement of Employer Sanctions." *Migration Information Source* (September).

Browning, Rufus P., Dale Rogers Marshall, and David H. Tabb. 1984. *Protest Is Not Enough: The Struggle of Blacks and Hispanics for Equality in Urban Politics.* Berkeley: University of California Press.

Bullock, Charles S., and M. V. Hood. 2006. "A Mile-Wide Gap: The Evolution of Hispanic Political Emergence in the Deep South." *Social Science Quarterly* 87(5): 1117–35.

Bump, Micah N. 2005. "From Temporary Picking to Permanent Plucking: Hispanic Newcomers, Integration, and Change in the Shenandoah Valley." In *Beyond the Gateway: Immigrants in a Changing America,* edited by Elzbieta M. Gozdziak and Susan F. Martin, pp. 137–76. Lanham, MD: Lexington Books.

Bump, Micah N., B. Lindsay Lowell, and Silje Pettersen. 2005. "The Growth and Population Characteristics of Immigrants and Minorities in America's New Settlement States." In *Beyond the Gateway: Immigrants in a Changing America,* edited by Elzbieta M. Gozdziak and Susan F. Martin, pp. 19–53. Lanham, MD: Lexington Books.

Burns, Peter, and James G. Gimpel. 2000. "Economic Insecurity, Prejudicial Stereotypes, and Public Opinion on Immigration Policy." *Political Science Quarterly* 115(2): 201–25.

Butcher, Kristin F. 1998. "An Investigation of the Effect of Immigration on the Labor-Market Outcomes of African Americans." In *Help or Hindrance? The Economic Implications of Immigration for African Americans,* edited by Daniel S. Hamermesh and Frank D. Bean, pp. 149–81. New York: Russell Sage.

Cacari Stone, Lisa. 2004. "Analysis of the Funding and Provision of Health Care to Immigrants After Welfare Reform: Local Consequences and Variation in New Mexico." Ph.D. diss., Department of Health Policy, Heller Graduate School of Social Welfare, Brandeis University, Waltham, MA.

Cady Hallett, Miranda. In progress. "Deferred Deportation, Community Transformation: Dynamics of Place-Identification and Legal Exclusion in Rural Arkansas." In *Latino Migrations to the U.S. Heartland: Redrawing Boundaries, Forging Communities, and Shaping Geographies,* edited by Linda Allegro and Andrew Wood. Durham, NC: Duke University Press.

Calafell, Bernadette Marie. 2003. "Disrupting the Dichotomy: 'Yo Soy Chicana/o' in the New Latina/o South." *Communication Review* 7(2): 175–204.

Callaway, Hadley. 2008. "That's Confidential." *News and Observer* (Raleigh, NC; August 7).

Caldwell, Edmond W. 2009. "The North Carolina Sheriff's Association's Perspective on the 287(g) Jail Enforcement Model." *Popular Government* 74(3): 2–18.

Camarillo, Albert M. 2004. "Black and Brown in Compton: Demographic Change, Suburban Decline, and Intergroup Relations in a South Central Los Angeles Community, 1950 to 2000." In *Not Just Black and White: Historical and Contemporary Perspectives on Immigration, Race, and Ethnicity in the United States,* edited by Nancy Foner and George M. Frederickson, pp. 358–76. New York: Russell Sage.

Cantu, Lionel. 1995. "The Peripheralization of Rural America: A Case Study of Latino Migrants in America's Heartland." *Sociological Perspectives* 38(2): 399–414.

Capps, Randy, Rosa Maria Castañeda, Ajay Chaudry, and Robert Santos. 2007. "Paying the Price: The Impact of Immigration Raids on America's Children." Washington, DC: Urban Institute and National Council of La Raza (October 31).

Capps, Randy, and Michael Fix. 2005. "Undocumented Immigrants: Myths and Reality." Washington, DC: Migration Policy Institute (October 25).

Card, David, and Ethan G. Lewis. 2007. "The Diffusion of Mexican Immigrants During the 1990s: Explanations and Impacts." In *Mexican Immigration to the United States*, edited by George J. Borjas, pp. 193–228. Chicago: University of Chicago Press.

Chavez, Leo T. 1998. *Shadowed Lives: Undocumented Immigrants in American Society* (2nd ed.). Fort Worth, TX: Harcourt Brace College.

———. 2007. "The Condition of Illegality." *International Migration* 45(3): 192–95.

———. 2008. *The Latino Threat: Constructing Immigrants, Citizens, and the Nation.* Stanford, CA: Stanford University Press.

Chishti, Muzaffar, and Claire Bergeron. 2009. "Policy Beat: Signs of Change in Immigration Enforcement Policies Emerging from DHS." *Migration Information Source* (March 16).

———. 2010. "Policy Beat: New Arizona Law Engulfs Immigration Debate." *Migration Information Source* (May 17).

Ciscel, David H., Barbara Ellen Smith, and Marcela Mendoza. 2003. "Ghosts in the Global Machine: New Immigrants and the Redefinition of Work." *Journal of Economic Issues* 37(2): 333–41.

Citrin, Jack, Donald P. Green, Christopher Muste, and Cara Wong. 1997. "Public Opinion Toward Immigration Reform: The Role of Economic Motivations." *Journal of Politics* 59(3): 858–82.

Cobb, James C. 2005. "Beyond the Y'all Wall: The American South Goes Global." In *Globalization and the American South*, edited by James C. Cobb and William Stueck, pp. 1–18. Athens: University of Georgia Press.

Cobb, James C., and William Stueck, eds. 2005. *Globalization and the American South.* Athens: University of Georgia Press.

Cohen, Elizabeth F. 2007. "Carved from the Inside Out: Immigration and America's Public Philosophy of Citizenship." In *Debating Immigration*, edited by Carol M. Swain, pp. 32–45. Cambridge, UK: Cambridge University Press.

Collins, Jane L. 2003. *Threads: Gender, Labor, and Power in the Global Apparel Industry.* Chicago: Chicago University Press.

Collins, Kristin. 2007a. "Sheriffs Help Feds Deport Illegal Aliens." *News and Observer* (Raleigh, NC; April 22).

———. 2007b. "UNC Joins Fray on Immigrant Tuition: The System Will Review Its Position on Whether to Give In-State Tuition to Those Who Come Here Illegally." *News and Observer* (Raleigh, NC; December 7).

———. 2008a. "Bizzell Has Not Spoken Publicly Since Issuing an Apology." *News and Observer* (Raleigh, NC; September 20).

———. 2008b. "County Cold to Migrant Influx." *News & Observer* (Raleigh, NC; May 25).

———. 2008c. "Immigrants Skeptical of Program." *News and Observer* (Raleigh, NC; June 8).

———. 2008d. "Immigration Arrest Raises Concerns." *News and Observer* (Raleigh, NC; July 30).

———. 2008e. "More Illegal Immigrants Driving Without N.C. License." *News and Observer* (Raleigh, NC; June 1).

———. 2008f. "Protesters Say Johnston Sheriff Should Go." *News & Observer* (Raleigh, NC; September 29).

———. 2008g. "Sheriffs to Check Status of Inmates." *News & Observer* (Raleigh, NC; May 31).

———. 2008h. "Tolerance Wears Thin: Johnston's Sheriff Says Hispanics Spread Crime and Dodge Taxes. Yet He Respects Their Hard Work and Expresses Pity for Their Plight." *News and Observer* (Raleigh, NC; September 7).

———. 2009. "Community College Board Hears Comments on Illegal Immigrant Admissions." *News & Observer* (Raleigh, NC; December 18).

Collins, Kristin, and Jane Stancill. 2008. "Colleges Shut Out Illegal Aliens: The Policy Is Among America's Toughest." *News and Observer* (Raleigh, NC; May 14).

Cordero-Guzmán, Hector R., Nina Martin, Victoria Quiroz-Becerra, and Nik Theodore. 2008. "Voting with their Feet: Nonprofit Organizations and Immigrant Mobilization." *American Behavioral Scientist* 52(4): 598–617.

Córdova Plaza, Rosío. 2009. "New Scenarios of Migration: Social Vulnerability of Undocumented Veracruzanos in the Southern United States." In *Latino Immigrants and the Transformation of the U.S. South*, edited by Mary E. Odem and Elaine Lacy, pp. 18–33. Athens: University of Georgia Press.

Cornelius, Wayne A., ed. 1998. "The Structural Embeddedness of Demand for Mexican Immigrant Labor: New Evidence from California." In *Crossings: Mexican Immigration in Interdisciplinary Perspectives*, edited by Marcelo Suárez-Orozco, pp. 113–44. Cambridge, MA: Harvard University Press.

———. 2001. "Death at the Border: Efficacy and Unintended Consequences of U.S. Immigration Control Policy." *Population and Development Review* 27 (4): 661–85.

———. 2002. "Ambivalent Reception: Mass Public Responses to the 'New' Latino Immigration to the United States." In *Latinos: Remaking America*, edited by Marcelo Suárez-Orozco and Mariela Páez, pp. 165–89. Berkeley: University of California Press.

———. 2009. "Keeping Migrants Here: Recent Research Shows Unintended Consequences of U.S. Border Enforcement." Washington, DC: Immigration Policy Center, Fact Check (June 17).

Cornelius, Wayne A., and Jessa M. Lewis, eds. 2007. *Impacts of Border Enforcement on Mexican Migration: The View from Sending Communities*. La Jolla: Center for Comparative Immigration Studies, University of California at San Diego.

Cornfield, Daniel B. 2009. "Immigrant Labor Organizing in a 'New Destination City':

Approaches to the Unionization of African, Asian, Latino, and Middle Eastern Workers in Nashville." In *Global Connections & Local Receptions: New Latino Immigration to the Southeastern United States*, edited by Fran Ansley and Jon Shefner, pp. 279–98. Knoxville: University of Tennessee Press.

Coutin, Susan Bibler. 2000. *Legalizing Moves: Salvadoran Immigrants' Struggle for U.S. Residency*. Ann Arbor: University of Michigan Press.

Cravey, Altha J. 1997. "The Changing South: Latino Labor and Poultry Production in Rural North Carolina." *Southeastern Geographer* 37(2): 295–300.

———. 2003. "Toque una Ranchera, Por Favor." *Antipode* 35: 603–21.

Crowley, Martha, Daniel T. Lichter, and Zhenchao Qian. 2006. "Beyond Gateway Cities: Economic Restructuring and Poverty Among Mexican Immigrant Families and Children." *Family Relations* 55(3): 345–60.

Cuadros, Paul. 2006. *A Home on the Field: How One Championship Team Inspires Hope for the Revival of Small Town America*. New York: HarperCollins.

———. 2008. "A George Wallace Moment." *News and Observer* (Raleigh, NC; June 8).

Cummings, Scott, and Thomas Lambert. 1997. "Anti-Hispanic and Anti-Asian Sentiments Among African Americans." *Social Science Quarterly* 78: 338–53.

Cunningham, Peter, Michelle Banker, Samantha Artiga, and Jennifer Tolbert. 2006. "Health Coverage and Access to Care for Hispanics in 'New Growth Communities' and 'Major Hispanic Centers.'" Washington, DC: Henry J. Kaiser Family Foundation (September).

Dahl, Robert Alan. 1961. *Who Governs? Democracy and Power in an American City*. New Haven, CT: Yale University Press.

Dale, Jack G., Susan Andreatta, and Elizabeth Freeman. 2001. "Language and the Migrant Worker Experience in Rural North Carolina Communities." In *Latino Workers in the Contemporary South*, edited by Arthur D. Murphy, Colleen Blanchard, and Jennifer A. Hill, pp. 93–104. Athens: University of Georgia Press.

Dawson, Michael C. 1994. *Behind the Mule: Race and Class in African-American Politics*. Princeton, NJ: Princeton University Press.

De Genova, Nicholas. 2005. *Working the Boundaries: Race, Space, and "Illegality" in Mexican Chicago*. Durham, NC: Duke University Press.

———. 2006. "Introduction: Latino and Asian Racial Formations at the Frontiers of U.S. Nationalism." In *Racial Transformations: Latinos and Asians Remaking the United States*, edited by Nicholas De Genova, pp. 1–20. Durham, NC: Duke University Press.

de Graauw, Els. 2008. "The Role of Nonprofit Organizations in Structuring Immigrant Political Incorporation in Urban America." In *Civic Hopes and Political Realities: Immigrants, Community Organizations, and Political Engagement*, edited by S. Karthick Ramakrishnan and Irene Bloemraad, pp. 323–50. New York: Russell Sage.

de la Garza, Rodolfo O., Angelo Falcón, and F. Chris García. 1996. "Will the Real Americans Please Stand Up: Anglo and Mexican-American Support of Core American Political Values." *American Journal of Political Science* 40(2): 335–51.

de la Garza, Rodolfo O., and John A. Garcia. 1992. *Latino Voices: Mexican, Puerto Rican, and Cuban Perspectives on American Politics*. Boulder, CO: Westview Press.

de la Garza, Rodolfo O., Martha Menchaca, and Louis DeSipio, eds. 1994. *Barrio Ballots: Latino Politics in the 1990 Elections*. Boulder, CO: Westview Press.

Delpar, Helen. 2008. "Alabama." In *Latino America: A State-by-State Encyclopedia*, edited by Mark Overmyer-Velásquez, pp. 1–12. Westport, CT: Greenwood Press.

Denning, Shea Riggsbee. 2009. "The Impact of North Carolina Driver's License Requirements and the REAL ID Act of 2005 on Unauthorized Immigrants." *Popular Government* 74(3): Online supplement (1–14). http://www.sog.unc.edu/popgov (last accessed May 11, 2010).

Denton, Nancy, and Jacqueline Villarrubia. 2007. "New Immigrants in the Hudson Valley: Newburgh and Poughkeepsie." Paper presented at the Annual Meeting of the Eastern Sociological Society, Philadelphia (March 15–18).

DeParle, Jason. 2009. "Downward Path Illustrates Concern About Immigrants' Children." *New York Times* (April 19).

Derose, Kathryn Pitkin, José J. Escarce, and Nicole Lurie. 2007. "Immigrants and Health Care: Sources of Vulnerability." *Health Affairs* 26(5): 1258–68.

Derthick, Martha. 1979. *Policymaking for Social Security*. Washington, DC: Brookings Institution Press.

DeSipio, Louis. 2001. "Building America, One Person at a Time: Naturalization and Political Behavior of the Naturalized in Contemporary American Politics." In *E Pluribus Unum? Contemporary and Historical Perspectives on Immigrant Political Incorporation*, edited by Gary Gerstle and John H. Mollenkopf, pp. 67–106. New York: Russell Sage.

———. 2006. "Latino Civic and Political Participation." In *Hispanics and the Future of America*, edited by Marta Tienda and Faith Mitchell, pp. 447–79. Washington, DC: National Academies Press.

Diamond, Jeff. 1998. "African-American Attitudes Towards United States Immigration Policy." *International Migration Review* 32(2): 451–70.

Donato, Katharine M. 2009. "Fishing Without a License: Effects of Immigration Enforcement in New U.S. Immigrant Destinations." Paper presented at the Annual Meeting of the American Sociological Association, San Francisco (August 8–11).

Donato, Katharine M., and Carl L. Bankston. 2008. "The Origins of Employer Demand for Immigrants in a New Destination: The Salience of Soft Skills in a Volatile Economy." In *New Faces in New Places: The Changing Geography of American Immigration*, edited by Douglas Massey, pp. 124–48. New York: Russell Sage.

Donato, Katharine M., and Dawn T. Robinson. 2001. "Immigration and the Organization of the Onshore Oil Industry: Southern Louisiana in the Late 1990s." In *Latino Workers in the Contemporary South*, edited by Arthur D. Murphy, Colleen Blanchard, and Jennifer A. Hill, pp. 105–13. Athens: University of Georgia Press.

Donato, Katharine M., Melissa Stainback, and Carl L. Bankston. 2005. "The Economic Incorporation of Mexican Immigrants in Southern Louisiana: A Tale of Two Cities." In *New Destinations: Mexican Immigration to the United States*, edited by Victor Zúñiga and Rubén Hernández-León, pp. 76–100. New York: Russell Sage.

Donato, Katharine M., Charles M. Tolbert, Alfred Nucci, and Yukio Kawano. 2007. "Recent Immigrant Settlement in the Nonmetropolitan United States: Evidence from Internal Census Data." *Rural Sociology* 72(4): 537–59.

———. 2008. "Changing Faces/Changing Places: The Emergence of Non-Metropolitan Immigrant Gateways." In *New Faces in New Places: The Changing Geography of American Immigration*, edited by Douglas S. Massey, pp. 75–98. New York: Russell Sage.

Drabenstott, Mark, Mark Henry, and Kristin Mitchell. 1999. "Where Have All the Packing Plants Gone? The New Meat Geography in Rural America." *Economic Review* 84(3): 65–82.

Drever, Anita. 2006. "New Neighbors in Dixie: The Community Impacts of Latino Migration to Tennessee." In *Latinos in the New South: Transformations of Place*, edited by Heather A. Smith and Owen J. Furuseth, pp. 19–36. Aldershot, UK: Ashgate Press.

———. 2009. "Tennessee: A New Destination for Latina and Latino Immigrants." In *Global Connections & Local Receptions: New Latino Immigration to the Southeastern United States*, edited by Fran Ansley and Jon Shefner, pp. 65–85. Knoxville: University of Tennessee Press.

DuBard, C. Annette, and Mark W. Massing. 2007. "Trends in Emergency Medicaid Expenditures for Recent and Undocumented Immigrants." *Journal of the American Medical Association* 297(10): 1085–92.

Duchón, Deborah A., and Arthur D. Murphy. 2001. "Introduction: From *Patrones* and *Caciques* to Good Ole Boys." In *Latino Workers in the Contemporary South*, edited by Arthur D. Murphy, Colleen Blanchard, and Jennifer A. Hill, pp. 1–9. Athens: University of Georgia Press.

Duncan, Cynthia M. 1999. *Worlds Apart: Why Poverty Persists in Rural America*. New Haven, CT: Yale University Press.

Dunn, Timothy J., Ana María Aragonés, and George Shivers. 2005. "Recent Mexican Immigration in the Rural Delmarva Peninsula: Human Rights Versus Citizenship Rights in a Local Context." In *New Destinations: Mexican Immigration to the United States*, edited by Victor Zúñiga and Rubén Hernández-León, pp. 155–83. New York: Russell Sage.

Durand, Jorge, Douglas S. Massey, and Chiara Capoferro. 2005. "The New Geography of Mexican Immigration." In *New Destinations: Mexican Immigration to the United States*, edited by Victor Zúñiga and Rubén Hernández-León, pp. 1–20. New York: Russell Sage.

Durand, Jorge, Edward Telles, and Jennifer Flashman. 2006. "The Demographic Foundations of the Latino Population." In *Hispanics and the Future of America*, edited by Marta Tienda and Faith Mitchell, pp. 66–99. Washington, DC: National Academies Press.

Dzidzienyo, Anani, and Suzanne Oboler, eds. 2005. *Neither Enemies Nor Friends: Latinos, Blacks, Afro-Latinos*. New York: Palgrave Macmillan.

Easterbrook, Michael. 2004a. "Crowds Crush DMV Offices." *News and Observer* (Raleigh, NC; January 24).

———. 2004b. "A New Border to Cross: Immigrants Line Up to Get Driver Licenses While Mexican Identification Card Is Still Valid." *News and Observer* (Raleigh, NC; January 17).

Easterbrook, Michael, and Jean P. Fisher. 2006. "Health Care Costly for Immigrants." (Fourth in the Series on "Illegal Immigration—Who Profits, Who Pays?") *News and Observer* (Raleigh, NC; March 1).

Eckes, Alfred E. 2005. "The South and Economic Globalization, 1950 to the Future." In *Globalization and the American South*, edited by James C. Cobb and William Stueck, pp. 36–55. Athens: University of Georgia Press.

Elliott, James R., and Marcel Ionescu. 2003. "Postwar Immigration to the Deep South Triad: What Can a Peripheral Region Tell Us About Immigrant Settlement and Employment?" *Sociological Spectrum* 23(2): 159–80.

Ellis, Mark, and Gunnar Almgren. 2009. "Local Contexts of Immigrant and Second-Generation Integration in the United States." *Journal of Ethnic and Migration Studies* 35(7): 1059–76.

Ellis, Mark, and Jamie Goodwin-White. 2006. "1.5 Generation Internal Migration in the U.S.: Dispersion from States of Immigration?" *International Migration Review* 40(4): 899–926.

Emery, Marla R., Clare Ginger, and Jim Chamberlain. 2006. "Migrants, Markets, and the Transformation of Natural Resources Management: Galax Harvesting in Western North Carolina." In *Latinos in the South: Transformations of Place*, edited by Heather A. Smith and Owen J. Furuseth, pp. 69–88. Aldershot, UK: Ashgate Press.

Engstrom, James. 2001. "Industry and Immigration in Dalton, Georgia." In *Latino Workers in the Contemporary South*, edited by Arthur D. Murphy, Colleen Blanchard, and Jennifer A. Hill, pp. 44–56. Athens: University of Georgia Press.

Erickson, Ken C. 1994. "Guys in White Hats: Short-Term Participant Observation Among Beef-Processing Workers and Managers." In *Newcomers in the Workplace: Immigrants and the Restructuring of the U.S. Economy*, edited by Louise Lamphere, Alex Stepick, and Guillermo Grenier, pp. 78–98. Philadelphia: Temple University Press.

Erie, Stephen. 1988. *Rainbow's End: Irish-Americans and the Dilemmas of Urban Machine Politics, 1840–1984*. Berkeley: University of California Press.

Erwin, Deborah O. 2003. "An Ethnographic Description of Latino Immigration in Rural Arkansas: Intergroup Relations and Utilization of Healthcare Services." *Southern Rural Sociology* 19(1): 46–72.

Eschbach, Karl, Jacqueline Hagan, Nestor Rodríguez, Rubén Hernández-León, and Stanley Bailey. 1999. "Death at the Border." *International Migration Review* 33(2): 430–54.

Espenshade, Thomas J. 1990. "Undocumented Migration to the United States: Evidence from a Repeated Trials Model." In *Undocumented Migration to the United States:*

IRCA and the Experience of the 1980s, edited by Frank D. Bean, Barry Edmonston, and Jeffrey S. Passel, pp. 159–81. Washington, DC: Urban Institute Press.

Espenshade, Thomas J., and Charles A. Calhoun. 1993. "An Analysis of Public Opinion Toward Undocumented Immigration." *Population Research and Policy Review* 12(3): 189–224.

Espenshade, Thomas J., and Katherine Hempstead. 1996. "Contemporary American Attitudes Toward U.S. Immigration." *International Migration Review* 30(2): 535–70.

Fabienke, David. 2007. "Beyond the Racial Divide: Perceptions of Minority Residents on Coalition Building in South Los Angeles." Los Angeles: Tomás Rivera Policy Institute (June).

Falcón, Angelo. 1988. "Black and Latino Politics in New York City: Race and Ethnicity in a Changing Urban Context." In *Latinos and the Political System*, edited by F. Chris Garcia, pp. 171–94. Notre Dame, IN: Notre Dame University Press.

Falk, William W., and Linda M. Lobao. 2003. "Who Benefits from Economic Restructuring? Lessons from the Past, Challenges for the Future." In *Challenges for Rural America in the Twenty-First Century*, edited by David L. Brown and Louis E. Swanson, pp. 152–65. University Park: Pennsylvania State University Press.

Fennelly, Katherine. 2005. "Latinos, Africans, and Asians in the North Star State: Immigrant Communities in Minnesota." In *Beyond the Gateway: Immigrants in a Changing America*, edited by Elzbieta M. Gozdziak and Susan F. Martin, pp. 111–36. Lanham, MD: Lexington Books.

———. 2006. "State and Local Policy Responses to Immigration in Minnesota." In *Immigration's New Frontiers: Experiences from the Emerging Gateway States*, edited by Greg Anrig and Tova Andrea Wang, pp. 101–42. New York: Century Foundation Press.

———. 2008. "Prejudice Toward Immigrants in the Midwest." In *New Faces in New Places: The Changing Geography of American Immigration*, edited by Douglas S. Massey, pp. 151–78. New York: Russell Sage.

Fennelly, Katherine, and Christopher M. Federico. 2008. "Rural Residence as a Determinant of Attitudes Toward US Immigration Policy." *International Migration* 46(1): 151–90.

Fennelly, Katherine, and Helga Leitner. 2002. "How the Food Processing Industry Is Diversifying Rural Minnesota." JSRI Working Paper No. 59. East Lansing: Julian Samora Research Institute, Michigan State University.

Fennelly, Katherine, and Myron Orfield. 2008. "Impediments to the Integration of Immigrants: A Case Study in the Twin Cities." In *Twenty-First Century Gateways: Immigrant Integration in Suburban America*, edited by Audrey Singer, Susan W. Hardwick, and Caroline B. Brettell, pp. 200–224. Washington, DC: Brookings Institution Press.

Fink, Deborah. 1998. *Cutting into the Meatpacking Line: Workers and Change in the Rural Midwest*. Chapel Hill: University of North Carolina Press.

Fink, Leon. 2003. *The Maya of Morganton: Work and Community in the Nuevo New South*. Chapel Hill: University of North Carolina Press.

Fischer, Mary J., and Marta Tienda. 2006. "Redrawing Spatial Color Lines: Hispanic Metropolitan Dispersal, Segregation, and Economic Opportunity." In *Hispanics and the Future of America*, pp. 100–137. Washington, DC: National Academies Press.

Fitzgerald, David. 2011. "Mexican Migration and the Law." In *Beyond* La Frontera: *The History of US-Mexico Migration*, edited by Mark Overmyer-Velásquez. New York: Oxford University Press.

Fix, Michael, ed. 2007. *Securing the Future: US Immigrant Integration Policy—A Reader*. Washington, DC: Migration Policy Institute.

Foley, Neil. 1997. *The White Scourge: Mexicans, Blacks, and Poor Whites in Texas Cotton Culture*. Berkeley: University of California Press.

Forman, Tyrone, Carla Goar, and Amanda Lewis. 2002. "Neither Black Nor White? An Empirical Test of the Latin Americanization Thesis." *Race & Society* 5: 65–84.

Fossett, Mark A., and K. Jill Kiecolt. 1989. "The Relative Size of Minority Populations and White Racial Attitudes." *Social Science Quarterly* 70(4): 820–35.

Fox, Cybelle. 2004. "The Changing Color of Welfare: How Whites' Attitudes Toward Latinos Influence Support for Welfare." *American Journal of Sociology* 110(3): 580–625.

———. 2007. "The Boundaries of Social Citizenship: Race, Immigration, and the American Welfare State, 1900–1950." Ph.D. diss., Departments of Sociology and Social Policy, Harvard University, Cambridge, MA.

———. 2009. "A New Nativism or an American Tradition: Federal Citizenship and Legal Status Restrictions for Medicaid and Welfare." Paper presented at the 2009 Meeting of the Robert Wood Johnson Foundation Scholars in Health Policy Program, Aspen, CO (May 27–30).

Fraga, Luis R., John A. Garcia, Rodney E. Hero, Michael Jones-Correa, Valerie Martínez-Ebers, and Gary M. Segura. 2010. *Latino Lives in America: Making It Home*. Philadelphia: Temple University Press.

Fremstad, Shawn, and Laura Cox. 2004. "Covering New Americans: A Review of Federal and States Policies Related to Immigrants' Eligibility and Access to Publicly Funded Health Insurance." Washington, DC: Kaiser Commission on Medicaid and the Uninsured (November).

Friedberg, Rachel M., and Jennifer Hunt. 1999. "Immigration and the Receiving Economy." In *The Handbook of International Migration: The American Experience*, edited by Charles Hirschman, Philip Kasinitz, and Josh DeWind, pp. 342–59. New York: Russell Sage.

Friedland, William H. 2002. "Agriculture and Rurality: Beginning the 'Final Separation'?" *Rural Sociology* 67(3): 350–71.

Fry, Richard. 2008. "Latino Settlement in the New Century." Washington, DC: Pew Hispanic Center (October 23).

Furuseth, Owen J., and Heather A. Smith. 2006. "From Winn-Dixie to Tiendas: The Remaking of the New South." In *Latinos in the New South: Transformations of Place*, edited by Heather A. Smith and Owen J. Furuseth, pp. 1–18. Aldershot, UK: Ashgate Press.

Fussell, Elizabeth. 2009. "Hurricane Chasers in New Orleans: Latino Immigrants as a Source of a Rapid Response Labor Force." *Hispanic Journal of Behavioral Sciences* 31(3): 375–94.

Gans, Herbert. 1992. "Second-Generation Decline: Scenarios for the Economic and Ethnic Futures of the Post-1965 American Immigrants." *Ethnic and Racial Studies* 15(2): 173–92.

———. 1999. "The Possibility of a New Racial Hierarchy in the Twenty-First-Century United States." In *The Cultural Territories of Race: Black and White Boundaries*, edited by Michèle Lamont, pp. 371–89. Chicago: University of Chicago Press.

García, Richard A. 1991. *Rise of the Mexican American Middle Class: San Antonio, 1929–1941*. College Station, TX: Texas A&M University Press.

Gardner, Trevor, and Aarti Kohli. 2009. "The C.A.P. Effect: Racial Profiling in the ICE Criminal Alien Program." Policy Brief. Berkeley: Chief Justice Earl Warren Institute on Race, Ethnicity & Diversity and University of California at Berkeley Law School.

Gartner, Erin. 2007a. "Hog-Plant Arrests Scare Many Away." *News and Observer* (Raleigh, NC; January 26).

———. 2007b. "Slaughterhouse Loses 300 Workers." *News and Observer* (Raleigh, NC; February 20).

Gay, Claudine. 2006. "Seeing Difference: The Effect of Economic Disparity on Black Attitudes Toward Latinos." *American Journal of Political Science* 50(4): 982–97.

Gelatt, Julia, and Michael Fix. 2007. "Federal Spending on the Immigrant Families' Integration." In *Securing the Future: US Immigrant Integration Policy—A Reader*, edited by Michael Fix, pp. 61–80. Washington, DC: Migration Policy Institute.

Gerstle, Gary, and John H. Mollenkopf. 2001. "The Political Incorporation of Immigrants, Then and Now." In *E Pluribus Unum? Contemporary and Historical Perspectives on Immigrant Political Incorporation*, edited by Gary Gerstle and John H. Mollenkopf, pp. 1–30. New York: Russell Sage.

Gill, Hannah, Mai Thi Nguyen, Katherine Lewis Parker, and Deborah Weissman. 2009. "Legal and Social Perspectives on Local Enforcement of Immigration Under the 287(g) Program." *Popular Government* 74(3): 2–18.

Gimpel, James G., and James R. Edwards. 1999. *The Congressional Politics of Immigration Reform*. Boston: Allyn and Bacon.

Giovagnoli, Mary. 2010. "Striking While the Iron Is Hot: Drop in Unauthorized Immigrant Population a Good Time for Immigration Reform." *Immigration Impact* (February 11).

Glaser, James M. 1994. "Back to the Black Belt: Racial Environment and White Racial Attitudes in the South." *Journal of Politics* 56(1): 21–41.

Gleeson, Shannon Marie. 2008. "The Intersection of Legal Status and Stratification: The Paradox of Immigration Law and Labor Protections in the United States." Ph.D. diss., Departments of Sociology and Demography, University of California at Berkeley.

Goldman, Dana P., James P. Smith, and Neeraj Sood. 2005. "Legal Status and Health Insurance Among Immigrants." *Health Affairs* 24(6): 1640–53.

———. 2006. "Immigrants and the Cost of Medical Care." *Health Affairs* 25(6): 1700–1711.

Gonzales, Roberto G. 2007. "Wasted Talent and Broken Dreams: The Lost Potential of Undocumented Students." *Immigration Policy in Focus* 5(3): 1–11.

———. 2009. "Young Lives on Hold: The College Dreams of Undocumented Students." New York: College Board Advocacy (April).

Gonzales, Roberto G., and Shannon Gleeson. 2009. "Membership, Opportunity, and Claims Making: Undocumented Immigrants Negotiating Bureaucracies." Paper presented at the Annual Meeting of the Law and Society Association, Denver, CO (May 31).

Gordon, Jennifer, and R. A. Lenhardt. 2008. "Rethinking Work and Citizenship." *UCLA Law Review* 55: 1161–1238.

Gouveia, Lourdes. 2006. "Nebraska's Responses to Immigration." In *Immigration's New Frontiers: Experiences from the Emerging Gateway States*, edited by Greg Anrig and Tova Andrea Wang, pp. 143–98. New York: Century Foundation Press.

Gouveia, Lourdes, Miguel A. Carranza, and Jasney Cogua. 2005. "The Great Plains Migration: Mexicanos and Latinos in Nebraska." In *New Destinations: Mexican Immigration to the United States*, edited by Victor Zúñiga and Rubén Hernández-León, pp. 23–49. New York: Russell Sage.

Gouveia, Lourdes, and Mary Ann Powell. 2007. "Second-Generation Latinos in Nebraska: A First Look." *Migration Information Source* (January).

Gouveia, Lourdes, and Rogelio Saenz. 2000. "Global Forces and Latino Population Growth in the Midwest: A Regional and Subregional Analysis." *Great Plains Research* 10: 305–28.

Gouveia, Lourdes, and Donald D. Stull. 1997. "Latino Immigrants, Meatpacking, and Rural Communities: A Case Study of Lexington, Nebraska." Working Paper No. 59. East Lansing: Julian Samora Research Institute, Michigan State University.

Gozdziak, Elzbieta M., and Micah N. Bump. 2004. "Poultry, Apples, and New Immigrants in the Rural Communities of the Shenandoah Valley: An Ethnographic Case Study." *International Migration* 42(1): 149–64.

———. 2008. *New Immigrants, Changing Communities: Best Practices for a Better America*. Lanham, MD: Lexington Books.

Gozdziak, Elzbieta M., and Susan F. Martin. 2005. "Challenges for the Future." In *Beyond the Gateway: Immigrants in a Changing America*, edited by Elzbieta M. Gozdziak and Susan F. Martin, pp. 277–83. Lanham, MD: Lexington Books.

Greenbaum, Susan. 1998. "Urban Immigrants in the South: Recent Data and a Historical Case Study." In *Cultural Diversity in the U.S. South: Anthropological Contributions to a Region in Transition*, edited by Carole E. Hill and Patricia D. Beaver, pp. 144–63. Athens: University of Georgia Press.

Grey, Mark A. 1995. "Pork, Poultry, and Newcomers in Storm Lake, Iowa." In *Any Way You*

Cut It: Meat Processing and Small Town America, edited by Donald D. Stull, Michael J. Broadway, and David Griffith, pp. 109–28. Lawrence: University Press of Kansas.

———. 1999. "Immigrants, Migration, and Worker Turnover at the Hog Pride Pork Packing Plant." *Human Organization* 58(1): 16–27.

———. 2006. "State and Local Immigration Policy in Iowa." In *Immigration's New Frontiers: Experiences from the Emerging Gateway States*, edited by Greg Anrig and Tova Andrea Wang, pp. 33–66. New York: Century Foundation Press.

Grey, Mark A., and Anne C. Woodrick. 2005. "'Latinos Have Revitalized Our Community': Mexican Migration and Anglo Responses in Marshalltown, Iowa." In *New Destinations: Mexican Immigration to the United States*, edited by Victor Zúñiga and Rubén Hernández-León, pp. 133–54. New York: Russell Sage.

Griffin, Larry J. 2006. "The American South and Self." *Southern Cultures* 12(3): 6–28.

Griffin, Larry J., Ranae J. Evenson, and Ashley B. Thompson. 2005. "Southerners All?" *Southern Cultures* 11(1): 6–25.

Griffin, Larry J., and Katherine McFarland. 2007. "'In My Heart I'm an American': Regional Attitudes and American Identity." *Southern Cultures* 13(4): 119–37.

Griffith, David. 1993. *Jones's Minimal: Low-Wage Labor in the United States*. Albany: State University of New York Press.

———. 1995a. "*Hay Trabajo*: Poultry Processing, Rural Industrialization, and the Latinization of Low-Wage Labor." In *Any Way You Cut It: Meat Processing and Small Town America*, edited by Donald D. Stull, Michael J. Broadway, and David Griffith, pp. 129–51. Lawrence: University Press of Kansas.

———. 1995b. "New Immigrants in an Old Industry: Blue Crab Processing in Pamlico County, North Carolina." In *Any Way You Cut It: Meat Processing and Small Town America*, edited by Donald D. Stull, Michael J. Broadway, and David Griffith, pp. 153–86. Lawrence: University Press of Kansas.

———. 2005. "Rural Industry and Mexican Immigration and Settlement in North Carolina." In *New Destinations: Mexican Immigration to the United States*, edited by Victor Zúñiga and Rubén Hernández-León, pp. 50–75. New York: Russell Sage.

———. 2006. *American Guestworkers: Jamaicans and Mexicans in the U.S. Labor Market*. University Park: Pennsylvania State University Press.

———. 2008. "New Midwesterners, New Southerners: Immigration Experiences in Four Rural American Settings." In *New Faces in New Places: The Changing Geography of American Immigration*, edited by Douglas S. Massey, pp. 179–210. New York: Russell Sage.

Griffith, David, Ed Kissam, Jeronimo Camposeco, Anna Garcia, Max Pfeffer, David Runsten, and Manuel Valdés Pizzini. 1995. *Working Poor: Farmworkers in the United States*. Philadelphia: Temple University Press.

Griffith, David, Alex Stepick, Karen Richman, Guillermo Grenier, Ed Kissam, Allan Burns, and Jeronimo Camposeco. 2001. "Another Day in the Diaspora: Changing Ethnic Landscapes in South Florida." In *Latino Workers in the Contemporary South*, edited by Arthur D. Murphy, Colleen Blanchard, and Jennifer A. Hill, pp. 82–92. Athens: University of Georgia Press.

Guinier, Lani, and Gerald Torres. 2002. *The Miner's Canary: Enlisting Race, Resisting Power, Transforming Democracy*. Cambridge, MA: Harvard University Press.

Guiraudon, Virginie. 2000. "The Marshallian Triptych Reordered: The Role of Courts and Bureaucracies in Furthering Migrants' Social Rights." In *Immigration and Welfare: Challenging the Borders of the Welfare State*, edited by Michael Bommes and Andrew Geddes, pp. 72–89. London: Routledge.

Guthey, Greig. 2001. "Mexican Places in Southern Spaces: Globalization, Work, and Daily Life in and Around the North Georgia Poultry Industry." In *Latino Workers in the Contemporary South*, edited by Arthur D. Murphy, Colleen Blanchard, and Jennifer A. Hill, pp. 57–67. Athens: University of Georgia Press.

Guthrie-Shimizu, Sayuri. 2005. "From Southeast Asia to the American Southeast: Japanese Business Meets the Sun Belt South." In *Globalization and the American South*, edited by James C. Cobb and William Stueck, pp. 135–63. Athens: University of Georgia Press.

Hagan, Jacqueline María. 1994. *Deciding to Be Legal: A Maya Community in Houston*. Philadelphia: Temple University Press.

Hagan, Jacqueline María, Nichola Lowe, and Christian Quingla. 2009. "Skills on the Move: A Study of Immigrant Social Mobility in the U.S. Construction Industry." Paper presented at the Labor Markets and Workplace Dynamics in New Destinations of Mexican and Latino Immigration Workshop, University of California at Los Angeles, Los Angeles (October 23).

Hagan, Jacqueline, Nestor Rodriguez, Randy Capps, and Kabiri Nika. 2003. "The Effects of Recent Welfare and Immigration Reforms on Immigrants' Access to Health Care." *International Migration Review* 37(2): 444–63.

Hakim, Danny. 2007. "Spitzer Tries New Tack on Immigrant Licenses." *New York Times* (October 28).

Hall, Bob. 1995. "The Kill Line: Facts of Life, Proposals for Change." In *Any Way You Cut It: Meat Processing and Small Town America*, edited by Donald D. Stull, Michael J. Broadway, and David Griffith, pp. 213–30. Lawrence: University Press of Kansas.

Hall, Kerry, Ames Alexander, and Franco Ordoñez. 2008. "The Cruelest Cuts: The Human Cost of Bringing Poultry to Your Table." *Charlotte Observer* (September 30).

Hamermesh, Daniel S., and Frank D. Bean, eds. 1998. *Help or Hindrance? The Economic Implications of Immigration for African Americans*. New York: Russell Sage.

Hansen, Art. 2005. "Black and White and the Other: International Immigration and Change in Metropolitan Atlanta." In *Beyond the Gateway: Immigrants in a Changing America*, edited by Elzbieta M. Gozdziak and Susan F. Martin, pp. 87–109. Lanham, MD: Lexington Books.

Hanson, Gordon. 2009. "The Economics and Policy of Illegal Immigration in the United States." Washington, DC: Migration Policy Institute (December).

Hartch, Todd. 2008. "Kentucky." In *Latino America: A State-by-State Encyclopedia*, edited by Mark Overmyer-Velásquez, pp. 335–45. Westport, CT: Greenwood Press.

Hartsoe, Steve. 2007. "Study: Emergency Health Care for Recent, Illegal Immigrants in N.C. Costly." *News and Observer* (Raleigh, NC; March 13).

Harwood, Edwin. 1986. "American Public Opinion and U.S. Immigration Policy." *Annals of the American Academy of Political and Social Science* 487: 201–12.

Haubert, Jeannie, and Elizabeth Fussell. 2006. "Explaining Pro-Immigrant Sentiment in the U.S.: Social Class, Cosmopolitanism, and Perceptions of Immigrants." *International Migration Review* 40(3): 489–507.

Hegeman, Roxana. 2007. "Undocumented Meatpackers Fear Raids." *Associated Press* (via *Yahoo News*; April 14).

Hernández-León, Rubén. 2004. "Restructuring at the Source: High-Skilled Industrial Migration from Mexico to the United States." *Work and Occupations* 31(4): 424–52.

———. 2008. *Metropolitan Migrants: The Migration of Urban Mexicans to the United States*. Berkeley: University of California Press.

———. 2010. "From Boomtown to Bust Town: The Impact of the U.S. Economic Crisis on Guanajuatense and Mexican Migration to Dalton, Georgia." Paper presented at the Latin American Migration: Transnational Perspectives and Regional Realities Conference, Institute for the Study of the Americas, University of North Carolina at Chapel Hill (March 26–27).

Hernández-León, Rubén, and Victor Zúñiga. 2000. "'Making Carpet by the Mile': The Emergence of a Mexican Immigrant Community in an Industrial Region of the U.S. Historic South." *Social Science Quarterly* 81(1): 49–65.

———. 2003. "Mexican Immigrant Communities in the South and Social Capital: The Case of Dalton, Georgia." *Southern Rural Sociology* 19(1): 20–45.

———. 2005. "Appalachia Meets Aztlán: Mexican Immigration and Inter-Group Relations in Dalton, Georgia." In *New Destinations: Mexican Immigration in the United States*, edited by Victor Zúñiga and Rubén Hernández-León, pp. 244–73. New York: Russell Sage.

Heyman, Josiah McC., Guillermina Gina Núñez, and Victor Talavera. 2009. "Healthcare Access and Barriers for Unauthorized Immigrants in El Paso County, Texas." *Family and Community Health* 32(1): 4–21.

Hiemstra, Nancy. 2008. "Spatial Disjunctures and Division in the New West: Latino Immigration to Leadville, Colorado." In *Immigrants Outside Megalopolis: Ethnic Transformation in the Heartland*, edited by Richard C. Jones, pp. 89–114. Lanham, MD: Lexington Books.

Higham, John. 1955. *Strangers in the Land: Patterns of American Nativism, 1860–1925*. New Brunswick, NJ: Rutgers University Press.

Hill, Carole E., and Patricia D. Beaver, eds. 1998. *Cultural Diversity in the U.S. South: Anthropological Contributions to a Region in Transition*. Athens: University of Georgia.

Hincapié, Marielena. 2009. "Aquí Estamos y No Nos Vamos: Unintended Consequences of Current U.S. Immigration Law." In *Global Connections & Local Receptions: New Latino Immigration to the Southeastern United States*, edited by Fran Ansley and Jon Shefner, pp. 89–128. Knoxville: University of Tennessee Press.

Hirschman, Charles, and Douglas S. Massey. 2008. "Places and Peoples: The New American Mosaic." In *New Faces in New Places: The Changing Geography of American Immigration*, edited by Douglas S. Massey, pp. 1–21. New York: Russell Sage.

Hochschild, Jennifer. 2007. "Pluralism and Intergroup Relations." In *The New Americans: A Guide to Immigration Since 1965*, edited by Mary C. Waters and Reed Ueda with Helen B. Marrow, pp. 164–75. Cambridge, MA: Harvard University Press.

Hoefer, Michael, Nancy Rytina, and Bryan C. Baker. 2009. "Estimates of the Unauthorized Immigrant Population Residing in the United States: January 2008." Population Estimates. Washington, DC: Department of Homeland Security, Office of Immigration Statistics (February).

———. 2010. "Estimates of the Unauthorized Immigrant Population Residing in the United States: January 2009." Population Estimates. Washington, DC: Department of Homeland Security, Office of Immigration Statistics (January).

Holthouse, David. 2009. "The Year in Hate: Number of Hate Groups Tops 900." *Intelligence Report*. Montgomery, AL: Southern Poverty Law Center (Spring).

Holzer, Harry. 1996. *What Employers Want: Job Prospects for Less-Educated Workers*. New York: Russell Sage.

Hopkins, Daniel J. 2010. "Politicized Places: Explaining Where and When Immigrants Provoke Local Opposition." *American Political Science Review* 104(1): 40–60.

Huntington, Samuel P. 2004. "The Hispanic Challenge." *Foreign Policy* 141 (March/April): 30–45.

Ignatiev, Noel. 1995. *How the Irish Became White*. New York: Routledge.

Immigration Policy Center (IPC). 2009. "Earned Legalization: Repairing Our Broken Immigration System." Washington, DC: Immigration Policy Center (November 5).

Itzigsohn, José. 2004. "The Formation of Latino and Latina Panethnic Identities." In *Not Just Black and White: Historical and Contemporary Perspectives on Immigration, Race, and Ethnicity in the United States*, edited by Nancy Foner and George M. Frederickson, pp. 197–216. New York: Russell Sage.

Jackson, Henry C. 2008. "Town Wonders If It's Next to Face Immigration Raid." *News and Observer* (Raleigh, NC; August 26).

Jacobson, Matthew Frye. 1998. *Whiteness of a Different Color: European Immigrants and the Alchemy of Race*. Cambridge, MA: Harvard University Press.

Jaramillo, Paola Andrea. 2007. "Hispana denuncia discriminación en supermercado." *La Conexión* (Raleigh, NC; August 13).

Jencks, Christopher, Lauri Perman, and Lee Rainwater. 1988. "What Is a Good Job? A New Measure of Labor-Market Success." *American Journal of Sociology* 93(6): 1322–57.

Jennings, James, ed. 1997. *Race and Politics in the United States: New Challenges and Responses for Black Activism*. London: Verso.

Jensen, Leif, Jeffrey H. Cohen, Jacqueline Almeida Toribio, Gordon F. De Jong, and Leila Rodríguez. 2006. "Ethnic Identities, Language, and Economic Outcomes Among Dominicans in a New Destination." *Social Science Quarterly* 87(5): 1088–99.

Jensen, Leif, Diane K. McLaughlin, and Tim Slack. 2003. "Rural Poverty: The Persisting Challenge." In *Challenges for Rural America in the Twenty-First Century*, edited by David L. Brown and Louis E. Swanson, pp. 118–31. University Park: Pennsylvania State University Press.

Jiménez, Tomás R. 2008. "Mexican-Immigrant Replenishment and the Continuing Significance of Ethnicity and Race." *American Journal of Sociology* 113(6): 1527–67.

———. 2010. *Replenished Ethnicity: Mexican Americans, Mexican Immigrants, and Identity.* Berkeley: University of California Press.

Johansen, Ingrid M. 2009. "Legal Requirements on Access to Elementary and Secondary Public Education for Children of Immigrants." *Popular Government* 74(3): 35–39.

Johnson, James H., Karen D. Johnson-Webb, and Walter C. Farrell. 1999. "A Profile of Hispanic Newcomers to North Carolina." *Popular Government* 69(1): 2–13.

Johnson, James H., and John D. Kasarda. 2009. "Hispanic Newcomers to North Carolina: Demographic Characteristics and Economic Impact." In *Latino Immigrants and the Transformation of the U.S. South*, edited by Mary E. Odem and Elaine Lacy, pp. 70–90. Athens: University of Georgia Press.

Johnson, Kenneth M. 2003. "Unpredictable Directions of Rural Population Growth and Migration." In *Challenges for Rural America in the Twenty-First Century*, edited by David L. Brown and Louis E. Swanson, pp. 19–31. University Park: Pennsylvania State University Press.

Johnson, Mark. 2010. "Migrants Get Colleges' Nod." *News and Observer* (Raleigh, NC; March 20).

Johnson-Webb, Karen D. 2003. *Recruiting Hispanic Labor: Immigrants in Non-Traditional Areas.* New York: LFB Scholarly.

Jones, Jennifer A. M. 2010. "Soul and Salsa: Social Exclusion and Linked Fate Among Mexicans and African-Americans in the South." Paper presented at the Annual Meeting of the American Sociological Association, Atlanta, GA (August 14–17).

Jones, Richard C., ed. 2008. *Immigrants Outside Megalopolis: Ethnic Transformation in the Heartland.* Lanham, MD: Lexington Books.

Jones-Correa, Michael. 1998. *Between Two Nations: The Political Predicament of Latinos in New York City.* Ithaca, NY: Cornell University Press.

———. 2005a. "Bringing Outsiders In: Questions of Immigrant Incorporation." In *The Politics of Democratic Inclusion*, edited by R. E. Hero and C. Wolbrecht, pp. 75–101. Philadelphia: Temple University Press.

———. 2005b. "The Bureaucratic Incorporation of Immigrants in Suburbia." Paper presented at the Immigration to the United States: New Sources and Destinations Conference, Russell Sage Foundation, New York (February 3–4).

———. 2008. "Race to the Top? The Politics of Immigrant Education in Suburbia." In

New Faces in New Places: The Changing Geography of American Immigration, edited by Douglas S. Massey, pp. 308–40. New York: Russell Sage.

———. 2009. "Commonalities, Competition and Linked Fate: Race Relations in New and Traditional Immigrant Receiving Areas." Paper presented at the Still Two Nations? The Resilience of the Color Line Conference, Duke University, Durham, NC (March 19–21).

Jones-Correa, Michael, and Katherine Fennelly. 2009. "Immigration Enforcement and Its Effects on Latino Lives in Two Rural North Carolina Communities." Paper presented at the Undocumented Hispanic Migration: On the Margins of a Dream Conference, Connecticut College, New London, CT (October 16–18).

Kammer, Jerry. 2009. "The 2006 Swift Raids: Assessing the Impact of Immigration Enforcement Actions at Six Facilities." Backgrounder. Washington, DC: Center for Immigration Studies (March).

Kandel, William A., and John Cromartie. 2004. "New Patterns of Hispanic Settlement in Rural America." Rural Development Research Report No. 99. Washington, DC: United States Department of Agriculture.

Kandel, William A., and Emilio A. Parrado. 2004. "Industrial Transformation and Hispanic Migration to the American South: The Case of the Poultry Industry." In *Hispanic Spaces, Latino Places: Community and Cultural Diversity in Contemporary America*, edited by Daniel D. Arreola, pp. 266–76. Austin: University of Texas Press.

———. 2006. "Hispanic Population Growth and Public School Response in Two New South Immigrant Destinations." In *The New South: Latinos and the Transformation of Place*, edited by Heather A. Smith and Owen J. Furuseth, pp. 111–34. Aldershot, UK: Ashgate Press.

Kanter, Rosabeth Moss. 1977. *Men and Women of the Corporation.* New York: Basic Books.

Kasarda, John D., and James H. Johnson. 2006. *The Economic Impact of the Hispanic Population on the State of North Carolina.* Chapel Hill, NC: Frank Hawkins Kenan Institute of Private Enterprise (January).

Kasinitz, Philip. 2004. "Race, Assimilation, and 'Second Generations,' Past and Present." In *Not Just Black and White: Historical and Contemporary Perspectives on Immigration, Race, and Ethnicity in the United States*, edited by Nancy Foner and George M. Frederickson, pp. 278–98. New York: Russell Sage.

Kasinitz, Philip, John H. Mollenkopf, and Mary C. Waters. 2002. "Becoming American/ Becoming New Yorkers: Immigrant Incorporation in a Majority Minority City." *International Migration Review* 36(4): 1020–36.

———, eds. 2004. *Becoming New Yorkers: Ethnographies of the New Second Generation.* New York: Russell Sage.

Kasinitz, Philip, John H. Mollenkopf, Mary C. Waters, and Jennifer Holdaway. 2008. *Inheriting the City: The Children of Immigrants Come of Age.* Cambridge, MA, and New York: Harvard University Press and Russell Sage.

Kaufmann, Karen. 2003. "Cracks in the Rainbow: Group Commonality as a Basis for Latino and African-American Political Coalitions." *Political Research Quarterly* 56(2): 199–210.

Kaushal, Neeraj. 2005. "New Immigrants' Location Choices: Magnets Without Welfare." *Journal of Labor Economics* 23(1): 59–80.

———. 2008. "In-State Tuition for the Undocumented: Education Effects on Mexican Young Adults." *Journal of Policy Analysis and Management* 27(4): 771–92.

Keiser, Lael R., and Joe Soss. 1998. "With Good Cause: Bureaucratic Discretion and the Politics of Child Support Enforcement." *American Journal of Political Science* 42(4): 1133–56.

Kelley, Daryl, and Carlos Chavez. 2004. "California Dreaming No More." *Los Angeles Times* (February 16).

Kerwin, Donald. 2007. "Immigrant Rights, Integration, and the Common Good." In *Securing the Future: US Immigrant Integration Policy—A Reader*, edited by Michael Fix, pp. 45–60. Washington, DC: Migration Policy Institute.

Key, V. O. 1984. *Southern Politics in State and Nation*. Knoxville: University of Tennessee Press (originally published New York: Knopf, 1949).

Kim, Claire Jean. 1999. "The Racial Triangulation of Asian Americans." *Politics and Society* 27(1): 105–38.

Kim, Nadia. 2004. "A View from Below: An Analysis of Korean Americans' Racial Attitudes." *Amerasia Journal* 30(1): 1–24.

Kirschenman, Joleen, and Kathryn M. Neckerman. 1991. "'We'd Love to Hire Them But . . .': The Meaning of Race for Employers." In *The Urban Underclass*, edited by Christopher Jencks and Paul Peterson, pp. 203–34. Washington, DC: Brookings Institution.

Kochhar, Rakesh. 2003. "Jobs Lost, Jobs Gained: The Latino Experience in Recession and Recovery." Washington, DC: Pew Hispanic Center (October 7).

———. 2006. "Latino Labor Report, 2006: Strong Gains in Employment." Washington, DC: Pew Hispanic Center (September 27).

———. 2008a. "Latino Labor Report, 2008: Construction Reverses Job Growth for Latinos." Washington, DC: Pew Hispanic Center (June 4).

———. 2008b. "Sharp Decline in Income for Non-Citizen Immigrant Households, 2006–07." Washington, DC: Pew Hispanic Center (October 2).

Kochhar, Rakesh, Roberto Suro, and Sonya Tafoya. 2005. "The New Latino South: The Context and Consequences of Rapid Population Growth." Washington, DC: Pew Hispanic Center (July 26).

Kohut, Andrew, Scott Keeter, Carroll Doherty, Roberto Suro, and Gabriel Escobar. 2006. "America's Immigration Quandary: No Consensus on Immigration Problem or Proposed Fixes." Washington, DC: Pew Research Center for the People and the Press and Pew Hispanic Center.

Konet, Dawn. 2007. "Unauthorized Youths and Higher Education: The Ongoing Debate." *Migration Information Source* (September).

Krissman, Fred. 2000. "Immigrant Labor Recruitment: U.S. Agribusiness and Undocumented Migration from Mexico." In *Immigration Research for a New Century: Multidisciplinary Perspectives*, edited by Nancy Foner, Rubén G. Rumbaut, and Steven Gold, pp. 277–300. New York: Russell Sage.

Ku, Leighton, and Demetrios G. Papademetriou. 2007. "Access to Health Care and Health Insurance: Immigrants and Immigration." In *Securing the Future: US Immigrant Integration Policy*, edited by Michael Fix, pp. 83–106. Washington, DC: Migration Policy Institute.

Kurotani, Sawa. 2005. "The South Meets the East: Japanese Professionals in North Carolina's Research Triangle." In *The American South in a Global World*, edited by James L. Peacock, Harry L. Watson, and Carrie R. Matthews, pp. 175–91. Chapel Hill: University of North Carolina Press.

Lacy, Elaine. 2007. "Mexican Immigrants in South Carolina: A Profile." Columbia, SC: Consortium for Latino Immigration Studies, University of South Carolina at Columbia (January).

———. 2008a. "Immigrants in the Southeast: Public Perceptions and Integration." Columbia: Consortium for Latino Immigration Studies, University of South Carolina at Columbia (February 1).

———. 2008b. "South Carolina." In *Latino America: A State-by-State Encyclopedia*, edited by Mark Overmyer-Velásquez, pp. 715–29. Westport, CT: Greenwood Press.

———. 2009. "Cultural Enclaves and Transnational Ties: Mexican Immigration and Settlement in South Carolina." In *Latino Immigrants and the Transformation of the U.S. South*, edited by Mary E. Odem and Elaine Lacy, pp. 1–17. Athens: University of Georgia Press.

Lacy, Elaine, and Mary E. Odem. 2009. "Popular Attitudes and Public Policies: Southern Responses to Latino Immigration." In *Latino Immigrants and the Transformation of the U.S. South*, edited by Mary E. Odem and Elaine Lacy, pp. 143–64. Athens: University of Georgia Press.

Lamont, Michèle. 2000. *The Dignity of Working Men: Morality and the Boundaries of Race, Class, and Immigration*. New York: Russell Sage.

Lamphere, Louise. 2005. "Providers and Staff Respond to Medicaid Managed Care: The Unintended Consequences of Reform in New Mexico." *Medical Anthropology Quarterly* 19(1): 3–25.

Lattanzi Shutika, Deborah. 2005. "Bridging the Community: Nativism, Activism, and the Politics of Inclusion in a Mexican Settlement in Pennsylvania." In *New Destinations: Mexican Immigration to the United States*, edited by Victor Zúñiga and Rubén Hernández-León, pp. 103–32. New York: Russell Sage.

———. 2008. "The Ambivalent Welcome: Cinco de Mayo and the Symbolic Expression of Local Identity and Ethnic Relations." In *New Faces in New Places: The Changing*

Geography of American Immigration, edited by Douglas S. Massey, pp. 274–307. New York: Russell Sage.

Leach, Mark. 2004. "Linking the Past to the Present: Mexican Migration to New Destination States." Unpublished manuscript, University of California at Irvine.

Leach, Mark, and Frank D. Bean. 2008. "The Structure and Dynamics of Mexican Migration to New Destinations in the United States." In *New Faces in New Places: The Changing Geography of American Immigration*, edited by Douglas S. Massey, pp. 51–74. New York: Russell Sage.

LeDuff, Charlie. 2000. "At a Slaughterhouse, Some Things Never Die: Who Kills, Who Cuts, Who Bosses Can Depend on Race." (Sixth in the Series on "How Race Is Lived in America.") *New York Times* (June 16).

Lee, Jennifer. 2002. *Civility in the City: Blacks, Jews, and Koreans in Urban America*. Cambridge, MA: Harvard University Press.

Lee, Jennifer, and Frank D. Bean. 2004. "America's Changing Color Lines: Immigration, Race/Ethnicity, and Multiracial Identification." *Annual Review of Sociology* 30: 221–42.

———. 2007. "Reinventing the Color Line: Immigration and America's New Racial/Ethnic Divide." *Social Forces* 86(2): 1–26.

———. 2010. *The Diversity Paradox: Immigration and the Color Line in Twenty-First Century America*. New York: Russell Sage.

Lee, Riane L., and Susan T. Fiske. 2006. "Not an Out-Group, Not Yet an In-Group: Immigrants in the Stereotype Content Model." *International Journal of Intercultural Relations* 30(6): 751–68.

Levitt, Peggy, Wendy Cadge, Sara Curran, B. Nadya Jaworsky, and Jessica Hejtmanek. 2008. "The City as Context: Spaces of Reception in New Immigrant Destinations." Paper presented at the Annual Meeting of the American Sociological Association, Boston (September 1–4).

Lewis, Paul G., and S. Karthick Ramakrishnan. 2007. "Police Practices in Immigrant-Destination Cities: Political Control or Bureaucratic Professionalism?" *Urban Affairs Review* 42(6): 874–900.

Lichter, Daniel T., and Kenneth M. Johnson. 2006. "Emerging Rural Settlement Patterns and the Geographic Redistribution of America's New Immigrants." *Rural Sociology* 71(1): 109–31.

———. 2009. "Immigrant Gateways and Hispanic Migration to New Destinations." *International Migration Review* 43(3): 496–518.

Lien, Pei-te, M. Margaret Conway, and Janelle Wong. 2004. *The Politics of Asian Americans: Diversity and Community*. New York: Routledge.

Light, Ivan. 2006. *Deflecting Immigration: Networks, Markets, and Regulation in Los Angeles*. New York: Russell Sage.

Lindsay, James M., and Audrey Singer. 2002. "Local Police Should Not Do a Federal Job." *New York Times* (May 8).

Linnartz, Hans Christian. 2008. "Point of View: Misinterpreting 'Public Benefits.'" *News and Observer* (Raleigh, NC; May 15).

Lippard, Cameron D. 2008. *Building Inequality: Race, Ethnicity, and Immigration in the Atlanta Construction Industry.* Saarbrüken, Germany: Vdm Verlag Dr Müller.

Lippard, Cameron D., and Charles A. Gallagher, eds. 2011. *Being Brown in Dixie: Race, Ethnicity, and Latino Immigration in the New South.* Boulder, CO: First Forum Press.

Lipsky, Michael. 1980. *Street-Level Bureaucracy: Dilemmas of the Individual in Public Services.* New York: Russell Sage.

Loewen, James W. 1988. *The Mississippi Chinese: Between Black and White.* Long Grove, IL: Waveland Press (originally published Cambridge, MA: Harvard University Press, 1971).

Logan, John. 2001. "The New Ethnic Enclaves in America's Suburbs." Albany: Lewis Mumford Center for Comparative Urban and Regional Research, State University of New York at Albany.

Lopez, Mark Hugo, and Michael T. Light. 2009. "A Rising Share: Hispanics and Federal Crime." Washington, DC: Pew Hispanic Center (February 18).

Lopez, Mark Hugo, and Susan Minushkin. 2008. "2008 National Survey of Latinos: Hispanics See Their Situation in U.S. Deteriorating, Oppose Key Immigration Enforcement Measures." Washington, DC: Pew Hispanic Center (September 18).

López-Sanders, Laura. 2009. "Trapped at the Bottom: Racialized and Gendered Labor Queues in New Latino Destinations." Paper presented at the Annual Meeting of the American Sociological Association, San Francisco (August 8–11).

Lovato, Roberto. 2008. "Juan Crow in Georgia." *The Nation* (May 9).

Luebke, Paul. 2011. "Anti-Immigrant Legislation." In *Being Brown in Dixie: Race, Ethnicity, and Latino Immigration in the New South,* edited by Cameron D. Lippard and Charles A. Gallagher, pp. 261–78. Boulder, CO: First Forum Press.

Luna, Guadalupe T., and Fran Ansley. 2009. "Global Migrants and Access to Local Housing: Anti-Immigrant Backlash Hits Home." In *Global Connections & Local Receptions: New Latino Immigration to the Southeastern United States,* edited by Fran Ansley and Jon Shefner, pp. 155–93. Knoxville: University of Tennessee Press.

MacLeod, Jay. 1995. *Ain't No Makin' It: Aspirations and Attainment in a Low-Income Neighborhood.* Boulder, CO: Westview Press.

Maguire, Marti. 2006. "Schools Bear Burden of Immigration." (Second in the Series on "Illegal Immigration—Who Profits, Who Pays?") *News and Observer* (Raleigh, NC; February 27).

———. 2007. "No Language Barrier for IRS: Immigrants Pay, Too." *News and Observer* (Raleigh, NC; April 14).

Major Cities Chiefs [MCC] Immigration Committee Members. 2006. "Recommendations for Enforcement of Immigration Laws by Local Policy Agencies." Houston, TX (June). http://www.houstontx.gov/police/pdfs/mcc_position.pdf (last accessed April 22, 2010).

Maldonado, Marta Maria. 2009. "'It Is Their Nature to Do Menial Labor': The Racialization of 'Latino/a Workers' by Agricultural Employers." *Ethnic and Racial Studies* 36(2): 1017–36.

Mantero, José María. 2008. *Latinos and the U.S. South.* Westport, CT: Praeger.

Markham, James M. 2009. "Other Responsibilities of Sheriff's Offices in Relation to the State's Foreign-Born Population." *Popular Government* 74(3): 15.

Marrow, Helen B. 2005. "New Destinations and Immigrant Incorporation." *Perspectives on Politics* 3(4): 781–99.

———. 2006. "Not Just Conflict: Intergroup Relations in a Southern Poultry Processing Plant." Paper presented at the Annual Meeting of the American Sociological Association (ASA), Montreal, Canada (August 11–14).

———. 2008. "Hispanic Immigration, Black Population Size, and Intergroup Relations in the Rural and Small-Town U.S. South." In *New Faces in New Places: The Changing Geography of American Immigration,* edited by Douglas S. Massey, pp. 211–48. New York: Russell Sage.

———. 2009a. "Immigrant Bureaucratic Incorporation: The Dual Roles of Professional Missions and Government Policies." *American Sociological Review* 74(5): 756–76.

———. 2009b. "New Immigrant Destinations and the American Colour Line." *Ethnic and Racial Studies* 36(2): 1137–57.

———. 2011a. "Intergroup Relations: Reconceptualizing Discrimination and Hierarchy." In *Being Brown in Dixie: Race, Ethnicity, and Latino Immigration in the New South,* edited by Cameron D. Lippard and Charles A. Gallagher, pp. 53–76. Boulder, CO: First Forum Press.

———. 2011b. "Race and the New Southern Migration, 1986 to the present." In *Beyond* La Frontera: *The History of Mexico-US Migration,* edited by Mark Overmyer-Velázquez. New York: Oxford University Press.

Marshall, Khiya J., Ximena Urrutia-Rojas, Francisco Soto Mas, and Claudia Coggin. 2005. "Health Status and Access to Health Care of Documented and Undocumented Immigrant Latino Women." *Health Care for Women International* 26(10): 916–36.

Marshall, T. H. 1964. "Citizenship and Social Class." In *Class, Citizenship, and Social Development,* edited by T. H. Marshall, pp. 65–122. Garden City, NY: Doubleday.

Massey, Douglas S. 2007. *Categorically Unequal: The American Stratification System.* New York: Russell Sage.

———. 2008a. "Assimilation in a New Geography." In *New Faces in New Places: The Changing Geography of American Immigration,* edited by Douglas S. Massey, pp. 343–353. New York: Russell Sage.

———, ed. 2008b. *New Faces in New Places: The Changing Geography of American Immigration.* New York: Russell Sage.

———. 2011. "The Past and Future of Mexico-U.S. Migration" In *Beyond* La Frontera: *The History of Mexico-US Migration,* edited by Mark Overmyer-Velázquez. New York: Oxford University Press.

Massey, Douglas S., and Chiara Capoferro. 2008. "The Geographic Diversification of American Immigration." In *New Faces in New Places: The Changing Geography of American Immigration*, edited by Douglas S. Massey, pp. 25–50. New York: Russell Sage.

Massey, Douglas S., Jorge Durand, and Nolan J. Malone. 2002. *Beyond Smoke and Mirrors: Mexican Immigration in an Era of Economic Integration*. New York: Russell Sage.

Massey, Douglas S., and Magaly Sánchez R. 2010. *Brokered Boundaries: Immigrant Identity in Anti-Immigrant Times*. New York: Russell Sage.

Maynard-Moody, Steven, and Michael Musheno. 2003. *Cops, Teachers, Counselors: Stories from the Front Lines of Public Service*. Ann Arbor: University of Michigan Press.

Mayo, Nikie. 2007. "County Supports 'Roundup' of Illegal Aliens: Richardson Calls for More Narcotics Officers." *Washington Daily Times* (Beaufort County, NC; March 22).

McClain, Paula D. 2006. "North Carolina's Response to Latino Immigrants and Immigration." In *Immigration's New Frontiers: Experiences from the Emerging Gateway States*, edited by Greg Anrig and Tova Andrea Wang, pp. 7–32. New York: Century Foundation Press.

———. In progress. "What's New About the New South? Race, Latino Immigration, and Intergroup Relations." Research Project, Russell Sage Foundation, New York (funded June 2006).

McClain, Paula D., Niambi M. Carter, Victoria M. DeFrancesco, J. Alan Kendrick, Monique L. Lyle, Shayla C. Nunnally, Thomas C. Scotto, Jeffrey D. Grynasviski, and Jason A. Johnson. 2003. "St. Benedict the Black Meets the Virgin of Guadalupe: Intergroup Relations in a Southern City." Paper presented at the Color Lines Conference, Harvard Law School, Cambridge, MA (August 29–September 1).

McClain, Paula D., Niambi M. Carter, Victoria M. Soto DeFrancesco, Monique L. Lyle, Jeffrey D. Grynasviski, Shayla C. Nunnally, Thomas C. Scotto, J. Alan Kendrick, Gerald F. Lackey, and Kendra Davenport Cotton. 2006. "Racial Distancing in a Southern City: Latino Immigrants' Views of Black Americans." *Journal of Politics* 68(3): 571–84.

McClain, Paula D., Monique L. Lyle, Niambi M. Carter, Victoria M. DeFrancesco Soto, Gerald F. Lackey, Kendra Davenport Cotton, Shayla C. Nunnally, Thomas C. Scotto, Jeffrey D. Grynasviski, and J. Alan Kendrick. 2007. "Black Americans and Latino Immigrants in a Southern City: Friendly Neighbors or Economic Competitors?" *Du Bois Review* 4(1): 97–117.

McClain, Paula D., and Steven C. Tauber. 2001. "Racial Minority Group Relations in a Multiracial Society." In *Governing American Cities: Inter-Ethnic Coalitions, Competition, and Conflict*, edited by Michael Jones-Correa, pp. 111–36. New York: Russell Sage.

McConnell, Eileen Diaz. 2008. "The Destinations of Contemporary Mexican Immigrants." *International Migration Review* 42(4): 767–802.

McConnell, Eileen Diaz, and Faranak Miraftab. 2009. "Sundown Town 'Little Mexico': Old-Timers and Newcomers in an American Small Town." *Rural Sociology* 74(4): 605–29.

McDaniel, Josh, and Vanessa Casanova. 2003. "Pines in Lines: Tree Planting, H2B Guest Workers, and Rural Poverty in Alabama." *Southern Rural Sociology* 19(1): 73–96.

McDermott, Monica. In progress. *Unstable Hierarchies: Race, Class and Immigration to the Southeastern United States.* Unpublished manuscript, Stanford University.

McGranahan, David A. 2003. "How People Make a Living in Rural America." In *Challenges for Rural America in the Twenty-First Century,* edited by David L. Brown and Louis E. Swanson, pp. 135–51. University Park: Pennsylvania State University Press.

McKinley, Jesse. 2006. "Immigrant Protection Rules Draw Fire." *New York Times* (November 12).

Meier, Kenneth J., Eric Gonzalez Juenke, Robert D. Wrinkle, and J. L. Polinard. 2005. "Structural Choices and Representational Biases: The Post-Election Color of Representation." *American Journal of Political Science* 49(4): 758–68.

Meier, Kenneth J., and Laurence J. O'Toole. 2006. "Political Control Versus Bureaucratic Values: Reframing the Debate." *Public Administration Review* 66(2): 177–92.

Mendelson, Margot, Shayna Strom, and Michael Wishnie. 2009. "Collateral Damage: An Examination of ICE's Fugitive Operations Program." Washington, DC: Migration Policy Institute (February).

Menjívar, Cecilia. 2006a. "Family Reorganization in a Context of Legal Uncertainty: Guatemalan and Salvadoran Immigrants in the United States." *International Journal of Sociology of the Family* 32(2): 223–45.

———. 2006b. "Liminal Legality: Salvadoran and Guatemalan Immigrants' Lives in the United States." *American Journal of Sociology* 111(4): 999–1037.

———. 2008. "Educational Hopes, Documented Dreams: Guatemalan and Salvadoran Immigrants' Legality and Educational Prospects." *Annals of the American Academy of Political and Social Science* 620(1): 177–93.

Merton, Robert K. 1972. "Insiders and Outsiders: A Chapter in the Sociology of Knowledge." *American Journal of Sociology* 78(1): 9–47.

Mexican Migration Project (MMP). 2009. "Crossing Costs, Adjusted to the 2009 (March) CPI." Princeton, NJ: Office of Population Research, Princeton University (April). http://mmp.opr.princeton.edu/results/results-en.aspx (last accessed February 9, 2010).

Migration Policy Institute (MPI) and New York University (NYU) School of Law. 2007. "Responses to Immigration: A Database of All State Legislation." Washington, DC: Migration Policy Institute.

Millard, Ann, and Jorge Chapa, eds. 2004. *Apple Pie and Enchiladas: Latino Newcomers in the Rural Midwest.* Austin: University of Texas Press.

Miller, Patrick M. 2010. "Racial Contact Effects in a High Latino Growth Context: Attitudes Toward Immigrants and Immigration in North Carolina." Paper presented at the Citadel Symposium on Southern Politics, Charleston, SC (March 4).

Mindiola, Tatcho, Yolanda Flores Niemann, and Nestor Rodríguez. 2002. *Black-Brown Relations and Stereotypes.* Austin: University of Texas Press.

Mohl, Raymond A. 2002. "Latinization in the Heart of Dixie: Hispanics in Late-Twentieth-Century Alabama." *Alabama Review* 55(4): 243–74.

———. 2003. "Globalization, Latinization, and the Nuevo New South." *Journal of American Ethnic History* 22(4): 31–66.

———. 2009. "Globalization and Latin American Immigration in Alabama." In *Latino Immigrants and the Transformation of the U.S. South*, edited by Mary E. Odem and Elaine Lacy, pp. 51–69. Athens: University of Georgia Press.

Montejano, David. 1987. *Anglos and Mexicans in the Making of Texas, 1836–1986*. Austin: University of Texas Press.

Morando, Sarah. 2009. "Paths to Mobility: The Mexican Second Generation at Work in a New Destination." Paper presented at the Labor Markets and Workplace Dynamics in New Destinations of Mexican and Latino Immigration Workshop, University of California at Los Angeles (October 23).

Morawska, Ewa. 2001. "Immigrant-Black Dissensions in American Cities: An Argument for Multiple Explanations." In *Problem of the Century: Racial Stratification in the United States*, edited by Elijah Anderson and Douglas S. Massey, pp. 47–96. New York: Russell Sage.

Morris, Frank, and James G. Gimpel. 2007. "Immigration, Intergroup Conflict, and the Erosion of African American Political Power in the 21st Century." Washington, DC: Center for Immigration Studies, Backgrounder (February).

Moss, Philip, and Chris Tilly. 2001. *Stories Employers Tell: Race, Skill, and Hiring in America*. New York: Russell Sage.

Motomura, Hiroshi. 2008. "Immigration Outside the Law." *Columbia Law Review* 108(8): 2037–97.

Murguia, Edward, and Rogelio Saenz. 2002. "An Analysis of the Latin Americanization of Race in the United States: A Reconnaissance of Color Stratification Among Mexicans." *Race & Society* 5: 85–101.

National Immigration Law Center (NILC). 2003. "Summary of Clear Law Enforcement for Criminal Alien Removal Act of 2003 (CLEAR) HR 2671." (July). www.nilc.org/imm lawpolicy/LocalLaw/clear03_secbysec_073103.pdf (last accessed June 18, 2010).

———. 2004a. "Driver's Licenses for All Immigrants: Quotes from Law Enforcement." (October). http://www.nilc.org/immspbs/DLs/index.htm (last accessed June 2, 2009).

———. 2004b. "Driver's Licenses for All Immigrants: Quotes from Religious Organizations and Leaders." (December). http://www.nilc.org/immspbs/DLs/index.htm (last accessed June 2, 2009).

———. 2005. "Summary of Clear Law Enforcement for Criminal Alien Removal Act of 2005 (CLEAR) HR 3137." (June 30). Source on file with the author.

———. 2008a. "FACT SHEET: Why Denying Driver's Licenses to Undocumented Immigrants Harms Public Safety and Makes Our Communities Less Secure." (January). http://www.nilc.org/immspbs/DLs/FactSheet_DLs_2008-01-16.pdf (last accessed June 2, 2009).

———. 2008b. "Questions and Answers About Driver's Licenses Now That Final REAL ID Regulations Have Been Issued." (February). http://www.nilc.org/immspbs/DLs /QA_re_DLs_post-regs_2008-02-27.pdf (last accessed June 2, 2009).

———. 2009a. "Basic Facts About In-State Tuition for Undocumented Immigrant Students." (February 23). Source on file with the author.

———. 2009b. "DREAM Act: Basic Information." (March 30). http://www.nilc.org/imm lawpolicy/DREAM/index.htm (last accessed March 12, 2009).

———. 2009c. "Overview of States' Driver's License Requirements." (April 27). http:// www.nilc.org/immspbs/DLs/index.htm (last accessed June 2, 2009). Earlier versions published on December 5, 2004, and January 31, 2007, on file with the author.

Neal, Micki, and Stephanie A. Bohon. 2003. "The Dixie Diaspora: Attitudes Toward Immigrants in Georgia." *Sociological Spectrum* 23(2): 181–212.

Nelson, Lise, and Nancy Hiemstra. 2008. "Latino Immigrants and the Renegotiation of Place and Belonging in Small Town America." *Social & Cultural Geography* 9(3): 319–42.

Newman, Katherine S. 1999. *No Shame in My Game: The Working Poor in the Inner City.* New York: Vintage Books and Russell Sage.

Newman, Katherine S., and Chauncy Lennon. 2004. "Working Poor, Working Hard: Trajectories at the Bottom of the Labor Market." In *Social Inequalities in Comparative Perspective*, edited by Fiona Devine and Mary C. Waters, pp. 16–40. Malden, MA: Blackwell.

Newton, Lina, and Brian E. Adams. 2009. "State Immigration Policies: Innovation, Cooperation, and Conflict." *Publius: The Journal of Federalism* 39(3): 408–31.

Ngai, Mae. 2004. *Impossible Subjects: Illegal Aliens and the Making of Modern America.* Princeton, NJ: Princeton University Press.

Nguyen, Mai Thi. 2007. "Anti-Immigration Ordinances in North Carolina: Ramifications for Local Governance and Planning." *Carolina Planning Journal* 32: 36–46.

Nguyen, Mai Thi, and Hannah Gill. 2010. "The 287(g) Program: The Costs and Consequences of Local Immigration Enforcement in North Carolina Communities." Chapel Hill, NC: The Latino Migration Project, Institute for the Study of the Americas and Center for Global Initiatives, University of North Carolina at Chapel Hill (February).

Nobles, Melissa. 2000. *Shades of Citizenship: Race and the Census in Modern Politics.* Stanford, CA: Stanford University Press.

North Carolina Administrative Office of the Courts (NCAOC). 2005. "Guidelines for the Use of Foreign Language Interpreting and Translating Services in the Court System." http://www.nccourts.org/Citizens/CPrograms/Foreign/Documents/Guidelines.html (last accessed June 2, 2009).

North Carolina Society of Hispanic Professionals (NCSHP). 2004. "Guidelines on the Admission of Undocumented Aliens." (November 12). Source on file with the author.

———. 2005. "Fact Sheet 2005-11: Community Colleges in North Carolina Admitting Undocumented Immigrants (UDI)." (April). Source on file with the author.

North Carolina Religious Coalition for Justice for Immigrants (NCRCJI). 2009. "Action Alert: Comment on Access to Community Colleges." (December 4). Electronic communication, on file with author.

Oboler, Suzanne. 1995. *Ethnic Labels, Latino Lives: Identity and the Politics of (Re)Presentation in the United States.* Minneapolis: University of Minnesota Press.

Odem, Mary E. 2004. "Our Lady of Guadalupe in the New South: Latino Immigrants and the Politics of Integration in the Catholic Church." *Journal of American Ethnic History* 23: 26–57.

———. 2008. "Unsettled in the Suburbs: Latino Immigration and Ethnic Diversity in Metro Atlanta." In *Twenty-First Century Gateways: Immigrant Integration in Suburban America,* edited by Audrey Singer, Susan W. Hardwick, and Caroline B. Brettell, pp. 105–36. Washington, DC: Brookings Institution Press.

———. 2009. "Latino Immigrants and the Politics of Space in Atlanta." In *Latino Immigrants and the Transformation of the U.S. South,* edited by Mary E. Odem and Elaine Lacy, pp. 112–25. Athens: University of Georgia Press.

Odem, Mary E., and Elaine Lacy. 2009. "Introduction." In *Latino Immigrants and the Transformation of the U.S. South,* edited by Mary E. Odem and Elaine Lacy, pp. ix–xxvii. Athens: University of Georgia Press.

Okamoto, Dina, and Kimberley Ebert. 2010. "Beyond the Ballot: Immigrant Collective Action in Traditional and New Destinations in the U.S." Unpublished manuscript, University of California at Davis.

O'Leary, Rosemary. 2006. *The Ethics of Dissent: Managing Guerrilla Government.* Washington, DC: CQ Press.

Oliver, J. Eric, and Janelle Wong. 2003. "Inter-Group Prejudice in Multiethnic Settings." *American Journal of Political Science* 47(4): 567–82.

Ordoñez, Franco. 2008. "Immigration Arrests Have Poultry Workers Afraid to Go to Jobs: House of Raeford Turns to Inmates to Fill Vacant Positions as Production Levels Slip." *Charlotte Observer* (October 3).

Ordoñez, Franco, and Ames Alexander. 2008. "Was Poultry Raid Just a Beginning? Federal Authorities Appear to Be Building Case Against Company's Managers, Immigration Experts Say." *Charlotte Observer* (October 13).

Ordoñez, Franco, and Bruce Henderson. 2008. "Fear, Uncertainty Follow Raid at Plant: Some Children Wait to See If Their Parents Were Arrested While Some Parents Reluctant to Pick Up Their Children." *Charlotte Observer* (October 8).

Orrenius, Pia M. 2004. "The Effect of U.S. Border Enforcement on the Crossing Behavior of Mexican Migrants." In *Crossing the Border: Research from the Mexican Migration Project,* edited by Jorge Durand and Douglas S. Massey, pp. 281–98. New York: Russell Sage.

Ortega, Alexander N., Hai Fang, Victor H. Perez, John A. Rizzo, Olivia Carter-Pokras, Steven P. Wallace, and Lillian Gelberg. 2007. "Health Care Access, Use of Services, and Experiences Among Undocumented Mexicans and Other Latinos." *Archives of Internal Medicine* 267(21): 2354–60.

Packer, Travis. 2010. "DREAMing of Immigration Reform." *Immigration Impact* (June 10).

Papademetriou, Demetrios G., and Brian Ray. 2004. "From Homeland to Home: Immigrants and Homeownership in Urban America." Washington, DC: Fannie Mae Occasional Papers.

Papademetriou, Demetrios G., and Aaron Terrazas. 2009. "Immigrants in the United States and the Current Economic Crisis." *Migration Information Source* (April).

Parrado, Emilio A., and William A. Kandel. 2008. "New Hispanic Migrant Destinations: A Tale of Two Industries." In *New Faces in New Places: The Changing Geography of American Immigration,* edited by Douglas S. Massey, pp. 99–123. New York: Russell Sage.

Parsons, Dan. 2007. "Hispanics Send Loud Message: Demonstrate Citizenship, Legal Residency During a Parade of Solidarity." *Washington Daily News* (Beaufort County, NC; June 5).

Passel, Jeffrey S. 2005. "Estimates of the Size and Characteristics of the Undocumented Population." Washington, DC: Pew Hispanic Center (March 1).

———. 2006. "The Size and Characteristics of the Unauthorized Migrant Population in the U.S.: Estimates Based on the March 2005 Current Population Survey." Washington, DC: Pew Hispanic Center (March 7).

Passel, Jeffrey S., and D'Vera Cohn. 2008. "Trends in Unauthorized Immigration: Undocumented Inflow Now Trails Legal Inflow." Washington, DC: Pew Hispanic Center (October 2).

———. 2009. "A Portrait of Undocumented Immigrants in the United States." Washington, DC: Pew Hispanic Center (April 14).

Patterson, Orlando. 2001. "Race by the Numbers." *New York Times* (May 8).

Peacock, James L., Harry L. Watson, and Carrie R. Matthews, eds. 2005. *The American South in a Global World.* Chapel Hill: University of North Carolina Press.

Penninx, Rinus. 2003. "Integration: The Role of Communities, Institutions, and the State." *Migration Information Source* (October).

Perez, Lorenzo. 2008. "Johnston Sheriff Apologizes: Sheriff Bizzell Says His Remarks About Mexican Immigrants Were 'Inappropriate.'" *News and Observer* (Raleigh, NC; September 8).

Perlmann, Joel. 2000. "Reflecting the Changing Face of America: Multiracials, Racial Classification, and American Intermarriage." In *Interracialism: Black-White Intermarriage in American History, Literature, and Law,* edited by Werner Sollors, pp. 506–33. Oxford, UK: Oxford University Press.

Perlmann, Joel, and Roger Waldinger. 1997. "Second Generation Decline? Children of Immigrants, Past and Present—A Reconsideration." *International Migration Review* 31(4): 893–922.

Perreira, Krista M. In progress. "Southern Immigrant Academic Adaptation Study." Research Project, Russell Sage Foundation, New York (funded November 2005).

Perreira, Krista M., Andrew Fuligni, and Stephanie Potochnick. 2010. "Fitting In: The Roles of Social Acceptance and Discrimination in Shaping the Academic Motivations of Latino Youth in the U.S. Southeast." *Journal of Social Issues* 66(1): 131–53.

Pew Hispanic Center. 2007a. "Construction Jobs Expand for Latinos Despite Slump in Housing Market." Washington, DC: Pew Hispanic Center (March 7).

———. 2007b. "2007 National Survey of Latinos: As Illegal Immigration Issue Heats Up, Hispanics Feel a Chill." Washington, DC: Pew Hispanic Center (December).

Piore, Michael J. 1979. *Birds of Passage: Migrant Labor and Industrial Societies.* Cambridge, UK: Cambridge University Press.

Porter, Eduardo. 2005. "Illegal Immigrants Are Bolstering Social Security with Billions." *New York Times* (April 5).

———. 2006. "Katrina Begets a Baby Boom by Immigrants." *New York Times* (December 11).

Portes, Alejandro. 2007. "The Fence to Nowhere: The Case for a Bilateral Labor Management Program." *The American Prospect* (October): 26–29.

Portes, Alejandro, and Robert L. Bach. 1985. *Latin Journey: A Longitudinal Study of Cuban and Mexican Immigrants to the United States.* Berkeley: University of California Press.

Portes, Alejandro, and Jozsef Borocz. 1989. "Contemporary Immigration: Theoretical Perspectives on Its Determinants and Modes of Incorporation." *International Migration Review* 23(3): 606–30.

Portes, Alejandro, and Patricia Fernández-Kelly. 2008. "No Margin for Error: Educational and Occupational Achievement Among Disadvantaged Children of Immigrants." *Annals of the American Academy of Political and Social Science* 620(1): 12–36.

Portes, Alejandro, Patricia Fernández-Kelly, and Donald W. Light. Forthcoming. "Life on the Edge: Immigrants Confront the American Health System." *Ethnic and Racial Studies.*

Portes, Alejandro, Donald W. Light, and Patricia Fernández-Kelly. 2009. "The U.S. Health System and Immigration: An Institutional Interpretation." *Sociological Forum* 24(3): 487–514.

Portes, Alejandro, and Rubén G. Rumbaut. 2001. *Legacies: The Story of the Immigrant Second Generation.* Berkeley: University of California Press.

———. 2006. *Immigrant America: A Portrait* (3rd ed., rev., expanded, and updated). Berkeley: University of California Press.

Portes, Alejandro, and Min Zhou. 1993. "The New Second Generation: Segmented Assimilation and Its Variants Among Post-1965 Immigrant Youth." *Annals of the American Academy of Political and Social Science* 530: 74–96.

Preston, Julia. 2007. "As Deportation Pace Rises, Illegal Immigrants Dig In." *New York Times* (May 1).

———. 2008a. "Employers Fight Tough Measures on Immigration." *New York Times* (July 6).

———. 2008b. "Facing Deportation but Clinging to Life in U.S." *New York Times* (January 18).

———. 2008c. "270 Illegal Immigrants Sent to Prison in Federal Push." *New York Times* (May 24).

Price, Marie, and Audrey Singer. 2008. "Edge Gateways: Immigrants, Suburbs, and the Politics of Reception in Suburban Washington." In *Twenty-First Century Gateways: Immigrant Integration in Suburban America*, edited by Audrey Singer, Susan W. Hardwick, and Caroline B. Brettell, pp. 137–68. Washington, DC: Brookings Institution Press.

Qian, Zhenchao. 2002. "Race and Social Distance: Intermarriage with Non-Latino Whites." *Race & Society* 5: 33–47.

Qian, Zhenchao, and Daniel T. Lichter. 2007. "Social Boundaries and Marital Assimilation: Interpreting Trends in Racial and Ethnic Intermarriage." *American Sociological Review* 72(1): 68–94.

Quill, Beth E., Lu Ann Aday, Carl S. Hacker, and Julie Kay Reagan. 1999. "Policy Incongruence and Public Health Professionals' Dissonance: The Case of Immigrants and Welfare Policy." *Journal of Immigrant Health* 1(1): 9–18.

Quillian, Lincoln, and Mary E. Campbell. 2003. "Beyond Black and White: The Present and Future of Multiracial Friendship Segregation." *American Sociological Review* 68(4): 540–66.

Raijman, Rebecca, and Marta Tienda. 1999. "Immigrants' Socioeconomic Progress Post-1965: Forging Mobility or Survival?" In *The Handbook of International Migration: The American Experience*, edited by Charles Hirschman, Philip Kasinitz, and Josh DeWind, pp. 223–38. New York: Russell Sage.

Ramakrishnan, S. Karthick. 2005. *Democracy in Immigrant America: Changing Demographics and Political Participation*. Stanford, CA: Stanford University Press.

Raphael, Steven, and Lucas Ronconi. 2007. "The Effects of Labor Market Competition with Immigrants on the Wages and Employment of Natives: What Does Existing Research Tell Us?" *Du Bois Review* 4(2): 413–32.

Redden, Elizabeth. 2008. "Admissions Control (Update)." *Chronicle of Higher Education* (May 13).

Redstone Akresh, Ilana. 2006. "Occupational Mobility Among Legal Immigrants to the United States." *International Migration Review* 40(4): 854–84.

Reed, John Shelton. 1986. *The Enduring South: Subcultural Persistence Mass Society* (3rd ed.). Chapel Hill: University of North Carolina Press.

———. 1993. *My Tears Spoiled My Aim and Other Reflections on Southern Culture*. San Diego: Harcourt Brace.

Reimers, David M. 2005. "Asian Immigrants in the South." In *Globalization and the American South*, edited by James C. Cobb and William Stueck, pp. 100–134. Athens: University of Georgia Press.

Rich, Brian L., and Marta Miranda. 2005. "The Sociopolitical Dynamics of Mexican Immigration in Lexington, Kentucky, 1977 to 2002: An Ambivalent Community Responds." In *New Destinations: Mexican Immigration to the United States*, edited by Victor Zúñiga and Rubén Hernández-León, pp. 187–219. New York: Russell Sage.

Rives, Karin. 2006. "Illegal Immigration—Jobs." (First in the Series on "Illegal Immigration—Who Profits, Who Pays?") *News and Observer* (Raleigh, NC; February 26).

Roberston, Gary D. 2007. "NC Governor Candidates Oppose Admissions Change for Immigrants." *News and Observer* (Raleigh, NC; November 29).

Rockquemore, Kerry Ann. 2002. "Negotiating the Color Line: The Gendered Process of Racial Identity Construction Among Black/White Biracial Women." *Gender & Society* 16(4): 485–503.

Rockquemore, Kerry Ann, and Patricia Arend. 2002. "Opting for White: Choice, Fluidity and Racial Identity Construction in Post Civil-Rights America." *Race & Society* 5: 49–64.

Rodríguez, Clara E. 2000. *Changing Race: Latinos, the Census, and the History of Ethnicity in the United States*. New York: New York University Press.

Rodríguez, Cristina. 2008. "The Significance of the Local in Immigration Regulation." *Michigan Law Review* 106(4): 567–642.

Rodríguez, Cristina, Muzaffar Chishti, Randy Capps, and Laura St. John. 2010. "A Program in Flux: New Priorities and Implementation Challenges for 287(g)." Washington, DC: Migration Policy Institute (March).

Rodríguez, Nestor. 1999. "U.S. Immigration and Changing Relations Between African Americans and Latinos." In *The Handbook of International Migration: The American Experience*, edited by Charles Hirschman, Philip Kasinitz, and Josh DeWind, pp. 423–32. New York: Russell Sage.

Roediger, David R. 1991. *The Wages of Whiteness: Race and the Making of the American Working Class*. London: Verso.

———. 2005. *Working Toward Whiteness: How America's Immigrants Became White: The Strange Journey from Ellis Island to the Suburbs*. New York: Basic Books.

Rogers, Reuel. 2004. "Race-Based Coalitions Among Minority Groups: Afro-Caribbean Immigrants and African-Americans in New York City." *Urban Affairs Review* 39(3): 283–317.

Rose, Mariel. 2007. "Appalachian *Mestizaje*: Race and Latino Immigration in Western North Carolina." In *Constructing Borders/Crossing Boundaries: Race, Ethnicity, and Immigration*, edited by Caroline B. Brettell, pp. 185–210. Lanham, MD: Lexington Books.

Rosenfeld, Michael J. 2002. "Measures of Assimilation in the Marriage Market: Mexican Americans 1970–1990." *Journal of Marriage and the Family* 64(1): 152–62.

Rosenfeld, Michael J., and Marta Tienda. 1999. "Mexican Immigration, Occupational Niches, and Labor Market Competition: Evidence from Los Angeles, Chicago, and Atlanta, 1970–1990." In *Immigration and Opportunity: Race, Ethnicity, and Employment in the United States*, edited by Frank D. Bean and Stephanie Bell-Rose, pp. 64–105. New York: Russell Sage.

Ruggles, Steven, Matthew Sobek, Trent Alexander, Catherine A. Fitch, Ronald Goeken,

Patricia Kelly Hall, Miriam King, and Chad Ronnander. 2004. *Integrated Public Use Microdata Series: Version 3.0* [machine-readable database]. Minneapolis: Minnesota Population Center (producer and distributor). http://www.ipums.org.

Rumbaut, Ruben G. 2008. "The Coming of the Second Generation: Immigration and Ethnic Mobility in Southern California." *Annals of the American Academy of Political and Social Science* 620(1): 196–236.

Rumbaut, Rubén G., and Alejandro Portes, eds. 2001. *Ethnicities: Children of Immigrants in America*. Berkeley: University of California Press.

Rural Sociological Society (RSS). 2006a. "The Challenges of Rural Poverty." Challenges for Rural America in the Twenty-First Century, Issue Brief No. 2. Source on file with the author.

———. 2006b. "The Changing Face of Rural America." Challenges for Rural America in the Twenty-First Century, Issue Brief No. 1. Source on file with the author.

Sabogal, Elena. 2005. "*Viviendo en la Sombra*: The Immigration of Peruvian Professionals to South Florida." *Latino Studies* 3(1): 113–31.

Saenz, Rogelio. 2000. "Earnings Patterns of Mexican Workers in the Southern Region: A Focus on Nonmetro/Metro Distinctions." *Southern Rural Sociology* 16: 60–95.

Saenz, Rogelio, Katharine M. Donato, Lourdes Gouveia, and Cruz C. Torres. 2003. "Latinos in the South: A Glimpse of Ongoing Trends and Research." *Southern Rural Sociology* 19(1): 1–19.

Saenz, Rogelio, and Cruz C. Torres. 2003. "Latinos in Rural America." In *Challenges for Rural America in the Twenty-First Century*, edited by David L. Brown and Louis E. Swanson, pp. 57–70. University Park: Pennsylvania State University Press.

Schildkraut, Deborah J. 2003. "American Identity and Attitudes Toward Official-English Policies." *Political Psychology* 24(3): 469–99.

Schlosser, Eric. 2001. *Fast Food Nation: The Dark Side of the All American Meal*. New York: Houghton Mifflin.

Schmid, Carol. 2003. "Immigration and Asian and Hispanic Minorities in the New South: An Exploration of History, Attitudes, and Demographic Trends." *Sociological Spectrum* 23(2): 129–57.

Schmidley, Diane. 2001. "Profile of the Foreign Born Population in the United States: 2000." Washington, DC: Government Printing Office, U.S. Census Bureau Current Population Reports Series, P-23-206.

Schoenholtz, Andrew I. 2005. "Newcomers in Rural Arkansas: Hispanic Immigrants in Rogers, Arkansas." In *Beyond the Gateway: Immigrants in a Changing America*, edited by Elzbieta M. Gozdziak and Susan F. Martin, pp. 213–38. Lanham, MD: Lexington Books.

Schumacher-Matos, Edward. 2010. "How Illegal Immigrants Are Helping Social Security." *Washington Post* (September 3).

Schur, Claudia L., Marc L. Berk, Cynthia D. Good, and Eric N. Gardner. 1999. "California's Undocumented Latino Immigrants: A Report on Access to Health Care Services." Washington, DC: Henry J. Kaiser Family Foundation (May).

Schwade, John. 2008. "Cops Need Informants, Illegal Immigrants Need Assurances." *News and Observer* (Raleigh, NC; June 7).

Sears, David O., and Victoria Savalei. 2006. "The Political Color Line in America: Many Peoples of Color or Black Exceptionalism?" *Political Psychology* 27(6): 895–924.

Seif, Hinda. 2004. "'Wise Up!' Undocumented Latino Youth, Mexican-American Legislators, and the Struggle for Higher Education Access." *Latino Studies* 2(2): 210–30.

Shahani, Aarti, and Judith Greene. 2009. "Local Democracy on Ice: Why State and Local Governments Have No Business in Federal Immigration Law Enforcement." Brooklyn, NY: Justice Strategies (February).

Shefner, Jon, and Katie Kirkpatrick. 2009. "Introduction: Globalization and the New Destination Immigrant." In *Global Connections & Local Receptions: New Latino Immigration to the Southeastern United States.* Edited by Fran Ansley and Jon Shefner, pp. xv–xl. Knoxville: University of Tennessee Press.

Shefter, Martin, ed. 1994. *Political Parties and the State: The American Historical Experience.* Princeton, NJ: Princeton University Press.

Shierholz, Heidi. 2010. "Immigration and Wages—Methodological Advancements Confirm Modest Gains for Native Workers." EPI Briefing Paper #255. Washington, DC: Economic Policy Institute.

Shklar, Judith. 1991. *American Citizenship—The Quest for Inclusion: The Tanner Lecture on Human Values.* Cambridge, MA: Harvard University Press.

Silver, Alexis. 2009. "Aging into Exclusion: Transitions to Adulthood for Undocumented Immigrant Youth." Paper presented at the Undocumented Hispanic Migration: On the Margins of a Dream Conference, Connecticut College, New London, CT (October 16–18).

Simon, Rita J., and Susan H. Alexander. 1993. *The Ambivalent Welcome: Print Media, Public Opinion, and Immigration.* Westport, CT: Praeger.

Sinclair, Upton. 1985. *The Jungle.* New York: Penguin (originally published 1906).

Singer, Audrey. 2004. "The Rise of New Immigrant Gateways." Washington, DC: Brookings Institution, Living Cities Census Series (February).

———. 2008. "Twenty-First Century Gateways: An Introduction." In *Twenty-First Century Gateways: Immigrant Integration in Suburban America,* edited by Audrey Singer, Susan W. Hardwick, and Caroline B. Brettell, pp. 3–30. Washington, DC: Brookings Institution Press.

Singer, Audrey, Susan W. Hardwick, and Caroline B. Brettell, eds. 2008a. "Afterword: Coming to Terms with Federal and Local Immigration Reform." In *Twenty-First Century Gateways: Immigrant Incorporation in Suburban America,* edited by Audrey Singer, Susan W. Hardwick, and Caroline B. Brettell, pp. 308–17. Washington, DC: Brookings Institution Press.

———. 2008b. *Twenty-First Century Gateways: Immigrant Incorporation in Suburban America*. Washington, DC: Brookings Institution Press.

Skaggs, Sheryl, Donald Tomaskovic-Devey, and Jeffrey Leiter. 2000. "Latino/a Employment Growth in North Carolina: Ethnic Displacement or Replacement." North Carolina State University. http://faculty.chass.ncsu.edu/leiter/LATINO.HTM (last accessed April 22, 2010).

Skillern, Peter, and Tanya Wolfram. 2005. "Transforming Trailers into Assets." *Popular Government* 70(2): 4–11.

Skrentny, John D. 2002. *The Minority Rights Revolution*. Cambridge, MA: Harvard University Press.

Smith, Barbara Ellen. 2003. "Across Races and Nations: Toward Worker Justice in the U.S. South." Paper presented at the Color Lines Conference, Harvard Law School, Cambridge, MA (August 29–September 1).

———. 2006. "Across Races and Nations: Social Justice Organizing in the Transnational South." In *Latinos in the New South: Transformations of Place*, edited by Heather A. Smith and Owen J. Furuseth, pp. 236–56. Aldershot, UK: Ashgate Press.

———. 2009. "Market Rivals or Class Allies? Relations Between African American and Latino Immigrant Workers in Memphis." In *Global Connections & Local Receptions: New Latino Immigration to the Southeastern United States*, edited by Fran Ansley and Jon Shefner, pp. 299–317. Knoxville: University of Tennessee Press.

Smith, Barbara Ellen, Marcela Mendoza, and David H. Ciscel. 2005. "The World on Time: Flexible Labor, New Immigrants, and Global Logistics." In *The American South in a Global World*, edited by James L. Peacock, Harry L. Watson, and Carrie R. Matthews, pp. 23–38. Chapel Hill: University of North Carolina Press.

Smith, Heather A. 2008. "The Untraditional Geography of Hispanic Settlement in a New South City: Charlotte, North Carolina." In *Immigrants Outside Megalopolis: Ethnic Transformation in the Heartland*, edited by Richard C. Jones, pp. 237–62. Lanham, MD: Lexington Books.

Smith, Heather A., and Owen J. Furuseth., eds. 2006a. *Latinos in the New South: Transformations of Place*. Aldershot, UK: Ashgate Press.

———. 2006b. "Making Real the Mythical Latino Community in Charlotte, North Carolina." In *Latinos in the New South: Transformations of Place*, edited by Heather A. Smith and Owen J. Furuseth, pp. 191–216. Aldershot, UK: Ashgate Press.

———. 2008. "The 'Nuevo South': Latino Place Making and Community Building in the Middle-Ring Suburbs of Charlotte." In *Twenty-First Century Gateways: Immigrant Integration in Suburban America*, edited by Audrey Singer, Susan W. Hardwick, and Caroline B. Brettell, pp. 281–307. Washington, DC: Brookings Institution Press.

Smith, James P., and Barry Edmonston, eds. 1997. *The New Americans: Studies on the Economic, Demographic, and Fiscal Effects of Immigration*. Washington, DC: National Academy Press.

Smith, Robert C. 2005. "Racialization and Mexicans in New York City." In *New Destina-*

tions: Mexican Immigration to the United States, edited by Victor Zúñiga and Rubén Hernández-León, pp. 220–43. New York: Russell Sage.

———. 2006. *Mexican New York: Transnational Lives of New Immigrants*. Berkeley: University of California Press.

Smith-Nonini, Sandy. 2005. "Federally Sponsored Mexican Migrants in the Transnational South." In *The American South in a Global World*, edited by James L. Peacock, Harry L. Watson, and Carrie R. Matthews, pp. 59–79. Chapel Hill: University of North Carolina Press.

———. 2009. "H2A Guest Workers and the State in North Carolina: From Transnational Production to Transnational Organizing." In *Global Connections & Local Receptions: New Latino Immigration to the Southeastern United States*, edited by Fran Ansley and Jon Shefner, pp. 249–78. Knoxville: University of Tennessee Press.

Solórzano, Armando. 2005. "At the Gates of the Kingdom: Latino Immigrants in Utah, 1900–2003." In *Beyond the Gateway: Immigrants in a Changing America*, edited by Elzbieta M. Gozdziak and Susan F. Martin, pp. 177–211. Lanham, MD: Lexington Books.

Staff Reports. 2008. "ACLU Suspects Bizzell of Anti-Latino Bias." *News and Observer* (Raleigh, NC; September 9).

Staiti, Andrea B., Robert E. Hurley, and Aaron Katz. 2006. "Stretching the Safety Net to Serve Undocumented Immigrants: Community Responses to Health Needs." Issue Brief No. 104. Washington, DC: Center for Studying Health System Change (February).

Stamps, Katherine, and Stephanie A. Bohon. 2006. "Educational Attainment in New and Established Latino Destinations." *Social Science Quarterly* 87(5): 1225–40.

Stancill, Jane. 2005. "Tuition Deal Provokes Outcry." *News and Observer* (Raleigh, NC; April 15).

———. 2007. "System Chief: Let Illegal Aliens In." *News and Observer* (Raleigh, NC; December 5).

Sterne, Evelyn Savidge. 2001. "Beyond the Boss: Immigration and American Political Culture from 1880 to 1940." In *E Pluribus Unum? Contemporary and Historical Perspectives on Immigrant Political Incorporation*, edited by Gary Gerstle and John H. Mollenkopf, pp. 33–66. New York: Russell Sage.

Striffler, Steve. 2005a. *Chicken: The Dangerous Transformation of America's Favorite Food*. New Haven, CT: Yale University Press.

———. 2005b. "We're All Mexicans Here: Poultry Processing, Latino Migration, and the Transformation of Class in the South." In *The American South in a Global World*, edited by James L. Peacock, Harry L. Watson, and Carrie R. Matthews, pp. 152–65. Chapel Hill: University of North Carolina Press.

———. 2009. "Immigration Anxieties: Policing and Regulating Workers and Employers in the Poultry Industry." In *Global Connections & Local Receptions: New Latino Immigration to the Southeastern United States*, edited by Fran Ansley and Jon Shefner, pp. 129–54. Knoxville: University of Tennessee Press.

Striffler, Steve, and Julie M. Weise. 2008. "Arkansas." In *Latino America: A State-by-State*

Encyclopedia, edited by Mark Overmyer-Velásquez, pp. 63–75. Westport, CT: Greenwood Press.

Studstill, John D., and Laura Neito-Studstill. 2001. "Hospitality and Hostility: Latin Immigrants in Southern Georgia." In *Latino Workers in the Contemporary South*, edited by Arthur D. Murphy, Colleen Blanchard, and Jennifer A. Hill, pp. 68–81. Athens: University of Georgia Press.

Stuesse, Angela C. 2009. "Race, Migration, and Labor Control: Neoliberal Challenges to Organizing Mississippi's Poultry Workers." In *Latino Immigrants and the Transformation of the U.S. South*, edited by Mary E. Odem and Elaine Lacy, pp. 91–111. Athens: University of Georgia Press.

Stull, Donald D. 1994. "Knock 'Em Dead: Work on the Killfloor of a Modern Beefpacking Plant." In *Newcomers in the Workplace: Immigrants and the Restructuring of the U.S. Economy*, edited by Louise Lamphere, Alex Stepick, and Guillermo Grenier, pp. 44–77. Philadelphia: Temple University Press.

Stull, Donald D., and Michael J. Broadway. 2004. *Slaughterhouse Blues: The Meat and Poultry Industry in North America*. Belmont, CA: Wadsworth.

———. 2008. "Meatpacking and Mexicans in the High Plains: From Minority to Majority in Garden City, Kansas." In *Immigrants Outside Megalopolis: Ethnic Transformation in the Heartland*, edited by Richard C. Jones, pp. 115–33. Lanham, MD: Lexington Books.

Stull, Donald D., Michael J. Broadway, and David Griffith, eds. 1995. *Any Way You Cut It: Meat Processing and Small Town America*. Lawrence: University Press of Kansas.

Subramanian, Ajantha. 2005. "North Carolina's Indians: Erasing Race to Make a Citizen." In *The American South in a Global World*, edited by James L. Peacock, Harry L. Watson, and Carrie R. Matthews, pp. 192–201. Chapel Hill: University of North Carolina Press.

Suro, Roberto. 2007. "Presidential Plenary: The Changing Nature of Inequality in America." Plenary presentation at the Annual Meeting of the Eastern Sociological Society, Philadelphia (March 15–18).

———. 2009. "America's Views of Immigration: The Evidence from Public Opinion Surveys." In *Migration, Public Opinion, and Politics*, edited by Bertelsmann Stiftung and Migration Policy Institute, pp. 52–76. Washington, DC: Transatlantic Council on Migration.

Suro, Roberto, and Audrey Singer. 2002. "Latino Growth in Metropolitan America: Changing Patterns, New Locations." Survey Series, Census 2000. Washington, DC: Brookings Institution.

Suro, Roberto, and Sonya Tafoya. 2004. "Dispersal and Concentration: Patterns of Latino Residential Settlement." Washington, DC: Pew Hispanic Center (December 27).

Swarns, Rachel L. 2006a. "In Georgia, Immigrants Unsettle Old Sense of Place." *New York Times* (August 4).

———. 2006b. "A Racial Rift That Isn't Black and White." *New York Times* (October 3).

Swift, Aisling. 2003. "DWI Laws Hit Language Barrier." *News and Observer* (Raleigh, NC; November 13).

Taylor, Marylee. 1998. "How White Attitudes Vary with the Racial Composition of Local Populations: Numbers Count." *American Sociological Review* 63(4): 512–35.

Taylor, Paul, and Richard Fry. 2007. "Hispanics and the 2008 Election: A Swing Vote?" Washington, DC: Pew Hispanic Center (December 6).

Telles, Edward E. 2004. *Race in Another America: The Significance of Skin Color in Brazil.* Princeton, NJ: Princeton University Press.

Telles, Edward E., and Vilma Ortiz. 2008. *Generations of Exclusion: Mexican Americans, Assimilation, and Race.* New York: Russell Sage.

Terrazas, Aaron. 2008. "Immigration Enforcement in the United States." *Migration Information Source* (October).

Thompson, Charles, and Cynthia Hill (producers and directors). 2005. "The Guestworker: Bienvenidos a Carolina del Norte." Documentary film presented at the Navigating the Globalization of the American South Conference, University of North Carolina at Chapel Hill, Chapel Hill, NC (March 3–4). Available at Filmakers Library, http://www.theguestworker.com/.

Tienda, Marta, and Haya Stier. 1998. "Immigration and Native Minority Workers: Is There Bad News After All?" In *Help or Hindrance? The Economic Implications of Immigration for African Americans,* edited by Daniel S. Hamermesh and Frank D. Bean, pp. 345–52. New York: Russell Sage.

Tilly, Chris. 1996. "The Good, the Bad, and the Ugly: Good and Bad Jobs in the United States at the Millennium." New York: Russell Sage (June). Source on file with the author.

Torres, Rebecca María, E. Jeffrey Popke, and Holly M. Hapke. 2006. "The South's Silent Bargain: Rural Restructuring, Latino Labor and the Ambiguities of Migrant Experience." In *The New South: Latinos and the Transformation of Place,* edited by Heather A. Smith and Owen J. Furuseth, pp. 37–68. Aldershot, UK: Ashgate Press.

Torres, Rebecca, Jeff Popke, Holly Hapke, Matilde Elisa Suarez, Heidi Serrano, Brian Chambers, and Paola Castaño. 2003. "Transnational Communities in Eastern North Carolina: Results from a Survey of Latino Families in Greene County." *North Carolina Geographer* 11: 88–107.

Tramonte, Lynn. 2009. "Debunking the Myth of 'Sanctuary Cities': Community Policing Policies Protect American Communities." Washington, DC: Immigration Policy Center (March).

Travel.State.Gov. 2010. "Visa Bulletin for May 2010." Washington, DC: U.S. Department of State, Bureau of Consular Affairs. http://travel.state.gov/visa/bulletin/bulletin_4805 .html (last accessed June 18, 2010).

Turnbull, Elizabeth. 2008. "North Carolina." In *Latino America: A State-by-State Encyclopedia,* edited by Mark Overmyer-Velásquez, pp. 611–26. Westport, CT: Greenwood Press.

Uhlaner, Carole. 1991. "Perceived Discrimination and Prejudice and the Coalition Prospects of Blacks, Latinos, and Asian Americans." In *Racial and Ethnic Politics in California*, edited by Byran O. Jackson and Michael B. Preston, pp. 339–71. Berkeley, CA: Institute for Governmental Studies Press.

U.S. Government Accountability Office (GAO). 2009a. "Immigration Enforcement: Better Controls Needed over Program Authorizing State and Local Enforcement of Federal Immigration Laws." GAO-09-109. Washington, DC: U.S. GAO (January 30).

———. 2009b. "Immigration Enforcement: Controls over Program Authorizing State and Local Enforcement of Federal Immigration Laws Should Be Strengthened." GAO-09-381T. Washington, DC: U.S. GAO (March 4).

Vallas, Steven P., and Emily Zimmerman. 2007. "Sources of Variation in Attitudes Toward Illegal Immigration." Fairfax, VA: Center for Social Science Research, George Mason University. http://cssr.gmu.edu/immigration/Immigration%20survey/immigration%20survey.html (last accessed April 22, 2010).

Van der Leun, Joanne. 2003. *Looking for Loopholes: Processes of Incorporation of Illegal Immigrants in the Netherlands*. Amsterdam: Amsterdam University Press.

———. 2006. "Excluding Illegal Migrants in the Netherlands: Between National Policies and Local Implementation." *West European Politics* 29(2): 310–26.

Van Hook, Jennifer, Susan K. Brown, and Frank D. Bean. 2006. "For Love or Money? Welfare Reform and Immigrant Naturalization." *Social Forces* 85(2): 643–66.

Vaquera, Elizabeth, and Elizabeth Aranda. 2009. "Criminalizing Borderlands: Determinants of Immigrants' Experiences with Immigration Officials." Paper presented at the Undocumented Hispanic Migration: On the Margins of a Dream Conference, Connecticut College, New London, CT (October 16–18).

Varsanyi, Monica W. 2008. "Immigration Policing Through the Backdoor: City Ordinances, the 'Right to the City,' and the Exclusion of Undocumented Day Laborers." *Urban Geography* 29(1): 29–52.

Vásquez, Manuel A., Chad E. Seales, and Marie Friedmann Marquardt. 2008. "New Latino Destinations." In *Latinas/os in the United States: Changing the Face of America*, edited by Hávidan Rodríguez, Rogelio Saenz, and Cecília Menjívar, pp. 19–35. New York: Springer.

Vaughn, Bobby. 2005. "Afro-Mexico: Blacks, Indígenas, Politics, and the Greater Diaspora." In *Neither Enemies Nor Friends: Latinos, Blacks, Afro-Latinos*, edited by Anani Dzidzienyo and Suzanne Oboler, pp. 117–36. New York: Palgrave Macmillan.

Vaughn, Bobby, and Ben Vinson. 2007. "Unfinished Migrations: From the Mexican South to the American South: Impressions on Afro-Mexican Migration to North Carolina." In *Beyond Slavery: The Multilayered Legacy of Africans in Latin America and the Caribbean*, edited by Darién J. Davis, pp. 223–45. Lanham, MD: Rowman and Littlefield.

Verdaguer, María Eugenia. 2008. "Virginia." In *Latino America: A State-by-State Encyclopedia*, edited by Mark Overmyer-Velásquez, pp. 821–38. Westport, CT: Greenwood Press.

Voss, Mike. 2007. "Board OKs Removal of Foreign-Language Materials." *Washington Daily News* (Beaufort County, NC; February 10).

Wade, Peter. 1997. *Race and Ethnicity in Latin America.* London: Pluto Press.

Wagley, Charles. 1965. "On the Concept of Social Race in the Americas." In *Contemporary Cultures and Societies in Latin America: A Reader in the Social Anthropology of Middle and South America*, edited by Dwight B. Heath. New York: Random House.

Wainer, Andrew. 2004. "The New Latino South and the Challenge to Public Education." Los Angeles: Tomás Rivera Policy Institute (November).

Walcott, Susan M., and Arthur D. Murphy. 2006. "Latino Communities in Atlanta: Segmented Assimilation Under Construction." In *The New South: Latinos and the Transformation of Place*, edited by Heather A. Smith and Owen J. Furuseth, pp. 153–66. Aldershot, UK: Ashgate Press.

Waldinger, Roger. 1996. *Still the Promised City? African Americans and New Immigrants in Post-Industrial New York.* Cambridge, MA: Harvard University Press.

———. 1999. "Network, Bureaucracy, and Exclusion: Recruitment and Selection in an Immigrant Metropolis." In *Immigration and Opportunity: Race, Ethnicity, and Employment in the United States*, edited by Frank D. Bean and Stephanie Bell-Rose, pp. 228–59. New York: Russell Sage.

———. 2001. "Up from Poverty? 'Race,' Immigration, and the Fate of Low-Skilled Workers." In *Strangers at the Gates: New Immigrants in Urban America*, edited by Roger Waldinger, pp. 80–116. Berkeley: University of California Press.

Waldinger, Roger, and Cynthia Feliciano. 2004. "Will the New Second Generation Experience 'Downward Assimilation'? Segmented Assimilation Re-Assessed." *Ethnic and Racial Studies* 27(3): 376–402.

Waldinger, Roger, and Michael I. Lichter. 2003. *How the Other Half Works: Immigration and the Social Organization of Labor.* Berkeley: University of California Press.

Waldinger, Roger, Nelson Lim, and David Cort. 2007. "Bad Jobs, Good Jobs, No Jobs? The Employment Experience of the Mexican American Second Generation." *Journal of Ethnic and Migration Studies* 33(1): 1–35.

Walker, Marlon A. 2008. "NC Sheriff's Slurs Snarl Locals' Immigration Work." *News and Observer* (Raleigh, NC; October 22).

Warren, Jonathan W., and France Winddance Twine. 1997. "White Americans, the New Minority? Non-Blacks and the Ever-Expanding Boundaries of Whiteness." *Journal of Black Studies* 28(2): 200–218.

Waterman, Richard W., and Kenneth J. Meier. 1998. "Principal-Agent Models: An Expansion?" *Journal of Public Administration Research and Theory* 8(2): 173–202.

Waters, Mary C. 1999. *Black Identities: West Indian Immigrant Dreams and American Realities.* Cambridge, MA: Harvard University Press.

Waters, Mary C., and Tomás R. Jiménez. 2005. "Assessing Immigrant Assimilation: New Empirical and Theoretical Challenges." *Annual Review of Sociology* 31: 105–25.

Watson, Harry L. 2005. "Southern History, Southern Future: Some Reflections and a

Cautious Forecast." In *The American South in a Global World*, edited by James L. Peacock, Harry L. Watson, and Carrie R. Matthews, pp. 277–88. Chapel Hill: University of North Carolina Press.

Weeks, Gregory B., John R. Weeks, and Amy J. Weeks. 2007. "Latino Immigration in the U.S. South: 'Carolatinos' and Public Policy in Charlotte, North Carolina." *Latino(a) Research Review* 6(1–2): 50–71.

Weise, Julie M. 2008. "Mississippi." In *Latino America: A State-by-State Encyclopedia*, edited by Mark Overmyer-Velásquez, pp. 445–61. Westport, CT: Greenwood Press.

Weissman, Deborah M., Rebecca C. Headen, Katherine Lewis Parker, Katherine Bandy, Catherine Currie, Evelyn Griggs, Jill Hopman, Nicole Jones, Rashmi Kumar, Marty Rosenbluth, and Christina Simpson. 2009. "The Policies and Politics of Local Immigration Enforcement Laws: 287(g) Program in North Carolina." Chapel Hill: American Civil Liberties Union of the North Carolina Legal Foundation and Immigration & Human Rights Policy Clinic at the University of North Carolina at Chapel Hill (February).

Wells, Miriam J. 2004. "The Grassroots Reconfiguration of U.S. Immigration Policy." *International Migration Review* 38(4): 1308–47.

White, Jesse L. 2004. "Economic Development in North Carolina: Moving Toward Innovation." *Popular Government* 69(3): 2–13.

Wilkes, Rima, and John Iceland. 2004. "Hypersegregation in the Twenty-First Century." *Demography* 41(1): 23–36.

Williamson, Abigail Fisher. 2009. "The Select Few: Immigrant Intermediaries and Immigrant Political Incorporation." Paper presented at the Undocumented Hispanic Migration: On the Margins of a Dream Conference, Connecticut College, New London, CT (October 16–18).

Willis, Rachel A. 2005. "Voices of Southern Mill Workers: Responses to Border Crossers in American Factories and Jobs Crossing Borders." In *The American South in a Global World*, edited by James L. Peacock, Harry L. Watson, and Carrie R. Matthews, pp. 138–51. Chapel Hill: University of North Carolina Press.

Wilson, James Q. 1989. *Bureaucracy: What Government Agencies Do and Why They Do It*. New York: Basic Books.

Wimberley, Ronald C., and Libby V. Morris. 2002. "The Regionalization of Poverty: Assistance for the Black Belt South?" *Southern Rural Sociology* 18(1): 294–306.

Winders, Jamie. 2005. "Changing Politics of Race and Region: Latino Migration to the U.S. South." *Progress in Human Geography* 29(6): 683–99.

———. 2008a. "Nashville's New 'Sonido': Latino Migration and the Changing Politics of Race." In *New Faces in New Places: The Changing Geography of American Immigration*, edited by Douglas S. Massey, pp. 249–73. New York: Russell Sage.

———. 2008b. "Tennessee." In *Latino America: A State-by-State Encyclopedia*, edited by Mark Overmyer-Velásquez, pp. 197–214. Westport, CT: Greenwood Press.

———. 2009a. "New Americans in a New South City? Immigrant and Refugee Politics in Nashville, Tennessee." In *Latino Immigrants and the Transformation of the U.S. South*, edited by Mary E. Odem and Elaine Lacy, pp. 126–42. Athens: University of Georgia Press.

———. 2009b. "Placing Latino Migration and Migrant Experiences in the U.S. South: The Complexities of Regional and Local Trends." In *Global Connections & Local Receptions: New Latino Immigration to the Southeastern United States*, edited by Fran Ansley and Jon Shefner, pp. 223–44. Knoxville: University of Tennessee Press.

Winn, Patrick. 2007. "Orange Won't Play Immigration Role." *News and Observer* (Raleigh, NC; January 26).

Wolfinger, Raymond. 1972. *Politics of Progress*. Englewood Cliffs, NJ: Prentice Hall.

Wong, Janelle S. 2006. *Democracy's Promise: Immigrants and American Civic Institutions*. Ann Arbor: University of Michigan Press.

Woodward, C. Vann. 1993. "The Search for Southern Identity." In *The Burden of Southern History*, edited by C. Vann Woodward, pp. 3–25. Baton Rouge: Louisiana State University Press (3rd ed., originally published 1960).

Yablon-Zug, Marcia Anne, and Danielle Holley-Walker. 2009. "Not Very Collegial: Exploring Bans on Undocumented Immigrant Admissions to State Colleges and Universities." *Charleston Law Review* 3: 101–17. http://ssrn.com/abstract=1360995 (last accessed August 19, 2009).

Yale-Loehr, Stephen, and Ted Chiappari. 2007. "Immigration: Cities and States Rush In Where Congress Fears to Tread." *New York Law Journal* (February 26).

Yancey, George A. 2003. *Who Is White? Latinos, Asians, and the New Black/Nonblack Divide*. Boulder, CO: Lynne Rienner.

Zarrugh, Laura. 2008. "The Latinization of the Central Shenandoah Valley." *International Migration* 46(1): 19–58.

Zezima, Katie. 2007. "Massachusetts Rescinds Deal on Policing Immigration." *New York Times* (January 12).

Zhou, Min. 1999. "Segmented Assimilation: Issues, Controversies, and Recent Research on the New Second Generation." In *The Handbook of International Migration: The American Experience*, edited by Charles Hirschman, Philip Kasinitz, and Josh DeWind, pp. 196–211. New York: Russell Sage Foundation.

Zhou, Min, and Carl L. Bankston. 1998. *Growing up American: How Vietnamese Children Adapt to Life in the United States*. New York: Russell Sage.

Zhou, Min, Jennifer Lee, Jody Agius Vallejo, Rosaura Tafoya-Estrada, and Yang Sao Xiong. 2008. "Success Attained, Deterred, and Denied: Divergent Pathways to Social Mobility in Los Angeles' New Second Generation." *Annals of the American Academy of Political and Social Science* 620(1): 37–61.

Zota, Sejal. 2009a. "Do State and Local Immigration Laws Violate Federal Law?" *Popular Government* 74(3): 22–30.

———. 2009b. "Immigration Enforcement in the Workplace." *Popular Government*

74(3): Online supplement (1–7). http://www.sog.unc.edu/popgov (last accessed May 11, 2010).

———. 2009c. "Unauthorized Immigrants' Access to Higher Education: Fifty States, Different Directions." *Popular Government* 74(3): 46–54.

Zúñiga, Elena, Xóchitl Castañeda, Al Averbach, and Steven P. Wallace. 2006. "Mexican and Central American Immigrants in the United States: Health Care Access." Los Angeles: Regents of the University of California and Mexican Secretariat of Health (SSA).

Zúñiga, Victor, and Rubén Hernández-León. 2001. "A New Destination for Old Migration: Origins, Trajectories, and Labor Market Incorporation of Latinos in Dalton, Georgia." In *Latino Workers in the Contemporary South*, edited by Arthur D. Murphy, Colleen Blanchard, and Jennifer A. Hill, pp. 126–36. Athens: University of Georgia Press.

———. 2005a. "Introduction." In *New Destinations: Mexican Immigration to the United States*, edited by Victor Zúñiga and Rubén Hernández-León, pp. xi–xxix. New York: Russell Sage.

———. 2005b, eds. *New Destinations: Mexican Immigration to the United States.* New York: Russell Sage.

———. 2009. "The Dalton Story: Mexican Immigrant and Social Transformation in the Carpet Capital of the World." In *Latino Immigrants and the Transformation of the U.S. South*, edited by Mary E. Odem and Elaine Lacy, pp. 34–50. Athens: University of Georgia Press.

Index

Page numbers in italic indicate illustrations (figures, maps, photographs, and tables).